Wolfgang Torge

Geodesy

Second Edition

 Walter de Gruyter
Berlin · New York 1991

Author
Wolfgang Torge, Univ. Prof. Dr.-Ing.
Institut für Erdmessung
Universität Hannover
Nienburger Strasse 6
D-3000 Hannover 1, Germany

‒

ISBN 3-11-007232-7   1st edition 1980, translated from the German by Christopher Jekeli, M.Sc.
Translation of the 2nd edition revised by Prof.Dr.-Ing. Delf Egge

This book contains 137 figures and 4 tables.

⊗ Printed on acid-free paper which falls within the guidelines of the ANSI to ensure permanence and durability.

Library of Congress Cataloging-in-Publication Data

Torge, Wolfgang.
  [Geodäsie. German]
  Geodesy / Wolfgang Torge. — 2nd ed.
    p.   cm.
  Translation of: Geodäsie.
  Includes bibliographical references and index.
  ISBN 0-89925-680-5
  1. Geodesy.   I. Title.
  QB281.T5815   1991   91-22158
  526′.1 — dc20   CIP

Die Deutsche Bibliothek Cataloging-in-Publication Data

Torge, Wolfgang:
  Geodesy / by Wolfgang Torge. Transl. from the German by Christopher Jekeli. — 2. ed. — Berlin ; New York : de Gruyter, 1991
    Dt. Ausg. u.d.T.: Torge, Wolfgang: Geodäsie
    ISBN 3-11-012408-4

Printed in Germany
Typesetting: Asco Trade Typesetting Ltd., Hong Kong / Printing: Ratzlow-Druck, Berlin
Binding: Dieter Mikolai, Berlin / Cover design: Rudolf Hübler, Berlin

Preface to the Second Edition

Since the first edition of this book was published about ten years ago, geodesy has experienced a remarkable development. This is mainly due to the continued progress in space technology leading to significant improvements in geodetic control surveying and gravity field modeling. Most remarkable is the fact that, for the first time in history, large-scale movements of tectonic plates have been derived from a global network. But also small-scale applications of space-techniques deserve mentioning, e.g. for monitoring recent crustal movements in areas of high geodynamic activity or for establishing geodetic control in engineering projects. Here, space techniques are frequently combined with refined terrestrial techniques. Changes in data acquisition systems and the still ongoing increase in computing power have triggered the development of more sophisticated data reduction and evaluation methods and have also led to refinements in theory.

As a consequence, this second edition has been thoroughly revised and, in parts, has been extended. The basic subdivision into six main chapters has been retained; however, some reorganization and supplements were appropriate in the parts referring to satellite geodesy, combined evaluation methods, and geodetic control. In order to represent the contents of the modified material more clearly, the headings of chapters 5 and 6 have been renamed to "Evaluation Methods, Global Geodesy" and "Geodetic Networks", respectively. Further updating refers to topics such as the International Earth Rotation Service, free-fall gravimeters, satellite laser ranging, the Navstar Global Positioning System, remove-restore methods for gravity field determination, earth models, geodynamic applications, and large-scale geodetic networks. SI-units are now used throughout the book. Historical notes, examples, and more detailed explanations have been set in smaller types. The reference list was expanded, 50% of which now consists of new entries.

During the past decade the interdisciplinary aspects of geodesy also received a remarkable strengthening. This refers to the geosciences, particularly to solid earth geophysics, oceanography and geology, and to astronomy, being one important root of geodesy. Interrelations to surveying engineering and terrestrial and space navigation also became stronger, which is mainly due to the efficiency of space-based methods. The main purpose of this second edition is again to serve as an introductory textbook for students of geodesy, geophysics, and surveying engineering. However, the book should also be a valuable reference for geoscientists and engineers facing geodetic problems in their professional tasks.

The contents of this book are partly based on courses given at the University of Hannover. The author is indebted to individuals and organizations for providing illustrations. He thanks Prof. D. Egge for checking the new English text passages. The help of the staff at the Institut für Erdmessung, Universität Hannover, is gratefully acknowledged. Finally, the long-standing good cooperation with the publisher continued during the preparation of this book.

Hannover, May 1991   Wolfgang Torge

Preface to the First Edition

This book is oriented in the first place toward graduate students whose areas of study include geodesy and surveying (also photogrammetry and cartography). To supplement the various specialized lectures, it is meant to provide a systematic overview of reference systems, and of the collection and processing of data in both global geodesy and geodetic surveying; in addition, it can serve as a text for reference. To the land surveyor who in his profession is often concerned only marginally with the problems that are treated here, this text offers a review of the rapid development which geodesy has experienced in the last two decades. For this reason, the more recent results and new, promising developments have also been presented.

Particular importance has been attached to the representation of temporal variations in the reference systems, the earth's surface, and the gravity field. In the future, geodesy will be engaged much more strongly in considering and investigating this area of geodynamics. Throughout, it has been attempted to view geodesy as a discipline of the geosciences which particularly in recent times have found themselves in closer association. The presentation can therefore provide the geoscientists in neighboring fields with insights to the problems and methods of geodesy.

The present text is the English translation of the book "Geodäsie", which in the German language appeared in 1975, as published by Walter de Gruyter, Berlin–New York.

A thorough revision was undertaken on the occasion of the translation. The latest theoretical and technological developments could thereby be taken into consideration, while it also enabled the inclusion of new global and regional results. Extensions and supplements were incorporated pertaining to such areas as marine geodesy, satellite geodesy, as well as lunar and planetary geodesy. The bibliography has been brought up to date and expanded considerably by adding to the German literature an increased number of references in the English language.

Wolfgang Torge, 1980

Contents

The references cited in the text that are marked with A are found in section A of the bibliography (p. 235 ff.) — text books, manuals, and symposia proceeding. References without special marking belong to the second section B (p. 238 ff.) — individual publications — of the bibliography.

1 Introduction

1.1 Definition and Classification of Geodesy

According to the classical definition of F. R. HELMERT (A1880), geodesy ($\gamma\eta$ = earth, $\delta\alpha\acute{\iota}\omega$ = I divide) is the *"science of the measurement and mapping of the earth's surface."* This definition has to this day retained its validity; it includes the determination of the earth's external gravity field, as well as the surface of the ocean floor. With this definition, which has to be extended to include temporal variations of the earth and its gravity field, geodesy may be included in the geosciences, and also in the engineering sciences, e.g. NAT. ACAD. SCIENCES (1978).

Triggered by the development of space exploration, geodesy turned in collaboration with other sciences toward the determination of the surfaces of other celestial bodies (moon, other planets). The corresponding disciplines are called *selenodesy* and *planetary geodesy* (BILLS and SYNNOT 1987).

Geodesy may be divided into the areas of global geodesy, national geodetic surveys, and plane surveying. *Global geodesy* is responsible for the determination of the figure of the earth and of the external gravity field. A *geodetic survey* establishes the fundamentals for the determination of the surface and gravity field of a country. This is realized by coordinates and gravity values of a sufficiently large number of control points, arranged in geodetic and gravimetric networks. In this fundamental work, curvature and gravity field of the earth must be considered. In *plane surveying* (topographic surveying, cadastral surveying, engineering surveying), the details of the terrain are obtained. As a *reference surface* for *horizontal positioning* the ellipsoid is used in geodetic surveying. In plane surveying, the horizontal plane is generally sufficient.

There is close interaction between global geodesy, geodetic surveying and plane surveying. The geodetic survey adopts the parameters determined by measurements of earth, and its own results are available to those who measure the earth. The plane surveys, in turn, are generally tied to the control points of the geodetic surveys and serve then particularly in the development of national map series and in the formation of real estate cadastres. Measurement and evaluation methods are largely identical in global geodesy and national geodetic surveys. Particularly space methods (satellite geodesy) enter more and more into regional and even local surveys. This also implies more detailed gravity field determination on regional and local scale.

With the corresponding classifications in the realms of the English and French languages, the concept of *"geodesy"* (la géodésie, "höhere Geodäsie" after *Helmert*) is to be referred only to global geodesy and geodetic surveying. The concept of *"surveying"* (la topométrie, Vermessungskunde or "niedere Geodäsie" after *Helmert*) shall encompass plane surveying.

In this volume, geodesy is treated only in the more restricted sense as explained above. An introduction to plane surveying is given by KAHMEN and FAIG (A1988).

1.2 The Problem of Geodesy

The problem of geodesy, generated from and partially supplementing Helmert's definition, may be described comprehensively as follows (DRAHEIM 1971, FISCHER 1975):

"The problem of geodesy is to determine the figure and the external gravity field of the earth and of other celestial bodies as functions of time; as well as, to determine the mean earth ellipsoid from parameters observed on and exterior to the earth's surface."

This *geodetic boundary-value problem* incorporates a geometric (figure of the earth) and a physical (gravity field) formulation of the problem; both are closely related.

By the *figure of the earth* we mean the physical and the mathematical surface of the earth.

The *physical* surface of the earth is the border between the solid or fluid masses and the atmosphere. Recently, the *ocean floor* has also been included in the formulation of the geodetic problem, being the bounding surface between the solid terrestrial body and the oceanic water masses. The extension of the problem to the oceans is designated *marine geodesy* (MOURAD 1977, SEEBER 1975). The irregular surface of the *solid earth* (continents and ocean floor) is incapable of being represented by a simple mathematical relation; it is therefore described point wise by the use of coordinates of the *control points*. On the other hand, the *ocean surfaces* (70% of the earth's surface) possess a simpler principle of formation. Under certain assumptions, they form a part of a level (equipotential) surface (surface of constant gravity potential) of the earth's gravity field. We may think of this surface as being extended under the continents and then identify it as the *mathematical figure* of the earth (HELMERT A1880/1884). J. B. LISTING (1873) designates this level surface as *geoid*.

C. F. Gauss had already referred to this surface: "What we call the surface of the earth in the geometrical sense is nothing more than that surface which intersects everywhere the direction of gravity at right angles, and part of which coincides with the surface of the oceans." (*C. F. Gauss:* "Bestimmung des Breitenunterschiedes zwischen den Sternwarten von Göttingen und Altona," Göttingen 1828), see also MORITZ (1977).

The majority of the observed parameters used in geodesy refers to the earth's *external gravity field*, whose study thereby becomes a concern of geodesy. The upper limit of space that is of interest is governed by the geodetic usage of artificial satellites and space probes, as well as the earth's moon. The physical aspect of the problem of geodesy follows from the consideration of the earth's surface and the geoid as bounding surfaces in the earth's gravity field. The external gravity field may be described by the infinite number of *level surfaces* extending completely or partially exterior to the earth's surface.

Reference systems are introduced in order to describe the motion of the earth in space (celestial system), and surface geometry and gravity field of the earth (terrestrial system). For global geodesy, the use of three-dimensional Cartesian coordinates in Euclidian space is adequate. In geodetic surveying, a *reference surface* is introduced in order to distinguish curvilinear surface coordinates and heights. Because of its

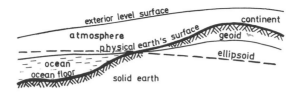

Fig. 1.1. Earth's surface and reference surfaces

simple equation, a rotational ellipsoid flattened at the poles is better suited as such a reference surface than the geoid, which is determined by the uneven distribution of the earth's masses. Particular significance is given to the *mean earth ellipsoid*, which is the optimal ellipsoid approximating the geoid. Because of its physical meaning, the *geoid* is well suited as reference surface for heights. Fig. 1.1 shows the mutual arrangement of the surfaces to be determined in geodesy.

The body of the earth and its gravity field are subject to *temporal variations* of secular, periodic, and abrupt nature, which can occur globally, regionally, and locally. The geodetic measurement and evaluation techniques today have advanced to the extent that they can detect a part of this change. Should average conditions be ascertained, observations must be corrected for these changes. With the detection of a part of the variations, geodesy also contributes to the investigation of the dynamics of the terrestrial body. The figure of the earth and the external gravity field are accordingly conceived as time dependent variables. This leads to the ideas of "four-dimensional geodesy" (ANGUS-LEPPAN 1973, MATHER 1973).

1.3 Historical Development of Geodesy

The formulation of the problem of geodesy expressed in [1.2] first developed in the course of the nineteenth century. However, the question of the figure of the earth had already been raised in antiquity. After the *sphere* first served as a model for the earth, the oblate *rotational ellipsoid* as figure of the earth asserted itself in the first half of the eighteenth century; cf. FISCHER (1975), BIALAS (A1982), LEVALLOIS (A1988).

1.3.1 The Spherical Earth Model

Various opinions on the form of the earth prevailed in the past; e.g. the notion of an *earth disk* encircled by Oceanus (*Homer's* Illiad, ~ 800 B.C., *Thales of Milet*, ~ 600 B.C.). *Pythagoras* (~ 580–500 B.C.) and his school, as well as *Aristotle* (384–322 B.C.), among others, expressed themselves for the spherical shape.

The founder of scientific geodesy is *Eratosthenes* (276–195 B.C.) of Alexandria, who under the assumption of a spherical earth deduced from measurements a radius for the earth (SCHWARZ 1975). The principle of the *arc measurement* method developed by him was still applied in modern ages: From geodetic measurement, the length ΔG of a meridian arc is determined; astronomical observations furnish the associated

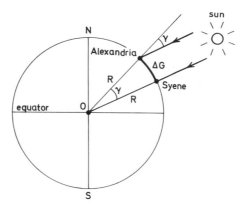

Fig. 1.2. Arc measurement of Eratosthenes

central angle γ (Fig. 1.2). The radius of the earth is then given by

$$R = \frac{\Delta G}{\gamma}. \tag{1.1}$$

Eratosthenes found that at the time of the summer solstice, the rays of the sun descended vertically into a well in Syene (Assuan, today); whereas in Alexandria, roughly on the same meridian, they formed an angle with the direction of the plumb line. From the length of the shadow of a vertical staff ("gnomon") produced in a hemispherical shell ("skaphe"), he determined this angle as 1/50 of a complete circle, i.e. $\gamma = 7°12'$. He estimated the distance from Syene to Alexandria to be 5000 stadia as taken from Egyptian cadastre maps which are based on the information of "bematists" (step counters). With the length of an Egyptian stadium as 157.5 m, we obtain an earth radius of 6267 km. This value departs from the radius of a mean spherical earth (6371 km) by -2%. A subsequent determination in antiquity is attributed to *Posidonius* (135–51 B.C.); using the meridian arc from Alexandria to Rhodes, he arrived at a radius of the earth deviating by -11%.

During the middle ages in Europe, the question of the figure of the earth was not pursued further. An arc measurement handed down by the Arabs was carried out (~ 827 A.D.) by the caliph of *al-Mámûn*, northwest of Bagdad ($+10\%$ deviation). At the beginning of the modern ages, the French physician *Fernel* in 1525 observed on the meridian through Paris the geographical latitudes of Paris and Amiens using a quadrant; he computed the distance from the number of rotations of a wagon wheel ($+0.1\%$ deviation).

The remaining arc measurements based on the notion of a spherical earth are characterized by fundamental advances in instrumentation technology (1611, *Kepler* telescope) and methodology. After the initial application of *triangulation* by *Gemma Frisius* (1508–1555) in the Netherlands, and by *Tycho Brahe* (1546–1601) in Denmark, the Dutchman *Willebrord Snellius* (1580–1626) conducted the first triangulation to determine the figure of the earth, Haasbroek (1968).

In 1615 with the triangulation applied by *Snellius* to the arc measurement between Bergen op Zoom and Alkmaar (Holland), the hitherto inaccurate estimate or direct measurement of the length of arc was replaced by a procedure of high precision. This method served into the

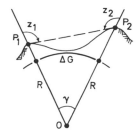

Fig. 1.3. Determination of the central angle from zenith angles

twentieth century for arc measurements and for the formation of principal control networks. For Snellius, the deviation with respect to the mean earth radius amounts to -3.4%.

Through the initiative of the Academy of Sciences, founded in Paris 1666, France in the seventeenth and eighteenth centuries assumed the leading role in geodesy. The French abbé *J. Picard* in 1669/70 carried out an arc measurement on the meridian through Paris between Malvoisine and Amiens with the aid of a triangulation network; he was the first to use a telescope with cross hairs. The value obtained by him for the radius of the earth (deviation of $+0.01\%$) aided *Newton* in the verification of the law of gravitation which he had formulated in 1665/66.

Another solution of the determination of the central angle, different in principle, namely by using *reciprocal zenith angles*, found application in 1645 by the Italians *Grimaldi* and *Riccioli* (Fig. 1.3). The angle may be computed from the zenith angles z_1 and z_2 observed at P_1 and P_2 according to

$$\gamma = z_1 + z_2 - \pi. \tag{1.2}$$

This procedure does not yield satisfactory results due to the insufficiently accurate determination of the curvature of light rays (refraction anomalies).

1.3.2 The Ellipsoidal Earth Model

In the sixteenth and seventeenth centuries, new observations and ideas from astronomy and physics decisively influenced the perception of the figure of the earth and its position in space. *N. Copernicus* (1473–1543) achieved the transition from the *geocentric* universe of *Ptolemy* to a *heliocentric* system (1543: "De revolutionibus orbium coelestium"), which *Aristarchus of Samos* (~ 320–250 B.C.) had already postulated. *J. Kepler* (1571–1630) discovered the laws of planetary motion (1609: "Astronomia nova ...", 1619: "Harmonices mundi"), and *Galileo Galilei* (1564–1642) developed modern mechanics (law of falling bodies, law of pendulum motion).

In 1666, the astronomer *J. D. Cassini* observed the flattening of the poles of Jupiter. The astronomer *J. Richer* in 1672 discovered on the occasion of an expedition to Cayenne to determine martian parallaxes, that he must shorten a one-second pendulum which had been regulated in Paris, in order to regain oscillations of one second. From this observation and on the basis of the law of pendulum motion, one can infer an increase in gravity from the equator to the poles. Building on these and on their own works, *Isaac Newton* (1643–1727) and *Christian Huygens* (1629–1695) developed earth models *flattened* at the poles and founded on principles of physics.

Newton (1687: "Philosophiae naturalis principia mathematica") obtained a rotational ellipsoid as an equilibrium figure for a homogeneous, fluid, rotating earth based on the validity of the law of universal gravitation. The flattening

$$f = \frac{a - b}{a} \tag{1.3}$$

(f for "flattening", a = semimajor axis, b = semiminor axis) in this case amounts to 1/230. At the same time, Newton postulated an increase in gravity acceleration from the equator to the poles proportional to $\sin^2 \varphi$ (φ = geographical latitude). *Huygens* (1690: "Discours de la Cause de la Pesanteur") shifts the source of the earth's attractive forces to the center of the earth and develops a rotationally symmetric equilibrium surface which possesses a meridian curve of fourth order with $f = 1/576$.

For a geometric verification of the ellipsoidal earth model, one has employed *arc measurements at various latitudes*. Namely, the length of a one-degree arc (meridian arc for a difference of 1° in latitude) in the case of flattened poles increases poleward from the equator. The ellipsoidal parameters a, b or a, f can be computed from two arc measurements [1.3.3].

An evaluation of the existing older arc measurements (*Snellius, Picard*, among others) led to an earth model elongated at the poles. The same result was obtained by *La Hire, J. D.* and *J. Cassini* (1683–1718) who extended the arc of Picard north to Dunkirk and south to Collioure (latitude difference of 8°20′). The computations from two arc segments yielded a "negative" flattening of $f = -1/95$, which can be attributed particularly to measurement errors of the astronomic latitudes. The intense dispute between the supporters of Newton and those of Cassini over the figure of the earth was resolved by two further arc measurements sponsored by the French Academy of Sciences.

Maupertuis and *Clairaut*, among others, participated in the expedition to *Lapland* (1736/37); the results of this arc measurement (average latitude 66°20′, latitude interval 57′.5) confirmed the polar flattening. In combination with the arc measurement on the meridian through Paris, revised by *Cassini de Thury* and *La Caille*, 1739/40, the result was $f = 1/183$. On a second expedition (1735–1744) to Peru (regions of today's Ecuador), an arc of average latitude 1°31′ S and 3°07′ amplitude was determined by *Godin, Bouguer*, and *La Condamine*. Combination with the Lapland arc led to $f = 1/210$. The flattening of the earth at the poles was thereby demonstrated by *geodetic* measurements.

A *synthesis* between the physical and geodetic substantiations of the ellipsoidal shape of the earth was finally achieved by *A.-C. Clairaut* (1713–1765) with the theorem (1743) named for him, which permits the computation of the flattening from two gravity measurements at different latitudes [3.5.2]. The practical application of this "*gravimetric method*" suffered until the twentieth century from the lack of accurate and well distributed gravity measurements and from the problem of reducing these data to the earth ellipsoid.

1.3.3 Arc Measurements

After the rotational ellipsoid had asserted itself as a model for the earth, numerous arc measurements were conducted until the middle of the nineteenth century to

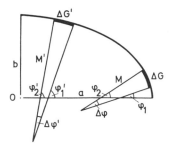

Fig. 1.4. Latitude arc measurement

determine the dimension of this earth ellipsoid. The arc length was invariably obtained by triangulation. We distinguish between arc measurements along an ellipsoidal meridian (latitude arc measurement), along a parallel (longitude arc measurement), and arc measurements oblique to the meridian.

For the computations in a *latitude arc measurement* (Fig. 1.4), the angles $\Delta\varphi = \varphi_2 - \varphi_1$, $\Delta\varphi' = \varphi_2' - \varphi_1'$ are formed from the observed geographic latitudes φ_1, φ_2, φ_1', φ_2'. The corresponding meridian arcs ΔG and $\Delta G'$ are obtained from triangulation networds. For short arcs one can replace the meridian ellipse by the osculating circle having the meridian radius of curvature $M = M(\varphi)$ evaluated at the mean latitude $\varphi = \frac{1}{2}(\varphi_1 + \varphi_2)$, where M is also a function of the ellipsoidal parameters a, f [3.4.2]. From $\Delta G = M\Delta\varphi$ and $\Delta G' = M'\Delta\varphi'$, a and f may be determined. The larger the latitude interval $\varphi' - \varphi$, the more accurate is the computed flattening; whereas, the accuracy of a depends in particular on the lengths of the meridian arcs.

Particular significance was attained by the measurement commissioned by the French National Assembly and carried out by *Delambre* and *Méchain* on the meridian through Paris between Barcelona and Dunkirk (1792–1798); it was supposed to serve for the definition of the meter as a natural unit of length. In combination with the Peruvian arc measurement, this yielded an ellipsoidal flattening of $f = 1/334$.

Of the numerous arc measurements carried out in the nineteenth and twentieth centuries, which were largely the foundations of geodetic surveys, we mention here only the older, historically important arcs of *Gauss* (arc measurement between Göttingen and Altona, 1821–1825, adjustment according to the least squares method) and of *Bessel* and *Baeyer* (arc measurement oblique to the meridian in East Prussia, 1831–1838). References to more recent and to some extent still currently significant works are made in the treatment of astrogeodetic methods [5.1.4].

1.3.4 The Geoid and the Ellipsoid

As *P.-S. Laplace* (1802), *C. F. Gauss* (1828), *F. W. Bessel* (1837), and others had already recognized, the assumption of an ellipsoidal earth model is not tenable under sufficiently high observational accuracy. Namely, one can no longer ignore the deviation (*deflection of the vertical*) of the physical plumb line, to which the measurements refer, from the ellipsoidal normal. By an adjustment of several arc measurements for the determination of the ellipsoidal parameters a and f, contradictions arise which exceed by far the observational accuracy.

An initial adjustment of arc measurements was carried out in 1806 by *A. M. Legendre* in his treatise "Sur la méthode des moindres carrées". *C. F. Gauss* was the first to adjust a triangulation network (in and around Brunswick, 1803–1807) by the method of least squares (GERARDY 1977).

Despite these discrepancies, numerous adjustments were undertaken until the mid-nineteenth century to determine the dimensions of the ellipsoid, whereby the deflections of the vertical, being physically caused, and hence, having systematic characteristics were treated as random observational errors. With the definition of geodesy [1.1] and the introduction of the geoid [1.2], *F. R. Helmert* made a transition to the current concept of the figure of the earth. Here, the deflections of the vertical are taken into account in the computation of the ellipsoidal parameters. The three-dimensional concept of geodesy was also introduced in that time (BRUNS 1878).

Friedrich Robert Helmert (1843–1917), one of the most distinguished geodesists of modern times, was professor of geodesy at the technical university at Aachen and director of the Prussian Geodetic Institute in Potsdam and of the central office of the "Internationale Erdmessung". Through his work, geodesy has experienced decisive impulses, which until today have their effect. In his fundamental monograph (A1880/1884) *Helmert* established geodesy as a proper science (WOLF 1970).

The determination of the geoid was for about 70 years (1880–1950) a major goal of geodesy. Its importance diminished after 1945 with the development of methods for the direct derivation of the physical surface of the earth; however, its determination still remains an essential problem of geodesy. In fact, the significance of the geoid has again increased with the establishment of three-dimensional continental and global systems [5.1.2], as well as with the requirements of marine geodesy [3.3.3].

1.4 Organization of Geodesy, Literature

1.4.1 National Organizations

The problems of *global geodesy* may be solved only with international cooperation of institutes which work at a national level, together with a few international services [1.4.2]. In some countries, governmental or academy research institutes (Federal Republic of Germany: Deutsches Geodätisches Forschungsinstitut in Munich and Frankfurt, Zentralinstitut Physik der Erde/Geodätisches Institut in Potsdam; U.S.S.R.: Central Scientific Research Institute of Geodesy, Aerial Survey, and Cartography in Moscow), as well as the geodetic institutes of universities are actively pursuing *research*. The *geodetic surveys* are carried out according to the structure of the official surveying system by decentralized institutes (Fed. Rep. of Germany: geodetic survey offices of the individual states) or by central agencies (Australia: Division of National Mapping; Canada: Surveys and Mapping Branch; France: Institut Géographique National; Great Britain: Ordnance Survey; India: Survey of India; Japan: Geographical Survey Institute; U.S.A.: National Geodetic Survey, National Oceanic and Atmospheric Administration (NOAA) — formerly Coast and Geodetic Survey).

In addition to these, a number of *nongeodetic* institutions exist which in the course of their special projects are also concerned with geodetic problems; indeed, they deal with the theory, and in particular, with the collection and evaluation of data. We mention here the institutes of space exploration and of astronomy (Goddard Space Flight Center of NASA, Greenbelt,

Md.; Centre National d'Études Spatiales, Brétigny-sur-Orge; Smithsonian Astrophysical Observatory (SAO), Cambridge, Mass.), geologic and hydrographic services (Geological Survey of Canada; Bundesanstalt für Geowissenschaften und Rohstoffe, Hannover; Bundesamt für Seeschiffahrt und Hydrographie, Hamburg; Bureau de Recherches Géologiques et Minières, Orleans; Institute of Geological Sciences and Institute of Oceanographic Sciences, U.K.; U.S. Geological Survey), university departments (Lamont-Doherty Geological Observatory, Columbia Univ., New York), and military agencies (U.S.A.: Defense Mapping Agency, Topographic Center DMATC and Aerospace Center DMAAC; U.S. Naval Oceanographic Office NAVOCEANO).

1.4.2 International Collaboration

At the beginning of the arc measurements in the kingdom of Hanover (1821), *C. F. Gauss* had already expressed his intensions. According to him, this net would be connected to neighboring triangulation networks, aiming toward an eventual merger of the European observatories. Organized international collaboration originates with the instigation by the Prussian general *J. J. Baeyer* (1794–1885): "*Über die Größe und Figur der Erde, eine Denkschrift zur Begründung einer Mitteleuropäischen Gradmessung*" (1861). In 1862, the "Mitteleuropäische Gradmessung" was founded in Berlin as the first international scientific association of significance; Baeyer was its first president. After expanding to the "Europäische Gradmessung" (1867) and to the "*Internationale Erdmessung*" ("Association Géodésique Internationale"), 1886, the association developed a fruitful activity, which was especially inspired by the works of *Helmert* as director of the central bureau (LEVALLOIS 1980).

After the dissolution of the "Internationale Erdmessung" during the first World War, the "*International Union of Geodesy and Geophysics*" (I.U.G.G.) which today (1987) has a membership of 77 countries was founded in 1919. It consists of one geodetic and six geophysical associations. The "*International Association of Geodesy*" (I.A.G.) is directed by a president who is elected every four years, and who has vice presidents and a general secretary at his side. I.U.G.G. and I.A.G. meet at general assemblies at four-year intervals; in addition, numerous symposia and scientific conferences which treat special themes are organized by the I.U.G.G., its associations and commissions.

The I.A.G. consists of five *sections*: Positioning, Advanced Space Technology, Determination of the Gravity Field, General Theory and Methodology, Geodynamics. *Commissions* are established for continuing problem, whereas, transient problems are treated by *special study groups*. In addition, the I.A.G., partly in collaboration with other scientific organizations maintains permanent institutions: International Earth Rotation Service (IERS) with the Central Bureau at the Observatoire de Paris, replacing since 1988 the Earth Rotation Service of the Bureau International de l'Heure (BIH) and the International Polar Motion Service (IPMS); Bureau International des Poids et Mesures (BIPM) Sèvres; Bureau Gravimétrique International (BGI), Toulouse; International Center of Recent Crustal Movements, Prague; International Center of Earth Tides, Brussels; Permanent Service for Mean Sea Level, Bidston on Merseyside, U.K.

For cooperative programmes of rocket and satellite research, an Inter-Union Committee on Space Research (COSPAR) was established by the International Council of Scientific Unions (ICSU).

1.4.3 Literature

A survey of the recent *text books* and *manuals* of geodesy is given in the bibliography on page 235. There also, references are listed to introductory mathematical works (potential theory, differential geometry, plane and spherical trigonometry, adjustment computations) and to literature pertaining to the neighboring disciplines of surveying, as well as to astronomy and geophysics. A list of geodetic publication series is given in Bulletin Géodésique *62*, no. 3, 381–393, 1988.

Among the *technical journals*, the "Bulletin Géodèsique" issued by the I.A.G. (Springer, Berlin-Heidelberg-New York) concerns itself exclusively with geodetic problems. After each general assembly of the I.A.G., the results are compiled in a general report; whereas, national reports contain information on the geodetic activities of the I.A.G. membership countries (*Proceedings of the I.A.G. — Travaux de l'A.I.G.*). Since 1990, the proceedings of IAG-symposia will be published in separate volumes by Springer. An international geodetic bibliography is published by the Technical University of Dresden. Prompt publication of research results is possible in the "Manuscripta Geodaetica", Heidelberg-New York. Queries in geodesy are further treated in the technical journals of *surveying*. The following are mentioned in particular: "Allgemeine Vermessungsnachrichten", Karlsruhe; "The Australian Surveyor", Sydney; "Bolletino di Geodesia e Scienze Affini", Florence; "The Canadian Surveyor", Ottawa; "Geodesy, Mapping and Photogrammetry", Washington (translation of the Russian journals "Geodeziya i Aerofotosyemka" and "Geodeziya i Kartografiya"); "GPS-World", Eugene, Oregon; "Marine Geodesy", New York; "Österreichische Zeitchrift für Vermessungswesen und Photogrammetrie", Vienna; "Vermessung, Photogrammetrie, Kulturtechnik", Baden-Dättwil; "Surveying and Mapping", Falls Church; "Survey Review", Tolworth, Surrey; "Vermessungstechnik", Berlin; "Zeitschrift für Vermessungswesen", Stuttgart. Geodetic articles also appear in the *geophysical* technical literature: "Bolletino di Geofisica teorica ed applicata", Trieste; "EOS Transactions American Geophysical Union", Washington; "Geophysical Journal", Oxford (combining Annales Geophysicae, The Geophys. J. of the Royal Astronom. Society, and Journal of Geophysics/Zeitschrift fur Geophysik); "Geophysical Research Letters", Washington, D.C.; "Surveys in Geophysics", Dordrecht; "Gerlands Beiträge zur Geophysik", Leipzig; "Journal of Geophysical Research", Washington; "Reviews of Geophysics and Space Physics", Washington; "Studia Geophysica et Geodaetica", Prague, "Tectonophysics", Amsterdam.

Reports are issued by geodetic universities and research institutes and by various scientific academies, as well as by some governmental agencies. We mention here: "Acta Geodaetica, Geophysica et Montanistica", Budapest; "Acta Geodaetica et Geophysica", Beijing; "Australian Journal of Geodesy, Photogrammetry and Surveying", Kensington N.S.W.; "Bull. d'Inform. Bureau Gravimetrique Internat.", Toulouse; "Bull. d'Inform. Marées Terrestres", Brussels; "Bull. of the Earthquake Research Institute", Univ. of Tokyo; "Bull. of the Geographical Survey Institute", Tokyo; "Defense Mapping Agency, Technical Rep.", Washington D.C.; "Mitt. d. Geodät. Inst. T. U. Graz.", "Mitt. Inst. f. Theor. Geod. Univ. Bonn"; "Nachrichten aus dem Karten- und Vermessungswesen", Frankfurt/Main; "NASA Goddard Space Flight Center Rep.", Greenbelt, Md.; "NOAA–NOS–National Geodetic Survey Technical Rep.", Rockville, Md.; "Publications of the Finnish Geodetic Institute", Helsinki; "Reports of the Department of Geodetic Science and Surveying", The Ohio State Univ., Columbus, Ohio; "Schriftenreihe der Hochschule der Bundeswehr", München; "Smithsonian Astrophysical Observatory: Special Reports"; "Unisurv G-Univ. of New South Wales Rep.", Kensington, NSW; "Veröff. der Bayer. Komm. für die Internationale Erdmessung der Bayer. Akad. der Wissenschaften", Munich; "Veröff. der Deutschen Geodätischen Kommission bei der Bayerischen Akad. der Wissenschaften", Munich and Frankfurt a.M.; "Veröff. des Zentralinstituts Physik der Erde", Potsdam; "Wiss. Arb. d. Fachr. Vermessungswesen d. Univ. Hannover".

2 The Gravity Field of the Earth

The significance of the external gravity field of the earth in geodesy may be described comprehensively as follows:

1. The external gravity field is the *reference system* for the overwhelming part of the measured quantities in geodesy. This field must be known in order to reduce the quantities into geometrically defined systems [5.1].
2. If the distribution of gravity values on the *surface of the earth* is known, then in combination with other geodetic measurements, the shape of this surface may be determined [5.2].
3. The most important reference surface for height measurements, the *geoid* [3.3], as an idealized ocean surface is a level surface of the gravity field.
4. The analysis of the external gravity field yields information on the structure and characteristics of the *interior* of the earth. In making the corresponding gravity field parameters available, geodesy becomes an auxiliary science of geophysics [5.5].

2.1 Components of the Gravity Field

A body rotating with the earth experiences the *gravitational* forces of the earth and of other celestial bodies, as well as the *centrifugal* force due to the earth's rotation. The resultant force is the *force of gravity*. It is a function of position, but also undergoes temporal variations.

For the geodetic use of *earth satellites*, one should note that a satellite does not partake in the rotation of the earth. Hence, only gravitation acts in this case.

The *unit of acceleration* in the SI-system (Système International d'Unités), MARKOWITZ (1973), is ms^{-2}. The acceleration of gravity can be measured with an accuracy of 10^{-7} to $10^{-8} ms^{-2}$; the deviations of the terrestrial gravity field from a "normal earth", in general, remain less than $2 \times 10^{-3} ms^{-2}$. Therefore, the sciences of geodesy and geophysics have until recently adopted the more suitable units

$$mgal = 10^{-5} ms^{-2}, \quad \mu gal = 10^{-8} ms^{-2} = 10 nms^{-2}.$$

They are derived from the unit "gal" (after Galilei) $= cm\ s^{-2}$ used in the cgs-system. In the sequel we shall mainly use the units

$$\mu ms^{-2} = 10^{-6} ms^{-2}, \quad nms^{-2} = 10^{-9} ms^{-2}.$$

2.1.1 Gravitation, Gravitational Potential

According to *Newton's law of gravitation* (1687), two point masses m_1 and m_2 attract each other with the gravitational force (attractive force)

$$K = -G\frac{m_1 m_2}{l^2}\frac{l}{l}, \tag{2.1}$$

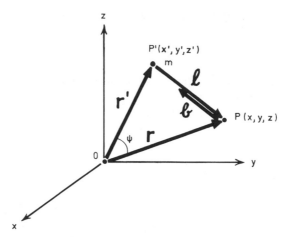

Fig. 2.1. Gravitation *b*

(G = gravitational constant, l = distance between point masses), where K and l point in opposing directions. The unit mass situated at the attracted point P (Fig. 2.1) in the gravitational field experiences a *gravitational acceleration* (henceforth, also termed "gravitation")

$$b = -G\frac{m}{l^2}\frac{l}{l},\tag{2.2}$$

due to the mass element at the attracting point P'. b lies on the line joining P and P' and is directed toward P'; l may be represented by the position vectors r and r', e.g. in the Cartesian x,y,z-system:

$$\left\{\begin{array}{l} l = r - r', \quad r = \begin{pmatrix} x \\ y \\ z \end{pmatrix}, \quad r' = \begin{pmatrix} x' \\ y' \\ z' \end{pmatrix}. \\ l = |l| = \sqrt{(x - x')^2 + (y - y')^2 + (z - z')^2}. \end{array}\right.\tag{2.3}$$

The value of the gravitational constant is (Committee on Data for Science and Technology — CODATA — system of physical constants 1986)

$$G = (6.67259 \pm 0.00085) \times 10^{-11} \text{ m}^3 \text{ kg}^{-1} \text{ s}^{-2}.$$

The first experimental determination of G was carried out in 1798 by *Cavendish*, who used the torsion balance. The goal of current work is to increase the relative accuracy of G to better than 1×10^{-4}. This includes investigations into a dependency of G on material, external influences, as well as distance and direction. Until today, these investigations have not rendered significant results (GILLIES 1987).

A body such as the earth, composed of an infinite number of mass elements, induces a gravitation on the unit mass at P which is computed by summing the individual accelerations (2.2) vectorially. The computations are simplified, if one changes from the vector field to a scalar field.

Because the gravitational field is *irrotational*,

$$\operatorname{curl} \boldsymbol{b} = \boldsymbol{0}, \tag{2.4}$$

$\boldsymbol{b}$ may be represented as the gradient of a potential (see e.g. KELLOGG A1929, SIGL A1985):

$$\boldsymbol{b} = \operatorname{grad} V. \tag{2.5}$$

With $\lim\limits_{l \to \infty} V = 0$, we introduce the *gravitational potential*

$$V = V(l) = \frac{Gm}{l} \tag{2.6}$$

as a positive quantity (as it is customary in geodesy). The value of the potential at the point P in the gravitational field indicates the work that must be done by the gravitation in order to move the unit mass from infinity ($V = 0$) to P.

The acceleration *potential* has the dimension of work per unit mass and it has the unit $\mathrm{m^2\,s^{-2}}$.

From the mass element m, we turn to the *earth* with continuously distributed elements

$$dm = \rho\, dv, \tag{2.7}$$

where $\rho = \rho(r')$ is the density and dv is the volume element. According to the superposition principle, the gravitational potential of the earth is given according to (2.6) by

$$V = V(r) = G \iiint\limits_{earth} \frac{dm}{l} = G \iiint\limits_{earth} \frac{\rho}{l} dv. \tag{2.8}$$

In the computation of V, one therefore has to assume that the density function $\rho = \rho(r')$ is completely known; in fact however, it is better known only for parts of the upper crust of the earth.

2.1.2 Gravitational Potential of a Spherically Symmetric Earth

To a first approximation, the earth can be viewed as a sphere with a centrally symmetric density structure. For the computation of the gravitational potential, we introduce the *spherical coordinates* r, ϑ, λ (Fig. 2.2) which are also required later. With the usual orientation of this system with respect to a global x,y,z-system (the $\vartheta = 0$ axis coincides with the z-axis which lies along the spin axis, the $\lambda = 0$ axis coincides with the x-axis which lies in the meridian plane of Greenwich), we have the following relationship

$$\boldsymbol{r} = \begin{pmatrix} x \\ y \\ z \end{pmatrix} = r \begin{pmatrix} \sin \vartheta \cos \lambda \\ \sin \vartheta \sin \lambda \\ \cos \vartheta \end{pmatrix}. \tag{2.9}$$

ϑ is then the spherical polar distance, λ is the geographical longitude.

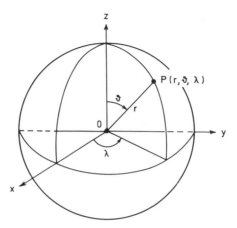

Fig. 2.2. Spherical coordinates r, ϑ, λ

In the subsequent derivation, the spherical coordinate system is oriented such that the $\vartheta = 0$ axis coincides with the line joining O and P (Fig. 2.3).

The potential of a homogeneous spherical shell of infinitesimal thickness dr' and density ρ and having a radius r' is given in analogy to (2.8) by

$$V' = G\rho\, dr' \iint_f \frac{df}{l},$$

where the integration is over the surface of the shell f and where

$$df = r'^2 \sin \vartheta'\, d\vartheta'\, d\lambda'$$

is the surface element. A distinction is made in the integration as to whether the attracted point is exterior or interior to the spherical shell.

For an attracted point lying in the *exterior*, the potential is given by

$$V'_e = 4\pi G\rho \frac{r'^2}{r}\, dr' = G\frac{dm'}{r}, \tag{2.10}$$

here

$$dm' = 4\pi\rho r'^2\, dr'$$

represents the mass of the spherical shell. The potential of the *spherical earth* composed of concentric homogeneous shells is

$$V_e = G \iiint_{earth} \frac{dm'}{r} = \frac{GM}{r}. \tag{2.11}$$

Hence, it is equal to the potential of the entire mass M of the earth concentrated at the center of mass.

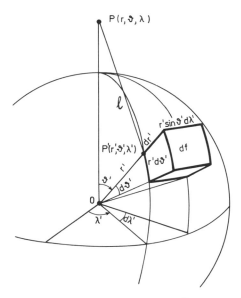

Fig. 2.3. Gravitational potential of a centrally symmetric sphere

With $GM = 398.6 \times 10^{12}$ m^3 s^{-2} and the radius of the earth $R = 6371$ km, the value of the potential at the surface of the earth $(r = R)$ amounts to $V = 6.26 \times 10^7$ m^2 s^{-2}, and the gravitation is $b = 9.82$ ms^{-2}.

For a point in the *interior*, we obtain for the potential of the spherical shell:

$$V_i' = 4\pi G\rho r' \, dr' = \frac{G \, dm'}{r'}. \tag{2.12}$$

V' here is constant; therefore, the gravitation is zero. The potential inside an *earth constructed of shells* is composed of the contribution (2.10) due to the masses interior to the sphere $r = $ const., as well as the contribution (2.12) from the spherical shell having thickness $R - r$:

$$V_i = \frac{4\pi G}{r} \int_0^r \rho r'^2 \, dr' + 4\pi G \int_r^R \rho r' \, dr'. \tag{2.13}$$

For a *homogeneous spherical earth* ($\rho = $ const.) we have

$$V_i = \frac{4}{3}\pi G\rho r^2 + 2\pi G\rho(R^2 - r^2) = 2\pi G\rho\left(R^2 - \frac{r^2}{3}\right). \tag{2.14}$$

2.1.3 Properties of the Gravitational Potential

We investigate the properties of the potential function V and its first and second derivatives.

If the attracted point P lies exterior to the attracting region, that is, the "physical body of the earth", then $l \geqslant 0$ always. Here we neglect the mass of the atmosphere

$M_{\text{Atm}} \approx 10^{-6} M$. The potential V (2.8) and the first derivatives (in view of (2.3))

$$\frac{\partial V}{\partial x} = V_x = -G \iiint\limits_{earth} \frac{x - x'}{l^3} \, dm \text{ etc.} \tag{2.15}$$

as well as the second derivatives

$$\frac{\partial^2 V}{\partial x^2} = V_{xx} = -G \iiint\limits_{earth} \frac{1}{l^3} \, dm + 3G \iiint\limits_{earth} \frac{(x - x')^2}{l^5} \, dm \text{ etc.} \tag{2.16}$$

are single-valued, finite, and continuous functions in the entire *exterior space*. They all vanish at infinity.

The unit of the *second derivative* of the potential is s^{-2}. In view of the magnitude of the second derivative and the measuring accuracy (10^{-8} to 10^{-9} s^{-2}), the units commonly used are 10^{-9} $s^{-2} = 1$ E(Eötvös) $= 1$ μms^{-2}/km $= 0.1$ mgal/km.

Applying the Laplacian operator $\Delta \equiv \frac{\partial^2}{\partial x^2} + \frac{\partial^2}{\partial y^2} + \frac{\partial^2}{\partial z^2}$ (here in Cartesian coordinates) to V yields the partial differential equation of second order which describes the gravitational field. With (2.16) we obtain *Laplace's differential equation*

$$\Delta V = 0. \tag{2.17}$$

Continuous functions having continuous first and second derivatives and which fulfill (2.17) are called *harmonic functions* or potential functions.

If the attracted point lies *inside* the body of the earth, then the case $l = 0$ is possible. This requires special attention because of the discontinuity of $1/l$.

To this end, we consider P enclosed by a sphere K (center at P_0, radius p); p is chosen sufficiently small, so that $\rho = \text{const.}$ inside this sphere (Fig. 2.4). The potential is composed of the contributions due to the masses lying interior and exterior to the sphere.

From (2.8) and (2.14) and using

$$R = p, \quad r = q = \sqrt{(x - x_0)^2 + (y - y_0)^2 + (z - z_0)^2},$$

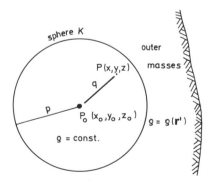

Fig. 2.4. Gravitational potential inside the earth

we find

$$V = G \iiint\limits_{earth-K} \frac{dm}{l} + 2\pi G\rho \left(p^2 - \frac{q^2}{3} \right).$$

In the limit $p \to 0$, $q \to 0$, agreement is obtained with the expression for the exterior potential (2.8). Differentiation of V yields

$$V_x = -G \iiint\limits_{earth-K} \frac{x - x'}{l^3} dm - \frac{4}{3}\pi G\rho(x - x_0) \text{ etc.}$$

As $q \to 0$, hence also $x - x_0 = y - y_0 = z - z_0 \to 0$, so that we again obtain agreement with the exterior case (2.15). The second derivatives are given by

$$V_{xx} = -G \iiint\limits_{earth-K} \frac{1}{l^3} dm + 3G \iiint\limits_{earth-K} \frac{(x - x')^2}{l^5} dm - \frac{4}{3}\pi G\rho \text{ etc.} \qquad (2.18)$$

The gravitational potential and its first derivatives are thus single-valued, finite, and continuous in the *interior* as well. The second derivatives, according to (2.18), exhibit discontinuities for sudden changes in density. For the interior of the earth, *Poisson's differential equation* is

$$\Delta V = -4\pi G\rho, \qquad (2.19)$$

which follows from (2.18).

2.1.4 Centrifugal Acceleration, Centrifugal Potential

The centrifugal force arises as a result of the rotation of the earth about its axis. We assume here a rotation of constant angular velocity ω about the rotational axis, which is further assumed to be fixed with respect to the earth. The centrifugal acceleration

$$z = \omega^2 p \qquad (2.20)$$

acting on a unit mass is directed outward perpendicularly to the spin axis (Fig. 2.5).

The *angular velocity*

$$\omega = 2\pi: 86164.10 \text{ s} = 7.292\,115 \times 10^{-5} \text{ rad s}^{-1}$$

is known with high accuracy from astronomy [4.1.3].

If the z-axis of an earth-fixed x,y,z-system coincides with the axis of rotation, then we have

$$p = \begin{pmatrix} x \\ y \\ 0 \end{pmatrix}, \qquad p = |p| = \sqrt{x^2 + y^2}.$$

With

$$z = \text{grad } \Phi \qquad (2.21)$$

we introduce the *centrifugal potential*

$$\Phi = \Phi(p) = \frac{\omega^2}{2} p^2. \qquad (2.22)$$

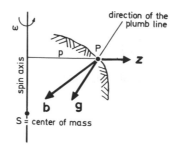

Fig. 2.5. Gravitation b, centrifugal acceleration z, gravity acceleration g

Differentiating twice and applying the Laplacian operator yields

$$\Delta\Phi = 2\omega^2. \tag{2.23}$$

The analytic function Φ, as opposed to V (2.17), is therefore not harmonic.

For points on the equator of the earth, the centrifugal potential has a value of $\Phi = 1.1 \times 10^5$ m^2 s^{-2} and the centrifugal acceleration is $z = |z| = 0.03$ ms^{-2} ($\approx 0.3\%$ of gravitation). At the poles $\Phi = 0$, $z = 0$.

2.1.5 Gravity Acceleration, Gravity Potential

The *gravity acceleration*, or *gravity* g (Latin: gravitas) is the resultant of gravitation b and centifugal acceleration z (Fig. 2.5):

$$g = b + z. \tag{2.24}$$

The direction of g is known as the *direction of the plumb line*; the magnitude $g = |g|$ is called the gravity intensity (often just gravity). Using (2.8) and (2.22), the *gravity potential* W of the earth becomes

$$W = W(r) = V + \Phi = G \iiint_{earth} \frac{\rho}{l}\, dv + \frac{\omega^2}{2} p^2. \tag{2.25}$$

The gravity acceleration is given by

$$g = \text{grad } W. \tag{2.26}$$

W and its first derivatives are single-valued, finite, and continuous as a consequence of the characteristics of V and Φ, with the exception of the uninteresting cases $r \to \infty$ (then also $\Phi \to \infty$) and $g = 0$ (direction of the plumb line is not unique). The second derivatives posses discontinuities at abrupt density variations.

In geodesy, the most important surface of discontinuity is the physical surface of the earth with a jump in density from $\rho = 0.0013$ g cm^{-3} (density of air) to $\rho = 2.7$ g cm^{-3} (mean density of the upper crust of the earth).

From (2.19) and (2.23), we obtain the *generalized Poisson differential equation*

$$\Delta W = -4\pi G\rho + 2\omega^2. \tag{2.27}$$

In the exterior space ($\rho = 0$, neglecting the density of the air), it turns into the *generalized Laplace differential equation*

$$\Delta W = 2\omega^2. \tag{2.28}$$

Because of the flattening at the poles and the centrifugal acceleration, g varies on the surface of an earth ellipsoid between 9.78 ms^{-2} (equator) and 9.83 ms^2 (pole).

2.2 Level Surfaces and Plumb Lines

2.2.1 Definition and Properties of Level Surfaces

The surfaces of constant gravity potential

$$W = W(r) = \text{const.} \tag{2.29}$$

are designated as *equipotential*, *level*, or *geopotential surfaces* (geops) of gravity. As a result of an elemental displacement ds, the potential difference of the differentially separated level surfaces (Fig. 2.6) is given, in view of (2.26), by

$$dW = \boldsymbol{g} \cdot d\boldsymbol{s} = g \, ds \cos(\boldsymbol{g}, d\boldsymbol{s}). \tag{2.30}$$

Therefore, the derivative of the gravity potential in a certain direction is equal to the projection of the gravity along this direction. If ds is taken along the level surface $W = W_p$, then it follows from $dW = 0$ that the gravity $\boldsymbol{g}$ is perpendicular to $W = W_p$. The level surfaces are intersected perpendicularly by the *plumb lines*; the tangent to the plumb line has already been defined in [2.1.5] as the *direction of the plumb line*. If ds is directed along the outer surface normal $\boldsymbol{n}$, then because $\cos(\boldsymbol{g}, \boldsymbol{n}) = -1$, the following important differential relationship exists:

$$dW = -g \, dn. \tag{2.31}$$

It provides the link between the potential difference (a physical quantity) and the difference in height (a geometric quantity) of neighboring level surfaces.

Since only the projection of ds along the plumb line enters in (2.30), dW is independent of the path. Hence, no work is done for a displacement along a level surface $W = \text{const.}$: the level surfaces are *equilibrium surfaces*.

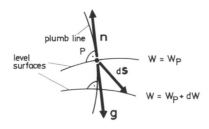

Fig. 2.6. Level surfaces and plumb lines

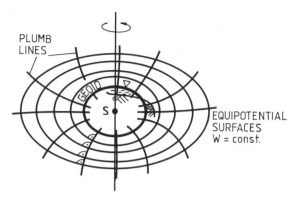

Fig. 2.7. Level (equipotential) surfaces and plumb lines near the earth

If g varies on a level surface, then according to (2.31) the distance dn to a neighboring level surface must also change. Therefore, the level surfaces are not parallel and the plumb lines are space curves. As a consequence of an increase of 0.05 ms^{-5} in gravity from the equator to the poles, the level surfaces of the earth *converge* toward the poles (Fig. 2.7).

The relative decrease of the distance between two level surfaces near the earth from the equator to the pole is on the order of 5×10^{-3}. Two level surfaces which are 100.0 m apart at the equator have a distance of only 99.5 m between them at the poles.

The level surfaces inside the earth and in its more immediate exterior space are closed, spheroidal (resembling a sphere) surfaces. As an outer limit in the realm of the *definition* of gravity, one may consider that level surface for which the gravitation and centrifugal accelerations in the equatorial plane cancel each other. The equatorial radius of this surface has a value of 42200 km.

The concept of a level surface was introduced by *MacLaurin* (1742); whereas, *Clairaut* (1743) thoroughly discussed "Level Surfaces and Plumb Lines" as a whole. BRUNS (1878) put forth the determination of the exterior level surfaces in their entirety as the fundamental problem of geodesy.

2.2.2 Analytical Representation of Level Surfaces

From the properties of the potential function $W = W(r)$ [2.1.5], it follows that the level surfaces extending completely in the *exterior* space are analytical surfaces; that is, they have no salient or singular points. Level surfaces extending partially or completely *inside* the earth exhibit discontinuities in the second derivatives at density irregularities. These surfaces can thus be constructed only from pieces of different analytical surfaces. For a continuous passage from one surface segment to another, the curvature [2.2.3] changes discontinuously with the second derivatives. The analytical parts of the level surfaces can be expanded in Taylor series.

We introduce a *local Cartesian system* at the attracted point P (Fig. 2.8). The z-axis coincides with the direction of the plumb line and points toward the zenith; the

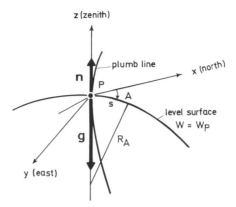

Fig. 2.8. Local cartesian coordinate system

x(north) and y(east) axes span the (horizontal) plane tangent to the level surface at P. This astronomically oriented reference system (left-handed system) is also known as the *local astronomic system*, cf. [3.2.2].

In the neighborhood of P, $W(x, y, z)$ is developed into a series:

$$W = W_p + W_x x + W_y y + W_z z + \frac{1}{2}(W_{xx}x^2 + W_{yy}y^2 + W_{zz}z^2) + W_{xy}xy$$

$$+ W_{xz}xz + W_{yz}yz + \cdots$$

Here, W_x, W_y, etc. represent the partial derivatives at P. If the calculation point is on the level surface, then neglecting terms of third and higher order, and because

$$W = W_p, \quad W_x = W_y = 0, \quad W_z = -g$$

it follows that the equation of this surface is

$$-gz + \frac{1}{2}(W_{xx}x^2 + W_{yy}y^2) + W_{xy}xy + \cdots = 0. \tag{2.32}$$

2.2.3 Curvature of the Level Surfaces

In order to derive the curvature of the level surface at the point P, we introduce the vertical plane defined by the surface normal (direction of the plumb line) at P and a second point. Its intersection with the level surface forms a plane curve, the *normal section*. The direction of the normal section is given by the angle measured in the horizontal plane between the x-axis and the normal section. This angle is called the *astronomic azimuth A* (Fig. 2.8). The curvature of the normal section (*normal curvature*) can be determined for small distances s from the geometrical relations of Fig. 2.8:

$$\frac{1}{R_A} = -\frac{2z}{s^2}. \tag{2.33}$$

Here, R_A is the radius of curvature. Introducing the plane polar coordinates

$$x = s \cos A, \quad y = s \sin A$$

and substituting (2.32) leads to

$$\frac{1}{R_A} = -\frac{1}{g}(W_{xx} \cos^2 A + 2W_{xy} \sin A \cos A + W_{yy} \sin^2 A). \qquad (2.34)$$

The normal curvature assumes is extreme values in the mutually perpendicular *directions of principal curvature*. From a consideration of extremas, we find that for their azimuths A_1 and $A_2 = A_1 \pm \dfrac{\pi}{2}$,

$$\tan 2A_{1,2} = 2\frac{W_{xy}}{W_{xx} - W_{yy}}. \qquad (2.35)$$

The curvatures in the x- and y-directions ($A = 0$ and $A = 180°$) are given by

$$\frac{1}{R_x} = -\frac{W_{xx}}{g}, \quad \frac{1}{R_y} = -\frac{W_{yy}}{g}, \qquad (2.36)$$

where R_x, R_y are the corresponding radii curvature. (2.34) to (2.36) reveal the connection between the curvature of the level surfaces and the second derivatives of the gravity potential.

2.2.4 Curvature of Plumb Lines

We start with the *curvature vector* of the plumb line

$$\mathbf{r}'' = \begin{pmatrix} x'' \\ y'' \\ z'' \end{pmatrix} = \kappa \begin{pmatrix} \cos A \\ \sin A \\ 0 \end{pmatrix}, \qquad (2.37)$$

which lies along the principal normal to the plumb line. Here $''$ denotes the second derivative with respect to the arc length of the plumb line, κ is the total curvature and A is the azimuth of the principal normal in the horizontal plane. We obtain the components of $\mathbf{r}''$ by differentiating the gravity vector

$$\mathbf{g} = g \begin{pmatrix} x' \\ y' \\ -z' \end{pmatrix} = \begin{pmatrix} W_x \\ W_y \\ -W_z \end{pmatrix}$$

and considering that $x' = y' = 0$, $z' = -1$:

$$\mathbf{r}'' = -\frac{1}{g} \begin{pmatrix} W_{xz} \\ W_{yz} \\ 0 \end{pmatrix}.$$

Substituting this into (2.37) yields the *curvature of the plumb line*

$$\kappa = -\frac{W_{xz}}{g \cos A} = -\frac{W_{yz}}{g \sin A}, \tag{2.38}$$

and the *azimuth* of its principal normal

$$A = \arctan \frac{W_{yz}}{W_{xz}}. \tag{2.39}$$

The curvatures of the projections of the plumb line on the xz- and yz-planes are given by

$$\kappa_x = -\frac{W_{xz}}{g}, \quad \kappa_y = -\frac{W_{yz}}{g} \tag{2.40}$$

respectively, where $\kappa = \sqrt{\kappa_x^2 + \kappa_y^2}$. (2.38) to (2.40) show that the curvature of the plumb lines also depends on the second derivatives of the gravity potential.

2.2.5 Gravity Gradient

The gravity vector expressed in the local astronomic system, cf. [3.2.2], is given by

$$\mathbf{g}^T = (\text{grad } W)^T = (W_x, W_y, -W_z), \tag{2.41a}$$

see also [2.2.4]. Differentiation yields the *gravity gradient tensor* (Eötvös tensor)

$$\text{grad } \mathbf{g} = \text{grad}(\text{grad } W) = \begin{pmatrix} W_{xx} & W_{xy} & -W_{xz} \\ W_{yz} & W_{yy} & -W_{yz} \\ -W_{xz} & -W_{yz} & -W_{zz} \end{pmatrix}. \tag{2.41b}$$

Since the gravity field is irrotational, we have

$$W_{xy} = W_{yx}, \quad W_{xz} = W_{zx}, \quad W_{yz} = W_{zy}. \tag{2.41c}$$

Taking Poisson's differential equation (2.27) into account, we recognize that (2.41b) only contains five mutually independent elements. They are closely related to the curvature of the level surfaces and the plumb lines.

The *gradient of gravity*

$$\text{grad } g = \begin{pmatrix} \partial g/\partial x \\ \partial g/\partial y \\ \partial g/\partial z \end{pmatrix} = -\begin{pmatrix} W_{xz} \\ W_{yz} \\ W_{zz} \end{pmatrix} \tag{2.41d}$$

describes the variation of gravity in the horizontal plane and in the vertical. The *horizontal gradient* (Fig. 2.9) formed by the components $\partial g/\partial x$ and $\partial g/\partial y$ points in the direction of the maximum increase in gravity in the horizontal plane.

The *vertical component* $\partial g/\partial z = -W_{zz}$ describes the variation of gravity with respect to height. If we combine the generalized Poisson differential equation (2.27) with the mean curvature

$$H^* = \frac{1}{2}\left(\frac{1}{R_x} + \frac{1}{R_y}\right) = -\frac{1}{2g}(W_{xx} + W_{yy}), \tag{2.42}$$

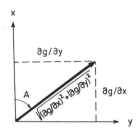

Fig. 2.9. Horizontal gradient of gravity

computed from (2.36), then we obtain the relation found by BRUNS (1878) between the vertical component of the gravity gradient and the *curvature of level surfaces*:

$$\frac{\partial g}{\partial z} = -2gH^* + 4\pi G\rho - 2\omega^2. \tag{2.43}$$

2.3 Spherical Harmonic Expansion of the Gravitational Potential

Because the density function $\rho = \rho(r')$ is not known well enough, the gravitational potential of the earth $V = V(r)$ cannot be computed using (2.8). However, as a solution of Laplace's differential equation (2.17), a series expansion of V is possible which is convergent in the space exterior to the earth (e.g. HOBSON A1931, SIGL A1985).

2.3.1 Expansion of the Reciprocal Distance

Applying the law of cosines in Fig. 2.1, we obtain

$$\frac{1}{l} = (r^2 + r'^2 - 2rr'\cos\psi)^{-\frac{1}{2}} = \frac{1}{r}\left(1 + \left(\frac{r'}{r}\right)^2 - 2\frac{r'}{r}\cos\psi\right)^{-\frac{1}{2}} \tag{2.44}$$

for the reciprocal distance, appearing in (2.8), between the attracted point P and the attracting point P'. Here, ψ is the central angle between P and P'.

If $1/l$ is expanded in a series converging for $r' < r$, and if the terms are arranged according to increasing powers of r'/r, then it follows that

$$\frac{1}{l} = \frac{1}{r}\sum_{l=0}^{\infty}\left(\frac{r'}{r}\right)^l P_l(\cos\psi). \tag{2.45}$$

The $P_l(\cos\psi)$ represent polynomials of lth degree in $\cos\psi$. They are known as *Legendre polynomials* (*zonal harmonic functions*) and they are computed for the argument $t = \cos\psi$ by means of

$$P_l(t) = \frac{1}{2^l \times l!} \times \frac{d^l}{dt^l}(t^2 - 1)^l. \tag{2.46}$$

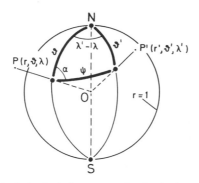

Fig. 2.10. Spherical distance and spherical coordinates

If we interpret ψ to be the spherical distance on a unit sphere between the attracted point and the attracting point, then according to Fig. 2.10 and using the spherical coordinates introduced in [2.1.2], the following relationship exists:

$$\cos \psi = \cos \vartheta \cos \vartheta' + \sin \vartheta \sin \vartheta' \cos(\lambda' - \lambda).$$

The corresponding decomposition of $P_l(\cos \psi)$ leads to

$$P_l(\cos \psi) = P_l(\cos \vartheta)P_l(\cos \vartheta')$$

$$+ 2 \sum_{m=1}^{l} \frac{(l-m)!}{(l+m)!}(P_{lm}(\cos \vartheta) \cos m\lambda \, P_{lm} \cos \vartheta') \cos m\lambda' \quad (2.47)$$

$$+ P_{lm}(\cos \vartheta) \sin m\lambda \, P_{lm}(\cos \vartheta') \sin m\lambda').$$

Here, the $P_l(t)$ are again the Legendre polynomials with argument $t = \cos \vartheta$ or $t = \cos \vartheta'$. The *associated Legendre functions of the first kind* $P_{lm}(t)$ (l = degree, m = order) are obtained by differentiating $P_l(t)$ m times with respect to t:

$$P_{lm}(t) = (1 - t^2)^{\frac{m}{2}} \frac{d^m}{dt^m} P_l(t). \quad (2.48)$$

We complete the expansion of $1/l$ by substituting (2.47) into (2.45).

The functions

$$P_{lm}(\cos \vartheta) \cos m\lambda, \quad P_{lm}(\cos \vartheta) \sin m\lambda \quad (2.49)$$

depending on ϑ and λ are known as (Laplace's) *surface harmonics*. They characterize the behavior of a function on a unit sphere.

2.3.2 Expansion of the Gravitational Potential

After substituting the spherical harmonic expansion (2.45), (2.47) of $1/l$, we obtain for the gravitational potential (2.8)

$$V = \frac{G}{r} \sum_{l=0}^{\infty} \sum_{m=0}^{l} k \frac{(l-m)!}{(l+m)!} \times \frac{1}{r^l} \left(P_{lm}(\cos \vartheta) \cos m\lambda \int\!\!\int\!\!\int_{earth} r'^l P_{lm}(\cos \vartheta') \cos m\lambda' \, dm \right.$$

$$\left. + P_{lm}(\cos \vartheta) \sin m\lambda \int\!\!\int\!\!\int_{earth} r'^l P_{lm}(\cos \vartheta') \sin m\lambda' \, dm \right), \quad k = \begin{cases} 1 & \text{for } m = 0 \\ 2 & \text{for } m \neq 0 \end{cases} . \tag{2.50}$$

For $l = 0$, the integration yields the potential of the earth's mass M concentrated at the center of mass (2.11). We extract this term, introduce the semimajor axis of the earth ellipsoid as a constant, and denote the integrals of the mass by C_{lm}, S_{lm} (harmonic coefficients). The gravitational potential expanded in spherical harmonics is then written as

$$V = \frac{GM}{r} \left(1 + \sum_{l=1}^{\infty} \sum_{m=0}^{l} \left(\frac{a}{r} \right)^l (C_{lm} \cos m\lambda + S_{lm} \sin m\lambda) P_{lm}(\cos \vartheta) \right), \tag{2.51}$$

where

$$C_{l0} = C_l = \frac{1}{M} \int\!\!\int\!\!\int_{earth} \left(\frac{r'}{a} \right)^l P_l(\cos \vartheta') \, dm,$$

$$\begin{Bmatrix} C_{lm} \\ S_{lm} \end{Bmatrix} = \frac{2}{M} \times \frac{(l-m)!}{(l+m)!} \int\!\!\int\!\!\int_{earth} \left(\frac{r'}{a} \right)^l P_{lm}(\cos \vartheta') \begin{Bmatrix} \cos m\lambda' \\ \sin m\lambda' \end{Bmatrix} dm \tag{2.52}$$

$$\text{for } m \neq 0.$$

Particularly in *satellite geodesy*, the coefficients

$$J_l = -C_l, \quad J_{lm} = -C_{lm}, \quad K_{lm} = -S_{lm} \tag{2.53}$$

are generally used.

The *fully normalized harmonics* $\bar{P}_{lm}(\cos \vartheta)$ are also employed frequently. These may be computed from the conventional harmonics (2.46), (2.48) according to

$$\bar{P}_{lm}(\cos \vartheta) = \sqrt{k(2l+1) \frac{(l-m)!}{(l+m)!}} P_{lm}(\cos \vartheta), \quad k = \begin{cases} 1 & \text{for } m = 0 \\ 2 & \text{for } m \neq 0. \end{cases}$$

In addition to the orthogonality relations for the surface harmonics, we now also have

$$\frac{1}{4\pi} \int\!\!\int_{\sigma} \left(\bar{P}_{lm} \begin{Bmatrix} \cos m\lambda \\ \sin m\lambda \end{Bmatrix} \right)^2 d\sigma = 1$$

over the unit sphere σ. Correspondingly, the harmonic coefficients $\bar{C}_{lm}$, $\bar{S}_{lm}$ of the expansion analogous to (2.51) of the gravitational potential are given by

$$\begin{Bmatrix} \bar{C}_{lm} \\ \bar{S}_{lm} \end{Bmatrix} = \sqrt{\frac{(l+m)!}{k(2l+1)(l-m)!}} \begin{Bmatrix} C_{lm} \\ S_{lm} \end{Bmatrix}, \quad k = \begin{cases} 1 & \text{for } m = 0 \\ 2 & \text{for } m \neq 0. \end{cases} \tag{2.52a}$$

The expansion (2.50) converges outside a sphere of radius $r = a$ which just encloses the terrestrial body. As an approximation, such a representation may also be applied on the surface of the earth. It should be noted that the harmonic expansion is in no case valid for the interior of the masses, since the interior is governed by Poisson's differential equation (2.19).

2.3.3 The Geometrical Meaning of the Surface Harmonics

We consider here the behavior of the *surface harmonics* (2.49) which appear in the harmonic expansion of the gravitational potential.

The condition $m = 0$ yields the special case of the Legendre polynomials $P_l(\cos \vartheta)$. Because of their independence of the geographical logitude λ, they divide the surface of the sphere into zones in which they have alternately positive and negative signs: *zonal harmonics*. These harmonics possses l real zeros in the interval $0 \leqslant \vartheta \leqslant \pi$, so that for even l, the sphere is divided symmetrically with respect to the equator $\vartheta = 90°$; and the case for odd l results in an asymetric division (Fig. 2.11). The $P_l(\cos \vartheta)$ up to $l = 3$ and computed according to (2.46) are given as follows:

$$P_0 = 1, \quad P_1 = \cos \vartheta, \quad P_2 = \frac{3}{2}\cos^2 \vartheta - \frac{1}{2}, \quad P_3 = \frac{5}{2}\cos^3 \vartheta - \frac{3}{2}\cos \vartheta. \quad (2.54)$$

The $P_{lm}(\cos \vartheta)(m \neq 0)$ have $(l - m)$ zeros in the interval $0 < \vartheta < \pi$. Because of the multiplication by $\cos m\lambda$ or $\sin m\lambda$, the surface harmonics are longitude dependent, furnishing $2m$ zeros in the interval $0 \leq \lambda < 2\pi$: *tesseral harmonics* (Fig. 2.12). For $P_{lm}(\cos \vartheta)$ up to $l = m = 3$, (2.48) yields

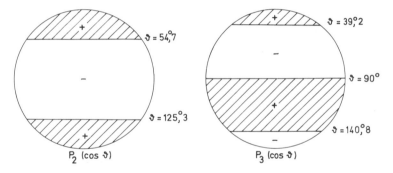

Fig. 2.11. Zonal harmonics

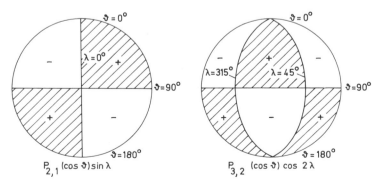

Fig. 2.12. Tesseral harmonics

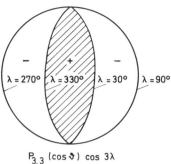

$$P_{3,3}\ (\cos \vartheta)\ \cos 3\lambda$$

Fig. 2.13. Sectorial harmonics

$$P_{1.1} = \sin \vartheta, \quad P_{2.1} = 3 \sin \vartheta \cos \vartheta, \quad P_{2.2} = 3 \sin^2 \vartheta,$$

$$P_{3.1} = \sin \vartheta \left(\frac{15}{2} \cos^2 \vartheta - \frac{3}{2} \right), \quad P_{3.2} = 15 \sin^2 \vartheta \cos \vartheta, \qquad (2.55)$$

$$P_{3.3} = 15 \sin^3 \vartheta.$$

Finally, for $m = l$, the dependence on ϑ disappears, and the sphere is divided into sectors of alternating signs: *sectorial harmonics* (Fig. 2.13).

The amplitudes of the terms given by the surface harmonics in the gravitational potential expansion are determined by the harmonic coefficients (2.52). For example, the series has only zonal harmonics for an earth rotationally symmetric with respect to the $\vartheta = 0$ axis; the C_{lm}, S_{lm} ($m \neq 0$) must all vanish. For a mass distribution which is symmetric with respect to the equator, the zonal harmonic coefficients with odd l must be absent.

Summarizing we state that the spherical harmonic expansion of the gravitational potential represents a *spectral decomposition* of the gravitational field. The field is separated into structures of wave-length $360°/l$, corresponding to a spatial resolution of $180°/l$. Contrary to the integral over all masses of the earth (2.8), the potential is now described by the elements of the series, with the harmonic coefficients as specific mass integrals. From well distributed observations of the potential or functionals of the potential, these coefficients ($l < \infty$) can be determined [5.2.3], [5.3.3.], [5.4.4].

2.3.4 Physical Meaning of the Lower Degree Harmonic Coefficients

Some of the mass integrals of lower degree have a simple physical interpretation. To see this, we substitute the harmonic functions P_l, P_{lm} for $l = 1, 2$ and $m = 0, 1, 2$ from (2.54) and (2.55) into (2.52) and subsequently transform the spherical coordinates into Cartesian coordinates using (2.9). This yields

$$C_1 = \frac{1}{aM} \iiint_{earth} z'\, dm, \quad C_{1.1} = \frac{1}{aM} \iiint_{earth} x'\, dm, \quad S_{1.1} = \frac{1}{aM} \iiint_{earth} y'\, dm. \qquad (2.56)$$

The integrals divided by M are the coordinates of the center of mass of the earth. If we place the origin of the coordinate system at the center of mass, as it is commonly done, then this gives

$$C_1 = C_{1.1} = S_{1.1} = 0. \tag{2.57}$$

For $l = 2$, we obtain

$$C_2 = \frac{1}{a^2 M} \iiint_{earth} \left(z'^2 - \frac{x'^2 + y^2}{2} \right) dm, \quad C_{2.1} = \frac{1}{a^2 M} \iiint_{earth} x'z' \, dm,$$

$$S_{2.1} = \frac{1}{a^2 M} \iiint_{earth} y'z' \, dm, \quad C_{2.2} = \frac{1}{4a^2 M} \iiint_{earth} (x'^2 - y'^2) \, dm, \tag{2.58}$$

$$S_{2.2} = \frac{1}{2a^2 M} \iiint_{earth} x'y' \, dm.$$

These expressions contain the *moments of inertia*

$$A = \iiint (y'^2 + z'^2) \, dm, \quad B = \iiint (x'^2 + z'^2) \, dm, \quad C = \iiint (x'^2 + y'^2) \, dm$$

and the *products of inertia*

$$D = \iiint y'z' \, dm, \quad E = \iiint x'z' \, dm, \quad F = \iiint x'y' \, dm$$

with respect to the coordinate axes. The z-axis contains the mean axis of rotation which, if polar motion [3.1] is neglected, coincides with one of the principal axes of inertia (maximum moment of inertia). Whence, $D = E = 0$ and C becomes a principal moment of inertia. If we let the x-axis coincide with one of the two principal axes of inertia in the plane of the equator, then A and B become principal moments of inertia with respect to these equatorial axes; furthermore $F = 0$. Since the locations of the principal axes of inertia in the equator are unknown, the usual reckoning of the geographic longitude λ from the Greenwich meridian is retained.

Using the moments of inertia A, B, C and the product of inertia F, the harmonic coefficients may be expressed as follows:

$$C_2 = \frac{1}{a^2 M} \left(\frac{A + B}{2} - C \right), \quad C_{2.1} = S_{2.1} = 0, \quad C_{2.2} = \frac{B - A}{4a^2 M}, \quad S_{2.2} = \frac{F}{2a^2 M}. \tag{2.59}$$

$J_2 = -C_2$ is also known as the *dynamic form factor*.

The flattening of the earth at the poles represents the greatest deviation from spherical symmetry. This is evident from the numerical value for C_2 which is three orders of magnitude larger than the values of the successive coefficients. $C_{2.2}$ and $S_{2.2}$ characterize the deviation of the terrestrial mass distribution from rotational symmetry (ellipticity of the equator) [3.5.4], [5.3.3].

2.4 Temporal Variations of the Gravity Field

Gravity changes with time may be divided into gravimetric earth tides and changes of earth rotation, on one hand, and temporal variations caused by terrestrial mass displacements, on the other.

Time dependent tidal accelerations are caused by the lunar and solar gravitational forces acting on different parts of the rotating earth, in combination with the effects of the revolutions of the moon about the earth and the earth about the sun. The accelerations produce variations in the terrestrial gravity field on the order of 10^{-7} *g*. A comprehensive description is given by MELCHIOR (A1983). Other variations of the gravity field in time generally are at least one order of magnitude smaller than the tidal effects.

2.4.1 Tidal Acceleration, Tidal Potential

For a *rigid* earth, the *tidal potential* may be determined from the law of gravitation and the orbital elements of the moon and the sun ("theoretical tides"), see e.g. BARTELS (A1957). The computations are carried out separately for the earth-moon and earth-sun systems; the results are subsequently added. The moon and the sun in this case may be regarded as point masses.

We introduce a coordinate system whose origin is at the earth's center of mass, moving with the earth in space, but not rotating (*revolution without rotation*). All points of the earth describe the same rotational motion in this system, with monthly (moon) or yearly (sun) periods. Hence, the centrifugal acceleration acts equally at all points. At the earth's center of mass S, it is compensated by the gravitation $\boldsymbol{b}_0$ of the moon and sun, respectively (equilibrium in the respective systems). At the other points of the earth, *tidal accelerations* $\boldsymbol{b}_t$ arise being the difference between the gravitational accelerations $\boldsymbol{b}$ and $\boldsymbol{b}_0$ (Fig. 2.14):

$$\boldsymbol{b}_t = \boldsymbol{b} - \boldsymbol{b}_0. \tag{2.60}$$

We make the transition from the acceleration to the *tidal potential* V_t:

$$\boldsymbol{b}_t = \text{grad } V_t = \text{grad } (V - V_0). \tag{2.61}$$

V is obtained from (2.6) as the gravitational potential of a point mass, in which, for the case of the moon, m is to be replaced by the mass of the moon M_M. For the determination of V_0, we introduce a rectangular coordinate system with its origin at S, and whose z-axis coincides with the line joining S and M. The potential of the homogeneous $\boldsymbol{b}_0$-field is then $|\boldsymbol{b}_0| \times z$.

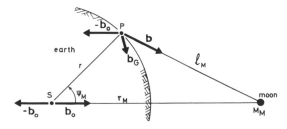

Fig. 2.14. Lunar tidal acceleration

With

$$|\boldsymbol{b}_0| = \frac{GM_M}{r_M^2} \quad \text{and} \quad z = r \cos \psi_M$$

and incorporating the constant GM_M/r_M (then the tidal potential as S becomes $V_t = 0$), one obtains

$$V_t = GM_M \left(\frac{1}{l_M} - \frac{1}{r_M} - \frac{r \cos \psi_M}{r_M^2} \right). \tag{2.62}$$

Since for points on the earth's surface $(r = R)$ we have the ratio $r/r_M = 1/60$ (for the sun the corresponding ratio is $1/23600$), the reciprocal distance

$$\frac{1}{l_M} = (r^2 + r_M^2 - 2rr_M \cos \psi_M)^{-\frac{1}{2}}$$

may be expanded, corresponding to (2.45), into spherical harmonics, with only degrees $l \geqslant 2$ being effective. For $l = 2$ and with *Doodson's* tidal constant

$$G_M(r) = \frac{3}{4} GM_M \frac{r^2}{\bar{r}_M^3} \tag{2.63}$$

($\bar{r}_M$ = mean distance to the moon) and $\cos^2 \psi_M = \frac{1}{2}(\cos 2\psi_M + 1)$, we get

$$V_t = G_M(r) \left(\frac{\bar{r}_M}{r_M} \right)^3 \left(\cos 2\psi_M + \frac{1}{3} \right). \tag{2.64}$$

A corresponding formula holds for the tidal potential due to the sun. For $r = R$ the *tidal constants* for the moon and the sun are

$$G_M(R) = 2.628 \ \text{m}^2\text{s}^{-2}, \quad G_s(R) = 1.208 \ \text{m}^2\text{s}^{-2}.$$

Hence, the solar tides amount to 46% of the lunar tides.

For stationary earth-moon and earth-sun systems, the level surfaces of the earth would experience a deformation that is constant with respect to time. Freely moving masses of water covering the entire earth would assume the form of one of these level surfaces: *equilibrium tide*. The variations in height of the level surfaces due to the tidal potential may be computed using (2.31). For the moon (sun), this gives an increase of 0.36 (0.16) m at $\psi = 0°$, $180°$ on the earth's surface; at $\psi = 90°$, $270°$, there is a decrease of 0.18 (0.08) m.

Differentiating (2.64) furnishes the *tidal acceleration*. The *radial component* (positive outward) for a mean distance to the moon ($r_M = \bar{r}_M$) is found to be

$$b_r = \frac{\partial V_t}{\partial r} = \frac{2}{r} G_M(r) \left(\cos 2\psi_M + \frac{1}{3} \right). \tag{2.65}$$

The *tangential component* (positive in the direction toward the moon) is

$$b_\psi = -\frac{\partial V_t}{r \partial \psi} = \frac{2}{r} G_M(r) \sin 2\psi_M. \tag{2.66}$$

The time dependent *change in gravity* $-b_r$ (r deviates only slightly from the direction of the plumb line) thus varies in the case of the moon (sun) between $-1.1(-0.5) \ \mu\text{ms}^{-2}$ and

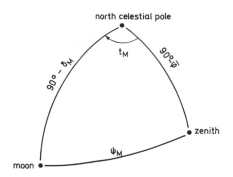

Fig. 2.15. Astronomic triangle

$+0.5(+0.3)$ μms^{-2}. The *direction of the plumb line* fluctuates on the order of b_ψ/g, hence about $\pm 0.''017(\pm 0.''008)$.

Formula (2.62) establishes the dependence of the tidal potential on the position of the moon (r_M, ψ_M). The variation of this field in time is more easily recognized if we change to an earth-fixed coordinate system, that is, one that *rotates* with the earth. According to Fig. 2.15, we have

$$\cos \psi_M = \sin \bar{\varphi} \sin \delta_M + \cos \bar{\varphi} \cos \delta_M \cos t_M$$

($\bar{\varphi}$ = geocentric latitude of the attracted point P, δ_M = declination and $t_M =$ $\Theta - \alpha_M$ = hour angle of the moon, α_M (right ascension) and δ_M are obtained for the sidereal time Θ from astronomic almanacs [4.1.2]). Substituting this into (2.64) yields

$$V_t = G_M(r)\left(\frac{\bar{r}_M}{r_M}\right)^3 \left(3\left(\frac{1}{3} - \sin^2 \bar{\varphi}\right)\left(\frac{1}{3} - \sin^2 \delta_M\right)\right.$$
$$\left. + \sin 2\bar{\varphi} \sin 2\delta_M \cos t_M + \cos^2 \bar{\varphi} \cos^2 \delta_M \cos 2t_M\right)$$

(2.67)

for the tidal potential of the moon (a corresponding equation may be obtained for the sun).

In (2.67), the quantities r_M, δ_M, t_M vary with various periods. The first term, which is in-dependent of the earth's rotation, exhibits long periodic oscillations (14 days; and 0.5 years for the sun). Its non-periodic part causes a permanent deformation of the level surfaces (they are lowered at the pole by about 0.20 m and raised at the equator by about 0.10 m). The second term oscillates with diurnal periods; the third with semidiurnal periods. In the present (1990) state of the art of tidal observations, the spherical harmonic expansion (2.67) must include terms up to $l = 4$ for the moon, and $l = 3$ for the sun.

For a comparison of the observed and theoretical (rigid earth) tides, DOODSON (1921) decomposed the tidal potential of the moon and sun into a sum of harmonic oscillations (*partial tides* or *waves*), which are determined by their frequencies, ampli-tudes, and phases. The expansion of CARTWRIGHT and TAYLER/EDDEN (1971/1973) contains 505 waves. The most important ones are the semidiurnal waves $M2$ (moon),

$S2$ (sun), $N2$ (eccentricity of the lunar orbit) and the diurnal waves $O1$ (moon), $P1$ (sun), $K1$ (lunisolar declination). More recent developments include more than 1000 tidal waves and enable the gravity tides to be computed to ±0.1 nms^{-2} and better (e.g. TAMURA 1987).

2.4.2 Earth Tides

The partially elastic body of the earth is deformed by the tides: *tides of the solid earth* (earth tides); see e.g. TOMASCHEK (A1957), MELCHIOR (1974), ZÜRN and WILHELM (1984). For a spherically symmetric, non-rotating elastic body, the earth's tides are described by the theory of *Love*.

Under the influence of the tidal potential V_t(2.64), the earth is deformed in a *radial* direction (Fig. 2.16) by a fraction of the variation Δr_t in the level surfaces

$$\Delta r_{el} = h\Delta r_t = h\frac{V_t}{g}. \tag{2.68}$$

As a consequence of the new distribution of mass, the *level surfaces* of the equilibrium tide $W + V_t = $ const. are *deformed*; the additional potential is proportional to V_t:

$$V_d = kV_t. \tag{2.69}$$

The deformations of the earth in the *horizontal* direction are proportional to the horizontal tidal accelerations ($x = $ north, $y = $ east):

$$\Delta x_{el} = \frac{l}{g}\frac{\partial V_t}{\partial\varphi}, \quad \Delta y_{el} = \frac{l}{g\cos\overline{\varphi}}\frac{\partial V_t}{\partial\lambda}. \tag{2.70}$$

In (2.68) to (2.70), the (dimensionless) *Love parameters* h, k, l (l is also called *Shida number*) enter as proportionality factors. They depend on the density and rigidity in the solid earth. For a *homogeneous spherical* earth, $k = 0.6h = 2l$.

For a point on the earth's surface, the gravity potential is altered by the amounts V_t, V_d due to the tides, and as a result of the change in potential due to Δr_{el}:

$$V_{el} = V_t + V_d - g\cdot\Delta r_{el} = V_t(1 + k - h). \tag{2.71}$$

By differentiating with respect to r, we obtain the *radial* component of the tidal acceleration. Under the assumption that V_d can be represented by a spherical har-

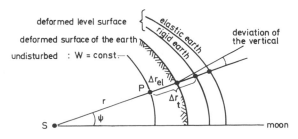

Fig. 2.16. Tides of the solid earth

monic of second degree, it is found, using (2.65), that

$$b_{r(el)} = \frac{\partial V_{el}}{\partial r} = \left(1 - \frac{3}{2}k + h\right)b_r. \tag{2.72}$$

The *tangential* component is given by

$$b_{\psi(el)} = -\frac{\partial V_{el}}{r\partial\psi} = (1 + k - h)b_\psi. \tag{2.73}$$

Therefore, due to the flexibility of the earth's surface, the observed *deviation of the vertical* $b_{\psi(el)}/g$ is smaller than the theoretical one.

The *amplitude factors* of the principal waves may be obtained by (2.72)

$$\delta = 1 - \frac{3}{2}k + h \tag{2.74}$$

using a gravimeter, and by (2.73)

$$\gamma = 1 + k - h \tag{2.75}$$

using a tiltmeter. Finally, extensometers deliver linear combinations of h and l. Together with these amplitude factors, one can determine the accompanying phase shift between the observed and the theoretical tides [4.2.6].

2.4.3 Other Temporal Variations of the Gravity Field

Besides the tides, the terrestrial gravity field is affected by a number of additional time dependent processes. Changes in gravitation are caused by the *shifting* of *mass* in the atmosphere, in the oceans, on the solid surface of the earth, and in its interior. These changes can occur in various forms (abrupt, periodic or quasi-periodic, secular). Their effect at the earth's surface can be local, regional, or global, with amplitudes seldom exceeding 10^{-8} g (e.g. TORGE A1989). Consequently, research and modeling in this field is still at its beginning. This refers also to a possible secular change of the gravitational constant. The causes of these processes, their variation in time, and how they are recorded will be taken up in the treatment of geodynamics [5.5.5]. The variations of the *centrifugal acceleration* caused both by polar motion [3.1] and by the changes in the earth's rotational velocity [4.1.3] could only be recognized in long-term gravity recordings of high accuracy.

3 Geodetic Reference Systems

From observed quantities and through subsequent geodetic computations, one attempts to determine the parameters of the physical earth's surface and the external gravity field, as well as the mean earth ellipsoid. To this end, reference systems have to be introduced. They consist of a coordinate system with defined metric and curvature, and its realization through a set of coordinates of reference points, cf. GAPOSCHKIN and KOLACZEK (A1981).

Because of the spatial formulation of the problem, *three-dimensional reference systems* are used in geodesy. The *terrestrial system* used for determining positions and the earth's gravity field, is fixed with respect to the earth's body. It is described in a global, spatial Cartesian coordinate system. The time variations of this system with respect to a quasi-inertial system are continuously monitored [3.1]. Terrestrial observations orientated in the earth's gravity field have to be transformed into this global system [3.2]. For applications in geodetic and plane surveying, as well as in most applications, heights are defined in the gravity field, and referred to the *geoid* as zero reference [3.3]. For describing positions on the curved surface of the earth, two-dimensional coordinate systems are introduced. They refer to the *rotational ellipsoid* as reference surface, and may easily be extended to three-dimensional ellipsoidal systems [3.4]. By including physical parameters, a *normal gravity field* is established for this ellipsoid which serves as a reference for the actual external field [3.5].

3.1 Global Spatial Cartesian System, Polar Motion

As a fundamental terrestrial coordinates system, one introduces an earth fixed spatial Cartesian system (X, Y, Z) whose origin is the earth's center of mass S (geocenter, center of mass including the mass of the atmosphere), Fig. 3.1. The Z-axis coincides with the *mean rotational axis* of the earth.

The mean equatorial plane perpendicular to this axis forms the XY-plane. The XZ-plane is generated by the mean meridian plane of Greenwich. The latter is defined by the mean rotational axis and the *zero meridian* of the BIH (Bureau International de l'Heure) adopted longitudes (*"mean" observatory of Greenwich*). The Y-axis is directed so as to obtain a right-handed system. The introduction of a mean rotational axis is necessary because in the course of time, the rotation of the earth changes with respect to the earth's body. This applies to the position of the earth's rotation axis (polar motion) and to the angular velocity of the rotation, cf. [4.1.3], MORITZ and MUELLER (A1987).

Polar motion consists of several components (LAMBECK A1980):

A somewhat circular motion of the instantaneous pole in a counterclockwise sense (as viewed from the north) with a period of about 430 days and an amplitude of 0."1 to 0."2 (*Chandler period*) is due to the fact that the principal axis of inertia of the earth does not coincide with

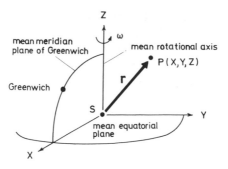

Fig. 3.1. Geocentric earth-fixed X,Y,Z-System

the spin axis. For a rigid earth, this leads to a gyration of the rotational axis about the principal axis of inertia with a period of $A/(C - A) = 305$ days (*Euler period*) and calculated from the principal moments of inertia $A = B$ and C. The difference between the Chandler and Euler periods is the consequence of the elastic yielding of the earth. A seasonal shifting of masses due to meteorological, oceanic and hydrological processes is the cause of an additional motion in the same direction with an *annual period* and an amplitude of $0\rlap{.}''05$ to $0\rlap{.}''1$. Finally, secular motions arise which, over geological epochs, attain large amounts: *polar wander*. The period from 1900 to 1970 witnessed a motion of about $0\rlap{.}''003$ per year proceeding approximately in the direction of the 80°W meridian.

With the superposition of these motions, the instantaneous pole describes a spiral curve with a slowly advancing midpoint. The deviations of the instantaneous position of the pole from the midpoint remain $< 0\rlap{.}''3$ over one year (Fig. 3.2).

The *Conventional Terrestrial System* (CTS) introduced above is based on a number of globally distributed observatories. They continuously monitor the earth's rotation in order to provide the necessary reductions to the mean rotation axis. As a space-

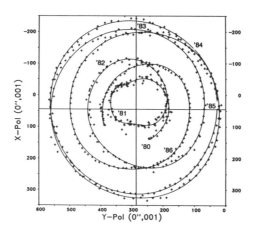

Fig. 3.2. Polar motion 1980 to 10/1986, solution ERP (DGFI I) 87L02, from SCHNEIDER (ed.) 1990

fixed reference, a *Conventional Inertial System* (CIS) as defined in astronomy, is used, cf. [4.1.2]. By international convention the mean rotational axis of CTS is defined by the mean pole position as determined between 1900.0 and 1906.0: *Conventional International Origin* (CIO). The position of the instantaneous (north) pole is determined by an international service (see below). It is given by the rectangular pole coordinates x_p, y_p with respect to CIO, defined in the plane tangential to CIO. The x_p-axis is in the direction of the Greenwich mean meridian, and the y_p-axis is directed along the 90°W meridian (Fig. 3.2).

Until the end of the 1980's, astronomic observatories performing high precision latitude and time determinations, served for materializing the CTS. Polar motion has been determined since 1899 by the five latitude observatories of the *International Latitude Service* (ILS). After extension to the *International Polar Motion Service* (IPMS), and through participation of the *Bureau International de l'Heure* (BIH), about 50 observatories finally contributed to the determination of polar motion and earth rotation (time). The results were given as 5d averages with a precision of about $\pm 0.''02$ for the pole coordinates, and ± 1 ms for earth rotation. Since 1967, polar motion was also determined from Doppler observations, within the U.S. NNSS (ANDERLE 1976), cf. [4.4.6].

The *mean meridian of Greenwich* has been defined through the geographic longitudes of the observatories, which participated in the BIH time service (BIH zero meridian), see [4.1.3] for the relations between longitude and time.

Since 1988, the *International Earth Rotation Service* (IERS) established by IAU and IUGG has replaced the IPMS and the earth-rotation section of BIH. Participating fundamental stations now employ advanced space methods, such as Very Long Baseline Interferometry, Lunar Laser Ranging, and Satellite Laser Ranging, cf. [4.4.5], [4.4.8]. The estimated precision is about $\pm 0.''002$ for polar motion, and ± 0.2 ms for earth rotation, for 1d average values. Geocentric positions of the fundamental stations are given with a precision of ± 0.1 m.

Consequently, the CTS is represented now by a global set of space stations through their instantaneous spatial coordinates (International Terrestrial Reference Frame ITRF). The reference to the conventional system or any other epoch will be made using time dependent models, as far as it is possible (MATHER 1974a; HEITZ 1978). These would include changes in the earth's rotation (polar motion and fluctuations in the rotation [4.1.3]), a displacement of the earth's center of mass, relative movements of the control points (model of plate tectonics [5.5.5]), and earth tides [2.4.2], [5.5.1].

3.2 Coordinate Systems in the Earth's Gravity Field

3.2.1 Global Astronomic System

A system of "natural" coordinates amenable to observations may be defined in the earth's gravity field (Fig. 3.3).

The *astronomic latitude* Φ (not to be confused with the potential of the centrifugal acceleration, introduced in [2.1.4]) is the angle measured in the plane of the meridian

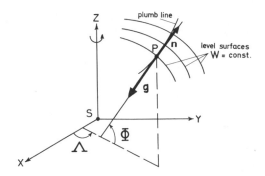

Fig. 3.3. Natural coordinates of the earth's gravity field

between the equatorial plane and the direction of the plumb line at the point P; it is positive from the equator northward, negative to the south. The angle measured in the equatorial plane between the Greenwich meridian plane and the plane of the meridian through P is designated the *astronomic longitude* Λ; it is positive toward the east. The *gravity potential* W [2.1.5] locates P in the system of level surfaces. The plane of the *astronomic meridian* here is spanned by the direction of the plumb line at P and a line parallel to the rotational axis. In German literature Φ and Λ are often denoted by φ, λ.

Determinations of astronomic positions provide the latitude Φ and the longitude Λ [4.1], thereby establishing the *direction of the vertical* at P with respect to the rotational axis. W cannot be measured directly; on the other hand, potential differences can be determined, without any further hypotheses, using spirit leveling in combination with gravity measurements [4.3.5]. Hence, P is usually specified by the potential or height difference with respect to a chosen level surface (the geoid), [3.3].

The point P in the curved space of the gravity field is determined by the intersection of the nonorthogonal *coordinate surfaces* ($\Phi = $ const., $\Lambda = $ const., $W = $ const.). The *coordinate lines* (Φ-line = astronomic meridian, Λ-line = astronomic parallel, W-line = isozenithal line) are space curves having double curvature.

The relationship between the global X, Y, Z-system and the Φ, Λ, W-system is obtained from (2.26) and Fig. 3.3:

$$\boldsymbol{g} = \text{grad } W = -g\boldsymbol{n} = -g \begin{pmatrix} \cos \Phi \cos \Lambda \\ \cos \Phi \sin \Lambda \\ \sin \Phi \end{pmatrix}, \tag{3.1}$$

where $\boldsymbol{n}$ is the outer surface normal to the level surface. From

$$W = W(X, Y, Z) \tag{3.2}$$

we obtain

$$\Phi = \text{arc tan } \frac{-W_Z}{\sqrt{W_X^2 + W_Y^2}}. \quad \Lambda = \text{arc tan } \frac{W_Y}{W_X}. \tag{3.3}$$

Therefore, the direction of the plumb line depends on the first derivatives of the gravity potential.

3.2.2 Local Astronomic Systems, Computations in the Earth's Gravity Field

The terrestrial geodetic measurements, with the exception of spatial distances, are tied to the direction of the plumb line at the point of observation, and thereby, to the earth's gravity field. They are particularly well represented in the local x, y, z Cartesian system introduced in [2.2.2], Fig. 3.4.

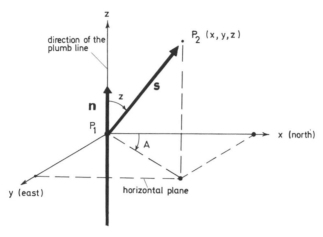

Fig. 3.4. Local astronomic x, y, z-system and terrestrial observations A, z, s

The *observed quantities* are the astronomic azimuth, the zenith angle, and the spatial distance. The angle which is measured in the horizontal plane between the astronomic meridian of P_1 and the vertical plane spanned by the vertical at P_1 and by point P_2 is the *astronomic azimuth A*. It is positive as measured from the x-axis (north) in a clockwise direction. Observed *horizontal directions* and *angles* may be regarded as azimuths lacking orientation to the north, and as azimuth differences, resp. The *zenith angle* (*zenith distance*) z is the angle measured in the vertical plane between the local vertical (direction of the plumb line) and the line joining P_1 and P_2; this angle is positive as measured from the outer surface normal. The *spatial distance s* is the length of the straight line joining P_1 and P_2.

For the vectorial arc element ds, it follows from Fig. 3.4 that

$$ds = \begin{pmatrix} dx \\ dy \\ dz \end{pmatrix} = ds \begin{pmatrix} \cos A \sin z \\ \sin A \sin z \\ \cos z \end{pmatrix}. \tag{3.4}$$

With a displacement ds, the orientation of the local system is altered because the plumb lines are not parallel. Computations in *one* local system are therefore admissible only in very limited areas.

The *transference of coordinates* in the curved global Φ, Λ, W-system using the observed polar coordinates (3.4) presupposes the knowledge of the second derivatives of the gravity potential. We have (e.g. GRAFAREND 1972, 1975)

$$\begin{pmatrix} d\Phi \\ d\Lambda \\ dW \end{pmatrix} = -\frac{1}{g} \begin{pmatrix} W_{xx} & W_{xy} & W_{xz} & dx \\ W_{yx}\cos\Phi & W_{yy}\cos\Phi & W_{yz}\cos\Phi & dy \\ 0 & 0 & g^2 & dz \end{pmatrix}. \tag{3.5}$$

As seen in [2.2.5], the matrix of second derivatives in (3.5) contains only five independent unknowns. They represent the curvature of level surface and plumb line, as well as the torsion of the astronomic meridian $-W_{xy}/g$, cf. [2.2.3] [2.2.4]. From (2.31) and (4.61) we recognize that with $dn = dz$ the results of geometric leveling are easily incorporated into (3.5).

In applying (3.5), numerous determinations of the second derviatives would have to exist, because of the irregular behavior of the curvature near the earth. However, only time-consuming gravity gradiometer (like torsion balance) measurements would be able to deliver these data [4.2.5], with results which are extremely sensitive to local mass anomalies. But even if the curvature of the gravity field were better known, the transference of coordinates would hardly be made in the Φ, Λ, W-system, since the structure of the transference formulas is complex.

A representation in differential geometry of the earth's gravity field and of the observations carried out therein has been developed by MARUSSI (1949, A1985). In this "Geodesia intrinseca", only quantities amenable to observations are used; reductions to other reference surfaces are unnecessary, see also HOTINE (A1969).

3.2.3 Local Astronomic and Global Cartesian System

The transference of coordinates in space is simplified by the transition to the global geocentric X, Y, Z-system [3.1]. For the position vector of P_2 in the local x, y, z-system of point P_1, we have from (3.4):

$$\begin{pmatrix} x \\ y \\ z \end{pmatrix} = s \begin{pmatrix} \cos A \sin z \\ \sin A \sin z \\ \cos z \end{pmatrix}. \tag{3.6}$$

The local system may be transformed into the global X, Y, Z-system by changing to a right-handed system and with rotations of $90° - \Phi$ and $180° - \Lambda$ (Fig. 3.5). An inversion yields

$$\begin{pmatrix} x \\ y \\ z \end{pmatrix} = C^{-1} \begin{pmatrix} \Delta X \\ \Delta Y \\ \Delta Z \end{pmatrix}, \tag{3.7}$$

where the inverse rotation matrix is

$$C^{-1} = \begin{pmatrix} -\sin\Phi\cos\Lambda & -\sin\Phi\sin\Lambda & \cos\Phi \\ -\sin\Lambda & \cos\Lambda & 0 \\ \cos\Phi\cos\Lambda & \cos\Phi\sin\Lambda & \sin\Phi \end{pmatrix}$$

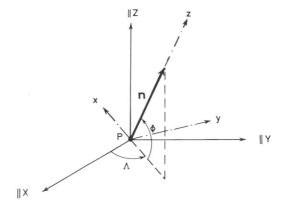

Fig. 3.5. Local x,y,z- and global X,Y,Z-system

and where

$$\Delta X = X_2 - X_1, \quad \Delta Y = Y_2 - Y_1, \quad \Delta Z = Z_2 - Z_1.$$

(3.6) and (3.7) relate the observed quantities, that is, distance, azimuth, and zenith angle to the global system. These formulas serve in the construction of observation equations in three-dimensional geodesy [5.1.2].

3.3 The Geoid as Reference Surface for Heights

3.3.1 Definition of the Geoid

We consider the waters of the ocean as freely moving homogeneous matter, which is subject only to the force of gravity of the earth. Upon attaining a state of equilibrium, the surface of such idealized oceans assumes a level surface of the gravity field; we may regard it as being extended under the continents (e.g. by a system of communicating tubes). This level surface is termed the *geoid*, cf. [1.2]. Its equation is given by

$$W = W(r) = W_0. \tag{3.8}$$

From [2.2], we see that the geoid is a closed and continuous level surface which extends partially inside the solid body of the earth. The curvature of the geoid displays discontinuities at abrupt density variations. Consequently, the geoid is not an analytic surface, and it is thereby eliminated as a reference surface for position determinations. However, it is well suited as a reference surface for heights defined in the gravity field, and easily supplied by spirit (geometric) leveling in combination with gravity measurements [4.3.5].

To establish the geoid, one utilizes the mean sea level, which may deviate by ± 1 to ± 2 m from a level surface [3.3.3]. In the case that one strives for ± 0.1 m accuracies, the classical *definition of the geoid* given above is no longer sufficient (RAPP 1983, RUMMEL and TEUNISSEN 1988). This kind of accuracy is attainable through the possibilities of satellite geodesy in the determination of heights of surface points and of the ocean surface (satellite altimetry), see [4.4]. The geoid as a *global reference surface for heights*, which is thus used for the representation of land and sea surface topography can then be defined as that level surface which best fits the mean sea level. In this respect, the potential and the elevation [3.3.2] of the geoid are obtained by applying a minimum condition for the deviations between the geoid and the mean sea level (MATHER 1978).

3.3.2 Geopotential Number and Orthometric Height

A surface point P can be determined in the system of level surfaces by its (negative) potential difference to the geoid. If P_0 is an arbitrary point on the geoid, then from (2.31) we obtain the integral

$$C = W_0 - W_P = - \int_{P_0}^{P} dW = \int_{P_0}^{P} g \, dn, \tag{3.9}$$

which is independent of path. C is known as the *geopotential number*.

To achieve good agreement with the numerical value of the height in meters, the unit of the geopotential number is chosen to be $100 \text{ m}^2 \text{ s}^{-2}$ (= kgal m), *geopotential unit* gpu. Because $g = 9.8 \text{ ms}^{-2}$, the values of the geopotential numbers are about 2% smaller than the values of the corresponding heights.

For geodetic and plane surveying, the geopotential number C is less suitable than the *orthometric height H*, which is the linear distance reckoned along the (curved) plumb line from the geoid to the surface point. If we expand the right-hand side of (3.9) in H and integrate along the plumb line from $P_0(H = 0)$ to $P(H)$, then for the orthometric height we obtain

$$H = \frac{C}{\bar{g}} \quad \text{with} \quad \bar{g} = \frac{1}{H} \int_0^H g \, dH. \tag{3.10}$$

For the computation of the mean gravity $\bar{g}$ along the plumb line, the actual values of gravity are required between the geoid and the earth's surface. Since a direct measurement of gravity inside the earth is not possible, a hypothesis regarding the mass distribution (density law) must be formed, with $\bar{g}$ then computed on this basis. Therefore, H can not be determined without an hypothesis. Because the level surfaces are not parallel, points of equal orthometric height are not situated on the same level surface.

If the geopotential number is divided by a constant gravity value (usually the normal gravity γ_0^{45} at sea level and for the geographic latitude $\varphi = 45°$ [3.5.2]), then without any hypothesis one obtains the *dynamic height*

$$H^{dyn} = \frac{C}{\gamma_0^{45}}. \tag{3.11}$$

Points on a level surface have the same dynamic height. Large corrections are necessary when converting leveled height differences into dynamic heights [5.1.5]. Because of this, the dynamic heights have not asserted themselves in geodesy.

Finally, the *normal heights* defined in [3.5.6] yield another height system without any hypothesis, which has attained considerable significance in geodetic surveying. The reference surface for normal heights is the quasigeoid which is close to the geoid.

3.3.3 Mean Sea Level

In order to establish the geoid according to [3.3.1] as a reference surface for heights, the ocean's water level is registered and averaged over longer intervals (≥ 1 year) using tide gauges (mareographs). The *mean sea level* (MSL) thus obtained represents an approximation to the geoid.

Since the tide gauge stations usually do not have an undisturbed link to the waters of the oceans, the recordings are frequently falsified by *systematic influences*. *The variations* of the sea level *with time*, as long as they are periodic or quasiperiodic, are largely eliminated by averaging the water level registrations. Satellite altimetry [4.4.9] furnishes data on the open seas which refer to the instantaneous water surface.

The height of the ocean surface above the geoid represents the *sea surface topography* (SST). Here, one distinguishes between the *instantaneous* sea surface topography and the *quasi-stationary* sea surface topography which results after accounting for the time dependent variations (MATHER 1975).

These variations include *ocean tides* which can deviate considerably from the theoretical values due to unequal water depths and because the continents impede the movement of water. The tidal amplitude on the open sea is less than 1 m; however, it can amount to several meters in coastal areas (Bay of Fundy, Nova Scotia: 21 m). Fluctuations which usually have yearly periods and attain values up to 1 m include those of a *meteorological* nature (atmospheric pressure, winds), those of an *oceanographic* nature (ocean currents, differences in water density as a function of temperature, salinity, and pressure), and those due to the *water budget* (changing water influx resulting from meltwater, monsoon rains, etc.). In addition, a secular sea level rise of about 1 mm per year has been observed during the past century.

Although the internal accuracy of the average annual values of the water level observations amounts to ± 1 cm, occasional deviations of ± 10 cm and higher may occur among the yearly averages (meteorological effects).

Even after reducing all dynamic components of SST by time averaging or modeling, the resulting *mean sea level does not form a level surface* of the earth's gravity field. Over larger areas, the deviations can amount to 1 m and more.

These deviations are caused by the non-periodic term of the tidal series expansion [2.4.1] and by the overall, approximately constant meteorological and oceanographic effects, which generate ocean currents.

The position of sea level with respect to a reference surface may be ascertained by the use of oceanographic and geodetic methods. An isobaric surface viewed as a level surface at great depths (1000 to 4000 m) serves as reference for *oceanic* (steric) *leveling*. Dynamic heights [3.3.2] of MSL with respect to the surface of a standard ocean are then computed using the fundamental hydrostatic equation and measured water densities (LISITZIN A 1974, STURGES 1974). A global approach is possible by the *hydrodynamic equation of motion* using measured water velocities. These computations reveal, among others, a global drop (1.0 to 1.5 m) of MSL from the equator to the polar zones — the maximum variation being about 2 m. Tying a *spirit leveling* net [4.3.5] to the tide gauges yields the inclination of MSL with respect to the reference level surface of the respective height system (~ geoid). The results (MATHER 1974b) agree partly with those of oceanography (e.g. an increase in MSL from the Atlantic to the Pacific coasts of the U.S.A. of 0.6 to 0.7 m; an increase from the Mediterranean Sea at Genoa northward to the Gulf of Bothnia by 0.6 m); however, the results disagree particularly and sometimes considerably in north-south directions. These discrepancies can perhaps be traced to the differently defined reference surfaces, to the particular characteristics of MSL in coastal areas, and to unknown systematic effects in the different methods (FISCHER 1977).

For the problematic nature of the determination of the mean sea level, see also ROSSITER (1967), LISITZIN (A1974).

3.4 Ellipsoidal Reference Systems

The earth's surface may be closely approximated by a rotational ellipsoid with flattened poles (height deviation from the geoid < 100 m). As a result, geometrically defined ellipsoidal systems are frequently used instead of the spatial Cartesian coordinate system [3.1].

3.4.1 Geometric Parameters and Coordinate Systems of the Rotational Ellipsoid

The rotational ellipsoid is created by rotating the meridian ellipse about its minor axis. The shape of the ellipsoid is thereby described by two *geometric parameters*; the *semimajor axis a* and the *semiminor axis b* (Fig. 3.6). Generally, *b* is replaced by one of a number of smaller quantities which is more suitable for series expansions: the (geometrical) *flattening f*, the *linear eccentricity ε*, the *first* and *second eccentricities e* and *e'*, respectively:

$$f = \frac{a-b}{a}, \quad \varepsilon = \sqrt{a^2 - b^2}, \quad e = \frac{\varepsilon}{a}, \quad e' = \frac{\varepsilon}{b}. \tag{3.12}$$

The following relations hold among these quantities:

$$\frac{b}{a} = 1 - f = \sqrt{1 - e^2} = \frac{1}{\sqrt{1 + e'^2}}. \tag{3.13}$$

We introduce a *spatial x, y, z Cartesian* coordinate system (Fig. 3.7). The origin of the system is situated at the center *O* of the figure, the *z*-axis coincides with the minor

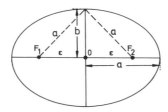

Fig. 3.6. Meridian ellipse

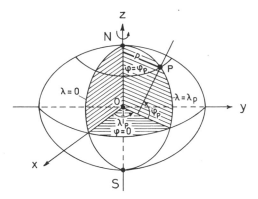

Fig. 3.7. Ellipsoidal geographic coordinates

axis of the ellipsoid. The equation of the surface of the ellipsoid is then given by

$$\frac{x^2 + y^2}{a^2} + \frac{z^2}{b^2} - 1 = 0. \tag{3.14}$$

The system of *ellipsoidal geographic coordinates* is defined by the *geographic latitude* φ and the *geographic longitude* λ. (also geodetic latitude and longitude). φ is the angle measured in the meridian plane between the equatorial plane (x,y-plane) of the ellipsoid and the surface normal at P, λ is the angle measured in the equatorial plane between the zero meridian (x-axis) and the meridian plane of P. Here, φ is positive northward and negative southward; and λ is positive as reckoned toward the east. The *ellipsoidal meridian plane* is formed by the surface normal and the z-axis.

In German literature, the notation B (= "Breite") and L (= "Länge") has been frequently used for φ and λ.

φ and λ are defined to have angular values, but they may also be considered as curvilinear surface coordinates. The *coordinate lines* of the orthogonal system are the meridians (λ = const.) and the parallels or circles of latitude (φ = const.).

With

$$x = p \cos \lambda, \quad y = p \sin \lambda \tag{3.15}$$

we introduce the radius of the circle of latitude

$$p = \sqrt{x^2 + y^2} \tag{3.16}$$

as a new variable (Fig. 3.7). Substituting this into (3.14) and differentiating yields the slope of the ellipsoidal tangent at P (Fig. 3.8)

$$\frac{dz}{dp} = -\left(\frac{b}{a}\right)^2 \frac{p}{z} = -\cot \varphi. \tag{3.17}$$

From (3.14) and (3.17) the *parametric representation of the meridian ellipse* follows:

$$p = \frac{a^2 \cos \varphi}{\sqrt{a^2 \cos^2 \varphi + b^2 \sin^2 \varphi}}, \quad z = \frac{b^2 \sin \varphi}{\sqrt{a^2 \cos^2 \varphi + b^2 \sin^2 \varphi}}. \tag{3.18}$$

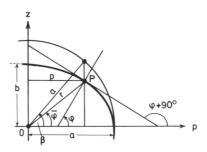

Fig. 3.8. Geographic latitude φ, reduced latitude β, geocentric latitude $\bar{\varphi}$

Using the *geocentric latitude* $\bar{\varphi}$ and the geocentric radius r (Fig. 3.8), the equation of the ellipse is given by

$$p = r \cos \bar{\varphi}, \quad z = r \sin \bar{\varphi}, \quad r = \sqrt{p^2 + z^2}. \tag{3.19}$$

Lastly, the *reduced latitude* is frequently used. It is obtained by projecting the ellipse on the concentric circle having the radius a (Fig. 3.8). Since the ratio of the elliptical ordinates to circular ordinates is b/a (ellipse as affine image of the circle), we have

$$p = a \cos \beta, \quad z = b \sin \beta. \tag{3.20}$$

Comparing (3.19) and (3.20) with (3.17) provides the transformations between the quantities $\varphi, \bar{\varphi}, \beta$:

$$\tan \bar{\varphi} = \left(\frac{b}{a}\right)^2 \tan \varphi, \quad \tan \beta = \frac{b}{a} \tan \varphi. \tag{3.21}$$

Using (3.13), we obtain series expansions for the differences between the various latitude parameters:

$$\varphi - \bar{\varphi} = \frac{e^2}{2} \sin 2\varphi + \cdots = 2(\varphi - \beta). \tag{3.22}$$

3.4.2 Curvature of the Rotational Ellipsold

The meridians and parallels are the lines of curvature of the rotational ellipsoid. The *principal radii of curvature* are therefore in the plane of the meridian (*meridian radius of curvature M*) and in the plane of the prime vertical, perpendicular to the meridian plane (*radius of curvature in the prime vertical N*), Fig. 3.9.

The curvature of the meridian $z = z(p)$ is

$$\frac{1}{M} = -\frac{d^2z/dp^2}{(1 + (dz/dp)^2)^{3/2}}. \tag{3.23}$$

Using (3.13) and substituting (3.17) and the second derivative obtained by considering (3.18) into (3.23) yields the *meridian radius of curvature*

$$M = \frac{a(1 - e^2)}{(1 - e^2 \sin^2 \varphi)^{3/2}}. \tag{3.24}$$

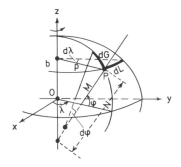

Fig. 3.9. Curvature of the rotational ellipsoid

The plane of a parallel circle (oblique section of the rotational ellipsoid) and the vertical plane in the same tangential direction intersect in P at the angle φ. The theorem of *Meusnier* (regarding surface curvature, see e.g. STOKER A1969) then provides the *radius of curvature in the prime vertical*:

$$N = \frac{p}{\cos \varphi}. \tag{3.25}$$

Because of rotational symmetry, the center of curvature is on the spin axis. Using (3.18), one obtains after some manipulations

$$N = \frac{a}{(1 - e^2 \sin^2 \varphi)^{\frac{1}{2}}}. \tag{3.26}$$

A comparison of (3.24) and (3.26) shows that $N \geq M$. At the poles ($\varphi = \pm 90°$), the polar radius of curvature becomes

$$c = M_{90} = N_{90} = \frac{a^2}{b}. \tag{3.27}$$

At the equator ($\varphi = 0°$), there is

$$M_0 = \frac{b^2}{a}, \quad N_0 = a. \tag{3.28}$$

The curvature of an arbitrary *normal section* at an azimuth α is computed according to *Euler's* formula by

$$\frac{1}{R_\alpha} = \frac{\cos^2 \alpha}{M} + \frac{\sin^2 \alpha}{N}. \tag{3.29}$$

Here, R_α is the radius of curvature. The *geodetic azimuth* α is defined as the angle measured in the horizontal plane between the ellipsoidal meridian plane of P_1 and the *vertical plane* determined by the normal to P_1 and by the point P_2; α is reckoned from north in the clockwise direction. The *mean curvature H^** is given by

$$H^* = \frac{1}{2}\left(\frac{1}{M} + \frac{1}{N}\right). \tag{3.30}$$

The *arc lengths of the coordinate lines* of the φ, λ-system are computed using M and N. For the arc elements of the meridian and parallel, respectively, we obtain (Fig. 3.9)

$$dG = M \, d\varphi, \quad dL = N \cos \varphi \, d\lambda. \tag{3.31}$$

From (3.24), the length of the *meridian arc* (starting at the equator) becomes

$$G = \int_{0}^{\varphi} M \, d\varphi = a(1 - e^2) \int_{0}^{\varphi} \frac{d\varphi}{(1 - e^2 \sin^2 \varphi)^{\frac{3}{2}}}. \tag{3.32}$$

(3.32) can be reduced to an elliptic integral of the second kind; and therefore, it is not representable in terms of elementary functions. The computations may be achieved through numerical integration. Another solution may be found by implementing a binomial expansion of the denominator of (3.32) and subsequently integrating term by term.

The length of the *arc of a circle of latitude* between the geographic longitudes λ_1 and λ_2 is given according to (3.31) by

$$\Delta L = \int_{\lambda_1}^{\lambda_2} N \cos \varphi \, d\lambda = N \cos \varphi (\lambda_2 - \lambda_1). \tag{3.33}$$

3.4.3 Spatial Ellipsoidal Coordinate System

For the spatial determination of points on the physical surface of the earth with respect to the rotational ellipsoid, the height h above the ellipsoid is introduced in addition to the geographic coordinates φ, λ; h is measured along the surface normal (Fig. 3.10).

The *spatial ellipsoidal coordinates* φ, λ, h are designated as *geodetic coordinates*. The point Q on the ellipsoid is obtained by projecting the surface point P along the ellipsoidal normal: *Helmert's projection.*

The *coordinate surfaces* (φ = const., λ = const., h = const.) of this system are orthogonal. The *coordinate lines* (φ-line = geodetic meridian, λ-line = geodetic parallel, h-line = ellipsoidal normal) represent planar curves.

If we substitute (3.25) into (3.15) and (3.17), and consider (3.13), then for the point Q on the ellipsoid if follows that

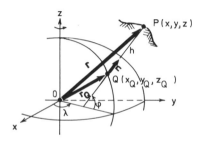

Fig. 3.10. Spatial ellipsoidal (geodetic) coordinates

$$r_Q = \begin{pmatrix} x_Q \\ y_Q \\ z_Q \end{pmatrix} = N \begin{pmatrix} \cos \varphi \cos \lambda \\ \cos \varphi \sin \lambda \\ (1 - e^2) \sin \varphi \end{pmatrix}.$$

For the surface point P, using (Fig. 3.10)

$$r = r_Q + hn, \quad n = \begin{pmatrix} \cos \varphi \cos \lambda \\ \cos \varphi \sin \lambda \\ \sin \varphi \end{pmatrix},$$

we obtain the relation

$$r = \begin{pmatrix} x \\ y \\ z \end{pmatrix} = \begin{pmatrix} (N + h) \cos \varphi \cos \lambda \\ (N + h) \cos \varphi \sin \lambda \\ ((1 - e^2)N + h) \sin \varphi \end{pmatrix}. \tag{3.34}$$

The inverse problem of φ, h is solved only by iteration; however, the system of equations converges quickly since $h \ll N$. From (3.34), we have

$$\left.\begin{array}{c} h = \dfrac{\sqrt{x^2 + y^2}}{\cos \varphi} - N, \quad \varphi = \text{arc tan} \dfrac{z}{\sqrt{x^2 + y^2}} \left(1 - e^2 \dfrac{N}{N + h}\right)^{-1} \\ \\ \lambda = \text{arc tan} \dfrac{y}{x}. \end{array}\right\} \tag{3.35}$$

BOWRING (1985) has given solutions for geodetic latitude and height which are particularly stable.

3.5 The Normal Gravity Field

3.5.1 The Normal Figure of the Earth, Level Ellipsoid

For the determination of the external gravity field [1.2], the *normal gravity field* is introduced as a reference system. The source of this field is an earth model which represents the normal figure of the earth; cf. the thorough investigations by LEDER-STEGER (1956) and MORITZ (A1990).

A *standard earth model* as a *geodetic* reference body should guarantee a good fit to the earth's surface and to the external gravity field; but also, it should possess a simple principle of formation. In this respect, the *rotational ellipsoid* [3.4], already introduced as a geometric reference surface, is well suited. In addition to the semimajor axis a and the flattening f as geometric parameters, we further introduce the total mass M and the rotational angular velocity ω as physical parameters. The gravity field is then formed as a result of gravitation and rotation. If we now require the surface of this ellipsoid to be a level surface of its own gravity field, then according to the theorem of *Stokes*, the gravity field is uniquely defined in the space exterior to this surface. This body is known as a *level* (or *equipotential*) *ellipsoid*. If the ellipsoidal parameters are given those values which correspond to the real earth, then this yields the optimum approximation to the geometry of the geoid and to the external gravity field: *mean earth ellipsoid* [5.4.4].

Theorem of G. G. Stokes (1819–1903): If a body of total mass M rotates with constant angular velocity ω about a fixed axis, and if S is a level surface of its gravity field enclosing the entire mass, then the gravity potential in the exterior space of S is uniquely determined (M, ω, S are Stokes' elements).

The standard model, however, should also comply with *geophysical* objectives. In particular, a comparison of the observed and normal gravity fields should admit inferences concerning the interior structure of the earth. This requires that the normal figure of the earth should be a spheroidal *equilibrium figure*. The level surfaces then coincide with the surfaces of equal density and equal pressure [5.5.2]. The hydrostatic equilibrium of the normal figure is created by a redistribution of the actual masses of the earth (regularization). The problem leads to the complex theory of equilibrium figures of rotating fluids (MORITZ 1989).

In the above definition of the *level ellipsoid*, nothing is stated regarding the interior mass distribution. But from the theory of equilibrium figures, it follows that only the *homogeneous* ellipsoids of *McLaurin* exist in equilibrium. On the other hand, the surface of an equilibrium figure constructed of shells, thus corresponding more to the *heterogeneous* structure of the earth, is not an ellipsoid. Nevertheless, as MORITZ (1968a) has shown, arrangements of the interior masses of the level ellipsoid are possible such that they are in good accordance with the actual structure of the earth. For an optimal approximation to an hydrostatic equilibrium figure, the maximum deviations between the level surfaces and the surfaces of equal density are on the order of f^2; the differences in stress for the ellipsoidal model remain considerably smaller than in the real earth. The level ellipsoid can then also serve as a bounding surface for a geophysical earth model [5.5.2], MARUSSI et al. (1974).

3.5.2 The Normal Gravity Field of the Level Ellipsoid

According to the theory of the level ellipsoid, developed by *P. Pizzetti* (1894), *C. Somigliana* (1929), and others, a closed representation of the normal gravity potential may be achieved in the system of ellipsoidal coordinates. To this end, we introduce an infinity of confocal ellipsoids with constant linear eccentricity ε (3.12). The point P (Fig. 3.11) is then specified by the *ellipsoidal coordinates* u (semiminor axis), β (reduced latitude), and λ (geographic longitude). From (3.20) and putting $\sqrt{u^2 + \varepsilon^2}$ for the semimajor axis, the transformation to the Cartesian system is given by

$$\begin{pmatrix} x \\ y \\ z \end{pmatrix} = u \begin{pmatrix} \sqrt{1 + (\varepsilon/u)^2} \cos \beta \cos \lambda \\ \sqrt{1 + (\varepsilon/u)^2} \cos \beta \sin \lambda \\ \sin \beta \end{pmatrix}. \tag{3.36}$$

For $\varepsilon = 0$, the u,β,λ-system with $u = r$, $\beta = 90° - \vartheta$ degenerates into the system of spherical coordinates (2.9).

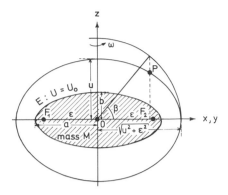

Fig. 3.11. Ellipsoidal coordinates u, β, λ and level ellipsoid $U = U_0$

We denote the vector of *normal gravity* by $\vec{\gamma}$ and the *potential of normal gravity* by U. In analogy to (2.26) we have

$$\vec{\gamma} = \text{grad } U. \tag{3.37}$$

Corresponding to (2.25), U is composed of the gravitational potential V and the potential of the centrifugal acceleration Φ

$$U = V + \Phi. \tag{3.38}$$

The notation V, Φ introduced in [2.1] for the gravitation and centrifugal potentials of the earth is retained here, since there is no risk of confusion.

The gravitational potential satisfies Laplace's differential equation (2.17) in the space exterior to the ellipsoid (semimajor axis a, semiminor axis b) containing the mass M. Corresponding to [2.3], it can therefore be expanded into spherical harmonics. If one imposes rotational sysmmetry on the normal gravity field, then the nonzonal terms in this expansion disappear. In addition, if the surface of the ellipsoid is considered to be a level surface, and if we add the expression for the centrifugal potential Φ using (2.22) and (3.36), then for the *potential of normal gravity* in the exterior space, we obtain the closed representation

$$U = \frac{GM}{\varepsilon} \text{ arc tan} \frac{\varepsilon}{u} + \frac{\omega^2}{2} a^2 \frac{q}{q_0} \left(\sin^2 \beta - \frac{1}{3} \right) + \frac{\omega^2}{2} (u^2 + \varepsilon^2) \cos^2 \beta. \tag{3.39}$$

Here q is an auxiliary quantity depending only on the geometric parameters ε and u; on the ellipsoid ($u = b$) it becomes q_0:

$$q = \frac{1}{2} \left(\left(1 + 3\frac{u^2}{\varepsilon^2} \right) \text{arc tan} \frac{\varepsilon}{u} - 3\frac{u}{\varepsilon} \right), \quad q_0 = q_{u=b}. \tag{3.40}$$

Hence, in agreement with *Stokes'* theorem [3.5.1], the normal gravity potential is determined by four parameters (a, b, M, ω). It is independent of the geographic longitude λ.

The surfaces of constant potential

$$U = U(r) = \text{const.} \tag{3.41}$$

are termed *spheropotential surfaces* (spherops). With the exception of the bounding surface E, they are not ellipsoids. If one puts $u = b$ and $q = q_0$ in (3.39), then the equation of the *level ellipsoid* reads

$$U = U_0 = \frac{GM}{\varepsilon} \text{arc tan} \frac{\varepsilon}{b} + \frac{\omega^2}{3} a^2. \tag{3.42}$$

The normal gravity $\vec{\gamma}$ is perpendicular to the level ellipsoid, so that in accordance with (3.37), only the orthogonal component appears in the derivative of U (3.39). If the geodetic latitude φ is used instead of the reduced latitude β (3.21), then for the *normal gravity on the ellipsoid* we obtain the formula of *Somigliana* (1929):

$$\gamma_0 = \frac{a\gamma_a \cos^2 \varphi + b\gamma_b \sin^2 \varphi}{\sqrt{a^2 \cos^2 \varphi + b^2 \sin^2 \varphi}}. \tag{3.43}$$

Here, the normal gravity which depends on latitude is represented by the four parameters a, b, γ_a (normal gravity at the equator), and γ_b (normal gravity at the pole). The ellipsoidal parameters $a, b, M, \omega, \gamma_a, \gamma_b$ appearing in (3.39) and (3.43) are interrelated according to the *theorem of Pizzetti*

$$2\frac{\gamma_a}{a} + \frac{\gamma_b}{b} = \frac{3GM}{a^2 b} - 2\omega^2 \tag{3.44}$$

and the *theorem of Clairaut*

$$f + \beta = \frac{\omega^2 a}{\gamma_a}(1 + e'^2)^{-\frac{1}{2}}\left(1 + e' \frac{3\left(1 + \frac{1}{e'^2}\right)\left(1 - \frac{1}{e'}\text{arc tan } e'\right) - 1}{\left(1 + \frac{3}{e'^2}\right)\text{arc tan } e' - \frac{3}{e'}}\right). \tag{3.45}$$

We see that there are only four independent quantities. In (3.45), besides the second eccentricity e' and the geometric flattening f (3.12), there is also the *gravity flattening*

$$\beta = \frac{\gamma_b - \gamma_a}{\gamma_a}. \tag{3.46}$$

The abbreviation β is used for both the reduced latitude and the gravity flattening; confusion is not to be anticipated.

The *normal gravity in the exterior space* is obtained by partial differentiation of (3.39). Near the ellipsoid, a Taylor series expansion with respect to the ellipsoidal height h is sufficient [3.5.3].

3.5.3 Series Expansions in the Normal Gravity Field

Application of the formulas for the normal gravity field (3.39) to (3.45) is facilitated through the use of series expansions with respect to f or some other quantity which characterizes the polar flattening.

We start with the spherical harmonic expansion (2.52), (2.53) of the gravitational potential V. Due to the symmetry with respect to the rotational axis (tesseral terms = 0) and the equatorial plane (odd zonal terms = 0), we obtain, upon adding the centrifugal potential (2.22) expressed in spherical coordinates, the *potential of normal gravity*

$$U = \frac{GM}{r}\left(1 - \sum_{l=2}^{\infty}\left(\frac{a}{r}\right)^{l} J_l P_l(\cos\vartheta)\right) + \frac{\omega^2}{2}r^2\sin^2\vartheta, \tag{3.47}$$

where l is even.

If P_2 is substituted from (2.54), the *expansion up to* $l = 2$ yields the normal gravity potential

$$U = \frac{GM}{r}\left(1 - \left(\frac{a}{r}\right)^{2} J_2\left(\frac{3}{2}\cos^2\vartheta - \frac{1}{2}\right) + \frac{\omega^2}{2GM}r^3\sin^2\vartheta\right). \tag{3.48}$$

Solving for r and setting $U = U_0$ gives the *radius vector to the level ellipsoid*, where we have put $r = a$ on the right side:

$$r = \frac{GM}{U_0}\left(1 - J_2\left(\frac{3}{2}\cos^2\vartheta - \frac{1}{2}\right) + \frac{\omega^2 a^3}{2GM}\sin^2\vartheta\right). \tag{3.49}$$

The *normal gravity* γ follows from the derivative of (3.47) with respect to r:

$$\gamma = \frac{GM}{r^2}\left(1 - 3\left(\frac{a}{r}\right)^{2} J_2\left(\frac{3}{2}\cos^2\vartheta - \frac{1}{2}\right) + \frac{\omega^2}{GM}r^3\sin^2\vartheta\right). \tag{3.50}$$

If we substitute either $\vartheta = 90°$ (equator) or $0°$ (pole) in (3.49) and (3.50), then we obtain either the semimajor axis a and the equatorial gravity γ_a or the semiminor axis b and the polar gravity γ_b of the ellipsoid. Using these, the *geometric flattening f* (3.12) and the *gravity flattening β* (3.46) may be computed according to

$$f = \frac{3}{2}J_2 + \frac{m}{2}, \quad \beta = -\frac{3}{2}J_2 + 2m. \tag{3.51}$$

Here

$$m = \frac{\omega^2 a^2 b}{GM} \approx \frac{\omega^2 a}{\gamma_a} \tag{3.52}$$

is the ratio of the centrifugal acceleration to the normal gravity at the equator.

From (3.50) and (3.51), we arrive at approximations to the *theorem of Pizzetti* (3.44)

$$GM = a^2\gamma_a\left(1 - f + \frac{3}{2}m\right) \tag{3.53}$$

and to *Clairaut's theorem* (3.45)

$$f + \beta = \frac{5}{2}m. \tag{3.54}$$

Substituting (3.51) and (3.52) into (3.50), we obtain *Newton's* gravity formula [1.3.2]

$$\gamma_0 = \gamma_a(1 + \beta\sin^2\varphi). \tag{3.55}$$

If two gravity values γ_0 are known on the ellipsoid and at different geographic latitudes φ, then γ_a and β may be computed from (3.55). With known values for the semimajor axis a and the angular velocity ω, (3.52) supplies the quantity m. Finally, *Clairaut's* theorem yields the geometric flattening f, which thus can be determined from gravity values. Application of this principle to the real earth — that is, deriving geometric form parameters from physical quantities — leads to the gravimetric method [5.2].

The relations above, linear in f, β and m may also be derived by series expansions of the closed formulas [3.5.2]. They had already been found by *A.-C. Clairaut* in his work "Théorie de la Figure de la Terre" (1743). For today's accuracy requirements, these expansions are not sufficient. Due to the rapid convergence of (3.47), the expansion up to $l = 4$ is in general adequate; that is, the expansion includes terms of order $f^2(O(f^2))$, etc. The most important relations then become (Burša 1970, Assoc. Int. de Geod. 1971):

$$f = \frac{3}{2}J_2 + \frac{m}{2} + \frac{9}{8}J_2^2 + \frac{15}{28}J_2 m + \frac{3}{56}m^2 \tag{3.56}$$

$$\beta = -f + \frac{5}{2}m - \frac{17}{14}fm + \frac{15}{4}m^2 \tag{3.57}$$

$$m = \frac{\omega^2 a^2 b}{GM} \tag{3.58}$$

$$\gamma_0 = \gamma_a(1 + \beta \sin^2 \varphi + \beta_1 \sin^2 2\varphi), \quad \beta_1 = \frac{1}{8}f^2 - \frac{5}{8}fm. \tag{3.59}$$

One of the first applications of *Clairaut's* theorem was made by *Helmert* (1901). An adjustment to the gravity formula (3.59) of about 1400 gravity values, modified by free-air reductions [5.2.4] yielded the parameters $\gamma_a = 9.7803 \text{ ms}^{-2}$ and $\beta = 0.005302$; with an ensuing flattening of $f = 1/298.3$.

The harmonic coefficients of second and fourth degree may be computed from f and m as follows:

$$J_2 = \frac{2}{3}f - \frac{m}{3} - \frac{1}{3}f^2 + \frac{2}{21}fm, \quad J_4 = -\frac{4}{5}f^2 + \frac{4}{7}fm. \tag{3.60}$$

Near the earth's surface, a Taylor series expansion with respect to the ellipsoidal height h is sufficient for the derivation of the *normal gravity* in the *exterior space*:

$$\gamma = \gamma_0 + \left(\frac{\partial \gamma}{\partial h}\right)_0 h + \frac{1}{2}\left(\frac{\partial^2 \gamma}{\partial h^2}\right)_0 h^2 + \cdots \tag{3.61}$$

$\partial \gamma / \partial h$ is obtained by applying *Bruns'* equation (2.43) to the exterior space:

$$\frac{\partial \gamma}{\partial h} = -2\gamma H^* - 2\omega^2, \tag{3.62}$$

where H^* is the mean curvature of the ellipsoid (3.30). A series expansion which neglects terms of $O(f^2)$ leads to the vertical component of the normal gravity gradient

$$\frac{\partial \gamma}{\partial h} = -2\frac{\gamma}{a}(1 + f + m - 2f \sin^2 \varphi) \tag{3.63}$$

and *normal gravity*

$$\gamma = \gamma_0 \left(1 - \frac{2}{a}(1 + f + m - 2f \sin^2 \varphi)h \right). \tag{3.64}$$

Series expansions up to $O(f^3)$ were carried out by COOK (1959).

The reference bodies derived from the spherical harmonic expansion of the gravitational potential (3.47) truncated at low degrees l are designated *level spheroids*. They may be considered as physically defined approximations to the normal figure of the earth [3.5.1]. Their boundary surfaces for $l = 2$ (*Bruns'* spheroid) and for $l = 4$ (*Helmert's* spheroid) are surfaces of fourteenth and twenty-second order, respectively. Consequently, they are less suitable as geometric reference surfaces. They deviate from rotational ellipsoids having the same axes by $O(f^2)$ for $l = 2$ and $O(f^3)$ for $l = 4$.

Of practical importance is the introduction of higher reference models (currently $l \leqslant 360$) in connection with gravity field computations in global geodesy [5.2] to [5.4], and in large-scale problems of geophysics and geodynamics [5.5].

3.5.4 The Triaxial Ellipsoid

A triaxial ellipsoid could conceivably form a better fit to the geoid than the biaxial rotational ellipsoid. Because of this, computations were repeatedly undertaken to determine the geometric and physical parameters of such a body.

If the spherical harmonic expansion (3.47) is written with different equatorial principal moments of inertia $A, B (A < B)$, then terms arise which depend on longitude. Furthermore, if the radii corresponding to the principal axes of inertia are denoted by a_1, a_2 ($a_1 > a_2$), then the normal gravity equation (3.59) generalizes to

$$\gamma_0 = \gamma_a \left(1 + \beta \sin^2 \varphi + \beta_1 \sin^2 2\varphi + \frac{f_a}{2} \cos^2 \varphi \cos 2(\lambda - \lambda_1) \right). \tag{3.65}$$

Here, λ_1 is the geographic longitude of the equatorial semimajor axis a_1 and $f_a = (a_1 - a_2)/a_1$ is the equatorial flattening of a triaxial ellipsoid whose axes are a_1, a_2, and b.

The parameters of such an ellipsoid were repeatedly determined by astrogeodetic [5.1.7] and gravimetric [5.2.8] methods. The results varied due to varying distributions of the observations on the earth's surface and because different methods were applied in the reduction to the ellipsoid [5.2.4]. The ellipsoidal parameters may also be derived from the harmonic coefficients as determined in satellite geodesy [5.3], since according to (2.59) these are related to the principal moments of inertia. As one result, we quote the values $a_1 - a_2 = 69$ m, $\lambda_1 = 345°15'$ (LUNDQUIST and VEIS 1966).

Since the deviations of the biaxial rotational ellipsoid from the geoid attain the same order of magnitude, the triaxial ellipsoid does not present a considerably better fit to the geoid and the gravity field. In contrast, the geodetic computations are encumbered by the intricate geometry. Lastly, the triaxial ellipsoid also is not suitable as a physical normal figure. Although triaxial rotational ellipsoids exist as equilibrium figures (homogeneous ellipsoids of *Jacobi*), such an ellipsoid would nevertheless yield a completely unnatural form when using the values for the angular velocity and mass of the earth. The triaxial ellipsoid thus is not appropriate as a reference body, with the exception of special purposes.

3.5.5 Geodetic Reference Systems

In order to make geodetic results mutually comparable and to provide coherent results to other sciences (astronomy, geophysics), geodetic reference systems are established by recommendation of the International Union for Geodesy and Geophysics (I.U.G.G.) [1.4.2].

In 1924 in Madrid, the general assembly of the I.U.G.G. introduced the ellipsoid determined by J. F. HAYFORD (1909) as the *International Ellipsoid* with the parameters

$$a = 6\,378\,388 \text{ m}, \quad f = 1/297.0. \tag{3.66a}$$

The general assembly in Stockholm (1930) adopted for this ellipsoid the *international gravity formula* established by G. Cassinis

$$\gamma_0 = 9.78049(1 + 0.005\,2884 \sin^2 \varphi - 0.000\,0059 \sin^2 2\varphi)\,\text{ms}^{-2}, \tag{3.66b}$$

corresponding to the normal gravity formula (3.59); thereby creating a level ellipsoid.

The geometric parameters a, f were calculated by *Hayford* from astrogeodetic observational material in the U.S.A. [5.1.7]. W. A. HEISKANEN (1928) had determined the equatorial gravity γ_a in (3.66b) from an adjustment of isostatically reduced gravity values [5.2.4]. Here, the gravity flattening β given according to (3.52) and (3.54) by a, f, γ_a, and ω was held fixed; ω existed with high accuracy from astronomic observations. The international reference system of 1924/1930 is thus defined by the four parameters a, f, γ_a, ω.

The corresponding ellipsoid has been applied in numerous geodetic surveys; also the normal gravity formula has found broad acceptance. However, according to present knowledge, the values for the parameters of the 1924/1930 system represent an insufficient approximation to the mean earth ellipsoid [5.4.4] for scientific purposes.

At the general assembly of the I.U.G.G. in Luzern (1967), the 1924/1930 reference system was replaced by the *Geodetic Reference System 1967* (ASSOCIATION INTERNATIONALE DE GÉODÉSIE 1971, MORITZ 1968b). It is defined by the following constants

$$a = 6\,378\,160 \text{ m}, \quad GM = 398\,603 \times 10^9 \text{ m}^3 \text{ s}^{-2}, \quad J_2 = 1082.7 \times 10^{-6}. \tag{3.67a}$$

The angular velocity of the earth's rotation

$$\omega = 7.292\,115\,1467 \times 10^{-5} \text{ rad s}^{-1}, \tag{3.67b}$$

not mentioned in the resolution, was adopted as the fourth parameter. The reference ellipsoid corresponding to this definition was declared to be a level ellipsoid.

On the orientation of the Geodetic Reference System 1967, the following is stipulated:
a) The minor axis of the reference ellipsoid shall be parallel to the direction with is defined by the conventional international origin (CIO) for polar motion.
b) The primary meridian shall be parallel to the zero meridian adopted by the BIH for the longitudes (= mean meridian of Greenwich).

The calculation of the semimajor axis a was based on astrogeodetic material over the entire earth which was transformed into a uniform system by gravimetric data. Observations of space probes yielded the geocentric gravitational constant GM. It includes the mass of the atmosphere $M_{\text{Atm}} = 0.89 \times 10^{-6}\ M$. The dynamic form factor J_2 was derived from orbit perturbations of artifical satellites. The angular velocity ω is known from astronomy with much higher accuracy than the other quantities. The accepted value refers to the second in mean solar time. The Geodetic Reference System 1967 represents a good approximation (as of 1964) to the mean earth ellipsoid. It has found application especially in the formulation of scientific problems and in the planning of new geodetic surveys.

At its general assembly in Canberra (1979), the I.U.G.G. recognized that the Geodetic Reference System 1967 no longer represented the size, shape and gravity field of the earth to an adequate accuracy. It was replaced by the *Geodetic Reference System 1980*, also based on the theory of the geocentric equipotential ellipsoid [3.5.2], [3.5.3], with the conventional constants:

$$a = 6378\,137 \text{ m}, \quad GM = 398\,600.5 \times 10^9 \text{ m}^3 \text{ s}^{-2}, \quad J_2 = 1\,082.63 \times 10^{-6},$$
$$\omega = 7.292\,115 \times 10^{-5} \text{ rad s}^{-1}, \tag{3.68}$$

where GM includes the atmosphere, and J_2 excludes the permanent tidal deformation [2.4.1]. There is no change in the orientation of the reference system (see above). The relative accuracy of these values amounts to $\pm 3 \times 10^{-7}(a)$, $\pm 1 \times 10^{-7}(GM)$, and $\pm 5 \times 10^{-6}(J_2)$, [5.4.4]. The new system is consistent with the 1976 I.A.U. System of Astronomical Constants.

Using the formulas given with respect to a level ellipsoid, the following quantities, among others, may be determined from the parameters (3.68) of the Geodetic Reference System 1980-rounded values-MORITZ (1984):

geometric ellipsoidal parameters [3.4.1]:

$$f = 1/298.2572, \quad b = 6356\,752.3 \text{ m}, \quad e^2 = 0.006\,694\,380;$$

radii of curvature at the pole and at the equator [3.4.2]:

$$c = 6399\,594 \text{ m}, \quad M_0 = 6335\,439 \text{ m}, \quad N_0 = a;$$

meridian and parallel arc lengths [3.4.2] for $\varphi = 50°$:

$$\Delta G(\Delta\varphi = 1°) = 111\,229 \text{ m}, \quad \Delta G(\Delta\varphi = 1') = 1853.8 \text{ m},$$
$$\Delta G(\Delta\varphi = 1'') = 30.90 \text{ m}, \quad \Delta L(\Delta\lambda = 1°) = 71\,696 \text{ m},$$
$$\Delta L(\Delta\lambda = 1') = 1194.9 \text{ m}, \quad \Delta L(\Delta\lambda = 1'') = 19.92 \text{ m};$$

physical parameters [3.5.2], [3.5.3]:

$$U_0 = 6.263\,6861 \times 10^7 \text{ m}^2 \text{ s}^{-2},$$
$$J_4 = -2.371 \times 10^{-6}, \quad J_6 = 0.006 \times 10^{-6}, \quad m = 0.003\,499\,786$$
$$\gamma_0 = 9.780\,327(1 + 0.005\,3024 \sin^2 \varphi - 0.000\,0058 \sin^2 2\varphi) \text{ ms}^{-2},$$
$$\left(\frac{\partial\gamma}{\partial h}\right)_0 = -0.30877(1 - 0.001\,42 \sin^2 \varphi) \times 10^{-5} \text{ s}^{-2}.$$

The normal gravity γ_0 depends on the influence of the total mass of the earth including the atmosphere. As far as values for normal gravity are required on the ellipsoid or within the range of the atmosphere, according to (2.12), the influence of the noneffective air masses lying above the attracted point must be subtracted. The correction for γ_0 amounts to $\partial\gamma = -8.7\ \mu ms^{-2}$ for $h = 0$ and $\partial\gamma = -0.1\ \mu ms^{-2}$ for $h = 30$ km (ECKER and MITTERMAYER 1969).

3.5.6 Normal Geographic Coordinates, Normal Heights

The *normal geographic coordinates* in the normal gravity field may be introduced (Fig. 3.12) in analogy to the definition of the astronomic latitude and longitude [3.2.1]. The *normal geographic latitude* φ^N is the angle measured in the meridian plane between the equatorial plane of the level ellipsoid and the direction of normal gravity at P. The *normal geographic longitude* λ^N is equivalent to the ellipsoidal quantity λ [3.4.1]. These coordinates are significant in the direct determination of the physical surface of the earth [5.2.5].

Since the spheropotential surfaces $U = $ const. are not parallel, the plumb lines of the normal gravity field are curved. Here, due to rotational symmetry, we have only a meridional component κ^N for the *normal curvature of the plumb line*. In a local ellipsoidal x,y,z-system (x = north, y = east, z = zenith of the normal plumb line) defined similarly as in [2.2.2], it follows, corresponding to (2.40), that

$$\kappa_x^N = -\frac{U_{xz}}{\gamma_0}, \quad \kappa_y^N = 0, \tag{3.69}$$

where $-U_{xz} = (\partial\gamma/\partial x)_0 = (\partial\gamma/M\partial\varphi)_0$, M = meridian radius of curvature (3.24). We substitute γ_0 (3.55) and its derivative, and using the gravity flattening β, we obtain the sufficient approximation

$$\kappa_x^N = \frac{\beta}{M}\sin 2\varphi. \tag{3.70}$$

From this, the *normal horizontal gravity gradient* on the ellipsoid of the Geodetic Reference System 1980 [3.5.5] is given by

$$\partial\gamma/\partial x = 8.2\sin 2\varphi\ ns^{-2}.$$

The *normal height* H^N introduced by *M. S. Molodenski* is of great importance for gravimetric methods and in geodetic surveying. It is defined analogously to the orthometric height (3.10), by the geopotential number C and the mean normal

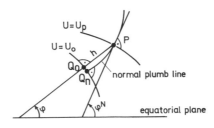

Fig. 3.12. Geodetic latitude φ and normal geographic latitude φ^N

gravity $\bar{\gamma}$

$$H^N = \frac{C}{\bar{\gamma}}, \quad \bar{\gamma} = \frac{1}{H^N} \int_0^{H^N} \gamma \, dH^N. \tag{3.71}$$

A point Q is determined by H^N as lying on the normal plumb line, or to a good approximation on the ellipsoid normal, which passes through the surface point P. In the normal gravity field, Q should have the same potential difference C (3.9) with respect to the level ellipsoid $U = U_0$ as the point P has with respect to the geoid in the gravity field of the earth:

$$C = U_0 - U_Q = W_0 - W_p. \tag{3.72}$$

If we require, as it is usual, that the potentials of the ellipsoid and the geoid be equal ($U_0 = W_0$), then we have $U_Q = W_p$. R. A. HIRVONEN (1960) calls the surface for which $U_Q = W_p$ holds for every point the *telluroid*. The normal height H^N of a point P is equivalent to the height of the corresponding telluroid point Q above the ellipsoid. The telluroid intersects the spheropotential surfaces $U = U_Q$; hence it itself is not a level surface of the normal gravity field. Its shape resembles that of the physical surface of the earth S, cf. [5.1].

If we substitute γ from (3.64) into (3.71) and integrate, then we see that

$$\bar{\gamma} = \gamma_0 \left(1 - \frac{1}{a}(1 + f + m - 2f \sin^2 \varphi)H^N \right). \tag{3.73}$$

Hence, $\bar{\gamma}$ may be computed rigorously (iteratively). Since C can be measured [5.1.5], the normal height is determined without any hypothesis. Extending the normal heights downward from the earth's surface yields the *quasigeoid* as reference surface for heights. It does not represent a level surface, but the deviations from the geoid are small, cf. [5.1.5].

4 Methods of Measurement in Geodesy

For the solution of the problem of geodesy formulated in [1.2], various geometric and physical quantities are observed on the surface of the earth and in the space exterior to it. They may be divided into four groups:

1. *Astronomic determinations* of latitude, longitude, and azimuth oriented with respect to the direction of the plumb line and obtained from direction measurements to the stars [4.1];
2. measurements of *gravity* and the components of the *gravity gradient* as well as *earth tide measurements* [4.2];
3. *geodetic measurements* of horizontal angles, distances, zenith angles, and height differences [4.3];
4. measurements independent of the direction of the plumb line to artificial earth satellites, the moon, and extragalactic radio sources, as well as height measurements from satellites to the earth's surface. Due to the importance of earth satellites, these measurements will be associated with the concept of "*satellite observations*" [4.4].

The methods of measurement (data collection) depend strongly on the *technological* possibilities. Substantial progress has been achieved through the development of electronics and the resulting change in measurement and evaluation techniques, the continuous establishment of satellite systems also for geodetic use, and the application of laser technology. The estimation of *accuracy* and the increase in accuracy in these methods deserve particular attention. Depending on the instrument, the accuracy obtained in the laboratory is usually not completely attainable when making geodetic measurements; this is due to external disturbing influences (microseismicity, temperature and pressure variations, magnetic effects, refraction, etc.).

4.1 Astronomic Measurements

Geodetic astronomy is concerned with the determination of the astronomic latitude Φ and longitude Λ [3.2.1], as well as the astronomic azimuth A [3.2.2] from observations of fixed stars; the basis for such work is *spherical astronomy* (Smart A1960, Mueller A1969, Eichhorn A1974, Sigl A1975).

4.1.1 Coordinate Systems of Spherical Astronomy

When observing fixed stars, the distance from the point of observation (topocenter) to the center of mass of the earth (geocenter) can be neglected in comparison to the distance to the star. If we circumscribe the *celestial sphere* (unit sphere) about the earth *E*, considered as a point (Fig. 4.1), then the positions of the fixed stars are determined on the sphere by two directions. Of the various coordinate systems in spherical astronomy, the equatorial and horizon systems are of particular interest in geodetic astronomy.

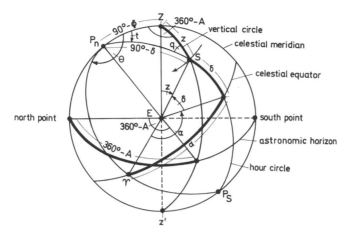

Fig. 4.1. Astronomic coordinate systems

The star-fixed *"equatorial system"* is formed by projecting the global terrestrial system [3.1] onto the celestial sphere. The extended rotational axis of the earth meets the celestial sphere at the celestial poles P_n and P_s (Fig. 4.1); the line of intersection of the earth's equatorial plane with the celestial sphere is the *celestial equator*. The great circles perpendicular to the celestial equator and containing the celestial poles are called *hour circles*; the small circles parallel to the celestial equator are termed celestial parallels.

The coordinates of a star S in this system are the *declination* δ and the *right ascension* α. δ is the angle measured in the plane of the hour circle between the equatorial plane and the line joining E and S (positive from the equator to P_n, negative to P_s). α is the angle measured in the plane of the equator between the plane of the hour circle of the vernal equinox Υ (intersection of the ecliptic and the equator where the sun passes from the southern to the northern hemisphere) and the plane of the hour circle of P (α is reckoned from Υ and positive in the direction opposite to the apparent daily motion of the celestial sphere).

By moving the local astronomic system that was introduced in [3.2.2] to the earth's center of mass and then projecting it onto the celestial sphere, we obtain the *horizon system*. The points of intersection of the extended direction of the plumb line with the celestial sphere are known as the *zenith Z* and the *nadir Z'*, respectively (Fig. 4.1). The intersection of the plane of the horizon with the celestial sphere is the *celestial horizon*. The great circles perpendicular to the horizon and including the zenith and nadir are called *vertical circles*; whereas, the small circles parallel to the horizon are known as *almucantars*. The vertical circle through the celestial poles is the *celestial meridian*; it intersects the horizon at the north and south points. The vertical circle perpendicular to the celestial meridian is the *prime vertical* and it contains the east and west points.

In the horizon system, the star is determined by the coordinates defined in [3.2.3]: the *zenith angle z* (rarely by the altitude $90°-z$) and the *astronomic azimuth A* (in astronomy this angle is usually reckoned from the south point and positive westward to the north; however, here in geodesy it is, as usual, positive from the north and in the clockwise direction). The coordinates of the horizon system depend on the observation station, and also on the time because of the earth's rotation.

If we rotate the α,δ-equatorial system about the polar axis by the angle of sidereal time Θ [4.1.3], then we obtain the time dependent (because the earth rotates) equatorial or *hour angle system* with the hour angle and declination as coordinates. Here, the *hour angle* t is the angle measured in the equatorial plane between the celestial meridian and the hour circle of S, reckoned from the upper meridian P_nZP_s toward W. For the determination of time, there is the fundamental relation

$$\Theta = t + \alpha. \tag{4.1}$$

The *astronomic triangle* P_nZS relates the hour angle system to the horizon system; in addition, it contains the astronomic latitude Φ (Fig. 4.1). For the calculation of the latitude, the time, and the azimuth, we have the important transformation

$$\begin{pmatrix} \cos A \sin z \\ \sin A \sin z \\ \cos z \end{pmatrix} = \begin{pmatrix} -\sin \Phi \\ 0 \\ \cos \Phi \end{pmatrix} \begin{pmatrix} 0 & \cos \Phi & \cos t \cos \delta \\ -1 & 0 & \sin t \cos \delta \\ 0 & \sin \Phi & \sin \delta \end{pmatrix}. \tag{4.2}$$

Differential formulas may be derived from the astronomic triangle (q = parallactic angle, A is reckoned in the positive sense from north) for the estimation of errors:

$$\left. \begin{aligned} d\Phi &= -\frac{\cos q}{\cos A} d\delta - \frac{dz}{\cos A} - \cos \Phi \tan A \, dt \\[2mm] dt &= -\frac{\cos q}{\sin A \cos \Phi} d\delta - \frac{dz}{\sin A \cos \Phi} - \frac{\cot A}{\cos \Phi} d\Phi \\[2mm] dA &= \frac{\sin q}{\sin z} d\delta + \frac{\cos q \cos \delta}{\sin z} dt + \cot z \sin A \, d\Phi. \end{aligned} \right\} \tag{4.3}$$

4.1.2 Variation of Stellar Coordinates, Star Catalogues

The stellar coordinates α, δ which until now have been considered as independent of time and the place of observation actually change due to movements of the earth's axis (precession, nutation), small motions of the stars on the celestial sphere (proper motion), as well as apparent displacements of the star's direction (parallaxes, aberration, refraction).

In *star catalogues*, the position α, δ of a star is given in a "mean" system for the epoch T_0, from which these variations have been for the most part removed: mean position (T_0). The transition from the *observed position* at epoch T to the mean position (T_0) is performed in several steps:

1. First, the position (T) of the star, observed at the topocenter, is transformed to the *apparent position* (T); this corresponds to a shift of the observer to the geocenter. Reductions are required due to atmospheric refraction and the earth's rotation.

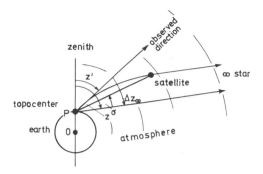

Fig. 4.2. Astronomic refractrion

Astronomic refraction Δz_∞ causes an apparent increase in the star's altitude (Fig. 4.2). The true zenith angle z is obtained from the observed quantity z' as

$$z = z' + \Delta z_\infty. \qquad (4.4)$$

Under the assumption that the atmosphere consists of spherically symmetric layers, Δz_∞ may be computed for $z' < 70°$ from the atmospheric pressure p(hPa) and the temperature T(K) at the place of observation:

$$\Delta z_\infty = \Delta z_0 \frac{p}{1013.25} \frac{273.15}{T}. \qquad (4.5)$$

Here Δz_0 which depends on z' is the standard refraction for $p = 1013.25$ hPa and $T = 273.15$K:

$$\Delta z_0 = 60.\!''2 \tan z' - 0.\!''06 \tan^3 z'. \qquad (4.6)$$

In the interval $0° < z' < 70°$, the uncertainty of Δz_∞ is approximately $\pm 0.\!''03$ to $\pm 0.\!''2$.

An apparent displacement in direction (*diurnal aberration*) results from the finite velocity of light and the relative velocity of the observer with respect to the stars due to the earth's rotation. This displacement is also taken into account by applying a correction.

The difference between the topocentric and geocentric directions (*geocentric parallax*) can be neglected in star observations.

2. The apparent position (T) depending on the motion and position of the earth in the ecliptic is transformed into the *true position* (T) corresponding to an observer at the origin of an heliocentric system. Here, reductions are required as a result of apparent directional changes (*annual aberration*) arising from the orbital motion of the earth around the sun, and due to the difference between the gecentric and helicentric directions (*annual parallax*).
3. The orientation of the α,δ-system, and thus, the true position (T) of a star changes due to the gravitation of the moon, the sun, and the planets.

The attractive forces of the moon and sun on the equatorial bulge of the earth create torques tending to turn the equatorial plane into the plane of the ecliptic (Fig. 4.3).

The combined effect of this and the moment of the earth's rotation produces a gyration of the earth's axis which describes a cone with a generating angle of $\varepsilon = 23°\!.5$ ($\varepsilon = $ obliquity of the ecliptic) about the pole of the ecliptic E_n. The vernal equinox Υ travels on the ecliptic

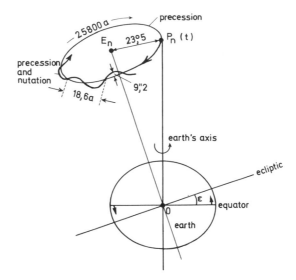

Fig. 4.3. Precession and nutation

at a rate of 50″4 per year, making a complete revolution in about 25800 years: *lunisolar precession.* The gravitation of the planets causes a dislocation of the earth's orbit, and thereby, an additional migration of ϒ along the equator, as well as a change in ε: *planetary precession.* The sum of the lunisolar and planetary precessions is termed *general precession.* It is superimposed by a periodic motion known as *nutation* (amplitude = 9″2, period = 18.6 years) which is principally due to the inclination of the orbit of the moon with respect to the ecliptic ($\sim 5°$).

By accounting for nutation, the true position is transformed into the *mean position* (T) (referred to the mean celestial equator and the mean vernal equinox at epoch T).

4. In the transition from the mean position (T) to the *mean position* (T_0) of the star catalogues, precession and proper motion between T and T_0 must be considered. Here, *proper motion* denotes the component of the spatial motion of the star which is tangent to the celestial sphere (generally $< 1''$ per year).

In addition to α, δ, the *star catalogues* generally contain information on the proper motion and apparent magnitudes of the stars. The astronomic system is defined by the coordinates of a number of very accurately observed *fundamental stars* (fundamental system), FRICKE (1985).

The fundamental catalogue $FK4$ (Astron. Recheninstitut Heidelberg 1963) contains the mean positions and proper motions of 1535 stars for the epochs 1950.0 and 1975.0. The corresponding entries for an additional 1987 stars (epoch 1950.0) are found in a supplement to this catalogue, $FK4$ *sup.* The new fundamental catalogue $FK5$ contains mean positions ($\pm\, 0''01 \ldots 0''02$) and proper motions ($\pm\, 0''05/cy$) for the FK4 stars and (in a supplement) additional stars up to the apparent magnitude 9.5, for the epoch J2000.0 (FRICKE et al. 1988). In addition, the coordinates of a few extragalactic radio sources are given in order to connect the stellar with the radio source system (accuracy of connection $\pm\, 0''1$), see below.

The *positional catalogues* list the mean places of a great number of stars in the fundamental system. These catalogues have been given considerable significance in geodetic astronomy when determining positions, but mainly in direction measurements of satellite geodesy where a dense and evenly distributed field of known fixed stars was required.

The *SAO* (Smithsonian Astrophysical Observatory) *star catalogue* (1966) represents a collection of some 260,000 star positions at the epoch 1950.0 covering the entire celestial sphere (average uncertainty $\pm$ 0.''5). It was prepared for use in optical satellite geodesy. The *AGK3* catalogue of the "Astronomische Gesellschaft" (1971) which is based on extensive old and new observational material contains over 200,000 star positions (epoch 1950.0, average uncertainty $\pm$0.''1 to $\pm$0.''2, northern hemisphere only).

In order to make comparisons with the observations, one requires the *apparent positions* of stars. They can be either computed from the mean positions of the star catalogues or taken from an *astronomic almanac* (only fundamental stars).

The almanac entitled *Apparent Places of Fundamental Stars* (Astron. Recheninstitut Heidelberg) contains the apparent places of *FK4* stars for a particular year. The apparent positions of the sun are found in the almanac known as the *Astronomical Ephemeris*.

With the *FK5*-system, in connection with the IAU (International Astronomical Union) 1976/1982 system of Astronomical Constants, an approximation to an inertial system is provided which is based on fixed stars: *Stellar-CIS*, see [3.1]. The accuracy of this system could hardly be improved beyond $\pm$0.''01, with earth-based optical astronomy. From astronomic space missions like the HIPPARCOS satellite and the space-telescope mission, a precision of $\pm$0.''001 may be expected. On the other hand, the direction to extragalactic radio sources can be determined to $\pm$0.''001 from earth-based Very Long Base Line Interferometry, see [4.4.8]. This offers the possibility to define a *Radio Source-CIS*, although the number of sources included will remain remarkable less than the number of fundamental stars (MORITZ and MUELLER A1987).

4.1.3 Time Systems

Determinations of time are required in geodetic astronomy and in satellite geodesy because of the relative motion of the target with respect to the place of observation. A high relative accuracy is needed in many applications when signal travel time of electromagnetic waves is used for distance measurements.

The unit of time, the *second* (s), was defined at the thirteenth general conference of the International Committee of Weights and Measures, 1967 by the oscillations of the cesium atom:

"One second is 9192631770 times the period of emitted radiation corresponding to the transition between two hyperfine levels of the fundamental state of the atom of cesium — 133".

This definition corresponds to the international *atomic time* scale. Its point of origin was established such that *atomic time* TAI (Temps Atomique International) agreed with universal time at midnight on Jan. 1, 1958. The definition of the time second given above has been included into the SI-system. The length of the SI-second has been fitted to the second of the *ephemeris time (ET)*, which was defined by the motion of the earth about the sun, and determined through long-term astronomic observations. TAI is realized by the atomic clocks (cesium time and frequency standards) of several standard laboratories, and by the average of their corresponding times calculated at the Bureau International des Poids et Mesures (BIPM), Sèvres (until 1985 at BIH) in Paris. Due to the high, short- and long-term relative frequency stability (10^{-12} to 10^{-13}) of the atomic clocks, they provide a good approximation to a uniform time scale.

In order to describe the motions of celestial bodies and artificial satellites, a strictly uniform time (inertial time) scale is needed. This is provided by the dynamical time. If referred to the geocenter it is denoted as *Terrestrial Dynamical Time* (TDT). Dynamical time is used as the argument for the astronomical ephemerides. With respect to atomic time *TAI*, we have $TDT = TAI + 32^{s}_{.}184$.

In order to relate earth based observations to a space-fixed system, time systems are used which are derived from the *rotation of the earth*: Sidereal and Universal (solar) time. Observations of the stars yield local or apparent *sidereal time* Θ (LAST) referring to the observer's meridian; this time is equal to the hour angle of the vernal equinox Υ (Fig. 4.1). The uniformly varying mean sidereal time (LMST) is obtained after accounting for the nutation [4.1.2] of Υ. LMST is used as time scale, with the mean sidereal day as fundamental unit.

For practical reasons, *solar time* is used in everyday life. It is related to the apparent diurnal motion of the sun about the earth. Since this revolution is nonuniform, a "mean" sun is introduced which moves with constant velocity along the equator; whereby the mean and true sun both pass through the vernal equinox at the same time. Mean solar time is then equal to the hour angle of the mean sun plus 12 hours. Mean solar time referring to the mean Greenwich meridian is termed *Universal Time UT*. The conversion of universal time to sidereal time is rigorously possible, e.g., MORITZ and MUELLER (A1987). Since the earth's orbital motion is about 1° per day, we have approximately 1 mean sidereal day = 1 mean solar day $-3^{m} 55^{s}_{.}91$.

Since 1988 Universal Time is obtained by about 50 observatories which participate in the *International Earth Rotation Service (IERS)*, cf. [3.1]. These UT0 times refer to the instantaneous rotational axis, and in order to compare them with one another, a correction to the astronomic longitude $\Delta\Lambda_P$ (4.12) due to polar motion [3.1] has to be applied. Considering the geographic longitudes of the observatories, we then obtain universal time UT1:

$$UT1 = UT0 + \Delta\Lambda_P, \quad \Delta\Lambda_P = -\frac{1}{15}(x_P \sin \Lambda + y_P \cos \Lambda) \tan \Phi. \qquad (4.7)$$

Universal Time UT1 hence refers to the Conventional Terrestrial System (mean pole CIO), cf. [3.1], thus providing the time scale for geodetic astronomy and satellite geodesy. The precision of *UT1* was about ± 1 ms (5d values) from astronomic methods, and is $\pm$ few 0.1 ms (1d values) with Lunar Laser Ranging and Very Long Baseline Interferometry. The longitudes of the stations which participate in the time service were last established in 1979: *BIH-system* 1979. They indirectly define the direction of the Greenwich Mean Meridian, cf. [3.1]. *UT1* still contains the variations of earth rotation, it does not represent a uniform time scale.

These variations are secular, periodic, or irregular in nature (LAMBECK A1980). A secular decrease in the angular velocity of the earth's rotation is caused mainly by tidal friction, lengthening the day by about 2 ms over 100 years. Fluctuations over decades have been also observed, reaching few ms changes in the length of day (*LOD*). Changes exhibiting annual and seasonal periods, and relative *LOD* changes of $O(10^{-9})$, mainly arise as a result of changing atmospheric mass distribution. Periodic tidal variations (annually to fortnightly) produce relative changes of the same order of magnitude. Finally it is presumed that terrestrial mass displacements produce irregular variations which have been observed over centuries or over just a few years (changes in the length of the day by several ms), as well as over weeks and months (changes by fractions of a ms).

Due to the secular decrease of earth rotation, $UT1$ and TAI continuously deviate from each other. This led to the introduction of the *Coordinated Universal Time UTC*. The time interval corresponds to atomic time TAI. In order to keep the difference $UTC\text{-}UT1 = DUT1 < 0.7$ s, "leap seconds" are introduced to UTC if necessary, thus fitting the epoch again to $UT1$. $DUT1$ is provided by the IERS, the time signal stations generally broadcast UTC.

Among the continuously broadcasting time signal stations in central Europe are DCF 77/Mainflingen (77.5 kHz), Y3S/Nauen (4525 kHz), HBG/Prangins (75 kHz), OMA/Liblice (50 kHz). For North America, the stations WWV/Ft. Collins, Colorado (2500–20000 kHz) and WWVH/Kauai, Hawaii (2500–15000 kHz) are the most important ones.

4.1.4 Observational Instruments

Direction and time measurements are required for the determination of latitude, longitude, and azimuth. The instruments are either permanently installed (observatories) or set up in the field.

Observations of the highest precision with *stationary* (observatory) instruments have been utilized by the former International Time Service [4.1.3] and International Polar Motion Service [3.1]. Among other instruments, the *photographic zenith tube* has been applied in this respect. In this case, stars near the zenith are photographed symmetrically with respect to the meridian. The zenith angles and the hour angles can be determined from the tracks of the stars. The direction of the vertical is established by a pool of mercury. Comparable precision ($\pm 0.''05$) may be achieved by the impersonal *Danjon prismatic astrolabe*. It is distinguished from the astrolabes that are designed for use in the field (see below) by a self-registering micrometer (MORITZ and MUELLER A1987).

For field measurements of first-order precision ($\pm 0.''1$ to $\pm 0.''3$) the *universal theodolite*, in particular, is brought into service. It consists of a precise theodolite [4.3.2] of very stable design, which with a few attachments can be used for astronomic observations (Fig. 4.4).

A broken telescope with a horizontal eyepiece permits observations near the zenith. To eliminate personal errors, the movable thread of the registering micrometer is driven to follow the star, such that impulses are generated and recorded at uniform intervals. The suspension or striding level serves to measure the tilt of the horizontal axis; whereas, the Horrebow level mounted at right angles to the horizontal axis registers any changes in the tilt of the telescope. Instruments of this kind include the astronomic DKM3-A universal theodolite (Kern, Aarau, Switzerland) and the Wild T4 universal theodolite (Wild, Heerbrugg, Switzerland). Due to a

Fig. 4.4. DKM3-A universal theodolite, courtesy of Kern and Co., Aaarau, Switzerland

built-in automatic stabilization, the levels mentioned above are not required on the geodetic-astronomic Theo 002 universal theodolite (Zeiss Jena), SIGL and BAUCH (1976).

Measuring accuracies of $\pm 0''\!.5$ to $\pm 1''$ may be reached when using the *prism astrolabe*. Here, one measures the transit times of those stars which cross the same almucantar [4.1.1]. The constant zenith distance (usually $\sim 30°$) is established by a prism placed in front of the telescope, and the direction of the vertical is defined by the surface of a pool of mercury or by a compensator pendulum.

Astrolabe attachments are particularly common. These are either mounted on a theodolite (e.g. the Wild T3 astrolabe with a mercury pool) or on an automatic level (Zeiss Ni2 astrolabe), DEICHL (1975), Fig. 4.5.

Fig. 4.5. ZEISS Ni2 level with prism astrolab, courtesy of Carl Zeiss, Oberkochen, Fed. Rep. Germany

Recently, *transportable zenith cameras* (Fig. 4.6) have also been used to rapidly determine astronomic latitude and longitude. Such an instrument consists of a

Fig. 4.6. Transportable zenith camera, IfE Hannover

camera oriented in the direction of the plumb line (focal length = 300 to 1000 mm, relative aperture of ~1 : 5) and which can be turned around this axis in any azimuth. In addition to a timing device, the instrument is also furnished with two levels that are arranged at right angles to each other (BIRARDI 1976, SEEBER and TORGE 1985), cf. [4.1.5].

In order to *measure time* at stations in the field, it is necessary to be equipped with a time signal receiver, a clock, and a recording device (chronograph).

The time signals [4.1.3] can be supplied by a *time signal receiver* that is tuned to a special frequency, or sometimes also by a radio receiver. The accuracy of the received signal depends on the fluctuations in the time of propagation and in the quality of the reception (± 1 to ± 2 ms). Clocks are required in order to interpolate the time between the received time signals. *Quartz crystal oscillators* with frequency stability of $10^{-7} \ldots 10^{-8}$ over few hours are used which are synchronized by time signals. In this way, the 1 ms accuracy needed in geodetic astronomy is provided.

Fig. 4.7. Portable quartz crystal chronometer, IfE Hannover

The function of *chronographs* is to record time. These instruments print the minutes, seconds, and hundredths of a second (printing chronograph, uncertainty ± 0.001 s). Small portable devices combining time receiver, quartz frequency standard and printer are available (Fig. 4.7). Time may also be taken from the signals transmitted by the world-wide radio navigation system OMEGA ($10 \ldots 14$ KHz), e.g. LAURILA (A1976). In astronomic positioning, the transit times of a star that crosses the horizontal or vertical threads of the telescope are recorded with the aid of a hand tappet or by using an "impersonal" micrometer (± 0.02 s).

4.1.5 Methods to Determine Astronomic Positions, Azimuth, and Time

Of the numerous methods, we mention here a few of those most frequently applied in geodesy. In determining the *astronomic latitude* Φ it is required, according to (4.2), to ascertain the zenith angle z and the hour angle t. It is seen from (4.3), that any error in z has a minimal effect for *transits on the meridian*; here an error in t has no effect on the latitude. For an upper culmination (the smaller zenith angle) of a northern star ($A = 0$) or a southern star ($A = 180°$), the latitude is given according to Fig. 4.1 by

$$\Phi = \delta_N - z_N \quad \text{and} \quad \Phi = \delta_S + z_S \tag{4.8}$$

respectively. Measuring the meridian zenith angle (e.g. to Polaris) is therefore most suitable for the determination of the latitude.

If one observes a pair of stars consisting of both a northern and a southern star having approximately the same zenith angle, then averaging (4.8) substantially eliminates the uncertainties in z due to refraction (*Sterneck method*). In the *Horrebow-Talcott method*, the (small) difference between the meridian zenith angle of the northern and southern stars in a star pair is measured by a registering micrometer. The optical axis in each case is adjusted to the same zenith angle using the Horrebow level that is mounted on the horizontal axis. Since accurate circle and time readings are not required, this method provides very precise results ($\pm 0.''1$ when about 20 star pairs are observed).

The *astronomic longitude* Λ is given by the difference between the local sidereal time Θ [4.1.3] and "Greenwich Sidereal Time" Θ_0 which refers to the Greenwich meridian (with 1 s $\triangleq 15''$):

$$\Lambda = \Theta - \Theta_0. \tag{4.9}$$

According to (4.1), Θ is related to the hour angle t which can be computed from the zenith angle using (4.2) if the latitude Φ is known:

$$\cos t = \frac{\cos z - \sin \Phi \sin \delta}{\cos \Phi \cos \delta}. \tag{4.10}$$

Comparing a clock with the time signal [4.1.3] yields universal time UT, which is then converted into Greenwich sidereal time Θ_0.

As seen from (4.3), the effect due to errors in z is minimal when observations are made on the *prime vertical*, while the effect here is zero for errors in Φ. The influence of refraction is largely eliminated when observing east and west stars of the same altitude and symmetric with respect to the meridian. Observing the *time of transit across the meridian* ($t = 0$) yields $\Theta = \alpha$. An accuracy of $\pm 0.^{s}01 \ldots \pm 0.^{s}02$ is obtained from approximately 30 transits.

The accuracy of the determination of longitude depends primarily on the systematic errors of the observer, the instrument, and the time comparison. If the longitude determinations are

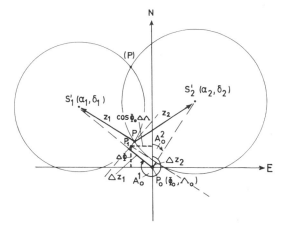

Fig. 4.8. Method of position lines

made by the same observer, who uses the same instrument and the same time signal transmitting station, as well as the same stars, then *longitude differences* are essentially free from these errors. Longitude determinations of high accuracy are thus carried out as measurements of differences in longitude with respect to a reference station of the BIH longitude system [4.1.3].

An economical method to determine simultaneously the *latitude and longitude* is known as the *method of position lines*.

The zenith angles z_1, z_2 of two stars $S_1(\alpha_1, \delta_1)$, $S_2(\alpha_2, \delta_2)$ are observed at sidereal times Θ_1, Θ_2 and at azimuths A_1, A_2. If S_1, S_2 are projected on the earth's surface, then the intersections of the circles centered at the projections S_1', S_2' and having radii z_1, z_2, respectively, represent two geometric positions P and (P) for the point of observation (Fig. 4.8). The circles can be replaced in the vicinity of P by their tangent lines (position lines); the intersection of these lines yields P_1 as an approximation to P. Computationally, one obtains the corrections $\Delta\Phi = \Phi - \Phi_0$ and $\Delta\Lambda = \Lambda - \Lambda_0$ upon introducing an approximate position P_0 (Φ_0, Λ_0). When observations are made with the prism astrolabe [4.1.4], the zenith angle, predetermined by the prism, is treated as an additional unknown. From about 20 stars, evenly distributed above the horizon, one obtains average accuracies from $\pm 0.''5$ to $\pm 1.''0$.

It is also possible to make simultaneous determinations of *latitude* and *longitude* using a *portable zenith camera* [4.1.4]. While also measuring the time, the field of stars near the zenith is photographed for two positions of the camera differing by 180° in azimuth (exposure time: 1 s). After the photographic plates are developed, the star tracks and the intersection of the lines connecting the fiducial marks are measured on a comparator. The transformation of the plate coordinates of the intersection into the α, δ-system [4.1.1] provides the coordinates α_z, δ_z of the zenith after averages are taken and corrections are made for the reading of the level. From Fig. 4.1, it is seen that $\Phi = \delta_z$, $\Theta = \alpha_z$ and (4.9) gives $\Lambda = \alpha_z - \Theta_0$. The observations (for several plates) require approximately one half to one hour (including instrument setup and disassembly); the attainable accuracy is $\pm 0.''5$.

If the latitude is known, then the *azimuth A* can be obtained, according to (4.2), from the hour angle t; that is, from (4.1) and a determination of sidereal time:

$$\tan A = \frac{\sin t}{\sin \Phi \cos t - \cos \Phi \tan\delta}. \tag{4.11}$$

(4.3) shows that an error in t has minimal effect for $\delta \approx 90°$ (stars near the pole). For some 10 observations, the standard deviation is $\pm 0.''3 \ldots \pm 0.''5$. The azimuth of a terrestrial target is obtained by measuring the angle between the directions to the star and the target.

The observations of latitude, longitude, and azimuth which refer to the instantaneous position of the rotational axis are to be transformed into the *CIO-system* [3.1] using the polar motion coordinates x_P, y_P:

$$\left.\begin{array}{l} \Phi_{CIO} = \Phi - (x_P \cos \Lambda - y_P \sin \Lambda) \\[2mm] \Lambda_{CIO} = \Lambda - (x_P \sin \Lambda + y_P \cos \Lambda) \tan \Phi \\[2mm] A_{CIO} = A - (x_P \sin \Lambda + y_P \cos \Lambda) \sec \Phi. \end{array}\right\} \tag{4.12}$$

4.2 Gravity Measurements

In these sections, we treat the measurements of gravity intensity (gravity) g [2.1.5], the gravity gradient [2.2.5], and body tides of the earth [2.4.2]. As a standard reference for gravimetry we mention TORGE (A1989). NETTLETON (A1976) describes the application of gravimetric techniques in applied geophysics, and MELCHIOR (A1983) discusses the methods of earth tide measurements.

4.2.1 Absolute Gravity Measurements

By an "absolute" gravity measurement, we mean the determination of g from the fundamental acceleration quantities length and time. The free-fall and the rise-and-fall methods, as well as the pendulum methods are significant in this respect (SAKUMA 1984, FALLER and MARSON 1988, see also TORGE 1990a).

Through the integration of $\ddot{z} = g$ for a *free-fall* experiment, one obtains the relation

$$z = z_0 + \dot{z}_0 t + \frac{g}{2} t^2 \tag{4.13}$$

between the path z and the fall time t. The constants of integration z_0, $\dot{z}_0$ represent the position and velocity of the body at $t = 0$. If the body falls through at least three planes (Fig. 4.9a), z and $\dot{z}_0$ can be eliminated. We have

$$g = 2\frac{(z_3 - z_1)(t_2 - t_1) - (z_2 - z_1)(t_3 - t_1)}{(t_3 - t_1)(t_2 - t_1)(t_3 - t_2)}. \tag{4.14}$$

For a symmetric *rise and fall* (Fig. 4.9b), it is sufficient to measure the crossing times t_1, t_2, t_3, t_4 at only two planes (separated by the distance Δz). (4.13) then yields

$$g = \frac{8 \Delta z}{(t_4 - t_1)^2 - (t_3 - t_2)^2}. \tag{4.15}$$

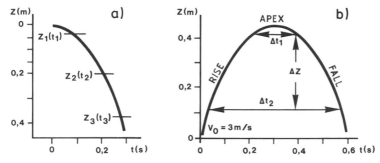

Fig. 4.9. Distance-time diagram a) free-fall method b) symmetrical rise and fall method, from TORGE (A1989)

If the relative error of a free-fall experiment is not to exceed $\pm 10^{-9}$ (corresponding to $\pm 1 \times 10^{-8}$ ms^{-2}), a falling distance of 0.5 m and a corresponding falling time of 0.3 s yield *accuracy requirements* of ± 0.5 nm and ± 0.2 ns. This can be achieved by interferometric measurements with laser light (He-Ne-laser) and electronic time measurement. All instruments in use today employ the simultaneous length and time measurement, with a *Michelson interferometer.* Two corner cube reflectors are the fundamental parts of the interferometer (Fig. 4.10). One of the reflectors is fixed and serves as a reference, the other can be moved in the vertical. By splitting the laser light into a measurement and a reference beam, and superimposing them again after parallel reflection, light interferences occur. The zero crossings of the fringe signal have a distance of $\lambda/2$ (wave-length $\lambda = 632.8$ nm). If n pulses (zero crossings) are counted, this corresponds to a falling distance of $\Delta z = n\dfrac{\lambda}{2}$. Time is measured with an atomic frequency standard (rubidium normal) after a large preset number of fringes has occurred (e.g. after 10000 fringes, which leads to approx. 60 time measurements during one drop over 0.5 m). Consequently, (4.13) has to be evaluated by a least squares adjustment (on-line processing).

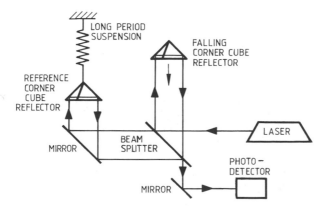

Fig. 4.10. Principle of Michelson interferometer used in the free-fall method, from TORGE (A1989)

In order to diminish *air pressure resistance*, the experiment has to be performed in vacuum ($10^{-3} \ldots 10^{-4}$ Pa). The effect of *microseismic movements* is partly absorbed by a long-period compensation device (e.g. spring with $T \geqslant 10$s). Randomization by performing many (e.g. 1000) experiments on one station leads to a further significant reduction of microseismics. In the *symmetric rise and fall* experiment, systematic errors which are proportional to the falling body's velocity, cancel (air drag, timing errors).

Since the first development (1951) of the free-fall method by *Volet* at the Bureau International des Poids et Mesures (BIPM) in Sèvres, various absolute determinations have been made at several institutes. At the National Physical Laboratory in Teddington, *Cook* achieved the first successful rise-and-fall experiment in 1965. Since 1965 *Sakuma* (BIPM) has performed a number of absolute determinations at the reference station in BIPM, Sevres. By continuously improving the rise-and-fall method, he has now approached the $\pm 10^{-9}$ precision. A first transportable absolute gravimeter was developed by *Faller* in 1968, and successfully employed during the measurements for the world network IGSN 71 [4.2.4], HAMMOND and FALLER (1971).

Since about 1970, more than ten *transportable* free-fall or rise-and-fall instruments have been constructed and brought into operation. We mention the rise-fall device of the Istituto di Metrologia "G. Colonnetti", Torino, and the GABL absolute gravimeter of the Institute of Automation and Electrometry, Siberian Branch, U.S.S.R. Academy of Sciences.

A recently developed system (FALLER et al. 1983) at *Joint Institute for Laboratory Astrophysics* (JILA), Boulder, was produced in a small series and is now operated by different institutions (Fig. 4.11). This instrument is characterized by a short falling distance (0.2 m), an additional chamber-in-chamber-technique in order to reduce residual air pressure effects. A special "super-spring" is installed to absorb microseismic acceleration, with an electronically generated oscillation period of about 30s. With 1000 to 2000 drops distributed in runs of 300 over one to two days (according to local microseismics), a standard deviation of $\pm 0.02 \ldots 0.03 \ \mu\text{ms}^{-2}$ is obtained for the mean value. Due to systematic errors (laser frequency stability,

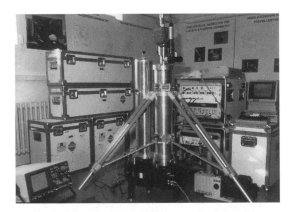

Fig. 4.11. JILA absolute gravimeter, IfE Hannover

timing errors, floor recoil) the accuracy of the final absolute value is estimated to be $\pm 0.1\ \mu\text{ms}^{-2}$ and better (e.g. TORGE et al. 1987).

The *pendulum method* is based on the measurement of the period and the length l of a freely swinging pendulum. For a *mathematical pendulum* (point mass suspended on a weightless wire), we have the differential equation

$$l\ddot{\varphi} + g \sin \varphi = 0, \qquad (4.16)$$

where φ is the phase (Fig. 4.12a). Integration leads to the period of oscillation

$$T = 2\pi \sqrt{\frac{1}{g}\left(1 + \frac{\varphi_0^2}{16} + \cdots\right)}. \qquad (4.17)$$

The amplitude φ_0 generally remains less than $30'$.

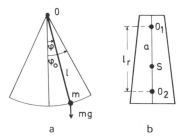

Fig. 4.12. Absolute pendulum principle a) mathematical pendulum b) reversible pendulum

The mathematical pendulum can not be strictly realized. However, (4.16) and (4.17) hold as well for the *physical pendulum*, if l is replaced by the reduced length of the pendulum

$$l_r = \frac{J}{ma}. \qquad (4.18)$$

Here, J is the moment of inertia with respect to the axis of rotation 0, and a is the distance between this axis and the center of mass S. For a *reversible pendulum* (Fig. 4.12b), l_r may be determined as the distance between the points of suspension 0_1 and 0_2 which give the same period of oscillation T.

Since 1817, when the English physicist *Kater* brought the reversible pendulum into operation, a limited number of observations was performed in the 19th century, with transportable devices developed in the 1860s (e.g. *Repsold* reversible apparatus). After the absolute determination in Potsdam, see [4.2.4], only a few further experiments were performed in this century.

Metal or quartz pendulums with lengths between 0.25 m and 1 m have been used. When measuring the time, the integration was performed over a large number of oscillations in order to increase the accuracy and to reduce microseismic disturbances. Geometric and elastic knife-edge effects as well as deformations of the pendulum during the oscillation, were particularly critical. The co-oscillation of the pendulum support could be essentially eliminated by letting two identical pendulums swing together with opposite phase and equal amplitude. The accuracy of the reversible pendulum method today amounts to $\pm 3\ \mu\text{ms}^{-2}$, when some observation series with several pendulums are performed (SCHÜLER et al. 1971). Due to the development of the free-fall method, the absolute pendulum method is no longer applied.

4.2.2 Relative Gravity Measurements

The measurement of a difference in gravity Δg by the direct or indirect observation of one of the two acceleration quantities time or length keeping the other one fixed, is known as a "relative" gravity measurement; it can be performed with considerably more ease than the "absolute" measurement of g. A distinction is made between pendulum and spring gravimeter measurements.

In a *pendulum* measurement, the periods of oscillation T_1, T_2 of the same pendulum are measured at two points $P_1(g_1)$ and $P_2(g_2)$. Assuming invariance of the length l of the pendulum, it follows from (4.17), after some simple manipulations that

$$\Delta g_{12} = g_2 - g_1 = -2g_1 \frac{T_2 - T_1}{T_2} + g_1 \frac{(T_2 - T_1)^2}{T_2^2}. \tag{4.19}$$

Thus the length measurement is not required here, as opposed to the case of the absolute determination, so that an arbitrary physical pendulum (generally, $l = 0.25$ m) can be used. As seen from (4.19), no calibration is needed for this dynamic method. Effects that are independent of time and position (knife edge errors) are cancelled. To eliminate the larger effects of co-oscillation in field measurements, two pendulums are always used which swing with opposite phase on the same support. Changes in the length of the pendulum during transport may be taken into account partly by employing several pairs of pendulums and through repeated measurements. The uncertainty of an observed gravity difference using pendulums amounts to $\pm 2\ \mu\text{ms}^{-2}$. The development of a portable pendulum originates with *R. v. Sterneck* (1887). With the invention of the spring gravimeter which is more exact and economical, the pendulum measurements have lost their importance (the time required to make a measurement including setup and disassembly of the pendulum apparatus is approximately one day, for the gravimeter it is about five minutes).

The (relative) spring *gravimeter* is based on the principle of a spring balance. The equilibrium position of a mass m is observed as it is influenced by the acceleration of gravity and by the counterforce of the elastic spring. If gravity changes the spring length will also change in order to reach static equilibrium again. According to *Hooke*'s law, the strain is proportional to the stress for small elongations. We differentiate between translational systems (seldom used) and rotational systems.

In a *translational system* (vertical spring balance), the condition of equilibrium (Fig. 4.13a) is given by

$$mg - f(l - l_0) = 0, \tag{4.20}$$

where f is the spring constant and $l(l_0)$ is the length of the spring with a load (without a load). Differentiating (4.20) furnishes a linear relationship between the change in gravity Δg and the observed difference in length Δl:

$$\Delta g = \frac{f}{m}\Delta l = \frac{g}{l - l_0}\Delta l. \tag{4.21}$$

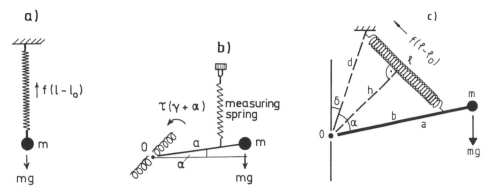

Fig. 4.13. Spring balance gravimeter principle a) vertical spring balance b) lever torsion spring balance c) general lever spring balance

In order to assess gravity changes with a relative accuracy of $\pm 10^{-8}$, length changes of a 0.1 m long spring have to be determined to ± 1 nm.

Rotational systems (lever spring balance) consist of a lever which supports a mass m and rotates about an axis O. Equilibrium is produced through a horizontal torsion spring or through a vertically or obliquely acting restoring spring. For the *lever torsion spring balance* (Fig. 4.13b), the equilibrium of the torques yields

$$mga \cos \alpha - \tau(\gamma + \alpha) = 0 \qquad (4.22)$$

where a = length of the lever, α = angle between the horizontal and the lever, τ = torsion constant, γ = pretension angle of the spring. For $\alpha = 0$, a linear relationship exists between Δg and the angle of deflection $\Delta \alpha$:

$$\Delta g = \frac{\tau}{ma} \Delta \alpha = \frac{g}{\gamma} \Delta \alpha. \qquad (4.23a)$$

At the *general lever spring balance* the spring counterforce $f(l - l_0)$ can act under an arbitrary angle on the lever carrying the mass m (Fig. 4.13c). The line connecting the rotation axis O with the point where the spring is mounted deviates by an angle δ from the vertical. The equilibrium condition for the torques reads

$$mga \sin(\alpha + \delta) - fbd \frac{l - l_0}{l} \sin \alpha = 0. \qquad (4.23b)$$

The sensivity of this non-linear system may be significantly improved by approximating the torques of gravity and of the elastic spring (*astatization*). With a zero-length ($l_0 = 0$) spring, this is achieved with a small angle δ, and $\alpha \approx 90°$. In order to obtain the $\pm 10^{-8}$ relative accuracy, we now need (at $a = 0.1$ m, $\alpha + \delta = 90°, \delta = 100''$) the displacement to be measured with ± 2 μm. Compared to the linear system the sensitivity is increased by the factor 2000.

The requirement on gravimeters to have accuracies of 0.1 μms^{-2} places high demands on their *pick-off* and *reading system*, as well as on the *constancy of the spring's elasticity.* Today the *zero-method* is used exclusively. Hereby the deflection is compensated by controlling the proof mass such that it remains in a defined zero position (corresponding to the orientation with respect to the vertical). The compensation is performed mechanically or electronically. The *mechanical compensation* is effected by a measurement screw, attached to the lever-spring-system by a weak spring (measuring spring) or via a transmission system. Optical and/or electrical *pick-off systems* are used to observe the beam position. The capacitive pick-off offers various advantages. These are the adaption of an external digital readout, and the combination with an *electronic feedback system*. Since the measurement screw is not moved, this is a purely electronic method and screw errors do not enter into the results (RÖDER et al. 1988).

The elasticity of the spring should exhibit a constancy of 10^{-8} (corresponding to 0.1 μms^{-2}) over several hours (the time interval required in the transport between two stations). The materials used for the spring include NiFe alloys (small thermoelastic coefficient) and quartz (large but linear thermoelastic coefficient, small coefficient of thermal expansion). In addition, the measuring system is protected against changes in the external environment (temperature, atmospheric pressure).

Of the many types of gravimeters developed since 1930, the most popular ones are the astatized instruments of *LaCoste-Romberg*, Austin, U.S.A. (Fig. 4.14; metal spring acting at a 45° inclination on the horizontal beam, thermostat, model G(D): direct measuring range of 70000 (2000) μms^{-2}, 10(1) μms^{-2} per rotation of the measurement screw) and of *Worden* (Texas Instruments), Houston, U.S.A. (quartz system with horizontal beam and vertical spring, with or without temperature stabilization accessory). Still in wide use for earth tide measurements is the linear *Askania* gravimeter (Bodenseewerk Geraetetechnik, Überlingen) (Fig. 4.15; horizontal beam and horizontal metal torsion spring, direct measuring range of 6000 μms^{-2} (Gs 15); for the type Gs 16, it is increased in steps of 900 to 30000 μms^{-2} by adding mass increments; double thermostat; calibration possibility using mass increments).

Despite all precautionary measures, temporal variations arise in the zero reading of the gravimeter: zero *drift* and sudden *tares*. The drift is caused by the aging of the

Fig. 4.14. LaCoste and Romberg gravimeter model *G* with battery and carrying case, courtesy of LaCoste and Romberg Gravity Meters Inc., Austin, Texas

Fig. 4.15. Askania gravimeter Gs15, courtesy of Bodenseewerk, Überlingen, Fed. Rep. Germany

spring (long-range drifts of 0.1 to 1 μms^{-2} per day), as well as by uncompensated temperature fluctuations, and by elastic aftereffects produced by locking and unlocking the lever. An important error source are vibrations and shocks acting on the measuring system during transportation. The resulting "transport drift" depends on the instrument, the transportation method and conditions (motor vehicle, aircraft, hand transport), and the shock protection used. It can be as much as 1 μms^{-2} per hour. These drifts and tares can be determined by *repeated measurements*, whereby one may distinguish between profile, star, and step methods, Fig. 4.16. The drift-function is then obtained graphically (Fig. 4.17) or numerically (low order polynomial approximation with respect to time). The observations are reduced beforehand for the effects of the radial component of the tidal acceleration [2.4.2].

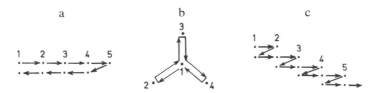

Fig. 4.16. Zero drift determination methods a) profile method b) star method c) step method

In order to convert the observed changes in lengths, angles or electrical units into gravity differences, one requires, according to (4.20) through (4.23), various parameters of the spring. Since they cannot be determined directly with the desired accuracy, the relationship between the gravimeter reading z (reading units) and the value of gravity g (ms^{-2}) must be obtained through a *calibration*. We develop the *calibration function*

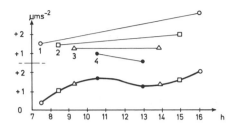

Fig. 4.17. Graphical drift determination (profile method)

$$g = F(z) \tag{4.24}$$

into a Taylor series. For a second degree calibration polynomial, the gravity difference between two points 1, 2 is given by

$$\Delta g_{12} = Y_1(z_2 - z_1) + Y_2(z_2^2 - z_1^2), \tag{4.25}$$

with the calibration coefficients Y_1, Y_2.

Discrete values of $dF(z)/dz$ can be determined by inclining the gravimeter by a known angle (tilting table) or by adding a mass increment which is known precisely and then measuring the deflection. This *laboratory calibration*, generally conducted by the manufacturer furnishes an approximation of the calibration function in (4.25). The approximate values are then converted into gravity differences by multiplying them by the "scale factor" Y_1. This factor is obtained by measuring a known difference of gravity (*calibration line*) (KANNGIESER et al. 1983), or derived from *absolute gravity values* of a global or regional gravity network adjustment, cf. [4.2.4], [6.3].

The *accuracy* in the difference of gravity as observed with gravimeters amounts to approximately ± 0.1 to ± 0.5 μms^{-2}.

The uncertainty can be reduced to ± 50 nms^{-2} by using *LaCoste-Romberg gravimeters* and measuring smaller gravity differences (McCONNELL et al. 1975). A further reduction to ± 20 to 30 nms^{-2} is possible at local ties using different instruments, equipped with electronic feedback systems (RÖDER and WENZEL 1986). High precision gravimetric techniques are discussed in GROTEN (1983) and TORGE (1984).

4.2.3 Gravity Measurements on the Ocean and in the Air

The application of the gravimetric method [5.2] and the development of earth models [5.5] presupposes the existence of the complete knowledge of the gravity field. Therefore, gravity measurements must also be made on the oceans (DEHLINGER A1978). Results are obtained more rapidly with airborne gravimeter measurements.

Ordinary gravimeters that are used on land [4.2.2], but which have been built into a pressure and water protected case, and equipped with remote control and recording devices are known as *underwater gravimeters*. They are transported and assembled on a ship and lowered to the ocean floor for measurements.

Underwater gravimeters have been developed since 1940 for research in applied geophysics. They can generally be used up to depths of 200 m, and at most 1000 m. Large areas of the continental shelves, as well as smaller water basins have been surveyed in this way (BEYER et al. 1966).

If gravity measurements are made on a ship or in an airplane, then one must solve the problems of *leveling* the instrument and separating the *perturbing accelerations* from the actual gravity.

These disturbing accelerations vary with peak periods of 5 to 10 s on a ship and 1 to 300 s on an airplane. The corresponding amplitudes can attain and exceed 0.5 ms^{-2} on the oceans and 0.05 ms^{-2} for airborne measurements. While the horizontal component of the disturbing acceleration can be reduced by instrumental or methodological measures, the vertical component enters completely into the observation.

The gravity meter may be *gimbal-suspended* or placed on a *gyro-stabilized platform*. In the first case, the resultant of g and the horizontal disturbing acceleration is measured (*Browne* effect), thereby requiring a correction that is often difficult to obtain. Today, the instruments are exclusively mounted on a stabilized platform (the uncertainty in leveling the instruments is $\pm 1'$). The *offleveling effect* caused by the remaining inclinations can generally be neglected. *Cross-coupling* effects may arise in measuring systems which are characterized by a horizontal lever, when the horizontal and vertical perturbing accelerations have the same period. If the horizontal component is measured, the effect can be taken into account computationally (cross-coupling computer).

The measuring systems must be strongly dampened due to the large *vertical accelerations*. The short-periodic perturbations are filtered out by taking averages over sufficiently long intervals of time (1 to 5 minutes). This low-pass filtering smoothes the data, and yields mean gravity values over the distance travelled during the averaging time interval.

In 1923, *F. A. Vening Meinesz* achieved the construction of a three-pendulum instrument, which could be used to measure gravity in a submerged submarine. *Sea gravimeters* (Askania Gss 20, Bodenseewerk Gss 30 with vertical restoring spring, LaCoste-Romberg) have been employed since around 1960; they operate according to the principles described in section [4.2.2], Fig. 4.18. In addition, dynamic sea gravimeters which operate on the *vibrating string* principle are used in Japan, the U.S.S.R., and in the U.S.A. Here, the gravity measurements are based on the fact that the vibrational frequency of a string under tension is proportional to $\sqrt{g}$ (BOWIN et al. 1972).

In the case of *airborne gravimeters*, particular difficulties arise as a result of long-periodic perturbations. They have to be monitored by continuous height determination of high precision (barometric and radar altimeter, GPS-heighting), and by computing the vertical component as the second derivative with respect to time. Airborne gravimetry at low altitudes has given satisfying results (BROZENA and PETERS 1988). Operated in a helicopter, air-sea gravimeters are successfully employed in geophysical exploration (HAMMER 1983).

The motion of a ship or airplane (velocity v, course azimuth α) causes inertial accelerations which affect the measurement value: *Eötvös-Effect*. The velocity component in the direction of the geodetic parallel increases (for a west-east course) the earth's angular velocity ω (Coriolis acceleration), Fig. 4.19. The meridional component of v causes an additional centrifugal acceleration. Therefore, the measured

Fig. 4.18. Gravity sensor Gss30 and gyrostabilized platform KT30, courtesy of Bodenseewerk Geosystem GmbH, Überlingen, Fed. Rep. Germany

gravity is actually too small. On the surface of a spherical earth ($r = R$), the Eötvös correction, given by

$$\delta g_E = 2\omega v \sin \alpha \cos \varphi + \frac{v^2}{R} = 4.0\ v \sin \alpha \cos \varphi + 0.0012\ v^2\ (10^{-5}\ \text{ms}^{-2}) \quad (4.26)$$

should be applied to the measured value of gravity; v has the units km/h. This correction can attain very large values; its accuracy is determined chiefly by the errors committed in measuring the velocity and course.

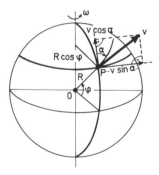

Fig. 4.19. Eötvös effect on gravity measurements

The *error sources* in sea and airborne gravimetry stem from instrumental effects, residual influences of vertical and horizontal disturbing accelerations, and uncertainties in the Eötvös-correction. With current sea gravimeters and good navigation, gravity field resolutions of 1 to 2 km and accuracies of $\pm 5 \dots 20\ \mu\text{ms}^{-2}$ can be achieved. Airborne gravimeter systems operated in helicopters provide resolutions of up to 1 km and an accuracy of $\pm 5\ \mu\text{ms}^{-2}$. In airborne applications, field resolutions of 10 to 20 km and accuracies of a few 10 μms^{-2} have been obtained. Kinematic

GPS-positioning using the carrier phase observable will further reduce these errors (BROZENA et al. 1989).

4.2.4 Gravity Reference Systems

The values of gravity required in geodesy and geophysics must refer to a global reference system. A *gravity reference system* is defined by values of gravity at a number of accurately surveyed gravity control points.

The gravity system is established through a global gravity network that is obtained from observations. The network must contain at least one absolute gravity measurement [4.2.1] to secure a gravity reference value. The "ms^{-2}-scale" is introduced by at least one calibration line with as large a difference in gravity as possible; it can be determined either by two absolute gravity measurements or (formerly) by relative pendulum measurements [4.2.2]. Measurements obtained by a gravimeter yield differences in gravity between the network points with high accuracy and less effort. The gravity control points should be placed, if possible, at undisturbed (geological and hydrological stability, little microseismicity) and permanent (scientific institutions) locations.

Redundant absolute and relative measurements are carried out, whenever possible, with different instruments, and are then adjusted to eliminate systematic errors and to increase the accuracy. The observed differences in gravity should form a network of closed loops; the drift of the instrument is determined from repeated measurements. The adjustment also provides the parameters of the gravimeters' drift and calibration functions, in addition to the gravity values (TORGE 1984).

The *Potsdam Gravity System* served as the international reference system from 1909 to 1971. It was based on reversible pendulum measurements that were made at the Geodetic Institute at Potsdam by *Kühnen* and *Furtwängler* (1898–1904). More recent absolute gravity determinations showed that the gravity value of Potsdam is 140 μms^{-2} too large. Therefore, between 1950 and 1970, a new global gravity system was constructed through international collaboration.

This *International Gravity Standardization Net* 1971 (IGSN71) was introduced in 1971 as the new reference system, at the General Assembly of the I.U.G.G. in Moscow. The network contains 1854 points (~ 500 primary stations) whose values of gravity were determined from ten new absolute and approximately 25000 relative measurements of gravity (including ~ 1200 relative pendulum measurements) with an overall uncertainty less than $\pm 1 \ \mu ms^{-2}$ (MORELLI et al. 1974), Fig. 4.20. Particularly high accuracy is associated with points of the densely observed gravimeter calibration lines (Euro-African, American, West Pacific) extending in the north-south direction (large differences in gravity). Regional gravity networks referred to other systems should be tied to the IGSN71. The transformation parameters (generally shift and scale) are derived from identical points, where data are available in both systems.

The I.A.G. has proposed an *International Absolute Gravity Basestation Network* (IAGBN), with 36 globally distributed stations (BOEDECKER and FRITZER 1986). Main purpose of this network is to monitor temporal gravity changes on a global scale,

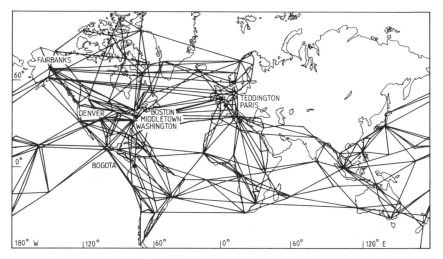

Fig. 4.20. International Gravity Standardization Net 1971 (I.G.S.N.71), absolute gravity stations and selected network ties, after MORELLI et al. (1974), from TORGE (A1989)

and to serve as a regional gravity control. Since 1987, the network is established with the help of transportable absolute gravimeters [4.2.1].

4.2.5 Determination of the Gravity Gradient

The gravity gradient [2.2.5] contains local gravity field information, which may be used in corresponding computations [3.2.2]. Gravity gradiometry may be applied in stationary or in kinematic mode.

The *torsion balance* represents a stationary gravity gradiometer. It consists of two equal masses situated at different heights and connected by a rigid system of negligibly small mass which is suspended by a torsional thread (Fig. 4.21). Due to the unequal

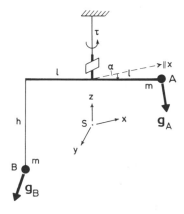

Fig. 4.21. Eötvös torsion balance principle

gravity accelerations at A and B, the suspended beam experiences a torsional moment and a tilt; the latter may be neglected. We introduce the local astronomic system [2.2.2] (origin at the center of mass S) and assume a linear variation in gravity around the area of the apparatus. For equilibrium of the torques, we then have

$$2\,m(W_y x - W_x y) - \tau(\vartheta - \vartheta_0) = 0. \tag{4.27}$$

Here, m is the mass at A and B, τ is the torsional constant of the thread, and $\vartheta - \vartheta_0$ is the angle of rotation of the suspended beam with respect to the initial position ϑ_0 (untwisted position). By expanding W_x and W_y about S in Taylor series and introducing also the azimuth α of the beam, the length of the beam $2l$, and the difference in heights of the masses, h, one obtains

$$\vartheta - \vartheta_0 = \frac{ml^2}{\tau}((W_{yy} - W_{xx})\sin 2\alpha + 2W_{xy}\cos 2\alpha) + \frac{mlh}{\tau}(W_{xz}\sin \alpha - W_{yz}\cos \alpha). \tag{4.28}$$

The deflection ϑ is recorded photographically, and the instrumental constants m, l, h, τ are provided by the manufacturer. Hence, the field quantities $W_{yy} - W_{xx}$, W_{xy}, W_{xz}, W_{yz}, as well as ϑ_0 can be determined by measuring ϑ for five different azimuths.

The development of a torsion balance suitable for field work was achieved around 1900 by the Hungarian physicist R. v. Eötvös; it was widely employed in applied geophysics between 1920 and 1940. An accuracy of ± 1 to $\pm 5 \times 10^{-9}$ s^{-2} can be attained for the field quantities (MUELLER et al. 1963). Due to the considerable effort that is required in making measurements and because of the large influence of nearby masses, the torsion balance has been superseded by the gravimeter.

Spring gravimeters can be used to approximate grad g by measuring small gravity differences. With station separations of 10 to 100 m, the horizontal gravity gradient can be derived (HAMMER 1979). For the measurement of the vertical gradient, special tripods are used with heights of up to 3 m (RÖDER et al. 1985). A precision of $\pm 10^{-8}$s^{-2} can be achieved with such measurements.

Any neighboring topographic masses influence these second derivatives quite strongly. *Topographic reductions* must therefore be applied. Terrestrial gradiometry fails in mountainous regions.

Gravity gradiometers are currently being developed particularly for use in aircraft and artificial earth satellites. They employ different numbers and configurations of accelerometer pairs, and use either conventional or superconducting electronics. The measurements are performed in a dense sequence (e.g. 1 s) and integrated over a time interval (e.g. 10 s) before further processing. These devices should furnish all second derivatives of the gravitational potential with uncertainties of a few 10^{-9}s^{-2} (aircraft), and about 10^{-12}s^{-2} (satellite), respectively (WELLS 1984). The results are largely free from the effects of topography since the measurements are made at a great distance above the earth's surface. The integration yields the detailed structure of the gravitational field, in the form of gravity anomalies and vertical deflections. Expected accuracies are ± 10 μms^{-2} and $\pm 0.''2$, for surface and airborne systems, and $\pm 20 \ldots 30$ μm^{-2} (resolution 50 km) for satellite gradiometers (RUMMEL and COLOMBO 1985, RUMMEL 1986).

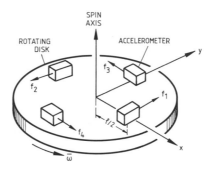

Fig. 4.22. Rotating gravity gradiometer unit principle, with accelerations *f* and carrier angular velocity $\bar{\omega}$; after JEKELI (1988)

We mention the *Gravity Gradiometer Survey System GGSS* (Bell Aerospace-Textron, Buffalo, New York) which is in the test phase (JEKELI 1988). It consists of three gradiometer units each equipped with two accelerometer pairs, mounted orthogonally on a slowly rotating disk (Fig. 4.22). These units are combined under different orientations on a gyro-stabilized platform. Linear combinations of the accelerometer outputs provide the components of grad **g**.

Among the planned *space missions* (satellite altitude about 200 km) are the ESA (European Space Agency) ARISTOTELES mission (GRADIO gradiometer, conventional electronics, $\approx 1994/95$, BALMINO and BERNARD 1986), and the NASA Superconducting Gravity Gradiometer Mission, ≈ 2000, PAIK et al. 1988). Non-gravitational accelerations which occur on moving platforms either cancel out in the differences for a pair of accelerometers, or they are separated by introducing additional attitude data (MORITZ 1968c). Main problems originate from residual attitude errors and from the drift of the accelerometers.

4.2.6 The Measurement of Earth Tides

Variations in the intensity of gravity which are caused by tides can be measured by gravimeters; other effects such as fluctuations in the direction of the plumb line are determined by tiltmeters, and crustal deformations are measured using extensometers (MELCHIOR A1983).

A spring-type field gravimeter [4.2.2] may be used as an earth-tide *recording gravimeter*. For this purpose it has to be equipped with a low-pass filter, a recording unit, and a quartz clock (WENZEL 1976, EDGE et al. 1986). Special tidal gravimeters (LaCoste-Romberg earth tide gravimeter, Askania Gs25, Geodynamics — modified North American Gravimeter) have great stability and a small measuring range.

Changes in the position of the lever are converted to electrical signals, generally by a capacitive detector; these are then amplified and recorded along with the time. Digital recording (with e.g. 10 s or 1 min. averaging and 10 min or 1 h output) is generally performed today. An analog output offers a convenient on-line control (Fig. 4.23). A calibration furnishes the relationship between the gravimeter reading and the recorded deflection; a relative accuracy of 1 to 2×10^{-3} can be obtained.

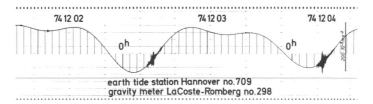

Fig. 4.23. Gravimetric earth tide record, obtained with LaCoste and Romberg gravimeter G 298, IfE Hannover

In the *superconducting gravimeter*, the force of gravity acting on a proof mass is compensated by a magnetic counterforce. A high long-term stability is achieved by the superconducting state of the system (Fig. 4.24). Vertical displacements of the mass are monitored by a capacitive detector and compensated through a feedback system, thereby admitting continuous recording . Instrumental long-term drift remains very small; the accuracy in the short-period (≤ 1 d) tidal band is better than ± 1 nms^{-2} (GOODKIND 1986, RICHTER 1987).

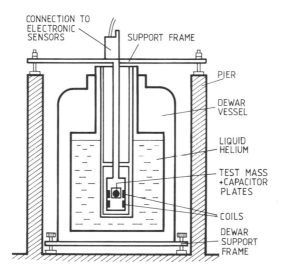

Fig. 4.24. GWR superconducting gravimeter principle, after GWR-Instruments, San Diego, California, information and RICHTER (1987), from TORGE (A1989)

Tiltmeters are designed as horizontal and vertical pendulums, and as water-tube levels. The fluctuations in the direction of the plumb line with respect to the earth's surface are determined from its two mutually perpendicular components (*NS, EW*).

The *horizontal pendulum* after *Zöllner* consists of two nearly vertical threads which support an approximately horizontal beam with an attached mass *m* (Fig. 4.25). Because of the small inclination *i* of the rotational axis with respect to the direction of the vertical, a horizontal force (fluctuation of the vertical, inclination of the support) acting perpendicularly to the beam causes a strongly amplified angular deflection. A further amplification is possible through an

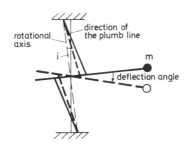

Fig. 4.25. Zöllner horizontal pendulum principle

illuminated pointer and a mirror attached to the beam. The deflections are registered photographically on film. By producing a known inclination and measuring the angle of deflection, one is able to calibrate the instrument ($\pm 1\%$), VAN RUYMBEKE (1976).

The Askania *vertical pendulum* (Bodenseewerk Geosystem GmbH, Überlingen) of *A. Graf* (length: 600 mm) is suspended such that it can swing freely. The deflections are sensed by two capacitive detectors at right angles to each other, and upon amplification, the signals are recorded by digital and analog means. The instrument is designed to operate in boreholes (20...60 m depth), FLACH (1976). Long *water-tube tiltmeters* have found only limited application (KÄÄRIÄINEN 1979).

Strain measurements are made with extensometers (strainmeters) (KING and BILHAM 1973). The strain, which depends on the tides, is on the order to 10^{-8} corresponding to 0.1 μm/10 m: therefore, an instrumental resolution of 1×10^{-10} is required. For the complete determination of the six independent components of the strain tensor, strainmeters must be oriented in different spatial directions. The results represent functions of the Love number h and the Shida number l [2.4.2].

Metal and quartz tube extensometers, as well as invar wires with lengths of 10 to 30 m are used for these purpose; laser interferometers allow lengths up to 1 km (BERGER and LEVINE (1974). Generally one end of the instrument is firmly attached to the earth's crust; the crustal displacements are measured at the other end.

Numerous *perturbing effects* are superimposed on the tidal signal:

As far as the *instrumental systematic errors* are concerned, the uncertainties associated with the determination of the calibration and frequency transfer function (frequency dependent damping and instrumental phase shift) represent a limit to the highest attainable accuracy. Direct effects of atmospheric pressure and temperature can either be held to a minimum by appropriate shielding, or determined and taken into account by regression analyses. *Instrumental drift* is obtained computationally in the evaluation: however, its influence complicates the analysis of long-periodic tides. The effects caused by *oceanic tides* are difficult to ascertain. They are composed of the direct attraction of the water masses and the induced crustal movements due to tidal loading. The semidiurnal partial tide is affected in particular (GROTEN and BRENNECKE 1973). The ocean tide loading effect can be determined for an elastic earth model if the ocean tide distribution is given. Global oceanic tidal models exist for the most important waves (e.g SCHWIDERSKI 1980, 1983). The loading effect has been modelled by FARRELL (1972). *Environmental* disturbing *effects* arise from the fluctuations in atmospheric pressure and temperature, as well as from varying solar radiation and the resulting tilt of the earth's surface. These effects bear in particular on the diurnal partial tides. Meteorological and hydrological effects also exhibit long-term behaviour.

The *gravimeters*, which are less sensitive to inclinations, already furnish good results when placed in temperature controlled cellars. *Tiltmeters* and *extensometers*, on the other hand, must be shielded from the surface influences by a sufficiently thick (several 10 m) rock cover. They are therefore installed in tunnels and mines, or in bore holes (vertical pendulum). Local effects resulting from variable elastic rock properties, anomalous topographic stress field, and cavity deformations, however, can affect the results of the inclination and strain measurements, thereby causing deviations from regionally valid values of 10 to 15% (HARRISON 1976).

For the evaluation of earth tide measurements, the recorded tidal signal is decomposed into partial tides and compared to the theoretical tides [2.4.1]. This *harmonic analysis* is based on a least squares adjustment, in order to derive the amplitude factors and phase shifts of the main waves (VENEDIKOV 1977, WENZEL 1976). With spring-type gravimeters, ten to twenty wave groups can be analyzed, depending on the length of the recording time. After several months of measurements, the factors δ (*gravimetric earth tides*) for the principal waves O1, K1, M2, S2 and K1, S2 as wave groups together with neighboring frequencies are obtained to an accuracy of ± 2 to $\pm 5 \times 10^{-3}$, and $\pm 0\overset{\circ}{.}1$ to $0\overset{\circ}{.}2$ for the accompanying phase shifts (TORGE and WENZEL 1977); the random errors amount to ± 5 to $\pm 20 \, \text{nms}^{-2}$. Standard deviations of $\pm$ a few $0.1 \, \text{nms}^-$ (5 min. samples) are obtained with digital recording (WENZEL and ZÜRN 1990). For superconducting gravimeters, registration series over five years and more are available. They also permit an analysis of long-periodic partial tides, and of the polar motion effect (RICHTER 1987).

The random error in measurements of *inclination* is about $\pm 0\overset{\prime\prime}{.}0002$, while the attainable instrumental accuracies for the factors γ and the phase shifts amount to roughly $\pm 1\%$ and $\pm 1\overset{\circ}{.}0$. respectively. Due to the local geological, topographic and cavity effects mentioned above, the results obtained from tiltmeters and extensometers are often not representative. This is particularly valid if the instrumental basis of these instruments is small (few decimeters to meters).

Gravimetric *tidal profiles* (duration of recordings of four months and more per station) for the past several years have been systematically established over the entire earth (MELCHIOR and DE BECKER 1983). The principal reference station in Brussels is available for a comparison of the various gravimeters that are being employed (DUCARME 1975).

4.3 Terrestrial Geodetic Measurements

Horizontal angles, distances, zenith angles, and height differences obtained from leveling are measured on the earth surface. These measurements determine the relative spatial positions of the surface points.

Distance measurements employing acoustic waves serve to position points on the ocean floor. One limitation on the accuracy is given by the uncertainties in accounting for atmospheric refraction, or in the propagation of acoustic waves through sea water.

Inertial surveying systems derive three-dimensional position differences from measurements of the vehicle's accelerations (SEEBER 1979, SCHWARZ A1986). The method is used for the interpolation of control points (standard deviation $\pm$ (0.1 m + 2 $\times$ 10^{-5}s), mainly for mapping purposes.

Due to the high accuracy and economy of satellite-based observation techniques, cf. especially [4.4.7], terrestrial geodetic measurements more and more serve for interpolation of satellite-derived results. Terrestrial surveying methods are treated in KAHMEN and FAIG (A1988). DEUMLICH (A1982) reviews the surveying instruments, while KAHMEN (A1978) concentrates on electronic measurement methods.

4.3.1 Atmospheric Refraction

In practially all terrestrial geodetic measurements, as in astronomic measurements and in satellite observations, electromagnetic waves serve as carriers of a signal. As they propagate through the atmosphere, they experience changes in velocity and in the curvature of the path (refraction), BRUNNER (A1984). The changes depend on the local *index of refraction* (refractive index) n. On the other hand, n is a function of the wave length λ. Ascertaining these changes presents considerable difficulties, since the index of refraction depends on position and time, and is not sufficiently stable in the lower kilometers of the atmosphere.

The wave path is determined by the minimum travel time Δt of the wave (*Fermat's principle*):

$$\Delta t = \frac{1}{c_0} \int_0^s n \, ds = \min. \tag{4.29}$$

For the electromagnetic distance measurements [4.3.3] we require the *velocity of the wave*:

$$c = \frac{c_0}{n}. \tag{4.30a}$$

The velocity of light in vacuum, c_0 has the value (XVIth General Assembly of the I.U.G.G., Grenoble 1975):

$$c_0 = 299\ 792\ 458 \pm 1.2 \ \text{ms}^{-1}. \tag{4.30b}$$

The mean velocity $\bar{c}$ along the path s of the ray is often introduced into the computations. It is given from the mean index of refraction $\bar{n}$ by

$$\bar{c} = \frac{c_0}{\bar{n}} \quad \text{with } \bar{n} = \frac{1}{s} \int_0^s n \, ds. \tag{4.31}$$

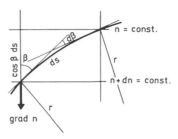

Fig. 4.26. Terrestrial refraction

Reducing the distance and direction measurements to the chord between the points presumes a knowledge of the *curvature of the light ray*. According to Fig. 4.26, it is given by

$$\frac{1}{r} = \frac{d\beta}{ds}.$$ (4.32)

Here, r is the local radius of curvature and β is the angle between the normal to the surface, $n = $ const., and the tangent to the light ray. Using

$$dn = \text{grad } n \cdot ds = |\text{grad } n| ds \cos \beta$$

and *Snell's* law

$$n \sin \beta = \text{const.}$$

from which the differential relation

$$\sin \beta \, dn + n \cos \beta \, d\beta = 0$$

follows, we obtain

$$\frac{1}{r} = -\frac{|\text{grad } n|}{n} \sin \beta.$$ (4.33)

The horizontal components of grad n cause *horizontal refraction* (lateral refraction), and affect horizontal angle measurements [4.3.2]. For rays which propagate higher above the ground (>25 m) and thereby avoid extreme horizontal temperature gradients, the effect on the observed direction remains generally less than 1".

If we neglect horizontal refraction, then for $n \approx 1$ and $\beta \approx 90°$, the *coefficient of refraction* κ (ratio of the curvature of the light ray to the earth's curvature) describes the *vertical refraction*:

$$\kappa = \frac{R}{r} = -R\frac{dn}{dh},$$ (4.34)

($R = $ radius of curvature of the ellipsoidal normal section). Vertical refraction affects distance measurements [4.3.3], zenith angles [4.3.4], and geometric leveling [4.3.5], and has to be accounted for by proper curvature reductions. When reducing zenith angles [4.3.4] one requires the *angle of refraction* δ (= angle between the tangent to the path of the light and the straight line joining the point of observation and the target). It is given by integrating $1/r$ or κ along the path. Regarding the light path as a circular arc, we have

$$\delta = \frac{s}{2r} = \frac{s}{2R}k. \tag{4.35}$$

k is designated the effective coefficient of refraction.

The *index of refraction n* is computed from empirically obtained relations (XIIIth General Assembly of the I.U.G.G., Berkeley, 1963).

The formula of *H. Barrell* and *J. E. Sears* furnishes the (frequency dependent) index of refraction for unmodulated monochromatic light. For wavelength λ (in μm), dry air, $T = 273$ K, $p = 1013.25$ hPa, and 0.03% CO_2 content, we have

$$(n - 1)10^6 = 287.604 + \frac{1.6288}{\lambda^2} + \frac{0.0136}{\lambda^4}. \tag{4.36}$$

Modulated light is used for electro-optical distance measurements. The group index of refraction providing the propagation of the maximum energy of a wave group is given by

$$n_g = n - \lambda \frac{dn}{d\lambda}. \tag{4.37}$$

For air temperature T(K), barometric pressure p(hPa) and partial pressure of water vapor, e(hPa), the equation

$$n_l - 1 = \frac{n_g - 1}{\alpha T}\frac{p}{1013.25} - \frac{4.1 \times 10^{-8}e}{\alpha T} \tag{4.38}$$

holds for the actual meteorological condition (α = coefficient of thermal expansion of air = 0.00366).

The index of refraction for *microwaves*, n_m, is obtained from the formula of *L. Essen* and *K. D. Froome* as

$$(n_m - 1)10^6 = \frac{77.62}{T}(p - e) + \frac{64.70}{T}\left(1 + \frac{5748}{T}\right)e. \tag{4.39}$$

If the error in the index of refraction caused by the meteorological parameters is not to exceed 10^{-6}, then under average conditions, one must obtain accuracies in the temperature to $\pm 1°$C, in the pressure to ± 3.5 hPa, and in the humidity to ± 30 hPa (light) or ± 0.2 hPa (microwaves).

If we form the derivatives of n_l and n_m with respect to the height h and substitute these into (4.34), then we arrive at the *curvature* of the ray as a function of the meteorological parameters. Using $n = 1.00029$, and assuming a condition of equilibrium in the atmosphere, we have for *light*:

$$\frac{1}{r_l}10^6 = \frac{78\,p}{T^2}\left(0.034 + \frac{dT}{dh}\right) + \frac{11}{T}\frac{de}{dh}. \tag{4.40}$$

Under average conditions (during the day with clear skies), there is

$$r_l = 8R, \qquad k_l = 0.13. \tag{4.41}$$

If the uncertainty in the angle of refraction should remain less than $0\rlap{.}''5$, then according to (4.35) for $s = 25$ km, k_l must be obtained with an accuracy of ± 0.001. Constraining the individual errors of the meteorological parameters in (4.40) to this limit, one must acquire accuracies for the average values for T of $\pm 1°$C, for p: ± 4 hPa, and for $\partial T/\partial h$: $\pm 2 \times 10^{-4}$ °C m^{-1}. Therefore, the curvature of the light rays is predominantly determined by vertical temperature gradients.

The curvature of the rays for *microwaves* is given approximately by

$$\frac{1}{r_m} 10^6 = \frac{1}{T^2} \left(77.6\, p + 7.4 \times 10^5 \frac{e}{T} \right) \frac{dT}{dh} + 2.7 \frac{p}{T^2} - \frac{3.7 \times 10^5}{T^2} \frac{de}{dh}. \tag{4.42}$$

For average conditions at day, we obtain

$$r_m = 4R, \qquad k_m = 0.25. \tag{4.43}$$

The temperature, the humidity (microwaves), and the vertical temperature gradient (curvature of light rays) are those *meteorological quanitities*, in particular, which strongly influence the index of refraction and the curvature. Especially in the atmospheric layers close to the ground, these quantitites exhibit large variations with respect to position (topography, vegetation, distance from the ground) and time (daily and yearly fluctuations) with effects that are both regular and irregular. By suitably designing measurements (to avoid larger anomalies) and by obtaining local meteorological data (measurements at the endpoints of distances; in exceptional cases, also using probes along the path of the ray), the regular effects can be ascertained to some extent from simple mathematical models. However, due to the complex nature of the meteorological parameters, they can be determined at times only statistically and then considered as a correlation between the observed quantities. The correlation may be reduced by repeating the measurements under different atmospheric conditions. The irregular effects of refraction are lessened with an accumulation of measurements.

It is possible to determine directly the *coefficient of refraction* by measuring reciprocal zenith angles [4.3.4]. Finally, one can take advantage of the dependence of the refraction index for light on the wavelength (*dispersion*). Using light of various wavelengths when measuring a distance furnishes, by equation (4.36), different distances and times of propagation; for zenith angle measurements, this procedure yields different vertical deviations of the target point. From these results, one may deduce the geometric length of the line [4.3.3] and the angle of refraction [4.3.4], respectively.

4.3.2 Horizontal Angle Measurements

The *horizontal angle* is defined as the angle measured in the horizontal plane of the local astronomic system [3.2.2] between two vertical planes. It is formed by the difference in *directions* to the target points which determine the vertical planes. A *theodolite* can be used for measuring directions. The principal components of this instrument are a horizontal (and a vertical) circle, a telescope capable of being rotated about the vertical axis and about the horizontal axis, and mechanisms for reading the circles. In order to orientate the theodolite with respect to the direction of the plumb line, it is equipped with precision spirit levels or compensators which automatically level the instrument.

We distinguish between optical and electronic theodolites. Classical *high precision theodolites* such as the DKM3 (Kern, Aarau) and the Wild T3 (Wild, Heerbrugg) are characterized by an especially stable construction, glass circles (80 to 250 mm diameter, reading capability to $0\rlap{.}{''}2$ ... $0\rlap{.}{''}5$, circle graduation error $<0\rlap{.}{''}5$), a coincidence microscope with optical micrometer for reading the circles, and a telescope with a lens aperture of 50 to 70 mm and a magnification of 30 to 80. An instrument which can also be used as a universal theodolite [4.1.4] is the Theo 002 (Jenoptik, Jena).

Electronic theodolites have telescopes and graduated circles similar to optical theodolites. The microscopes are replaced by optical-electronic scanning systems (resolution $\sim 0\rlap{.}{''}5$), A microprocessor controls and evaluates the instrument's operation. By combination with an electronic distance measurement unit [4.3.3], an electronic theodolite can be extended to a "total station". The T3000 (Wild Leitz Ltd., Heerbrugg) is an example for a high precision electronic theodolite (Fig. 4.27).

For precise angle measurements in 1. order control networks (30 to 60 km spacing of the stations), the theodolite was set on an *observation pillar*. The targets were made discernible by using *light signals*. A spotlight or (seldom) sunlight reflected by a heliotrope served as the luminous device.

Special structures (steel or wooden towers with heights of 30 m or more) had to be erected in flatlands. Because the direction measurements are sensitive to any vibrations, these towers consisted of two independent frames: an inner frame for the instrument, and an outer frame

Fig. 4.27. High precision electronic theodolite Wild T3000, courtesy of Wild Leitz Ltd., Heerbrugg, Switzerland

for the support of the observer and the target. One source of error was the twisting of the inner structure by uneven solar radiation (up to 1″ per 5 min.).

With the availability of electronic distance meters [4.3.3] and GPS satellite methods [4.4.7], first order horizontal control networks are no longer determined by angle measurements, cf. [6.1.1]. The application of the theodolite is thus reduced to station distances of less than 10 to 20 km (mountains), or even a few km (flat areas with intervisibility problems). Consequently, optical or electronic *precision theodolites* (aperture of 40 to 45, magnification of 30, circle reading 1″) such as the Wild T2 (optical), Wild T2002 (electronic) or Zeiss ETh2 (electronic) can be employed, Fig. 4.28. The observation procedure developed for first order triangulation (see below) may be modified according to the less stringent demands (stand. dev. $\pm 0.''5$) for shorter lines of sight.

Fig. 4.28. Electronic precision theodolite ZEISS E Th2, courtesy of Carl Zeiss, Oberkochen, Fed. Rep. Germany

To determine horizontal angles, one conducts either *direction measurements* (successive observations to all directions for both positions of the telescope (1 set) for several sets or *angle measurements* (separate measurements of two directions, each with both telescope positions and for several sets).

Large station separations (some 10 km) pose severe problems for theodolite observations due to the often unfavourable visibility condition. In order to avoid an observation time of some weeks per station, special methods had been developed for 1. order triangulation. We mention the observation of *incomplete direction sets* combined by at least one common direction, the *angle measurement in all combinations* after *Schreiber* (results in equally weighted and uncorrelated directions), and the *Swiss sector method*. In the latter, a few readily visible directions, approximately evenly distributed along the horizon, form the principal angles, into which additional directions are included by further angle measurements.

In order to increase the accuracy, and especially, to decrease the effects of horizontal refraction [4.3.1], the horizontal angles of high-precision networks should be observed under different meteorological conditions. A standard deviation of $\pm 0\!\!''\!2$ to $\pm 0\!\!''\!4$ can be achieved for a direction after a station adjustment (1. order net).

4.3.3 Distance Measurements

Distance measurements establish the scale of geodetic networks. Arranged as networks or traverses they also provide geometrical relations between the observation stations.

The *unit of length* is the *meter*. According to the definition of the Eleventh General Conference for Weights and Measure, 1960, it is 1650763.73 times the wavelength of the radiation emitted in vacuum corresponding to the transition of the ^{86}Kr atom from the $5d_5$ state to the $2p_{10}$ state.

The previously accepted definition was based on the definition of the meter as the ten millionth part of the meridian quadrant through Paris; its length was derived from an arc measurement by *Delambre* and *Méchain* [1.3.3]. This definition at first (1799) was used for the *legal meter* (realized in the less durable mètre des archives) and later (International Meter Convention, Paris 1875) for the *international meter*. The latter was defined by the length of the meter prototype (platinum — iridium bar) preserved by the Bureau International des Poids et Mesures in Sèvres.

Until about 1960, the scale of triangulation networks, constructed from angle measurements [4.3.2] was derived from *base lines* having lengths of 5 to 10 km. Measuring rods and (as of 1900) wires or tapes served to measure distances. In the method specified by *Jäderin* (1880), freely hanging metal wires 24 m in length were used; they were made of the NiFe alloy, invar (very small coefficient of thermal expansion). The relative accuracy of the more recent base lines amounts to $\pm 10^{-6}$. This quite elaborate but lengthy method of mechanically measuring the distance has today become obsolete as a result of the use of electromagnetic distance measurements.

For field calibrations of wires and tapes, several international calibration lines were established during the last decades by *interferometric methods*. Starting from the length of a standard meter, the *Väisäla* light interference comparator provided an optical multiplication up to baseline lengths of 864 m (relative accuracy $\pm 10^{-7}$).

In *electromagnetic distance measurements* (RINNER 1974), light waves ($\lambda = 0.36$ to 0.78 μm) and microwaves ($\lambda = 1$ cm to 10 cm) serve as carriers of the measuring signal. The travel time of the signal serves as measure for the distance. Time measurement can be performed by pulse or phase comparison methods.

When the *pulse method* is used, the transmitter emits a pulse, which is reflected at the target (reflector) and observed at the receiver. An accurate timer measures the time of propagation Δt which the signal requires to travel forth and back along the distance D. We have

$$D = \frac{\bar{c}}{2}\Delta t. \tag{4.44}$$

$\bar{c}$ is the average velocity of propagation along the path of the ray (4.31). If the uncertainty in distance is to remain less than 5 mm, then the time of propagation should be obtained to an accuracy of ± 0.03 ns. This high accuracy demand poses problems with respect to the pulse generation. The method is extensively applied at satellite laser ranging [4.4.5]. It was also used for airborne ranging over long distances (see below).

Due to its high accuracy, the *phase comparison techniques* are favored today. The high-frequency carrier waves are *modulated* (amplitude or frequency modulation), and the modulation frequency $f(7.5$ to 150 MHz) is used as a "yardstick" in the measurement. Main components of the *distance meter* are transmitter and receiver, phase meter, and microprocessor. If a digital phase detector is used, the measurement process can be made fully automatic. At the target station, a reflector has to be installed. After reflection, a phase shift $\Delta\varphi$ of the signal is measured at the receiver. It corresponds to a propagation time

$$\Delta t = \frac{r + \Delta\varphi/2\pi}{f}. \tag{4.45}$$

The number of the complete periods r in the time t is determined by applying several, slightly different modulation frequencies. Substituting (4.45) into (4.44) yields

$$D = \frac{\bar{c}}{2f}\left(r + \frac{\Delta\varphi}{2\pi}\right). \tag{4.46}$$

The *calibration* of electronic distance measuring devices consists of checking the modulation frequency with a frequency meter, and determining the instrumental constants (zero correction and possible cyclic errors of electro-optical devices) on short ($\leqslant 1$ km) test lines.

The lengths of these *calibration lines*, which are usually partitioned into several sections, are determined by a laser interferometer or an electro-optical short range distance meter of high precison.

Instruments of this type are the Mekometer ME 3000 (FROOME 1971) and its latest successor, the Geomensor CR 234 (Com-Rad Electronic Equipment Ltd., U.K.), Fig. 4.29. White light (Xenon flash tube) is used as carrier. The modulation wave length (30 cm) is automatically adjusted such that the distance is an integer number of wavelengths, and measured with a frequency meter. A meteorological sensor unit provides the data for a meteorological correction, external data can be included, cf. [4.3.1]. With 7 reflectors, the maximum range is 10 km. The instrumental precision is $\pm(0.1$ mm $+ 0.1 \times 10^{-6}D)$, and the meteorological error part may be reduced to $\pm 0.5 \times 10^{-6}D$ (DODSON and FLEMING 1988).

The *measurement range* of distance meters depends on the curvature of light and microwaves, and on the absorption in the atmosphere. The range may be increased by erecting towers for the instrument and reflector, as well as by amplifying the transmitted energy. In this respect, the requirements for stability are less stringent if microwaves are used instead of the more strongly bundled light waves.

Fig. 4.29. High precision short-range distance meter Geomensor CR 234, courtesy of Com-Rad Electronic Equipment Ltd., Mid Glamorgan, U.K.

For the long-range *electro-optical distance meters* (first developed by *E. Bergstrand* in 1948), the strongly bundled light waves from the light source (generally He-Ne-gas laser, $\lambda = 632.8$ nm) are amplitude modulated using KDP (potassium dihydrogen phosphate) crystals. The light is transmitted through emitting optics, reflected at the other end by a (passive) prism reflector, and directed through the receiving optics to a secondary electron multiplier. The phase of the modulated oscillations thus obtained is then compared with a phase meter to the phase of the emitted modulation frequency. To determine the meteorological conditons, temperature and pressure measurements are necessary [4.3.1]. The range is limited by the disturbances in the visibility (haze, fog); nevertheless, in using laser light, one can span distances up to 60 km on clear days and 60 to 80 km at night.

Among the laser distance meters are the Geodimeter 600 (30 MHz modulation frequency) of AGA in Sweden, the Geodolite 3G (49 MHz) of Spectra-Physics, U.S.A., and the Rangemaster III (15 MHz) of Laser Systems and Electronics Inc., U.S.A. The Geodimeter 6000 (Geotronics AB) employs an infrared LED GaAs diode, with 14.98 MHz modulation frequency (range with 16 prisms and clear weather up to 20...30 km), Fig. 4.30.

For the long-range *microwave distance meters* (first developed by *T. L. Wadley* 1956), a klystron (older instruments) or a Gunn oscillator creates the carrier wave ($\lambda = 8$ mm to 10 cm) which is frequency modulated by a quartz oscillator and emitted through a transmitter at the master station. At the remote station, the active reflector

Fig. 4.30. Long-range laser distance meter Geodimeter 6000, mounted on optical theodolite, courtesy of Geotronics AB, Danderyd, Sweden

(transponder), which is designed both as a receiver and transmitter, retransmits a new carrier wave. The received signal, weakened in the atmosphere, is modulated on this wave. Upon reception at the master station, the phase difference to the oscillator's reference signal is measured. Higher carrier frequencies are more easily focused, the loss in energy and the effect of ground reflection (ground sing) are thereby reduced (changing from 10 cm to 3 cm and 8 mm waves). Through the latest developments, the measuring procedure has been essentially automated with digital readout. At present, the errors in determining the humidity [4.3.1] restrict the accuracy of the longer lines. Since microwaves are hardly absorbed in the atmosphere, one can attain a range of 50 to 75 km and more regardless of the weather, during the day and at night.

With large parabolic antennas the range can be extended to 100 km and more. Some instruments have separate measuring and antenna units, which enable the antenna to be elevated on a high mast. For particular weather conditions, a supernormal coefficient of refraction ($k > 1$) may develop over the ocean. Measurements with this kind of wave guide (duct) can be made over very long ranges, more than 100 km (SPELLAUGE 1972).

Included among the microwave distance meters (modulation frequency 7.5 and 15 MHz at earlier developments, 75 and 150 MHz at more recent instruments) of this type are the Tellurometer MRA6 (1.8 cm carrier wave) and the CA 1000 (3 cm, 25 MHz, weight: 1.6 kg), manufactured by Tellurometer (U.K.) Ltd.; and the SIAL MD 60 (3 cm, the high modulation frequency of 150 MHz is hardly affected by ground reflection) by Siemens Albis AG. Zürich, Fig. 4.31.

Fig. 4.31. Long-range microwave distance meter SIAL MD60C, courtesy of Siemens Albis AG, Zürich, Switzerland

The *accuracy of the phase measuring method* is determined in part by errors which do not depend on distance (errors in the phase measurement and in the zero reading), and partly by errors increasing with distance (errors in the modulation frequency, in the velocity in vacuum, and in the mean index of refraction $\bar{n}$). For *large* distances, the predominant error is caused by the uncertainty in $\bar{n}$. Under normal conditions, the standard deviation *in distance* for *laser light* measurements is given by

$$m_D = \pm(1 \ldots 5 \text{ mm} + 1 \ldots 2 \times 10^{-6} \, D) \qquad (4.47)$$

and for measurements using *microwaves*, it is

$$m_D = \pm(10 \ldots 15 \text{ mm} + 3 \times 10^{-6} \, D). \qquad (4.48)$$

The *correlation* between measurements which were conducted under the same atmospheric conditions can attain values up to $r = +0.9$. For observations under different conditions it reduces to $+0.0 \ldots 0.4$ (HÖPCKE 1965).

Systematic *scale differences* (2×10^{-6} and larger) are frequently discovered between simultaneous light and microwave distance measurements, where the distances which are determined using microwaves prove to be shorter. It is assumed that this is caused by locally disturbed meteorological parameters which therefore are not representative of the entire distance (KUNTZ and MÖLLER 1971). Refraction effects thus remain a limiting factor in precise electromagnetic distance measurements (ILIFFE and DODSON 1987).

Long-distance measurements are time-consuming, even if weather-independent microwaves are used. In addition, GPS-positioning has proved to be efficient already at distances of a few km, cf. [4.4.7]. Consequently, *medium-range* electronic *distance meters* gained importance in the establishment or improvement of horizontal control networks. They can be combined with a theodolite, or even manufactured as a closed unit (electronic total station), cf. [4.3.2]. In this way, differences of threedimensional coordinates can be obtained, which refer to the local astronomic systems [3.2.2]. These instruments use infrared or visible light as carrier of the measuring signal. Electronic *precision total stations* (e.g. Wild Tachymat TC2000, Zeiss Elta 2, Geodimeter 440) have a maximum range of 5 to 7 km, and yield standard deviations of

$$m_D = \pm (2\ldots3 \text{ mm} + 2\ldots3 \times 10^{-6}D)$$

and $\pm 0\rlap{.}''5\ldots1''$ resp., Fig. 4.32. Employing the timed pulse method (e.g. Wild Distomat DI3000, Zeiss Eldi 10, Fig. 4.33) leads to maximum ranges of about 15 km and a standard deviation of

$$m_D = \pm (3\ldots5 \text{ mm} + 1\ldots3 \times 10^{-6}D),$$

within few seconds of measurement time.

Fig. 4.32. Electronic precision total station ZEISS Elta 2, courtesy of Carl Zeiss, Oberkochen, Fed. Rep. Germany

In the 1950s and early 1960s, *airborne microwave methods* were developed in order to measure long distances with "m"-accuracies. They were employed for the rapid establishment of large-scale control networks, and for bridging broad water areas, cf. [6.1.1]. In these "line-crossing" methods, the distance meter (master station) is located on the airplane, at least two ground

Fig. 4.33. Electronic distance meter Wild Distomat DI3000, courtesy of Wild Leitz Ltd., Heerbrugg, Switzerland

stations P_1, P_2 are equipped with transponders (Fig. 4.34). With the *Aerodist* system (carrier wave 0.25 m, max. range 300 km, modulation frequency 1.5 MHz, $\pm(1\text{ m} + 1 \times 10^{-5}D))$, flying across the line between P_1 and P_2, the phase difference is continually monitored. The minimum of the slant ranges is subsequently reduced using the heights h_1, h_2, h to the chord s (line crossing).

Shoran (Short Range Navigation) and *Hiran* (High Precision Shoran) used the pulse measuring mode (10^{-6} to 10^{-7}s pulses modulated on m-wavelength carrier, timing accuracy $\pm 10 \dots . 100$ ns corresponding to $\pm 1.5 \dots 15$ m, ranges of 300 to 900 km).

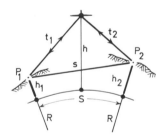

Fig. 4.34. Line crossing method

Before the observed distances can be processed further, and after employing frequency and zero corrections (see above), it is necessary to apply physical and geometric *reductions* (HÖPCKE 1966), (Fig. 4.35). The distance D' which is either computed from a measurement of the propagation time or is merely read on the instrument, is based on a standard index of refraction n_0. With the first and second *velocity corrections*, it is amended such that it is in accordance with the mean index of refraction $\bar{n}$ and the curved path of the ray (coefficient of refraction k):

$$D = D' + D'(n_0 - \bar{n}) - (k - k^2)\frac{D'^3}{12\,R_\alpha^2} \qquad (4.49)$$

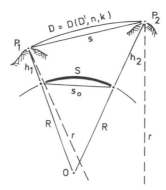

Fig. 4.35. Reduction of the measured distance D

(R_α is the radius of curvature of the arc S at an azimuth α (3.29)). The chord distance s, required for three-dimensional computations is corrected for the *curvature* of the path of the ray (assumed to be a spherical arc):

$$s = D - k^2 \frac{D^3}{24 R_\alpha^2}. \qquad (4.50)$$

The length of the *normal section* S [6.1.3] essential in two-dimensional ellipsoidal calculations, is given by

$$S = 2 R_\alpha \arcsin \frac{s_0}{2 R_\alpha} \quad \text{with} \quad s_0 = \sqrt{\frac{s^2 - (h_2 - h_1)^2}{(1 + h_1/R_\alpha)(1 + h_2/R_\alpha)}}. \qquad (4.51)$$

Without actually measuring the meteorological parameters, the length of the curved distance can be determined using simultaneously two or three *different wavelengths*. With lightwaves, two measured distances will differ because of dispersion [4.3.1]; and therefore, the observed difference in the distance, according to (4.38), depends particularly on the influences which the temperature and atmospheric pressure have on the average index of refraction. On the other hand, the difference with respect to an additional measurement using *microwaves*, in view of (4.39), mainly reveals the effects of the partial pressure of water vapor. From these differences between the measured distances D_{l_1}', D_{l_2}', D_m' which are obtained with light and microwaves, the geometric length of the path (without the curvature correction) is

$$D = D_{l_1}' - A(D_{l_2}' - D_{l_1}') - B(D_m' - D_{l_1}'). \qquad (4.52)$$

The coefficients A, B may be computed using the meteorological parameters of a standard atmosphere. If only two lightwaves are used, then the effect of water vapor pressure must be estimated.

A two-wave instrument (He — Cd laser 441.6 nm, He-Ne laser 632.8 nm) has been developed, to measure distances with a precision of ± 0.1 mm (HUGGETT 1981). From extensive application in California, a few 10^{-7} relative accuracy has been obtained for distances up to 10 km (LANGBEIN et al. 1987). By adding a microwave, the relative uncertainty can be reduced to $< 10^{-7}$ (HUGGETT and SLATER 1975).

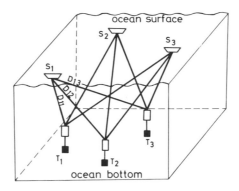

Fig. 4.36. Positioning on the ocean floor (T = transponder, S = position of ship and transmitter)

Control points on the ocean floor are important for the determination of accurate positions on the oceans. To establish their positions with respect to points on the ocean surface, exclusive use is made of *sound waves* because of the special properties of wave propagation through water. Acoustic transponders, powered by batteries or sources of nuclear energy serve as marks (life time of a few years, range up to 30 km). From the time of propagation Δt, which an acoustic signal (sound waves of 5 to 20 kHz, pulse length 10 to 20 ms) requires in travelling forth and back between the ship-borne transmitter and the transponder, we obtain the slant range

$$D = \frac{\bar{v}}{2}\Delta t. \tag{4.53}$$

The average velocity of sound $\bar{v}$ along the path depends on the temperature, salinity, and pressure of the water. It should be determined with the aid of measured data. In addition, a curvature correction must be applied due to the deflection of the path. The transponders are usually arranged in arrays (3 to 4 instruments, separated by 5 to 10 km). The methods of "line-crossing" and spatial trilateration (geometric position given by the intersection of the spheres having centers S and radii D, Fig. 4.36) serve then, in particular, to establish the position with respect to the ship. Further geometric configurations are given by RINNER (1977). A relative accuracy of ± 3 to ± 5 m is attainable even for great depths (MOURAD et al. 1972).

Different methods are available for the *absolute positioning* of a ship (INGHAM A1975, SEEBER 1985). The satellite navigation systems NNSS [4.4.6] and GPS [4.4.7] allow worldwide determinations (± 50 m). Radio navigation systems such as Loran C and Decca ($\pm$ some 100 m resp. $\pm$ some 10 m) cover large marine areas. High-precision systems ($\pm$ few m) as Syledis and Hi-Fix are operated in some near-shore regions. Geodetic angle and distance measurements from land also serve to determine positions in coastal proximity.

4.3.4 Zenith Angle Measurements, Trigonometrically Determined Heights

The zenith angle [3.2.2] is measured with the vertical circle of a theodolite.

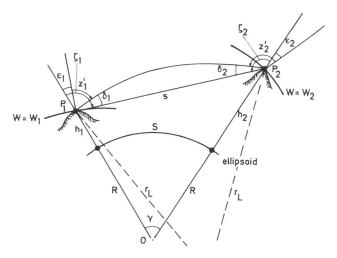

Fig. 4.37. Trigonometric heighting

For measurements of control networks, precise theodolites [4.3.2] are used. Levels or compensators serve to bring the reading device into the horizontal. Reading accuracy is $\pm 0.''2$ to $\pm 0.''5$ for high-precision instruments, and $\pm 1''$ for precision theodolites. .

The observed zenith angle z' refers to the local direction of the plumb line and the curved ray of light (Fig. 4.37).

Considering the angle of refraction δ [4.3.1] and the component of the deflection of the vertical ε [5.1.1] in the direction of side s at an azimuth A, the *ellipsoidal zenith angle* referring to the chord s is given by

$$\zeta = z' + \delta + \varepsilon. \tag{4.54}$$

The *difference in ellipsoidal heights* between the two points P_1, P_2 is computed from *Jordan's* formula for heights:

$$\Delta h_{12} = h_2 - h_1 = S\left(1 + \frac{h_1 + h_2}{2R}\right)\cot\zeta_1 + \frac{S^2}{2R\sin^2\zeta_1}. \tag{4.55}$$

S is the length of the normal section (4.51).

According to (4.35), δ depends on the coefficient of refraction k, and thereby, on the meteorological conditions, particularly on the vertical gradient of temperature (4.40). At present δ is generally derived from meteorological data taken only at the endpoints of the line. This leads to errors of a few seconds of arc, or more, for distances larger than a few km. In this way, the applicability of trigonometric heights over longer lines is considerably restricted.

Using *reciprocal zenith angles*, the effect of the uncertainties in refraction is reduced. From the central angle

$$\gamma = S/R = \zeta_1 + \zeta_2 - \pi \tag{4.56}$$

and equation (4.54), the law of tangents as applied to the triangle OP_1P_2 (Fig. 4.37) yields the difference in height

$$\Delta h_{12} = S\left(1 + \frac{h_1 + h_2}{2R} + \frac{S^2}{12R^2}\right) \times \tan\frac{1}{2}((z_2' + \delta_2 + \varepsilon_2) - (z_1' + \delta_1 + \varepsilon_1)) + \cdots$$

$$(4.57)$$

Only the differences in the angles δ and ε appear in this equation. For a symmetrical light path, $\delta_1 = \delta_2, \varepsilon_1 = \varepsilon_2$, and the height difference is then affected only by random errors.

An approximately *symmetric effect of refraction* is to be expected for *simultaneous* observations, if in the case of cloudy weather, these are conducted prior to the isothermal conditions of the evening, and if the ray of light is more than 15 to 20 m above the ground. The uncertainties in refraction then remain less than $1''$ ($s < 25$ km). Height differences observed under similar meteorological conditions may be highly correlated (up to r = $\pm$ 0.9). This correlation is strongly reduced if the measurements are divided into time periods of various meteorological conditions, then $-0.1 < r < 0.1$ (TEGELER 1971).

The *coefficient of refraction* can be determined from reciprocal zenith angle measurements assuming a symmetric line of sight. From (4.54), (4.56) and (4.35), we have

$$k = 1 - \frac{R}{s}(z_1' + z_2' - \pi). \qquad (4.58)$$

In this way, C. F. *Gauss* obtained an average value of $k = 0.13 \pm 0.04$ on the occasion of the arc measurement of 1823 in Hanover; this value was applied extensively. However, it is approximately valid only for lines of sight with a large ground clearance; close to the ground, k can assume values between -1.0 and $+1.0$. The variation in k is reduced to between -0.1 and $+0.4$ for a line of sight at a height of 25 m (first-order triangulation). In mountainous regions, the variation usually remains less than 0.01.

Trigonometric leveling has been introduced in order to increase the accuracy of trigonometric height determination (RUEGER and BRUNNER 1982). Station spacing is reduced to $200\ldots300$ m, and a combined precision theodolite/distance meter [4.3.3] is used for measuring zenith angles and distances. As lines of sight are short and run parallel to the surface, refraction errors reduce significantly. The effect of varying vertical deflections may be neglected. The method is particularly effective if separate vehicle transport with specially mounted instrument and targets is used: *motorized* trigonometric leveling (BECKER 1987), The accuracy of $\pm 1\ldots2$ mm $\sqrt{s_{km}}$ is comparable to geometric leveling [4.3.5].

For the *direct* determination of the *angle of refraction* the dispersion of the light [4.3.1] may be utilized; whereby, light having a short wave-length is more strongly curved than light of long wavelength. Employing *two different wavelengths* causes a dispersion angle (the difference between the two angles of refraction) at the target point. This angle depends on the individual effective coefficients of refraction along the light path. Considering the (small) influence of the water vapor pressure, the dispersion angle is proportional to the refraction angle which is about two orders of magnitude greater. Main error source is atmospheric turbulence. Up to now, experiments with distances not greater than 20 km have given uncertainties of $\pm 1''$ to $\pm 2''$ in the angle of refraction. Future application of dispersometers might be restricted to distances of a few km (WILLIAMS and KAHMEN 1984).

4.3.5 Leveling

In *geometric leveling*, the differences in height are determined using horizontal lines of sight between points in close proximity to each other (for precise leveling, the station spacing is $\leqslant 30 \ldots 40$ m). Due to the short spacing, the systematic influence of refraction is smaller than in the case of the trigonometric heights [4.3.4]. Hence, when a number of leveled height differences are summed, the accuracy of the leveling is about two orders of magnitude higher than for the trigonometrically determined heights, with zenith angles measured over long distances.

Leveling is conducted with a *leveling instrument* (a level) and with the aid of *leveling rods*. The instrument consists primarily of a measuring telescope capable of rotation about the vertical axis. The line of sight is brought into the horizontal using a bubble in conjunction with a tilting screw or automatically by a compensator (optical-mechanical part with a gravity pendulum as main component).

For leveling of highest accuracy, *precision levels* are used with a telescope objective aperture of 45 to 60 mm and a power of magnification of 35 to 50. Some instruments have a coincidence bubble — e.g. Nabon (Breithaupt, Kassel), Plani (Fennel, Kassel), N3 (Wild, Heerbrugg) — which has a sensitivity of $\sim 10''/2$ mm and a setting accuracy of $\pm 0''.2$. The setting accuracy of the compensators in the automatic levels, e.g. NiA3 (MOM, Budapest), Ni1 (Zeiss, Oberkochen, Fig. 4.38), Ni 002 (Jenoptik, Jena) amounts to $\pm 0''.1 \ldots \pm 0''.2$. In adjusting to the graduation mark of the measuring rod, the line of sight is raised or lowered in a parallel manner by a parallel plate which is mounted in front of the objective lens; the amount of displacement is measured by a micrometer. The measuring rods in use are 3 m invar rods with two opposing and staggered graduations.

The *leveled height difference* δn between the rod stations is given by the difference between the backsight R and the foresight V readings (Fig. 4.39):

Fig. 4.38. Precise level ZEISS Ni1, courtesy of Carl Zeiss, Oberkochen, Fed. Rep. Germany

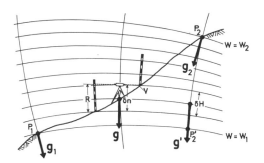

Fig. 4.39. Geometric leveling

$$\delta n = R - V. \tag{4.59}$$

Because of the quasi-differential distance between the rod stations, one may neglect the convergence of the equipotential surfaces [2.2.1], as well as the change in curvature of the level surface which passes through the telescope. Then, δn corresponds to the separation of the level surfaces that pass through the rod stations.

Summing the observed δn's between the control points P_1 and P_2 yields the leveled height difference

$$\Delta n_{12} = \sum_1^2 \delta n. \tag{4.60}$$

Δn depends on the path taken, since the level surfaces are not parallel; the result of leveling does not correspond to a difference in orthometric heights (3.10) $H_2 - H_1$. A definitive determination of height is possible only by considering the gravity g; that is, by turning to *potential differences* ΔW. Then, corresponding to (3.9), we have

$$\Delta W_{12} = W_2 - W_1 = -\int_1^2 g\, dn = -\int_{2'}^2 g'\, dH \approx -\sum_1^2 g\, \delta n, \tag{4.61}$$

where g' is gravity along the plumb line $P_2' P_2$. Therefore, ΔW can be determined *without further hypothesis* from leveled height differences δn and surface gravity values g. Reductions involving gravity must be applied in order to obtain differences from the δn's referring to a specific system of heights [5.1.5].

The sum of the leveled height differences of a closed circuit (error of closure), in addition to the measuring errors, consists of the path dependent *orthometric excess*

$$\varepsilon = \oint dn. \tag{4.62}$$

On the other hand, the line integral $\oint dW = 0$.

The *accuracy of precise leveling* depends on personal, instrumental, topographical, and atmospherical influences. Since the difference in height Δn between two control points is composed of numerous individual observations δn, particular attention must be afforded to the propagation of errors. The most important error sources are (e.g. KUKKAMÄKI 1980):

1. *Vertical refraction.* This depends mainly on the vertical gradient of temperature [4.3.1]. The irregular part (shimmer) has the effect of a random error (± 0.01 mm under cloudy skies). Systematically acting influences occur particularly for measurements in terrain with steep slopes, or close to the ground (0.01 to 0.1 mm per 1 m difference in height). As first shown by KUKKAMÄKI (1938), these can be represented in part by a *refraction correction.* More sophisticated refraction models are available, which include meteorological and hydrological data, terrain slope, and orientation with respect to the sun (ANGUS-LEPPAN 1984).

2. *Vertical movements* of the instrument and rods. These depend on the firmness of the ground and on the manner in which the instrument is set up; movements of 0.01 to 0.1 mm per station are possible. Movements proportional to the time during which the measurements are made at a station are cancelled by the succession of observations: $R_I V_I V_{II} R_{II}$ (I, II = scales of the rod). In addition, from the average of forward and backward leveling runs, those movements of the rods are eliminated which are proportional to time and which occur while the instrument is brought to the next station.

3. *Leveling-error of the instrument.* The random errors which depend on the instrument (uncertainty in setting the bubble or compensator) are less than 0.01 to 0.03 mm per station. Errors resulting from the centered bubble or freely swinging compensator being out of adjustment cause a departure of the line of sight from the horizontal; these errors are not realized when the instrument is set up half way between rods.

4. *Error in leveling the rod* (inclination of the rod). Random and systematic errors can be kept sufficiently small by centering the circular bubble and carefully holding the rod in the vertical position.

5. *Rod graduation error.* Errors in scale are determined by routine calibrations and are taken into account by subsequent corrections. The random part remains generally less than 0.01 mm.

6. *Variations in the direction of the plumb line due to the tides* [2.4.2]. These cause time dependent inclinations of the line of sight which are computed by reducing the tangential tidal component to the direction of the leveling line. The difference in height between two points which are separated by a distance s includes additively the displacements of the backsight and foresight. Using (2.66) and (2.73), the *tidal correction* is given for the moon (for the sun, the correction is 46% of this) by

$$v_M = 0.06 \sin 2\psi_M \cos(A_M - A) \times s \quad \text{(mm/km)}. \tag{4.63}$$

Here, A_M is the moon's azimuth and A is the azimuth of the leveling line. For longer runs, these influences are partly cancelled (KUKKAMÄKI 1949).

In order to eliminate or reduce the various systematic sources of error, precise leveling is always conducted twice in opposing directions and under different meteorological conditions. The lengths of the sights for the nearly equal back- and foresights ("leveling from the middle") should not be too large and should accommodate the atmospheric conditions, such that the lowest air layers that are close to the ground (less than 0.5 m above the ground) are avoided. For a 1 km double-run leveling, one can attain a standard deviation of ± 0.3 to 1.0 mm. The systematic effects of vertical movements and refraction which cannot be taken into account through modeling and through the measurement procedure cause correlations of $r = +0.1$ between the height differences of the forward and backward leveled runs (LUCHT 1972).

An acceleration of the rather time-consuming procedure of precise leveling with an accompanying comparable accuracy is particularly desirable for the detection of vertical crustal movements [5.5.5]. To this end, *a motorized precise leveling* was developed at the Technical University of Dresden, whereby the level (Ni 002, Jenoptik, Jena) and the rods are transported by specially equipped motor vehicles (PESCHEL 1974). Meanwhile, this method is used in several countries, with modified equipment (BECKER 1987). Due to the rapid progress of the survey, time dependent errors are reduced. Asymmetric refraction has less influence, as the line of sight is more remote from the earth's surface.

In leveling across *broad waterways* and *inlets of the sea*, several methods are suitable in addition to the one of trigonometric heights [4.3.4]; these include reciprocal leveling and hydrostatic, as well as hydrodynamic leveling.

In *reciprocal leveling*, approximately horizontal sights to specially marked targets are taken simultaneously with a precise level from both sides of the waterway. For longer series of observations including a change of instruments, the total difference in height over 1 to 2 km can be determined to a precision of ± 1 to ± 2 mm (JELSTRUP 1955, KAKKURI 1966).

Hydrostatic leveling is based on the principle of communicating tubes. A hose filled with water (free of air bubbles, uniform temperature) is laid between the shores of the watercourse to be bridged. The levels of water measured at the vertical ends of the hose are situated in the same level surface. This method may be applied for ranges up to 20 km. In the Netherlands, it is used in an operational mode (some km range, $\pm 0.5 \ldots 1$ mm), WAALEWIJN (1964). Large water crossings as over the Fehmarn-Belt (20 km) require remarkable efforts (ANDERSEN et al. 1991).

In *hydrodynamic leveling*, the height is transferred over the waterway utilizing the water level. As natural waters are under hydrodynamic equilibrium, tide gauge records have to be reduced for the effects of sea surface topography, cf. [3.3.3]. This implies the development of a hydrodynamic model, which takes water velocity, wind drag, water depth and bottom friction, atmospheric pressure, water density, gravity and Coriolis force into account. As yet, this method has been applied only seldom. A transfer of heights over the channel between Ramsgate and Dunkirk (70 km) has been achieved with a precision of ± 1.5 cm (CARTWRIGHT and CREASE 1963). An equivalent accuracy was achieved at the Fehmarn-Belt crossing (WÜBBELMANN 1991).

4.4 Satellite Observations

In this group of measurements, one utilizes targets and sensors which are not attached to the earth's body. Artificial earth satellites possess the greatest significance in this respect. Observations of distant cosmic objects (the earth's moon, extragalactic radio sources) are also included here (KAULA A1966, SCHNEIDER A1988, SEEBER A1989/1992).

4.4.1 The Unperturbed Motion of a Satellite

After the satellite has separated from the carrier rocket, it begins its unrestrained revolution about the earth. The satellite's orbit is determined by the initial conditions and the force fields which are in effect. Fundamental theory is provided by celestial mechanics (BROUWER and CLEMENCE A1961, SCHNEIDER A1984).

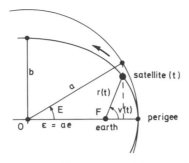

Fig. 4.40. Orbital system of the satellite

For the time being, we regard the motion in a gravitational field of an earth whose structure is spherically symmetric [2.1.2].

The mass of the satellite can be neglected in comparison to the earth's mass M. From the derivative of the gravitational potential V (2.11), we obtain the *equation of motion*

$$\ddot{r} = \text{grad } V = -\frac{GM}{r^2}\frac{r}{r}. \tag{4.64}$$

r is the geocentric position vector; the dots denote differentiation with respect to time.

According to Kepler's laws, the satellite moves in an *elliptical orbit*. One focal point of the ellipse (with semimajor axis a, and first eccentricity e) coincides with the center of gravitation (=center of mass of the earth). In the *orbital system* of Fig. 4.40, the position of the satellite is described by the *distance r from the center of mass* and the *true anomaly v* (=geocentric angle between the directions to the satellite and to perigee). Using the *eccentric anomaly E* as an auxiliary quantity, we obtain

$$r = a(1 - e \cos E), \qquad \tan v = \frac{\sqrt{1 - e^2}\sin E}{\cos E - e}. \tag{4.65}$$

We introduce Kepler's third law via the *mean (angular) velocity* (mean motion)

$$\bar{n} = \sqrt{\frac{GM}{a^3}} \tag{4.66}$$

and the *mean anomaly*

$$\overline{M} = \bar{n}(t - T) \tag{4.67}$$

which increases linearly with time t. T is the epoch of the passage through perigee, the closest approach to the earth. E can then be computed iteratively using *Kepler's equation*:

$$\overline{M} = E - e \sin E. \tag{4.68}$$

The orbital system is transformed into the space-fixed *equatorial system* [4.1.1] by the rotations of Ω (=right ascension of the ascending node), i (=inclination of the orbital plane with respect to the equatorial plane), and ω (=argument of perigee),

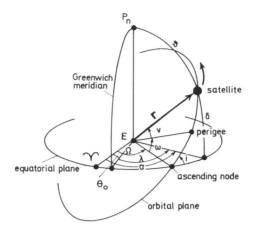

Fig. 4.41. Satellite orbit and equatorial system

Fig. 4.41. The *geocentric position vector* is found to be

$$\mathbf{r} = r\begin{pmatrix} \cos\delta\cos\alpha \\ \cos\delta\sin\alpha \\ \sin\delta \end{pmatrix} = r\begin{pmatrix} \cos(\omega + v)\cos\Omega - \sin(\omega + v)\sin\Omega\cos i \\ \cos(\omega + v)\sin\Omega + \sin(\omega + v)\cos\Omega\cos i \\ \sin(\omega + v)\sin i \end{pmatrix}, \quad (4.69a)$$

with

$$r = \frac{a(1 - e^2)}{1 + e\cos v}. \tag{4.69b}$$

With equations (4.66) through (4.69), the orbit of the satellite is given by the 6 *Keplerian elements* a, e, Ω, i, ω, T. a and e determine the size and shape of the ellipse. Ω and i establish the orbital plane in the equatorial system. ω orients the ellipse in the orbital plane, T (or equivalently $\overline{M}$ or v) furnishes the epochal orientation of the satellite in its orbit. The 6 orbital elements correspond to the constants of integration which result from the two integrations of (4.64).

4.4.2 The Perturbed Motion of the Satellite

The actual orbit of the satellite departs from the Keplerian orbit due to the effects of various "disturbing forces" of gravitational and nongravitational type. The disturbing forces cause variations with time in the orbital elements (*orbital perturbations*) of secular, long, and short periodic nature. The orbit can be viewed as the envelope of Keplerian ellipses (osculating ellipses) which are given at each instant by the actual orbital elements.

In order to account for the complete *gravitation of the earth*, the gravitational potential of a spherically symmetric earth must be amended by the "disturbing function" R':

$$V = \frac{GM}{r} + R'. \tag{4.70}$$

According to equations (2.51)–(2.53), R' contains the harmonic coefficients J_{lm}, K_{lm} ($l \geqslant 2$) of the spherical harmonic expansion of V. The spherical coordinates r, ϑ, λ are replaced by the orbital elements using (4.65) and the spherical relations between ϑ, λ and Ω, i, ω, v as inferred from Fig. 4.34; we thereby arrive at

$$R' = R'(a, e, \Omega, i, \omega, \overline{M}; J_{lm}, K_{lm}). \tag{4.71}$$

Next, we substitute (4.70), (4.71) into (4.64) and obtain the *equation of motion*

$$\ddot{r} = -\frac{GM}{r^2}\frac{r}{r} + \operatorname{grad} R'. \tag{4.72}$$

This vectorial differential equation or the corresponding system of scalar second-order differential equations can be converted to an equivalent system of first-order differential equations, cf. [5.3.3]. The differential equations can be solved numerically or analytically.

The *numerical integration* is based on a standard orbit computation method. A numerical mathematics procedure is applied to the equation of motion including all disturbing effects. *Analytical integration* uses the Lagrangian equations for the variation of the orbital elements in response to the disturbing function R'. With the spherical harmonic expansion (4.71), these variations become a function of the harmonic coefficients J_{lm}, K_{lm}. Analytical integration then gives the changes in the orbital elements between the initial epoch t_0 and the time t. In adding these orbital perturbations to the orbital elements a_0, e_0, Ω_0, i_0, ω_0, $\overline{M}_0$ of the initial epoch, the *geocentric position vector* (4.69) becomes a function of these elements, the time t, and the parameters of the gravitational field:

$$r = r(a_0, e_0, \Omega_0, i_0, \omega_0, \overline{M}_0; t; GM, J_{lm}, K_{lm}). \tag{4.73}$$

Hence, one can predict the position of the satellite at time t from the observed vector r_0 and an (approximate) knowledge of the gravitational field. Approximate orbital data for selected satellites are published by responsible agencies; navigation satellites transmit their own orbital data, cf. [4.4.6], [4.4.7]. This information serves in the determination of the orientation of the instruments which observe the satellite. Precise orbit determinations are necessary if the positions of terrestrial points are to be derived from satellite positions, cf. [5.3.4].

The orbit of the satellite experiences secular and periodic perturbations (amplitude of up to 100 m and more for a 3h-orbit) due to *lunisolar gravitation*, which affects the earth and the satellite unequally. These perturbations can be computed by extending the disturbing function (4.71) to include the tidal potential. *Earth and ocean tides* affect low-flying satellites.

Nongravitational orbital perturbations are caused primarily by atmospheric drag and solar radiation pressure. *Air drag* brakes the satellite, finally changing its orbit into a circular path and then into a spiralling motion, leading to its fall to the earth. The perturbations depend on the velocity of the satellite, on the atmospheric density, and on the effective cross-sectional area to mass ratio. For altitudes greater than 1000 km, the air drag on satellites may be neglected, with the exception of balloon satellites [4.4.3]. The influence of air drag is generally considered by applying corrections, although they are affected by errors in the atmospheric density model. The

CIRA (COSPAR International Reference Atmosphere) 1972 is an empirical, high-altitude atmospheric model, whereas the U.S. Standard Atmosphere 1962, with supplements 1966, gives more detail in the neighborhood of the earth's surface. In addition, *electromagnetic interactions* occur in the ionosphere, which lead to small perturbations that are difficult to ascertain. High-altitude satellites are accelerated by *radiation pressure* due to the incident photons. These perturbations depend on the attitude of the satellite with respect to the sun and on the area to mass ratio; they are taken into account through corrections. Particularly large perturbations arise in the case of balloon satellites.

With good satellite tracking, and with the present gravitational models of the earth [5.4.4], and also taking into account the nongravitational perturbations, the satellite's ephemeris can be determined with m-accuracy for short arcs (fractions of a day) and with approximately 10 m-accuracy for long arcs (few days). The orbits of laser-tracked satellites can be calculated with dm-accuracy.

4.4.3 Artificial Earth Satellites, Time Measuring Systems

Since the launch of Sputnik I (1957), artificial earth satellites have been available to geodesy as targets at high altitude. Because the irregularities of the terrestrial gravitational field affect the orbit of the satellite [4.4.2], this field, in turn, can be derived from satellite observations (satellites as sensors). While Sputnik delivered a remarkably improved value for the earth's flattening, the satellite Vanguard I (1958) furnished the earliest information about deviations from the ellipsoidal shape (different flattening at the poles).

The following aspects should be considered when *designing geodetic satellites and establishing* their *orbits*:
1. The nongravitational perturbing effects are minimized for small cross-sectional surface and large mass [4.4.2]. A rotationally symmetric shape reduces the influence of uneven air drag.
2. For precise positioning, the satellite should have a high altitude.
3. For gravitational field determination, satellites at low altitudes are required, the lower limit is governed by the perturbing air drag. Orbits with different inclinations must be available in order to separate the effects of the harmonic coefficients.

With respect to the *instrumentation*, we distinguish between active and passive satellites. *Active satellites* carry transmitters of various types; thus, there is also the problem of energy supply. *Passive satellites* reflect incident light. Geodetic satellites or satellites for partial geodetic use can be equipped with the following:

Flashing light devices to transmit short (1 ms) light flashes of high intensity; transponders to receive and transmit microwaves from ground stations or from other satellites for distance measurements; transmitters which continuously emit radiowaves with stable frequencies for measurements of Doppler shifts; transmitters for emitting radar carrier waves with signals and data information; quartz or rubidium resp. cesium clocks for timing resp. transmission of time signals; laser reflectors (retroreflector arrays of fused silica corner cubes) to reflect laser light pulses; a radar altimeter for

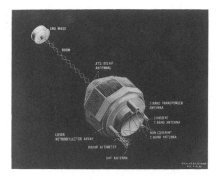

Fig. 4.42. Artifical earth satellite GEOS3 (National Aeronautics and Space Administration NASA)

distance measurements to the ocean surface; a gravity field related stabilization to maintain the satellite's orientation with respect to the earth's surface.

Satellites that are important in geodesy include the GEOS (Geodetic) satellites 1–3 (U.S.A. 1965, 1968, 1975). GEOS 3 (1975–1978, $h \approx 840$ km, $i = 115°$), Fig. 4.42, carried a radar altimeter (± 1 m) for height measurements over the oceans, laser reflectors, a Doppler transmitter, a C-Band transponder, as well as a satellite-to-satellite tracking system (S-Band) for measurements to the geostationary satellite ATS 6 ($h \approx 36{,}000$ km). The oceanographic satellites SEASAT 1 (1978) and GEOSAT (U.S. Navy, 1985–1989) carried improved altimeter systems ($h \approx 800$ km, $i = 108°$). Among the scheduled satellite missions which include a radar altimeter is the European Remote Sensing Satellite ERS-1 (1991) and the NASA/CNES TOPEX-POSEIDON project (1992), cf. [4.4.9]. A number of additional satellites equipped with reflectors ($h \approx 600$ to 5900 km, $i = 15°$ to 80°) are available. The satellites Starlette (France, 1975, $h \approx 800$ to 1100 km, $i = 50°$) and Lageos (U.S.A., 1976, $h \approx 5900$ km, $i = 110°$) are of particular importance. They are spherical in shape (diameter 0.2 and 0.6 m resp.) and possess a very favorable surface to mass ratio, Fig. 4.43.

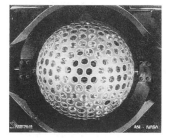

Fig. 4.43. Artifical earth satellite LAGEOS (National Aeronautics and Space Administration NASA)

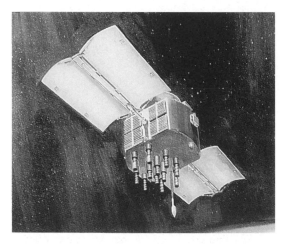

Fig. 4.44. GPS (Global Positioning System) satellite view

The Transit system satellites (since 1964, $h \approx 1000$ km, $i \approx 90°$) transmit frequencies which are suitable for Doppler measurements [4.4.6]; the Secor satellites carried Secor transponders [4.4.4]. The NAVSTAR Global Positioning System (since 1978, $h \approx 20\,000$ km, $i \approx 55°$) will finally (1992) consist of 24 satellites, Fig. 4.44, cf. [4.4.7]. A DISCOS (Displacement Compensation System) has been implemented into the latest NNSS-satellites [4.4.6], and will be of value for future low-flying satellites. A massive test mass floats freely within a surrounding shell, and is thus shielded against external surface forces. By measuring the variable distances between mass and shell, gravitation can be separated from surface forces.

Until about 1970, direction measurements were made to satellites (e.g. GEOS1, 2) emitting light flashes, and to spherically shaped *balloon satellites*, with a coated external skin reflecting incident sunlight. If the observer is located in the earth's shadow, then the satellite forms an illuminated target which is suitable for optical observations. Intensities of 0^m to 5^m have been achieved (m = a unit on the astronomic scale of light intensity). These passive satellites are strongly perturbed by nongravitational forces. Their lifetime is also relatively short. Among these satellites were Echo 1 and Echo 2 (1960–1968 and 1964–1969, respectively, $h \approx 1600$ km and 1100 km, $i = 47°$ and $81°$, balloon diameter of 30 m and 41 m). The satellite Pageos was of considerable importance (1966–1972, $h \approx 2800$–5600 km, $i = 87°$, diameter of 30 m) [5.3.2]. The polyhedral Japanese satellite EGS (also *Ajisai*, 1986, $h \approx 1500$ km, $i = 50°$) is covered by mirror elements and a set of laser reflectors. Incident sunlight is reflected periodically (two flashes per second) by rotation of the satellite around its axis.

Due to the large velocity of an artificial earth satellite, great demands are placed on the *measurement of time for orbit determination*. The *mean orbital velocity* $\bar{v}$ of a satellite that is moving in a circular ($r = a$) orbit is given from (4.66) by $\bar{v} = a\bar{n} = (GM/a)^{1/2}$. For a satellite close to the earth ($h = 1000$ km), we obtain with $a = R + h = 7370$ km a value of $\bar{v} = 7.4$ km s^{-1}. Kepler's third law yields the period of revolution $U = 104$ min. In order to keep orbital errors less than 1 cm, time (epoch) must be determined to ± 1 μs. If distances to satellites are determined from signal travel time (laser light pulses), cm-accuracy requires time measurements (time interval) to ± 1 ns. Rubidium or cesium frequency standards which are tied to UTC

[4.1.3] with the aid of time signals are capable of this type of accuracy. Precise quartz oscillators can be used in satellite receivers, if an external time control is provided, e.g. through the satellite system, cf. [4.4.7].

4.4.4 Direction Measurements, Early Distance Measurements

Until about 1970, *optical-photographical* measurements of direction prevailed. The satellite is depicted, as a result of a photographic exposure, with the fixed stars in the plane of a film or plate. Observations included those of light flashes from active satellites, reflected laser light, and reflected sunlight [4.4.3].

The *cameras* with which the photographs are taken should have a large *focal length*, since for a given positional uncertainty of the satellite's images, the directional accuracy depends on this focal length. A large *relative aperture* is also required so that even faint satellites and stars are discernible. Further, a *field of view* having reasonable size ensures that a sufficiently long section of the satellite's track and a large number of stars are represented. Cameras which do not follow the satellite come equipped with a *special shutter* that chops the light trail of the satellite into dots or short segments.

The distinction between ballistic, astronomic, and orbital cameras is made according to the mount. *Ballistic cameras* are mounted azimuthally, thereby allowing for rotation in the horizon system [4.1.1.]. They have shorter focal lengths (300 to 1000 mm) and larger fields of view (30° to 10°). These instruments are easy to use and portable, so that they are well suited for mobile stations. *Astronomic cameras* are mounted equatorially, and thus are able to rotate in the equatorial system [4.1.1]. They possess large focal lengths ($\geqslant 1000$ mm) and small fields of view ($<10°$ to 5°). Since the camera is able to follow the motion of the stars, even faint stars (up to 13^m) can be detected. It is possible for *orbital cameras* to follow also the motion of a satellite. In this case, the satellite's orbit is computed from the orbital elements, and the camera follows along in the orbital plane (triaxial camera). Motions deviating from the orbital plane can also be pursued if a fourth axis is available. Faint satellites (up to 12^m) are discernible when followed in this way. These heavy cameras are only used in the stationary mode.

Included among the ballistic cameras is the Wild BC4 camera, which consists of the Wild RC5 aerial camera mounted on the base of a Wild T4 Universal Theodolite. Especially developed for satellite observations are the equatorially mounted Zeiss BMK 46 and BMK 75 cameras with $f = 460(750)$ mm and a relative aperture of 1 : 2 (1 : 2.5), Fig. 4.45. Exposures with these cameras are made on glass plates, 18×18 cm in dimension. The Baker-Nunn cameras employed by the SAO (triaxial Schmidt reflector, $f = 500$ mm, 1 : 1) used 56 mm film. The SBG 760 camera (Schmidt reflector, $f = 760$ mm, 1 : 1.8, 9×12 cm, glass plates) of Jenoptik. Jena has a mount with four axes.

An *illuminating laser* is required when conducting direction measurements with *laser light* to correspondingly equipped satellites [4.4.3]. The laser system may be provided by a corresponding distance measurement instrument [4.4.5].

Upon developing the photographs and identifying the stars, the satellite and stellar image points are measured on a precise comparator (uncertainty of ± 1 to ± 2 μm).

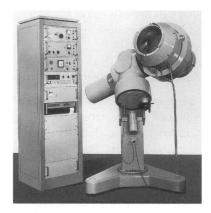

Fig. 4.45. Ballistic camera measuring system BMK 46/18/1:2 with time measuring station ZMS, courtesy of Carl Zeiss, Oberkochen, Fed. Rep. Germany

The measured x, y *photocoordinates* of the satellite are subsequently transformed to the *spatial directions*, right ascension α and declination δ. The transformation parameters are determined by the photocoordinates of the stars. The results of the transformation are the *topocentric directions* α^*, δ^* to the satellite.

Known *systematic effects* (distortion, comparator errors, astronomic refraction) are considered prior to the transformations. Since the satellite is not situated at infinity, the angle of astronomic refraction is diminished by the *parallactic refraction* σ (Fig. 4.2). The direction to the satellite is corrected accordingly. For $z < 45°$ and $h > 1000$ km, we have approximately

$$\sigma = \frac{2.3}{h_{(m)}} \tan z = 0''\!\!.48 \frac{\tan z}{h_{(1000\,km)}}. \tag{4.74}$$

The *accuracy* of the satellite's direction is determined by the uncertainty of the stellar positions [4.1.2] and the coordination of time, as well as by comparator measuring errors, by scintillations due to atmospheric turbulences ($1''$ to $5''$, period <1 s), and by distortions of the photographic emulsion (± 1 μm). The accuracy amounts to $\pm 0''\!\!.2 \ldots \pm 2''$, an increase of which does not seem to be possible.

An accuracy of $\pm 0''\!\!.2$ corresponds to an along-track orbital error of ± 1.5 m, for a satellite of 1500 km altitude. This is far behind the accuracy of laser distance measurements [4.4.5]. Nevertheless as satellite directions refer to the conventional inertial system, cf. [3.1], they have contributed to stabilize satellite orbits at earth model computations, cf. [5.4.4].

The *Secor* (Sequential Collation of Range) *system*, developed in the U.S.A. worked on the principle of phase measurements with *microwaves* [4.3.3] (CULLEY 1965). Between 1964 and 1970, several satellites have been equipped with SECOR transponders. Two-way distance measurements have been performed following a standard scheme of spatial trilateration, cf. [5.3.2]. In the case of the fully automated measuring process, several thousand measured values were obtained during one pass of the satellite. *Reductions* were required mainly because of the refraction in the troposphere ($h < 30$ km, $n > 1$) and the ionosphere ($h > 60$ km, $n < 1$). The *accuracy* of a single measured distance depends essentially on the knowledge of the refraction; the average distance could be obtained to ± 3 m. This laborious method, for which an increase in accuracy does not seem possible, has been superseded by laser distance measurements, cf. [4.4.5].

The determination of the orbit of an artificial earth satellite requires a sequence of observations in rapid succession which do not depend on the time of day or on the weather conditons. In this respect, *radar measurements* in the S-Band (2 to 4 GHz) and C-Band (4 to 6 GHz) range are suitable. They were made using either a stationary or a mobile apparatus and provided distances with an uncertainty of ± 2 to ± 5 m, in addition to (less accurate) directions and range rates.

4.4.5 Laser Distance Measurements

Laser distance measurements to satellites (Satellite Laser Ranging SLR) are feasible when the satellite is equipped with laser reflectors [4.4.3]. After measuring the time of propagation of the laser pulse as it travels from the emitter to the reflector, and back, the distance is computed according to (4.44). A *laser distance measuring system* (third generation) consists of a Nd:YAG laser (yttrium-aluminium-garnet crystal doped with neodymium ions), the transmitting and receiving optics (optical telescopes), the mechanical mounting, optical-electronic system for detecting the laser pulses, an electronic time counter, and an electronic control system with process computer. The laser pulse is emitted through the transmitting optics; at the same instant, the time counter begins to record the time. The reflected pulse collected by the receiving telescope is channeled, upon amplification in a secondary-electron multiplier, to the time counter. The laser and receiving telescope are mounted such that they can automatically follow the satellite, according to the precalculated orbit, e.g. WILSON (1982).

Fig. 4.46. Neodymium-YAG laser distance measuring system with Contraves-Goerz mounting, Fundamentalstation Wettzell, Fed. Rep. Germany, courtesy of Forschungsgruppe Satellitengeodäsie, München

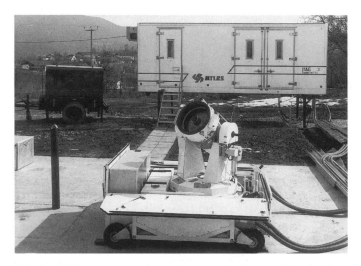

Fig. 4.47. Mobile laser distance measuring system MTLRS-1, Institut für Angewandte Geo-däsie, Frankfurt a.M., Fed. Rep. Germany, courtesy of Forschungsgruppe Satellitengeodäsie, München

First-generation laser instruments (since 1965) operated with pulse lengths of 10 to 40 ns, and used ruby lasers. A special pulse analysis allowed to reduce the pulse length to 2...5 ns, for second-generation lasers. The Nd:YAG laser (since 1977) can generate giant pulses with steep edges and a high repetition rate, with a pulse length of 200 ps (laser wavelength 532 nm, pulse repetition rate 1 to 4 Hz, pulse energy 150 mJ, pulse power 1 GW, beam divergence 10^{-3} to 10^{-4} rad). The pulse travel time is measured by an electronic counter (resolution 10 ps), which is controlled by rubidium and cesium clocks, or hydrogen masers (connection to UTC with ± 1 μs).

The *accuracy* of laser distance measurements depends primarily on the pulse width, the stability of the photomultiplier, and the time resolution. The effects of refraction [4.3.1] are taken into account by corrections. Depending on the satellite's altitude, some 100 to some 1000 distances are measured during one passage, with an accuracy of $\pm$ a few m (first generation) to ± 5 cm (third generation). By compressing the data to "normal points" (average over 0.5 to 2 min), an accuracy of ± 1 cm is achieved.

Third generation laser systems are being operated, among others, by the Goddard Space Flight Center of NASA, and by the "Forschungsgruppe Satellitengeodäsie", München/Frankfurt a.M./Bonn (Fundamental Station Wettzell), Fig. 4.46. *Mobile systems* have been developed in the U.S.A. (NASA, Silverberg 1978), in the U.S.S.R., and in F.R.G./Netherlands (Wilson and Conrad 1982), Fig. 4.47. These systems operate with low energy (4 to 10 mJ) and single photon detection (1 to 3 pulses per second).

The laser reflectors deposited on the *moon* (first by the Apollo 11 mission in 1969, and later by Apollo 14, 15 and Luna 21/Lunokhod 2) provide accurately defined targets for *laser distance measurements*, Bender et al. (1973). *Lunar Laser Ranging* (LLR) contributes to the investigation of the dynamics of the earth-moon-system, and of geodynamic processes. The observations are made with pulsed lasers having a tightly bundled beam and a powerful telescope to recapture the weak returning signal (single photon technique).

Observations have been carried out regularly since 1969 by the McDonald Observatory, Univ. of Texas (2.7 m telescope, second generation pulsed ruby laser, one pulse every 3 s). Lunar laser ranging systems further operate in Australia, in France, and in Hawaii; additional systems are under construction.

An accuracy of 0.15 m has been achieved for a single distance. By changing to shorter pulse lengths, one anticipates $\pm 1 \ldots 3$ cm normal point accuracies (DICKEY et al. 1984).

The advantages of laser measurements reside in the high accuracy, and in not having to rely on satellite-borne sources of energy. As in any method which utilizes light, it is necessary that the target can be optically seen.

4.4.6 Doppler Frequency Shift Measurements

For Doppler measurements (ANDERLE 1973), a transmitter aboard a satellite S emits, at time t, a signal in the ultrashort-wavelength range and with a constant frequency f_s (Fig. 4.48). The observer receives the frequency f_E at time $t + \Delta t$. Due to the relative velocity $\dot{s}$ of the satellite, f_E is displaced with respect to f_S (Doppler frequency shift). We have

$$f_E = f_S - \frac{f_S}{\bar{c}} \dot{s}, \tag{4.75}$$

where $\bar{c}$ is the mean velocity of electromagnetic waves (4.31). The frequency shift

$$\Delta f = f_E - f_S = -\frac{f_S}{\bar{c}} \dot{s} \tag{4.76}$$

is proportional to $\dot{s}$; a reversal in the sign of Δf occurs at the time of closest approach of the satellite to the observing station ($\dot{s} = \Delta f = 0$).

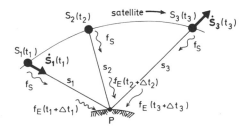

Fig. 4.48. Doppler measurements

The continuously transmitted frequency f_s is amplified by the receiving equipment and compared to a constant reference frequency f_0 which is generated by the receiver and is in the neighborhood of f_s. The difference $f_0 - f_E$ (beat frequency) is integrated by an electronic counter over the time intervals $(t_2 + \Delta t_2) - (t_1 + \Delta t_1)$, etc. This yields

$$s_2 - s_1 = \frac{\overline{c}}{f_0} N_{12} - \overline{c} \frac{f_0 - f_s}{f_0}(t_2 - t_1). \tag{4.77}$$

The *range difference* can then be computed from the output of the counter (Doppler count) N_{12} and the difference in time $t_2 - t_1$.

Doppler observations have been used for orbit determinations of the GEOS satellites (GEOS3: 162 and 324 MHz). The most important application has been made with the *Navy Navigation Satellite System* (*NNSS*) or *TRANSIT System* (KOUBA 1983a). It operates since 1964 generally on a basis of 4 to 6 Transit satellites. Primarily established for U.S. Navy navigation, it became available for the public in 1967. The system will be maintained until 1995 when the GPS system will be fully operational, cf. [4.4.7]. The orbit planes of the *TRANSIT* satellites are evenly distributed in longitude. Because of the earth's rotation, a satellite will be visible at least every two hours (equatorial region). Two carrier waves are continuously transmitted, with 150 and 400 MHz frequency. Since 1981 three NOVA satellites equipped with the DISCOS system [4.4.3], have replaced some of the older OSCAR satellites.

In order to determine the satellites' orbit, Doppler measurements are made to the satellite at four ground stations in the U.S.A., thereby providing the data to compute the orbital elements [4.4.1]. These satellite-ephemerides refer to the geodetic datum [5.1.2] of the tracking stations [5.3.4]. The orbital data, computed for 12 hours in advance, are transferred to the satellite and stored there. The satellite, in turn, transmits a time signal and this *"broadcast ephemeris"* (± 10 to ± 30 m) at two-minute intervals. Upon receiving this information, the position of the observer can be determined [5.3.4] with the help of the measured Doppler count. 1 to 2 Transit satellites are continually tracked by 20 stations which constitute the global *Transit Network* (TRANET) of the U.S. Defense Mapping Agency. The resulting *"precise ephemeris"* (± 1 to ± 2 m) obtained by interpolation are later made available to a limited group of users.

A number of *Doppler receivers* for geodetic purposes are available as mobile units (BROWN 1976a, STANSELL 1979). The portable systems (weight: 10 to 20 kg) consist of a receiver with reference oscillator, microprocessor and data recording unit (usually a magnetic tape cassette), an antenna and an energy supply (batteries).

Doppler counts are formed over 4.6 s, 30 s, or 2 min. with the aid of the internal oscillator. After eliminating nearly horizontal observations (because of uncertainties in refraction for zenith angles $> 70°$ to $80°$) and disturbed signals, a single pass of the satellite provides some 10 to 15 usable Doppler counts (integration interval: 30 s). In the middle latitudes, one can observe on the average as many as 15 suitable passes per day.

Included among the *portable* instruments are the Geoceiver (Magnavox, Torrance, U.S.A.), Fig. 4.49, the CMA (Canadian Marconi Co., Montreal) and the JMR (JMR Instr. Inc., Chatsworth, Cal.) devices.

The *error budget* for the Transit system contains the ephemeris errors (gravitational model and surface forces, the latter effect is strongly reduced at the NOVA satellites),

Fig. 4.49. Doppler satellite receiver system Magnavox MX1502, courtesy of Magnavox Co., Torrance, California

refraction errors and errors in the receiver, including variation of the antenna phase center (calibration). The tropospheric refraction is computed using an atmospheric model and, if possible, also observed meteorological data. The influence of iono-spheric refraction is, to a first approximation, inversely proportional to the frequency of the carrier wave. Therefore, it can be determined by using the two transmitted frequencies. A frequency drift is taken into account in the ensuing adjustment by introducing a frequency offset for each pass.

The *accuracy* of the station coordinates obtained at a single satellite pass, is $\pm 10 \dots$ 30 m. The accuracy is significantly improved by observing a multitude of passes (absolute positioning), or by simultaneous observation of two stations (relative positioning), cf. [5.3.4].

Doppler measurements, as any technique which operates with radio waves, are independent of the weather and the time of day, so that an abundance of data is accumulated within a short interval of time. The digital recording of data simplifies their automatic processing.

Doppler measurements may also be used to determine distance variations between two satellites (*satellite to satellite tracking* SST). Monitoring low-altitude (few 100 km) satellites particularly permits to derive the earth's gravitational field to a high resolution and accuracy (RUMMEL et al. 1978). High-low (one high- and one low- flying satellite) and low-low (two low-flying satellites) configurations have been designed and tested.

After successful experiments (e.g. at the GEOS-3 mission, cf. [4.4.9]) several SST missions have been proposed for the 1990's. One of them is the NASA Geopotential Research Mission GRM. With two DISCOS [4.4.3] equipped satellites (160 km height, 150 to 550 km mutual distance, resolution 1 μm/s), the gravitational field should be determined in a 6 months mission with 100 km spatial resolution, and $\pm 10 \dots 30 \, \mu\mathrm{ms}^{-2}$ and ± 0.1 m (geoid), resp. (SCHUTZ et al. 1987).

4.4.7 Global Positioning System GPS

The *NAVSTAR/GPS* (Navigation System with Time and Ranging/Global Positioning System) is a radionavigation system based on satellites. Is has been under development by the U.S. Department of Defense since 1973, and will be fully operational after 1992. The system provides real time navigation and positioning by one-way microwave distance measurements between the GPS satellites and the receiver. Early on, its use for geodetic applications was investigated, and today it is already extensively employed in geodesy (BOSSLER et al. 1980).

In 1992, the system's space segment will consist of 21 *GPS satellites* (1991: 6 experimental and 10 operational satellites), and later be extended to 24 satellites, cf. [4.4.3]. They are arranged in six nearly circular orbits ($i = 55°$, 12h period of revolution), with an altitude of approx. 20000 km, Fig. 4.50. The final constellation will have at least 4 satellites above the horizon during 24 hours, at every location of the earth.

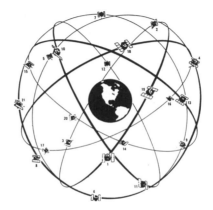

Fig. 4.50. Global Positioning System (GPS) constellation for 21 satellites

The GPS satellites carry an *atomic clock* (rubidium, cesium) as high-precision oscillator (10.23 MHZ, $\pm 10^{-12} \ldots 10^{-13}$). By multiplication, the $L1$ (1575.42 MHz $\triangleq$ 19.05 cm) and the $L2$ (1227.60 MHz $\triangleq$ 24.45 cm) microwaves carrier waves are derived from the fundamental frequency, and continuously emitted. They serve as carrier waves for two code modulations and for a data signal (navigation message). The *codes* are given as binary signals ($+1$/or -1 sequence) in a pseudo-random noise form. The *P*-code (precise) is modulated on $L1$ and $L2$ (length 267 days, frequency 10.23 MHz $\triangleq$ 29.31 m), and serves for accurate navigation. It is made available only to a limited group of users. The C/A-code (coarse acquisition) is on the $L1$ wave only (length 1 ms, 1.023 MHz $\triangleq$ 293.1 m). The codes serve to measure a signal's propagation time from the satellite to the receiver, and for the identification of the satellite. The *navigation message* is transmitted on $L1$ and $L2$, and contains the data needed for navigation. It includes the satellite's ephemeris, a clock correction with respect to GPS-time (see below), corrections for atmospheric refraction, and information about the status of the satellite.

The operation of the GPS-satellites is maintained by the *control segment*. It consists of the master control station (Colorado Springs, U.S.A.) and five monitoring stations with global distribution. These stations receive the signal of the satellites and transfer them to the master station. After computation of the satellite orbits and clock corrections, these data (extrapolated broadcast ephemeris with ± 20 m accuracy, GPS-time with ± 1 ms) are transmitted to the satellites for storage and retransmission to the users.

The *GPS-time* is defined by the cesium clocks of the control segment stations. It agreed with UTC [4.1.3] in January 1980, the actual difference is part of the navigation message. The GPS ephemeris refers to an earth-fixed geocentric system, cf. [3.1.]. This *World Geodetic System 1984 WGS84* (DMA 1987) is defined by the coordinates of the monitoring stations (± 1 m). It includes a gravity field model (complete through degree and order 180, published through 12, 12), and the parameters of a level ellipsoid, which are identical with the Geodetic Reference System 1980, cf. [3.5.5], KUMAR (1988).

The *GPS receiver* carries a quartz clock, which is approximately synchronized with GPS-time. The signals transmitted from the satellite are received through an antenna. Using time measurement and the satellite message (see below) the observations are transformed into the three-dimensional position of the antenna, by means of the software implemented in the receiver's micro-processor.

We distinguish between *code* and *carrier phase measurements*.

The *code measurement* employs the travel time Δt of a signal, between the satellite and the receiver. Correlation techniques applied to a code copy generated in the receiver, serve for the determination of Δt. Multiplication of Δt with the propagation velocity $\bar{c}$, cf. [4.3.3], gives only pseudoranges, as the clocks of the satellite and of the receiver are not perfectly synchronized:

$$\bar{c} \cdot \Delta t = s + \bar{c} \cdot \delta t_r, \tag{4.78a}$$

with δt_r = receiver clock correction, and the distance

$$s = ((X_s - X_p)^2 + (Y_s - Y_p)^2 + (Z_s - Z_p))^{1/2}. \tag{4.78b}$$

X_s, Y_s, Z_s and X_p, Y_p, Z_p are the geocentric coordinates of the satellite and the ground station (antenna), respectively. With the broadcast ephemeris transmitted from the satellite, simultaneous measurements of signal travel times to four satellites deliver the coordinates X_p, Y_p, Z_p and the clock correction δt_r, by spatial resection. This method is applied mainly for navigation. It gives a real-time position accuracy of ± 10 m (*P*-code with noise $\pm 0.6 \dots 1$ m), resp. ± 20 m (C/A -Code with noise ± 10 m). Starting in March 1990, the U.S.DoD degraded the GPS orbital data and the satellite clock ("selective availability"). GPS positioning accuracy was thus reduced for civil users to ± 100 m.

A corresponding navigation system *GLONASS* is under development in the USSR, and will be fully operational until 1995 (MOSKVIN and SOROCHINSKY 1990). Its space segment will comprise 21 (+ 3)satellites ($h = 19100$ km), arranged in three circular orbits ($i = 64.°8$) which are spaced 120° apart from each other. The emitted carrier waves (1602.5625 and 1615.5 MHz) serve for time and Doppler shift measurements. A common use of GPS/GLONASS and the development of integrated receivers is under discussion, mainly for international civil aviation.

Geodesy and surveying require accuracies which should be at least two orders of magnitude better than in navigation. This can be achieved by *phase measurements* of the *carrier waves* (shorter wavelength, noise only $\pm 2 \ldots 3$ mm). The method has found wide application and should be even more important when the system becomes fully operational (KING et al. A1987, WELLS et al. A1987), see also SEEBER (1984) and BEUTLER et al. (1988). The phase is detected by comparing the carrier wave with the reference signal in the receiver. In most receivers, the codes are used for reconstruction of the carrier wave. Following (4.45) and (4.46), we have

$$\Delta \varphi = \frac{2\pi}{\lambda}(s - r\lambda + \bar{c}\delta t_r),\tag{4.79}$$

with r = integer number of waves within the range s. Through the unknown number r, an ambiguity problem enters into (4.79), which poses problems. Since the change of r with time is counted in the receiver, the ambiguity may be expressed by a constant bias parameter for each observation epoch. Difficulties arise when the phase lock is lost due to signal obstruction (cycle slips).

The *error budget* of GPS is composed of errors from the satellite's position (orbital errors and clock errors), errors entering during the signal's travel through the atmosphere (ionospheric and tropospheric refraction, multipath propagation in the antenna's vicinity), and errors originating from the receiver (phase center variations, phase delays, cycle slips, receiver noise), SEEBER A1989/1992. The influence of these error sources is partly reduced by modelling and estimating the model parameters together with the antenna coordinates. This strategy may firstly be applied to orbit corrections. Orbital errors enter into terrestrial baselines with the proportion baseline-length/ satellite altitude. Consequently, a ± 20 m error gives a 10 cm effect, in a 100 km baseline. By orbital parameter corrections for short arcs, or by an orbit post-processing (precise ephemeris), the orbit errors can be reduced to ± 2 m. This procedure is recommended particularly if actual tracking data are made available by simultaneous observations at "fiducial points" established in and around the survey area, possibly even occupied by SLR [4.4.5] or VLBI [4.4.8] equipment. Ionospheric refraction is derived from the different results of the L1 and the $L2$ wave, using the frequency dependence of the refractive index at phase propagation, cf. [4.4.6]. Tropospheric refraction is taken into account by a troposphere model, often with the inclusion of observed meteorological data.

Geodetic *GPS receivers* must permit to measure the phase difference, and they should have access to both frequencies $L1$ and $L2$ (BOUCHER 1987). If only station distances < 10 km have to be measured, a single frequency receiver can also provide "cm"-accuracy. Code reading is necessary for real time navigation purposes (*code dependent receivers*). One channel receivers have to employ sequential or other techniques in order to switch from one satellite to the next. Multi-channel receivers allow the simultaneous observation of several satellites. *Code-free receivers* use the signals of the satellites without the codes. Consequently they are independent from possible code changes or restrictions. Since orbital data and time are not supplied from the satellites, the satellites' ephemeris must be taken from other sources, and time synchronization has to be performed by comparison of the receivers.

Fig. 4.51. GPS satellite receiver system Wild Magnavox WM102, courtesy of WM Satellite Survey Company, Heerbrugg, Switzerland

Among the *code-dependent* (*L*1 and *L*2, P and C/A-code) receivers we have the TI4100 GPS Navigator (Texas Instruments; receiver 24 kg, 37 × 44 × 21 cm; recorder: 7 kg, 36 × 21 × 20 cm, Seeber et al. 1985), and the Wild Magnavox WM102 (Wild/Heerbrugg and Magnavox/Torrance, Cal.; receiver + battery 17 kg, 51 × 39 × 17 cm, up to 6 satellites can be tracked simultaneously on 7 *L*1 and 1 *L*2 channels), standard deviation of differential positioning is $\pm(5\text{mm} + 10^{-6}\,s)$, Fig. 4.51. The Trimble 4000SL GPS Surveyor (Trimble/Sunnyvale, Cal.) can be upgraded to the *L*2 frequency (simultaneous tracking of 5 satellites), Fig. 4.52.

Fig. 4.52. GPS satellite receiver system Trimble 4000 SST, courtesy of Trimble Navigation Europe Ltd., Tonbridge, Kent, U.K.

The Trimble 4000 ST Field Surveyor includes 8 channels of $L1$ with options of 12 channels of $L1$, and 8 or 12 channels of $L1$ and $L2$. The 12-channel Ashtech XII dual frequency receivers (Ashtech Inc., Sunnyvale, Cal.) are provided with an optional P-code tracking module. The 3 DF Direction Finding System Receiver (24 channels in four 6-channels groups with separate antennas) allows to determine also attitude angles as azimuth. The Macrometer II (Litton Aero Service, two frequencies) is a code-free receiver.

Although the final stage of the NAVSTAR/GPS system has not yet been reached, *GPS-positioning* already has remarkably *influenced* and changed geodetic and survey-ing methods (TORGE 1988). On one hand, this is due to the high relative accuracy, which is comparable to terrestrial techniques already at station distances of a few km. As no direct visibility between the stations is needed, and as the method is weather independent and applicable day and night, GPS positioning offers significant eco-nomic advantages. Among the draw-backs are the problems which occur in urban areas, forests, and mountains (lacking visibility to the satellites). In addition, it has to be recognized that GPS after corresponding transformation provides ellipsoidal heights (height differences), cf. [3.4.3]. In order to transform them into gravity field related heights [3.3.2] which are needed in practice, geoid or quasigeoid heights have to be subtracted, cf. [5.1.5].

4.4.8 Very Long Baseline Interferometry

Extragalactic radio sources (*quasars* = quasi-stellar radio sources, radio galaxies) emit waves in the cm-to dm-range which are detected by large antennas (radio telescopes) that are used in radio astronomy. A receiving system (Fig. 4.53) consists of two widely separated (a few 1000 to 10000 km) radio telescopes P_1 and P_2, and thus has a high resolution ($\approx 0.''001$) due to the long baseline b (resolution $\approx$ wave-length/telescope diameter).

The radio wave arrives at P_2 with a phase difference $\Delta\varphi(t)$ with respect to P_1:

$$\Delta\varphi = 2\pi \frac{\bar{c}}{\lambda}\tau = 2\pi v\tau. \tag{4.80a}$$

Here, $\bar{c}$ is the mean wave velocity, $\lambda(v)$ is the wavelength (frequency) of the received signal, and τ is the time delay which the wave requires to travel the distance:

$$\Delta s = -\mathbf{b}\cdot\mathbf{s} = -(\mathbf{r}_2 - \mathbf{r}_1)\cdot\mathbf{s}, \tag{4.80b}$$

with $\mathbf{b}$ = baseline vector between the radiotelescopes, and $\mathbf{s}$ = unit vector in the direction to the radio source. With

$$\Delta s = \tau\bar{c} \tag{4.80c}$$

we obtain the observation equation

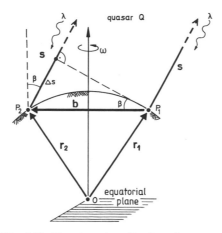

Fig. 4.53. Very long baseline interferometry

$$\tau(t) = -\frac{1}{c}\mathbf{b}\cdot\mathbf{s}(t), \tag{4.80d}$$

for deriving the baseline **b** from τ.

Interferences are obtained by comparing the two wave trains. Since $\Delta\varphi$ changes in time t as a result of the earth's rotation, the interferences are recorded as having the fringe frequency

$$F(t) = \frac{1}{2\pi}\frac{d(\Delta\varphi)}{dt} = \frac{1}{\lambda}\frac{d(\Delta s)}{dt} = v\frac{d\tau(t)}{dt}, \tag{4.81}$$

or, with (4.80)

$$F(t) = -\frac{v}{c}\mathbf{b}\cdot\mathbf{\mathring{s}}(t). \tag{4.82}$$

From the measured delay time τ and the delay rate $d\tau/dt$, the components of the baseline vector (earth-fixed equatorial system) can be derived according to (4.79)–(4.81). The direction **s** is given through the coordinates α, δ of the radio source.

This method is known as *Very Long Baseline Interferometry* (*VLBI*), CAMPBELL and WITTE (1978), CARTER et al. (1985).

Due to the large distance between antennas, a direct comparison of the wave trains arriving at P_1 and P_2 is not possible. Therefore, the signals are recorded on magnetic tape, along with a time signal which is generated by the frequency standards at the respective stations. The interferences are later recovered by a digital correlator; a correlation analysis furnishes the delay time τ and its variation in time $d\tau/dt$, as well as the fringe frequency F from equations (4.80), (4.81). Corrections must be applied due to the systematic differences in the frequency standards, and because of the

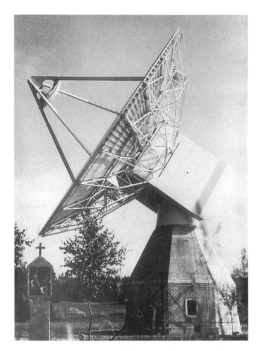

Fig. 4.54. 20m-radio telescope, Fundamentalstation Wettzell, Fed. Rep. Germany, courtesy of Forschungsgruppe Satellitengeodäsie, München

influences of tropospheric refraction and diurnal aberration [4.1.2]. The accuracy of this method depends on the time measurement ($\pm 0.01 \ldots 0.001$ ns), the stability of the frequency standard ($\pm 10^{-14}$ with the hydrogen maser), the ability to account for the effects of refraction, and the quality of the correlation.

The data of about 10 radio telescopes are evaluated for the determination of earth rotation parameters and baseline vectors, with stations in U.S.A., Western Europe, (including Wettzell, F. R. G., see Fig. 4.54), and Japan (CAMPBELL 1990). In connection with the NASA Crustal Dynamics Program, some mobile radiotelescopes have been developed. They are particularly employed in regions of recent geodynamics, such as California and the Eastern Mediterranean.

The *accuracy* of the baseline component determinations (24 h observations, 10 quasars) is a few cm. The mean values of baselines, computed over few years, have standard deviations of $\pm$ few mm, cf. [5.5.5].

4.4.9 Satellite Altimetry

The method of satellite altimetry is based on a *satellite-borne altimeter* which transmits radar pulses in the vertical direction to the earth's surface. These are reflected perpendicularly by the surface of the ocean (Fig. 4.55). Then according to (4.44), a measurement of the propagation time furnishes the height h_a of the satellite above the instantaneous sea surface. The radar altimeters operate in the 14 GHz frequency

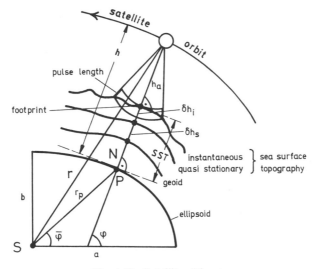

Fig. 4.55. Satellite altimetry

range (2 cm-wave-length) with pulse lengths of about 10 ns to few ns, and a resolution of 1 m to a few cm.

The effects of beam divergence and a finite pulse length result in measurements that refer to a mean surface within a circular "footprint" (few km diameter); short-wavelength features of the ocean (i.e., waves) are thereby smoothed out. The observations must be corrected for instrumental effects (through calibration in the laboratory and in test areas), for the influence of the atmosphere, and for the oceanic tides (tide model). The "quasi-stationary" sea surface topography [3.3.3] is obtained when considering the temporal variations of oceanographic and meteorological type, and in the water budget. With an accurate determination of the orbit, the position of this surface can be established in the geocentric coordinate system [5.3.5]. On longer satellite missions, the sea surface can be covered several times with approximately uniform profiles.

If the satellite's ellipsoidal height h is calculated from its ephemeris, we have (Fig. 4.55)

$$h_a = h - (N + SST), \quad \text{with} \quad SST = \delta h_i + \delta h_s. \tag{4.83}$$

The radar altimeter observation thus carries information about the geoid (geoid height N) and the sea surface topography (SST), $\delta h_i =$ instantaneous SST, $\delta h_s =$ quasi-stationary SST.

After the successful experiments on the Skylab mission (1973), the first global survey with a radar altimeter was accomplished by the GEOS 3 satellite (STANLEY 1979). The average over 2 seconds of measurements (footprint spacing of ~ 15 km) is accompanied by an accuracy of ± 0.5 m. This measuring accuracy has been increased in the SEASAT 1 mission (1978) to ± 0.1 m by changing to a shorter pulse length (TAPLEY et al. 1982).

The results of the first 18 months of the US Navy GEOSAT mission (± 3 cm precision, 7 km ground track interval) remained classified. The subsequent Exact Repeat Mission (ERM) delivered repeated ground tracks every 17 days which retrace the SEASAT tracks (McADoo and SANDWELL 1988), cf. [4.4.3].

The Radar altimeters of the ERS-1 (1991, $h = 700$ km, $i = 98.°5$, sun synchronized orbit) and the TOPEX-POSEIDON (1992, $h = 1330$ km, $i = 63°$) satellites should deliver accuracies better than 10 cm.

5 Methods of Evaluation, Global Geodesy

The problem in global geodesy is to determine the figure of the earth and the dominant features of the external gravity field, as well as to derive the mean earth ellipsoid (BOMFORD A1980, HEISKANEN and MORITZ A1967, GROTEN A1979, MORITZ A1980, VANÍČEK and KRAKIWSKY A1986).

In this section, we treat, in the first place, the *methods of evaluation* which have been developed for the various groups of measurement: the *astrogeodetic methods* [5.1] use astronomic [4.1] and the *gravimetric methods* [5.2] employ gravity measurements [4.2], both of them in connection with terrestrial geodetic measurements [4.3]. The *methods of satellite geodesy* [5.3] are based on satellite observations [4.4]. These methods have different advantages and disadvantages; *combining* them is an important problem of geodetic theory [5.4]. Evaluation methods developed for global geodesy are also employed for solving regional geodetic problems, sometimes with admissible simplifications, cf. [6].

The figure of the earth and the external gravity field contain information regarding the interior of the earth; but also, the ideas developed in the geosciences in turn affect the formulation of the problem of geodesy. Hence, in [5.5] the *structure and dynamics of the earth's body* are treated. Contributions of geodesy to geodynamics research are also discussed here. Finally, section [5.6] briefly reviews the methods and results of *lunar geodesy* (selenodesy) and *planetary geodesy*.

5.1 Astrogeodetic Methods

Observations for the astrogeodetic computations include astronomic latitudes and longitudes, astronomic azimuths [4.1], as well as horizontal angles, distances, zenith angles, and leveled height differences [4.3]. The gravity intensity [4.2] is required for reduction purposes in the determination of the geoid and the quasigeoid, and also the orthometric and normal heights.

The x,y,z-system or, upon introducing a reference ellipsoid, the φ,λ,h-system [3.4.3] serves as a reference system for spatial computations.

5.1.1 Deflection of the Vertical, Geoid Undulation, Height Anomaly

With the exception of distances, the observed quantities refer to the earth's gravity field [3.2]. The geodetic computations are simplified with the introduction of the normal gravity field [3.5] and the ellipsoidal reference system [3.4]. By forming the (small) differences between actual and normal gravity field quantities (disturbing quantities) we obtain linear relations between observations and unknown parameters (e.g. TORGE 1985).

To the point P in the actual gravity field (on a level surface $W =$ const.) we assign a point Q in the normal gravity field (on a level surface $U =$ const.) [3.5]. The angle between the surface normals at P (direction of the actual plumb line) and at Q (direction of the normal plumb line) is designated the (total) *deflection of the vertical* Θ, which is a vector quantity.

We make the following distinctions:

1. The deflection of the vertical Θ, defined by *Helmert* as the angle at the *surface of the earth* between the directions of the plumb line and the ellipsoidal normal through P (Fig. 5.1). The point Q_0 on the ellipsoid is assigned to the point P as defined by the ellipsoidal normal. The actual or normal gravity fields between Q_0 and P are not required.

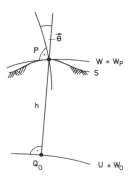

Fig. 5.1. Surface deflection of the vertical

2. The deflection of the vertical Θ_0, defined by *Pizzetti* as the angle at the *geoid* between the directions of the plumb line and the ellipsoidal normal through the point P_0 on the geoid (Fig. 5.2). P_0 is assigned to the surface point P by the curved plumb line. The ellipsoid should possess the same potential W_0 as the geoid. The height difference between the ellipsoid and the geoid is designated the *geoid undulation N* (geoid height).

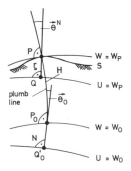

Fig. 5.2. Deflection of the vertical θ^N, after Molodenski, deflection of the vertical θ_0, after Pizetti, height anomaly ζ, geoid undulation (geoid height) N

3. The deflection of the vertical Θ^N, defined by *Molodenski* as the angle at the *surface of the earth* between the directions of the plumb line at P and the surface normal of that spheropotential surface which has the same potential W_P as the geopotential surface through P. According to [3.5.6], the points Q, thus determined, establish the telluroid. The height difference between the telluroid and the physical surface of the earth is known as the *height anomaly* ζ.

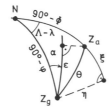

Fig. 5.3. Components ξ, η of the deflection of the vertical

In the following elaborations, the deflection of the vertical Θ, being a vector, is decomposed into two mutually perpendicular components. We assume that the minor axis of the reference ellipsoid is *parallel* to the mean rotational axis of the earth, and that the zero meridian of the ellipsoidal system is *parallel* to the mean meridian plane of Greenwich, see [5.1.2]. If the axes are then brought into coincidence by parallel displacements and if a unit sphere is centered at point P ($N =$ point of intersection of the coinciding rotational axes with the unit sphere), then Θ enters as the spherical distance between the points on this sphere which correspond to the astronomic zenith Z_a and the geodetic zenith Z_g (Fig. 5.3). The *north-south component* along the astronomic meridian is denoted by ξ (positive when Z_a is north of Z_g), and the *east-west component* in the prime vertical is denoted by η (positive when Z_a is east of Z_g). From the spherical relations

$$\sin\varphi = \cos\eta \sin(\Phi - \xi), \qquad \sin\eta = \cos\varphi \sin(\Lambda - \lambda)$$

and using

$$\cos\eta \approx 1, \quad \sin\eta \approx \eta, \quad \sin(\Lambda - \lambda) \approx \Lambda - \lambda,$$

the components of the deflection of the vertical are given by

$$\xi = \Phi - \varphi, \quad \eta = (\Lambda - \lambda)\cos\varphi. \tag{5.1}$$

The element

$$\varepsilon = \xi\cos\alpha + \eta\sin\alpha \tag{5.2}$$

is the component in azimuth α.

The derivation above is valid for Helmert's deflection of the vertical Θ. For the deflection Θ_0, we must introduce, in place of Φ and Λ, the astronomic coordinates as they are defined on the geoid; they differ from the surface quantities by the *curvature of the plumb line* [5.1.6]. For the surface deflection Θ^N, the direction of reference is given by the normal geodetic coordinates φ^N, λ^N [3.5.6]. They differ from φ, λ by the *normal curvature of the plumb line* (Fig. 3.12),

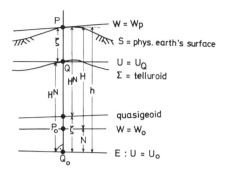

Fig. 5.4. Physical earth's surface, telluroid, quasigeoid, geoid, ellipsoid

producing the angles

$$\delta\varphi^N = \varphi - \varphi^N, \quad \delta\lambda^N = \lambda - \lambda^N = 0. \tag{5.3}$$

If we integrate over this normal curvature (3.70), then for the Geodetic Reference System 1980, we have

$$\delta\varphi^N = -\int_0^{H^N} \kappa_x^N \, dH^N = -\frac{\beta}{M} \sin 2\varphi \, H^N = -0.''00017 \sin 2\varphi \, H^N_{(m)}. \tag{5.4}$$

Therefore, when computing the deflection of the vertical in (5.1), the difference between φ and φ^N generally remains below the accuracy of the determination of astronomic latitude [4.1.5].

The geodetic coordinates φ, λ, required in (5.1) and (5.3), may be derived through threedimensional or ellipsoidal computations [5.1.2], [5.1.4].

If the deflection of the vertical and the curvature of the plumb line are neglected, then the *geoid undulation N* can be computed from the ellipsoidal height h and the orthometric height H (Fig. 5.4):

$$N = h - H. \tag{5.5}$$

The *height anomaly ζ* is obtained as the corresponding difference between h and the normal height H^N (3.71):

$$\zeta = h - H^N. \tag{5.6}$$

The deflections of the vertical and the height anomalies (geoid undulations), according to (5.1) through (5.6), depend on the ellipsoidal coordinates, and hence, on the parameters of the reference ellipsoid and on its position with respect to the earth (geodetic datum [5.1.2]). If they refer to the geocentrically situated mean earth ellipsoid [5.4.6], then they are referred to as *absolute* quantities; otherwise, they are *relative* quantities. The absolute deflections of the vertical assume values of 1″ to 10″ in flat terrain and in the highlands; in mountainous areas, they remain under 30″ to 1′. The absolute geoid undulations rarely exceed 100 m.

5.1.2 Three-Dimensional Computations, Geodetic Datum

The astronomic azimuth A and zenith angle z are measured in the local astronomic system [3.2.2]; through a rotation, horizontal angles are transformed into azimuths.

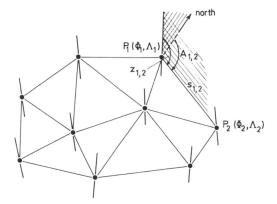

Fig. 5.5. Spatial terrestrial network

With the observed spatial distances (chord s), these quantities establish the shape and scale of a spatial network. The orientation with respect to the earth's gravity field is given at every point by the astronomic latitude Φ and the astronomic longitude Λ (Fig. 5.5).

The *observation equations*

$$
\left.
\begin{aligned}
A &= \text{arc tan } \frac{-\sin \Lambda\, \Delta X + \cos \Lambda\, \Delta Y}{-\sin \Phi \cos \Lambda\, \Delta X - \sin \Phi \sin \Lambda\, \Delta Y + \cos \Phi\, \Delta Z} \\
z &= \text{arc cos } \frac{\cos \Phi \cos \Lambda\, \Delta X + \cos \Phi \sin \Lambda\, \Delta Y + \sin \Phi\, \Delta Z}{(\Delta X^2 + \Delta Y^2 + \Delta Z^2)^{\frac{1}{2}}} \\
s &= (\Delta X^2 + \Delta Y^2 + \Delta Z^2)^{\frac{1}{2}},
\end{aligned}
\right\}
\tag{5.7}
$$

follow from (3.6) and (3.7). At every point of measurement, Φ and Λ enter as orientation parameters which refer to the axes of the global X,Y,Z-system, cf. [3.2.1]. Consequently, the observations A, z, s are related to the coordinate differences ΔX, ΔY, ΔZ in this system. Corresponding, but quite unwieldly, equations may be constructed as well for the φ, λ, h-system by taking (3.34) into account. The differential relationships between A, z, s and X, Y, Z or φ, λ, h that are required for an adjustment can be derived by differentiating (5.7) and (3.34) (WOLF 1963b).

The dependence of A and z on the plumb line direction, given by Φ, Λ, is of particular interest. It reads

$$dA_{12} = \sin A_{12} \cot z_{12} d\Phi_1 + (\sin \Phi_1 - \cos \Phi_1 \cos A_{12} \cot z_{12})\, d\Lambda_1,$$

$$dz_{12} = -\cos A_{12} d\Phi_1 - \cos \Phi_1 \sin A_{12} d\Lambda_1.$$

Changing from differentials to (small) differences δ, we interpret the $\delta\Phi$, $\delta\Lambda$, δA, and δz at a point P as discrepancies between the quantities Φ, Λ, A, and z in the astronomic system and φ, λ, α, and ζ (ζ = zenith angle) in the ellipsoidal system. Then we obtain

$$A - \alpha = \sin \Phi \, (\Lambda - \lambda)$$

$$+ (\sin A \, (\Phi - \varphi) - \cos A \cos \Phi \, (\Lambda - \lambda)) \cot z$$

$$z - \zeta = -\cos A \, (\Phi - \varphi) - \sin A \cos \Phi \, (\Lambda - \lambda).$$

By introducing the deflections of the vertical using (5.1) and replacing the astronomic quantities by ellipsoidal ones in the coefficients, we get

$$A - \alpha = \eta \tan \varphi + (\xi \sin \alpha - \eta \cos \alpha) \cot \zeta \qquad (5.8a)$$

$$z - \zeta = -(\xi \cos \alpha + \eta \sin \alpha). \qquad (5.8b)$$

Equ. (5.8a) is employed for *reducing* observed azimuths and horizontal angles or directions to the corresponding ellipsoidal quantities [5.1.4]. Equ. (5.8b) reduces zenith angles to be used in trigonometric heighting [4.3.4]. In addition, equ. (5.8) serve as *orientation equations*. As the definition of ξ, η implies the parallelism of the axes in the geocentric and the ellipsoidal system, they orientate a side of the geometric network in space. (5.8a) is known as *Laplace's equation*; (5.8b) furnishes the component ε of the deflection of the vertical in azimuth α (5.2), VANÍČEK and WELLS (1974), TORGE (1985).

A geometrical interpretation reveals that (5.8) prevents rotations about the vertical and horizontal axes of a theodolite. In addition, a rotation about the line joining P_1 and P_2 must finally be forestalled to guarantee the parallelism of the axes of the global astronomic and ellipsoidal systems. This is accomplished if one of the conditions above is enforced at another (preferably distant) side of the network. Using at least three independent condition equations (5.8) — generally of types (5.8a) — it is thus achieved that the spatial computations take place in a φ,λ,h-system whose axes are parallel to the global X,Y,Z-system.

The *geodetic datum* defines the orientation of a conventional φ,λ,h- or x,y,z-system with respect to the global X,Y,Z-system, and hence, with respect to the body of the earth, cf. [5.4.5]. The parallelism of the axes of the system is already secured by the

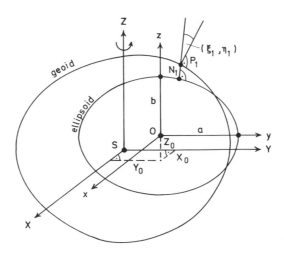

Fig. 5.6. Geodetic datum, with parallelism of axes

type of equations of (5.8); therefore, rotations are excluded. The three translational parameters are determined (in classical terrestrial networks) by the deflections of the vertical ξ_1, η_1 and the geoid undulation N_1 at an initial (origin) point P_1 (Fig. 5.6).

Finally, the ellipsoidal parameters a, f, denoting the semimajor axis and flattening, are included in the definition of the geodetic datum. Relations for the definition of a geodetic datum through terrestrial data are given in [5.1.7]. Instead of ξ_1, η_1, N_1, the ellipsoidal system can also be established by the coordinates of its origin X_0, Y_0, Z_0 with respect to the earth's center of mass. This formulation is adequate for the results of satellite geodesy, cf. [5.4.5].

The point wise determination of the surface of the earth using a spatial polyhedron was suggested by BRUNS (1878); however, three-dimensional computations were rarely carried out due to the uncertainty of trigonometric height transfer over large distances, cf. [4.3.4]. The concept of "three-dimensional geodesy" was revived by MARUSSI (1949) and HOTINE (A1969). Detailed derivations are given by WOLF (1963a, b), CHOVITZ (1974), TORGE (1980a), among others. The application of terrestrial spatial networks or traverses has been restricted to special test areas and points less than 20 km apart (RAMSAYER 1971, TORGE and WENZEL 1978, HRADILEK A1984).

5.1.3 Geometric-astronomic Leveling

Geometric leveling [4.3.5] may be incorporated into three-dimensional computations [5.1.2], if the observed height difference $\delta n \approx dn$ can be transformed correspondingly. From (5.5) follows

$$dh = dH + dN, \qquad (5.9)$$

being the differential relationship between the ellipsoidal height h, the orthometric height H, and the geoid undulation N. According to Fig. 5.7, dH consists of dn and the "orthometric correction" dE [5.1.5]:

$$dH = dn + dE. \qquad (5.10)$$

From Fig. 5.7, we obtain for dN:

$$dN = -\varepsilon \, ds - dE. \qquad (5.11)$$

Here, ε is the component of Helmert's surface deflection of the vertical [5.1.1] in azimuth α. The negative sign prefixing ε is based on the sign definition inherent in (5.1), and on the following convention: We obtain a positive dN if the level surface $W = $ const. rises above the level surface $U = $ const.

Substituting (5.10) and (5.11) into (5.9) and subsequently integrating yields the ellipsoidal height difference

$$\Delta h_{12} = h_2 - h_1 = \int_1^2 dn - \int_1^2 \varepsilon \, ds. \qquad (5.12a)$$

Thus, Δh may be determined without further hypothesis from leveling and surface deflections of the vertical; and therefore, it can be included as an "observation" in spatial computations (HEITZ 1973). This method is referred to as *geometric-astronomic leveling*.

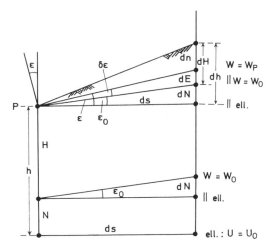

Fig. 5.7. Geometric-astronomic leveling

(5.12a) represents an "observed" difference in unknown heights in the φ,λ,h-system. In the x,y,z-system, the relation (not representable in closed form) between Δh and the unknowns is obtained from (3.35); differentiation of (3.34) provides a suitable differential relationship. With parallelism of axes in the x,y,z- and the X,Y,Z-system we have

$$d(\Delta h_{12}) = dh_2 - dh_1 = \cos \varphi_2 \cos \lambda_2 \, dX_2 - \cos \varphi_1 \cos \lambda_1 \, dX_1$$
$$+ \cos \varphi_2 \sin \lambda_2 \, dY_2 - \cos \varphi_1 \sin \lambda_1 \, dY_1$$
$$+ \sin \varphi_2 \, dZ_2 - \sin \varphi_1 \, dZ_1. \tag{5.12b}$$

(5.12b) allows ellipsoidal height differences as derived from (5.12a), to be included into an adjustment, with global geocentric coordinates as unknowns.

Whereas, the first integral in (5.12a) can be computed by summing the δn's, the evaluation of the second integral presents some difficulties. The question of interpolating the deflection of the vertical is connected to these problems and is treated in [5.1.6]. It is noted that both integrals in (5.12a) are formed over the *same path*.

5.1.4 Positional Systems

In three-dimensional computations, the zenith angles and the ellipsoidal height differences, introduced in [5.1.3], are afflicted by greater uncertainties (refraction and errors in interpolating the deflection of the vertical, respectively), which affect *all* coordinates in the global x,y,z-system. If ellipsoidal coordinates are used, the positional coordinates φ, λ are obtained more accurately than the height h by one order of magnitude On the other hand, users require heights which are defined in the gravity field, such as orthometric or normal heights. They may be determined with geometric leveling to the same accuracy as φ and λ. Therefore, the determinations in position and height have been generally separated.

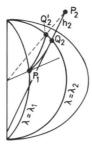

Fig. 5.8. Reduction of the normal section due to the height of the target point (skew normal reduction)

The reference surface for *positional determinations* is the *rotational ellipsoid* [3.4]. The observations, which are made on the earth's surface, are projected onto the ellipsoid with the aid of ellipsoidal normals.

The *astronomical azimuth A* is reduced to the ellipsoidal quantity α using the deflections of the vertical (5.8a). If the target point is not situated on the ellipsoid, but at a height h_2, then a further geometric reduction must be applied to A. Namely, the vertical plane through the ellipsoidal normal at the observation point P_1 and through the target point P_2, in general, does not contain the ellipsoidal normal through P_2 (Fig. 5.8). Therefore, the ensuing ellipsoidal normal section does not pass through the footpoint Q_2, instead it passes through Q'_2. A is reduced by the angle $Q'_2 P_1 Q_2$ which can be determined from the equations of the two vertical planes. We obtain (quantities with no index refer to P_1)

$$\alpha = A - \eta \tan \varphi - (\xi \sin \alpha - \eta \cos \alpha) \cot \zeta + \frac{e^2}{2b} h_2 \cos^2 \varphi \sin 2\alpha. \qquad (5.13)$$

The first term in the reduction is independent of direction. It corresponds to a twist in the observed set of directions: it has no effect on the horizontal *angles*. The second term can be viewed as an error in setting up the theodolite and depends on the deflection of the vertical; for $\xi = 5''$, $\alpha = 90°$, and $\zeta = 88°$, it has a value of $-0''.17$. The third term (skew normal reduction) must be considered only for high elevations of the target point; for $\varphi = 50°$, $\alpha = 45°$, $h_2 = 1000$ m, it attains a value of just $+0''.04$.

The measured *spatial distance s* is independent of the direction of the plumb line; it is converted to the length S of the ellipsoidal normal section using ellipsoidal heights (4.51).

According to [5.1.2], the geodetic datum can be defined by a, f, ξ_1, η_1, N_1. Considering (5.1), *Laplace's equation* (5.8a) for $\zeta = 90°$ (which is fulfilled to a good approximation in 1. order control networks) simplifies to

$$A - \alpha = (\Lambda - \lambda) \sin \varphi. \qquad (5.14)$$

As the zenith angle equation (5.8b) should be automatically fulfilled by the reduction to the ellipsoid, the parallelism of the axes of the ellipsoidal and global systems is in principle ensured if (5.14) is satisfied at least in the initial point, thus preventing an azimuthal rotation. Hence, at these *Laplace stations*, it is ncessary to measure the astronomic azimuth (Laplace azimuth) and astronomic longitude.

Using (5.14), the orientation of the geodetic network can be controlled and improved; thereby in particular, counteracting the systematic effects of horizontal refraction [4.3.1]. *Laplace stations* have been distributed with separations of at least 200 km in some terrestrial networks.

The *horizontal control networks of geodetic surveys* are coordinated according to two-dimensional ellipsoidal computations. Continental control systems were developed from the more recent arc measurements [1.3.3] and the unification of national geodetic networks [6.1.7].

Of the more recent *long arc measurements*, the following are mentioned: the American meridian arc (Alaska-Tierra del Fuego), the West European–African meridian arc along the meridian of Paris (Shetland-Algeria), the Arctic Ocean–Mediterranean Sea meridian arc (Hammerfest–Crete) and the African meridian arc tied to it at 30° east longitude (Cairo–Cape Town), the European–Asiatic longitude arc measurements at 48° latitude (Brest–Astrakhan) and at 52° latitude (Ireland–Ural Mountains), as well as the latitude and longitude arc measurements in India.

Table 5.1 lists the ellipsoidal parameters and origin points of several of the approximately 50 more significant astrogeodetic systems (MUELLER 1974, DMA 1987):

Tab. 5.1. Reference Ellipsoids and Origin Points of Several Astrogeodetic Systems

Geod. Datum	Ellipsoid Name	semimajor axis a (m) flattening f	Origin Point Name	latit. φ	longit. λ
Australian Geodetic 1966	Australian National = GRS 67	6 378 160 1/298.25	Johnston	$-25°57'$	$133°13'$
European 1950 (ED 50)	Internat. 1924	6 378 388 1/297.0	Potsdam Helmertturm	$52°23'$	$13°04'$
North American 1927 (NAD 27)	Clarke 1866	6 378 206 1/294.98	Meades Ranch	$39°13'$	$261°27'$
Pulkovo 1942	Krassovski 1942	6 378 245 1/298.3	Pulkovo Observatory	$59°46'$	$30°20'$
South American 1969 (SAD 69)	South Amer. 1969 = GRS 67	6 378 160 1/298.25	Chua	$-19°46'$	$311°54'$

GRS 67 = Geodetic Reference system 1967 [3.5.5]

5.1.5 Height Systems

The *geoid* and the *quasigeoid* serve as reference surfaces for the determination of heights on a continental basis. The geopotential numbers and orthometric heights [3.3.2] refer to the geoid; whereas, the normal heights [3.5.6] refer to the quasigeoid. The leveled height differences $\delta n \approx dn$ [4.3.5] must be converted into these systems.

According to (3.9), the *geopotential number* is given by

$$C = \int_{P_0}^{P} g \, dn. \tag{5.15}$$

Should the error resulting from the uncertainty in the gravity g remain less than 10^{-3} m^2 s^{-2} (≈ 0.1 mm), then only for height differences greater than 100 m must g be known with at most a 10 μms^{-2} uncertainty. Hence, the leveled differences δn for larger sections may be combined and multiplied by an average value of gravity. The desired accuracy is attained if the gravity measurements are made 15 to 25 km apart in flat terrain and 5 to 10 km apart in the highlands. In particular, those points should be included for which the variation in gravity departs from linearity (variations in slope, changes in the direction of the leveling line, gravity anomalies), RAMSAYER (1959).

Orthometric heights and normal heights can be computed from the geopotential numbers using equations (3.10) and (3.71), respectively. However, in geodetic surveys, the leveled *height differences* are generally converted into the respective height systems and then adjusted. From (3.9) and (3.10), which are expanded using (3.11), the *orthometric height difference* is given by

$$\Delta H_{12} = H_2 - H_1 = \int_{1}^{2} dn + E_{12}, \tag{5.16}$$

where the *orthometric correction* is

$$E_{12} = \int_{1}^{2} \frac{g - \gamma_0^{45}}{\gamma_0^{45}} \, dn + \frac{\bar{g}_1 - \gamma_0^{45}}{\gamma_0^{45}} H_1 - \frac{\bar{g}_2 - \gamma_0^{45}}{\gamma_0^{45}} H_2. \tag{5.17}$$

E consists of a path dependent, rigorously obtainable part and two terms depending on position which are subject to an hypothesis due to the appearance of the mean gravity $\bar{g}$ (3.10). The first term transforms the leveled height difference into a dynamic height difference (3.11); it can have cm to dm values. On the other hand, the total orthometric correction attains only mm to cm values.

To compute the *average gravity* $\bar{g}$ between the geoid and the point P (height H), we introduce the gravity g' at a point P' (height H') varying along the plumb line:

$$g' = g - \int_{H'}^{H} \frac{\partial g}{\partial H} \, dH. \tag{5.18}$$

Into (5.18) we substitute *Bruns'* formula (2.43) for the vertical component of the gravity gradient $\partial g / \partial H$ with the mean curvature of the ellipsoid and the average crustal density of 2.67 g cm^{-3}; integration yields

$$g' = g + 0.848 \times 10^{-6}(H - H')(\text{ms}^{-2}). \tag{5.19}$$

Substituting g' into (3.10) and integrating gives

$$\bar{g} = g + 0.424 \times 10^{-6} H \text{ (ms}^{-2}). \tag{5.20}$$

The second term on the righthand side corresponds to a reduction of g to the height $H/2$, with the topography modeled by a Bouguer plate, cf. [5.2.4].

If a relative accuracy of $\pm 10^{-5}$ (corresponding to ± 1 mm/100 m) in height is desired, then $\bar{g}$ must be determined with an accuracy of ± 100 μms^{-2}. Using (5.20), this is attainable in flat terrain and in the highlands; here, the errors in the density hypothesis remain small, cf. [6.2.2].

In analogy to (5.16) and (5.17), we obtain from (3.71) the *normal height difference*

$$\Delta H_{12}^N = H_2^N - H_1^N = \int_1^2 dn + E_{12}^N, \tag{5.21}$$

with the *normal correction*

$$E_{12}^N = \int_1^2 \frac{g - \gamma_0^{45}}{\gamma_0^{45}} \, dn + \frac{\bar{\gamma}_1 - \gamma_0^{45}}{\gamma_0^{45}} H_1^N - \frac{\bar{\gamma}_2 - \gamma_0^{45}}{\gamma_0^{45}} H_2^N. \tag{5.22}$$

E^N has the same order of magnitude as the orthometric correction E, but the former can be computed without an hypothesis [3.5.6]. The normal heights are used in the unified height system of eastern Europe (U.S.S.R., Poland, former GDR, etc.); the reference surface is determined by the tide gauge at Kronstadt.

According to (5.17) and (5.22), the difference between the orthometric and normal heights, and thus also between the geoid and the quasigeoid is due to the deviation of the actual average gravity $\bar{g}$ from the normal gravity $\bar{\gamma}$:

$$H^N - H = N - \zeta = \frac{\bar{g} - \bar{\gamma}}{\bar{\gamma}} H, \tag{5.22a}$$

where $\bar{g} - \bar{\gamma}$ corresponds to a gravity anomaly defined as mean value along the plumb line, from the surface to the geoid. The differences are usually on the order of a few cm to dm in magnitude; the geoid and quasigeoid coincide on the oceans.

5.1.6 Astrogeodetic Determination of the Geoid and Quasigeoid

Differences in the geoid undulations or height anomalies can be determined by combining trigonometric height measurements and geometric leveling, or by integrating the deflections of the vertical along the path (astronomic leveling).

By comparing the ellipsoidal height difference Δh (4.55), computed from *zenith angles* with the orthometric height difference ΔH (5.16) or the normal height difference ΔH^N (5.21), and using (5.5) and (5.6), respectively, one obtains the differences in the geoid undulation and in the height anomaly:

$$\Delta N = \Delta h - \Delta H, \quad \Delta \zeta = \Delta h - \Delta H^N. \tag{5.23}$$

These relations, also known as the *theorem of Villarceau* (1875), furnish sufficient accuracy only in mountainous areas because of the refraction-dependent uncertainty of the zenith angles. *GPS-heighting* also delivers ellipsoidal height differences, thus providing another strategy to derive geoid height differences, cf. [5.3.4].

In *astronomic leveling*, which was developed by *Helmert*, the deflection of the vertical is integrated along the path P_1 to P_2. If Helmert's *surface deflections of the vertical* ε [5.1.1] are used, then we have (Fig. 5.7)

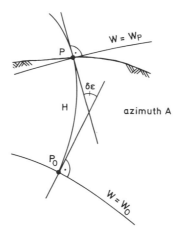

Fig. 5.9. Curvature of the plumb line

$$\Delta N_{12} = N_2 - N_1 = -\int_{1}^{2} \varepsilon \, ds - E_{12}, \qquad (5.24a)$$

where E_{12} is the orthometric correction (5.17); for the sign of ε, cf. [5.1.3]. Integration of the deflections of the vertical ε_0 defined on the *geoid* yields (Fig. 5.7)

$$\Delta N_{12} = -\int_{1}^{2} \varepsilon_0 \, ds. \qquad (5.24b)$$

Here, the "observed" ε should be reduced to the geoid because of the *angle of curvature of the plumb line* $\delta\varepsilon$ (Fig. 5.9):

$$\varepsilon_0 = \varepsilon + \delta\varepsilon. \qquad (5.25)$$

$\delta\varepsilon$ is given by integrating the curvature of the plumb line (2.38). At the azimuth of the chord s, we obtain

$$\delta\varepsilon = -\int_{0}^{H} \kappa_s \, dH = -\int_{0}^{H} \frac{1}{g} \frac{\partial g}{\partial s} \, dH. \qquad (5.26a)$$

Hence, according to (3.31), the *components of the angle of curvature of the plumb line* in the directions of the meridian and prime vertical are given to a spherical approximation (earth radius R) by

$$\delta\Phi = -\frac{1}{R} \int_{0}^{H} \frac{1}{g} \frac{\partial g}{\partial \Phi} \, dH, \quad \cos\Phi \, \delta\Lambda = -\frac{1}{R \cos\Phi} \int_{0}^{H} \frac{1}{g} \frac{\partial g}{\partial \Lambda} \, dH, \qquad (5.26b)$$

with

$$d\Phi = \Phi_0 - \Phi, \quad \delta\Lambda = \Lambda_0 - \Lambda, \qquad (5.26c)$$

Φ_0, Λ_0 = astronomic latitude and longitude, resp., defined on the geoid, cf. [5.1.1].

The gravity g and the horizontal gravity gradient $\partial g/\partial s$ along the plumb line are computed by postulating hypotheses on the values of gravity between the surface and the geoid, cf. [5.1.5]. The curvature of the plumb line can attain values from a few $0\rlap{.}''1$ (flat terrain) to $10''$ (mountainous areas); the uncertainty in its determination amounts to $\pm 0\rlap{.}''1$ to $\pm 1''$. The laborious model computations of $\delta\varepsilon$ (based on a digital terrain and density model) are eliminated by utilizing the surface deflections of the vertical (5.24). A comparison of (5.24a) with (5.24b) and (5.25) shows that the orthometric correction E is the line integral of the angle of curvature of the plumb line $\delta\varepsilon$.

To determine the differences in the *height anomalies* $\Delta\zeta$, we combine equations (5.23) and substitute (5.16), (5.21), and (5.24a). This yields

$$\Delta\zeta_{12} = \zeta_2 - \zeta_1 = - \int_1^2 \varepsilon\, ds - E_{12}^N, \tag{5.27}$$

where E^N is the normal correction (5.22).

The evaluation of the line integrals in (5.24), (5.27), and (5.12a) assumes, first of all, a complete knowledge of the deflections of the vertical along the corresponding line. Since astronomic determinations of the deflection of the vertical (measurements of astronomic latitude and longitude) are generally conducted at larger intervals for reasons of economcy (e.g. in primary control networks), assumptions must be made on the behavior of the deflections between these observation points: *interpolation of the deflection of the vertical*. The surface deflections, depending on the topographic masses, exhibit irregular characteristics, particularly in mountainous terrain; whereas, the deflections on the geoid may be interpolated more easily.

For an *arithmetic interpolation* in the simplest case, we presume a linear variation of the deflection of the vertical between the endpoints P_1 and P_2. The integration of (5.24a) then results in (by neglecting the curvature of the plumb line)

$$\Delta N_{12} = - \frac{\varepsilon_1 + \varepsilon_2}{2} s. \tag{5.28}$$

The geoid can also be approximated by a *surface polynomial* (VANIČEK and MERRY 1973). The coefficients of the polynomial are computed from the corresponding polynomial expansion of the components of the deflection of the vertical. According to (5.24), these components represent the partial derivatives of N in the directions of the meridian and parallel arcs; compare also (5.40). For a spherical approximation (radius of curvature R), equations (3.31) give us

$$\xi = - \frac{1}{R}\frac{\partial N}{\partial\varphi}, \quad \eta = - \frac{1}{R\cos\varphi}\frac{\partial N}{\partial\lambda}. \tag{5.29a}$$

Further differentiation of (5.29a) furnishes the *condition of integrability*

$$\frac{\partial\xi}{\cos\varphi\,\partial\lambda} = \frac{\partial\eta}{\partial\varphi}, \tag{5.29b}$$

which should be heeded in any analytic representation of ξ, η.

To estimate the optimal values at a point for which no observations were made, a *prediction* can be made, in analogy to [5.2.7], using all observed deflections of the vertical (HEITZ 1969).

One obtains better results if additional information is included on the behavior of the deflections. The gravimetric deflections of the vertical (5.60), computed from gravity anomalies, are acquired for a *gravimetric interpolation* of the deflections. This method may be extended to astrogravimetric leveling [5.4.1]; it provides good results even for a larger spacing (100 to 200 km) of the stations (uncertainty in the interpolated deflection: $\pm 0\rlap{.}{''}5$ to $1''$).

In *topographic* or *topographic-isostatic interpolation*, one computes for the points of observation and for the intermediate points the deflections of the vertical which arise from the gravitation of the topographic and possibly also isostatically compensating masses [5.5.4]. The differences between the observed and the computed deflections are largely unaffected by the irregular influence of topography; they may be interpolated linearly. The accuracy of this method ($\pm 1''$ to $\pm 2''$) depends on how accurately the density can be estimated and on how well one can account for the topography.

Finally, observed and refraction corrected *reciprocal zenith angles* deliver the differences of the vertical deflection component ε, in the direction of the connecting side S. From (4.54) and (4.56), and taking the sign of ε into account, we obtain

$$\varepsilon_2 - \varepsilon_1 = z_1 + z_2 - S/R - \pi. \tag{5.29c}$$

The geoid is determined either in profiles (north-south and east-west) or areally. The computed geoid undulations and height anomalies refer, as the deflections of the vertical, to the geodetic datum of the ellipsoidal φ,λ,h-system; hence, they are "relative" quantities [5.1.1].

The method of astronomic leveling was first applied under the direction of *Helmert* in the Harz mountains. Detailed investigations of the geoid in alpine regions were conducted in Switzerland (geoid profile along the meridian of the Saint Gotthard, station spacing of 3 to 4 km) where it was also possible to apply an interpolation by reciprocal zenith angles (KOBOLD 1955). For a densely surveyed area of deflections of the vertical (control points separated by 3 to 5 km in mountainous regions, 5 to 10 km in highlands, and 10 to 20 km in flat terrain), differences in the geoid can be determined to accuracies of a few cm over several tens of kilometers (TORGE 1977). The distance between control points may be increased in mountainous areas, when including a topographic (-isostatic) interpolation of the deflection of the vertical. By now, geoid determinations exist for several countries, where the first-order triangulation points are generally also stations at which the deflection of the vertical is measured. The uncertainty in the differences amounts to ± 0.1 to ± 0.3 m.

A detailed geoid computation covering varying topography from flat areas to high mountains was performed in Austria. Based on 700 observed vertical deflections (average station separation 10 to 15 km, accuracy $\pm 0\rlap{.}{''}5$), the deflection field was smoothed by removing a global gravity model part, cf. [5.4.2], and the topographic-isostatic part (high resolution digital terrain model and surface density model). Astronomic leveling (ERKER 1987), and least squares collocation [5.4.3] resp. (SÜNKEL et al. 1987) were applied, giving geoid differences with a precision of $\pm 0.05 \ldots 0.1$ m/100 km.

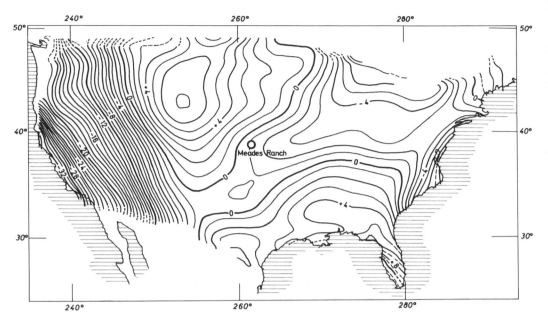

Fig. 5.10. Astrogeodetic geoid of the United States of America, referred to NAD 1927, origin point at Meades Ranch, contour line interval 2 m, after CARROLL and WESSELS (1975)

Combining the systems of the deflections of the vertical from the individual countries results in continental astrogeodetic representations of the geoid. The geoid of Europe, North Africa, and the Near East which was computed by BOMFORD (1972) is based on the European Datum 1950 [6.1.7]. A revised geoid (typical accuracy of ± 2 m) was derived by LEVALLOIS and MONGE (1978). Fig. 5.10 shows an astrogeodetic geoid of the United States of America, referring to the North American Datum 1927 [6.1.7], CARROLL and WESSELS (1975). Geoid representations (10 m and sometimes 5 m contour lines) of America, Australia, and Africa/Asia/Europe were prepared by FISCHER et al. (1968).

5.1.7 Orientation of Astrogeodetic Systems, Best Fitting Ellipsoids

The fit of an astrogeodetic system to the geoid may be improved by determining the deflections of the vertical and geoid undulations for a large number of network points, instead of for just one origin point, and applying a minimum condition onto these data.

In the *three-dimensional method*, three spatial displacements of the ellipsoid with respect to the geoid and a variation in the ellipsoidal parameters are permitted; the parallelism of the axes of the geodetic and global systems is maintained. The corresponding changes $\delta\xi_1, \delta\eta_1, \delta N_1, \delta a, \delta f$ in the parameters of the geodetic datum [5.1.2] create changes in the ellipsoidal coordinates and, by considering (5.1), (5.5), also in the deflection of the vertical $\delta\xi, \delta\eta$ and in the geoid undulation δN of all network points. $\delta\xi, \delta\eta$, and δN are then given by the *equations of* F. A. VENING MEINESZ (1950), (spherical approximation, for the derivation see [5.4.5]):

$$\begin{aligned}
\delta\xi = {}& (\cos\varphi_1\cos\varphi + \sin\varphi_1\sin\varphi\cos(\lambda - \lambda_1))\delta\xi_1 \\
& - \sin\varphi\sin(\lambda - \lambda_1)\delta\eta_1 \\
& - (\sin\varphi_1\cos\varphi - \cos\varphi_1\sin\varphi\cos(\lambda - \lambda_1)) \\
& \times\left(\frac{\delta N_1}{a} + \frac{\delta a}{a} + \sin^2\varphi_1\delta f\right) - 2\cos\varphi(\sin\varphi - \sin\varphi_1)\delta f \\
\delta\eta = {}& \sin\varphi_1\sin(\lambda - \lambda_1)\delta\xi_1 + \cos(\lambda - \lambda_1)\delta\eta_1 \\
& + \cos\varphi_1\sin(\lambda - \lambda_1)\left(\frac{\delta N_1}{a} + \frac{da}{a} + \sin^2\varphi_1\delta f\right) \\
\delta N = {}& -a(\cos\varphi_1\sin\varphi - \sin\varphi_1\cos\varphi\cos(\lambda - \lambda_1))\delta\xi_1 \\
& - a\cos\varphi\sin(\lambda - \lambda_1)\delta\eta_1 \\
& + (\sin\varphi_1\sin\varphi + \cos\varphi_1\cos\varphi\cos(\lambda - \lambda_1)) \\
& \times(\delta N_1 + \delta a + a\sin^2\varphi_1\delta f) - \delta a \\
& + (\sin^2\varphi - 2\sin\varphi_1\sin\varphi)a\delta f.
\end{aligned}$$
(5.30)

The deflections ξ', η' or geoid undulations N' may be available for a number of points of an initial geodetic datum. We set

$$\xi = \xi' + \delta\xi, \quad \eta = \eta' + \delta\eta, \quad N = N' + \delta N,$$
(5.31)

where $\delta\xi$, $\delta\eta$, and δN are given by (5.30). The minimum condition

$$\sum(\xi^2 + \eta^2) = \min.$$
(5.32)

or, in view of (5.24b), the equally valid condition

$$\sum N^2 = \min.$$
(5.33)

then furnishes the corrections $\delta\xi_1$, $\delta\eta_1$, δN_1, δa, δf to the initial geodetic datum. Subsequently, (5.30) reveals the changes in ξ, η, N at every point.

The two-dimensional *translational method*, developed by *Helmert*, uses quantities which are reduced to the ellipsoid [5.1.4]. A network shift $(\delta\xi_1, \delta\eta_1)$, an associated rotation of the network due to the Laplace equation, a scale change, and an ellipsoid transition $(\delta a, \delta f)$ are permitted in this method. The relationship between the changes $\delta\xi$, $\delta\eta$ in the network points and the corrections to the datum is given by the *translational equations of the deflection of the vertical* corresponding to (5.30). An adjustment of the deflections of the vertical using (5.32) yields the changes in the datum, cf. also [6.1.7].

Employing areally distributed measurements (area method), *J. F. Hayford* (1909) [3.5.5] and *T. N. Krassowski* (1942), among others, determined ellipsoids from adjustments of the deflections of the vertical. In this respect, by assuming the isostatic compensation theory of *Pratt* [5.5.4] HAYFORD (1909) corrected the observed deflections in the U.S.A. for the influence of the topographic-isostatic masses; he thus obtained ellipsoidal parameters that are unperturbed by any irregular masses. *Krassowski* used astrogeodetic material from the U.S.S.R., U.S.A., and Europe in computing a triaxial ellipsoid [3.5.4]. The parameters $a = 6378245$ m, $f = 1/298.3$ were then used to define a biaxial ellipsoidal which is the basis for geodetic surveys in East European countries (IZOTOV 1959).

Computations for a geodetic datum from astrogeodetic deflections and geoid undulations can only be carried out on the continents. They provide ellipsoids which best fit the dimensions and position of the geoid in their respective regions (*best fitting ellipsoids*); the mean earth ellipsoid can not be determined in this way. A geocentric position of these systems is as well not obtainable. Nevertheless, the deflections of the vertical or geoid undulations remain small in an optimally fitted region, so that there are only small reductions of the distances (4.51) and horizontal directions (5.13) to the ellipsoid.

Since geocentric coordinates for a great number of points are available today, along with good values for the mean earth ellipsoid, the methods for determining astrogeodetic datums have lost their significance. The system of equations (5.30) serves in the transformation to a given global datum, compare also [5.4.5].

5.2 Gravimetric Methods

Gravimetric methods use measurements of gravity [4.2] and potential differences as derived from geometric leveling [4.3.5]. The reference system is the normal gravity field of the level ellipsoid [3.5].

5.2.1 Geodetic Boundary-Value Problem, Disturbing Potential, Gravity Anomaly

The *geodetic boundary-value problem* (boundary-value problem of physical geodesy) comprises the determination of the physical surface of the earth or the geoid, as well as the external gravity field from the gravity potential W and gravity acceleration $g = \mathrm{grad}\ W$ on the earth's surface. According to *M. S. Molodenski* (1945), this problem may be represented by a nonlinear integral equation of the second kind in W (MOLODENSKI 1958):

$$-2\pi W + \iint\limits_{S} \left(W \frac{\partial}{\partial n} \left(\frac{1}{l} \right) - \frac{1}{l'} \frac{\partial W}{\partial n_S} \right) dS + 2\pi\omega^2 (X^2 + Y^2) + 2\omega^2 \iiint\limits_{v} \frac{dv}{l'} = 0, \quad (5.34)$$

where v denotes the volume enclosed by the earth's surface S; n is the outer surface normal to S, and ω is the angular velocity of the earth's rotation. l and l' denote the distances between the attracted point and the attracting point either on the surface or interior to the earth, respectively. If W and $\partial W/\partial n$ are known on S, then S represents the unknown quantity of the problem.

Equation (5.34) exemplifies an application of Green's third identity in potential theory. Therefore, the geodetic boundary-value problem corresponds to the classical *third boundary-value problem* (the determination of an harmonic function [2.1.3], given a linear combination of this function and its normal derivative on a bounding surface). The problem at hand, however, differs from the latter in that the geometry of the bounding surface is not known and the

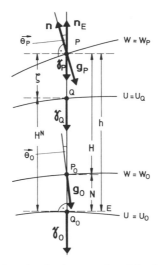

Fig. 5.11. Gravity acceleration in the actual and in the normal gravity field

derivatives (gravity values) are not along the surface normals, but in the direction of the plumb line (free and oblique boundary-value problem, GRAFAREND and NIEMEIER 1971).

(5.34) can be solved by a suitable *linearization*. To this end, we approximate the gravity potential W by the potential U (3.38) of normal gravity and define the *disturbing* or *anomalous potential* at P by

$$T_P = W_P - U_P. \tag{5.35}$$

The gravity acceleration $\boldsymbol{g}_P$ at P is approximated by the normal gravity $\vec{\gamma}_Q$ at the point Q on the spheropotential surface $U = U_Q$ (Fig. 5.11). We define the *gravity anomaly* (vector) as

$$\Delta\boldsymbol{g} = \boldsymbol{g}_P - \vec{\gamma}_Q. \tag{5.36}$$

Neglecting the deflection of the vertical Θ_P, we obtain the (scalar) gravity anomaly used in gravimetric methods:

$$\Delta g = g_P - \gamma_Q. \tag{5.37}$$

It is the difference between the observed gravity intensity at P and the normal gravity computed by (3.64) at Q.

We expand the normal potential at P according to Taylor's theorem and truncate the series at the linear term:

$$U_P = U_Q + \left(\frac{\partial U}{\partial n_E}\right)_Q \zeta_P + \cdots$$

Here, n_E is the ellipsoidal normal and ζ_P is the distance between the spheropotential surface $U = U_Q$ and the level surface $W = W_P$ (Fig. 5.11). It was introduced as height anomaly in [5.1.1]. Using $\gamma = -(\partial U/\partial n_E)$ and (5.35), it follows that

$$\zeta_P = \frac{T_P - (W_P - U_Q)}{\gamma_Q}. \tag{5.38}$$

Letting $U_Q = W_P$, cf. [5.2.8], we obtain *Bruns' theorem*

$$\zeta_P = \frac{T_P}{\gamma_Q}. \tag{5.39}$$

It relates the physical quantity T to the geometric quantity ζ.

The components of the *deflection of the vertical* Θ_P are given by the derivatives of N_P in the directions of the meridian and the prime vertical, respectively; cf. (5.29a). By introducing the arc elements (3.31) in these directions, equation (5.39) yields

$$\xi_P = -\frac{1}{M\gamma_Q}\frac{\partial T}{\partial \varphi}, \qquad \eta_P = -\frac{1}{\bar{N}\cos\varphi\,\gamma_Q}\frac{\partial T}{\partial \lambda}, \tag{5.40}$$

where $\bar{N}$ is the radius of curvature in the prime vertical (3.26).

5.2.2 Linearization of the Geodetic Boundary-Value Problem

We shall derive the relationship between the disturbing potential T and the gravity anomaly Δg. From evident relations in Fig. 5.11

$$g = -\frac{\partial W}{\partial n}, \quad \gamma = -\frac{\partial U}{\partial n_E} = -\frac{1}{\cos\Theta_P}\frac{\partial U}{\partial n},$$

and since $\cos\Theta_P \approx 1$, the derivative of (5.35) in the direction of the plumb line, n, is

$$\left(\frac{\partial T}{\partial n}\right)_P = -g_P + \gamma_P. \tag{5.41}$$

The difference $g_P - \gamma_P$ defined at P is termed the *gravity disturbance*. An application of Taylor's theorem provides

$$\gamma_P = \gamma_Q + \left(\frac{\partial \gamma}{\partial n_E}\right)_Q \zeta_P + \cdots$$

for the normal gravity at P. Substituting this into (5.41) and taking note of (5.37) and (5.39), we obtain

$$-\left(\frac{\partial T}{\partial n}\right)_P + \frac{1}{\gamma_Q}\left(\frac{\partial \gamma}{\partial n_E}\right)_Q T = \Delta g. \tag{5.42}$$

This first-order partial differential equation in T is known as the *fundamental equation of physical geodesy*.

With *spherical approximation* and the introduction of a spherical reference surface (radius R), quantities on the order of the flattening are neglected, and we have $\partial/\partial n = \partial/\partial r$. From (3.50), it follows that

$$\gamma = \frac{GM}{r^2} \text{ and } \frac{\partial \gamma}{\partial r} = -2\frac{GM}{r^3} = -2\frac{\gamma}{r}. \tag{5.43}$$

Substituting this into (5.42) gives

$$-\frac{\partial T}{\partial r} - \frac{2}{r} T = \Delta g. \tag{5.44}$$

Since Δg can be derived only on the earth's surface, (5.42) or (5.44) each represents only a boundary condition for the determination of T. The differential equation to be solved for T is obtained if we equate the centrifugal potential of the ellipsoid with the centrifugal potential of the earth. This is possible since ω is known to high accuracy, cf. [2.1.4]. T is then an harmonic function, being the difference of two gravitational potentials in the space exterior to the earth. *Laplace's differential equation* (2.17)

$$\Delta T = 0 \tag{5.45}$$

is the defining equation of T.

The problem given by (5.44) and (5.45) can also be formulated as an *integral equation* using (5.34). In this regard, we replace W by T and note that T has no terms depending on the earth's rotation. Then we get

$$-2\pi T + \iint_S \left(T \frac{\partial}{\partial n_s}\left(\frac{1}{l}\right) - \frac{1}{l}\frac{\partial T}{\partial n_s} \right) dS = 0. \tag{5.46}$$

The gravity anomaly Δg is used in classical gravimetric geodesy, as only orthometric heights H or normal heights H^N are supposed to be known. Consequently normal gravity can be transferred only from Q_0 to Q with H^N, and actual gravity from P to P_0 with H, cf. [5.2.3]. The gravity disturbance δg can be computed if the position of P in space (ellipsoidal height h) and hence the normal gravity γ_P is known. This applies for positions of artificial earth satellites and points on the earth's surface derived thereof. As a consequence of the increasing use of satellite techniques, the boundary-value problem may be formulated using gravity disturbances (bounding surface is known), cf. [5.2.6].

5.2.3 Solution of the Geodetic Boundary-Value Problem for the Geoid

If we remove the topographic masses outside the geoid by a gravity reduction [5.2.4], then due to (5.45), the disturbing potential T may be expanded in a series of spherical harmonic functions in the space exterior to the geoid. We assume that the masses of the geoid and the equipotential ellipsoid are equal; in addition, the center of the ellipsoid is defined to coincide with the center of mass of the earth. According to (2.51) and (2.57), the terms of zero and first order then vanish; compare this to [5.2.8]. The *spherical harmonic expansion of T* can be represented in abbreviated form using surface harmonic functions T_l by

$$T(r, \vartheta, \lambda) = \sum_{l=2}^{\infty} \left(\frac{R}{r}\right)^{l+1} T_l(\vartheta, \lambda). \tag{5.47}$$

Differentiation with respect to r furnishes

$$\frac{\partial T}{\partial r} = -\frac{1}{r} \sum_{l=2}^{\infty} (l+1)\left(\frac{R}{r}\right)^{l+1} T_l(\vartheta, \lambda). \tag{5.48}$$

Substituting (5.47) and (5.48) into (5.44) yields the spherical harmonic expansion of the gravity anomaly

$$\Delta g(r, \vartheta, \lambda) = \frac{1}{r} \sum_{l=2}^{\infty} (l-1)\left(\frac{R}{r}\right)^{l+1} T_l(\vartheta, \lambda). \tag{5.49}$$

For a spherical approximation, we have $r = R$ on the *geoid*; (5.47) and (5.49) then become

$$T(\vartheta, \lambda) = \sum_{l=2}^{\infty} T_l(\vartheta, \lambda) \tag{5.50}$$

and

$$\Delta g(\vartheta, \lambda) = \frac{1}{R} \sum_{l=2}^{\infty} (l-1) T_n(\vartheta, \lambda). \tag{5.51}$$

Here, the $\Delta g(\vartheta, \lambda)$ are gravity anomalies referring to the geoid (Fig. 5.11):

$$\Delta g = g_0 - \gamma_0. \tag{5.52}$$

If we substitute the expansions (2.51) and (3.47) for W and U (where $C_l = -J_l$) into (5.35), then with $a = r = R$, the *disturbing potential* is given by

$$T(\vartheta, \lambda) = \frac{GM}{R} \sum_{l=2}^{\infty} \sum_{m=0}^{l} (\delta C_{lm} \cos m\lambda + \delta S_{lm} \sin m\lambda) P_{lm}(\cos \vartheta). \tag{5.53}$$

As a result of the properties of the expansion for U [3.5.3], we have (with generally sufficient accuracy) $\delta C_2 = C_2 - C_{2(Ell.)}$, $\delta C_4 = C_4 - C_{4(Ell.)}$ and $\delta C_{lm} = C_{lm}$, $\delta S_{lm} = S_{lm}$ for all remaining coefficients.

A comparison of (5.50) with (5.53) supplies T_l. By substituting this into (5.51), we obtain for the *gravity anomaly*:

$$\Delta g(\vartheta, \lambda) = \frac{GM}{R^2} \sum_{l=2}^{\infty} \sum_{m=0}^{l} (l-1)(\delta C_{lm} \cos m\lambda + \delta S_{lm} \sin m\lambda) P_{lm}(\cos \vartheta). \tag{5.54a}$$

The coefficients δC_{lm}, δS_{lm} in this expansion can be determined up to degree $l < \infty$, if there exists a sufficient number of points with known gravity anomaly values and distributed evenly over the earth. Each value then provides an equation for the determination of δC_{lm}, δS_{lm}. For a complete coverage of gravity anomalies over the earth, the coefficients δC_{lm}, δS_{lm} can be computed by integrating Δg over the earth's surface. The corresponding solution for the coefficients in (5.54a) is obtained with the aid of the orthogonality relations for the harmonic functions. We have

$$\begin{Bmatrix} \delta C_{lm} \\ \delta S_{lm} \end{Bmatrix} = \frac{k}{4\pi\gamma_m} \frac{(2l+1)}{(l-1)} \frac{(l-m)!}{(l+m)!} \iint_{\sigma} \Delta g \, P_{lm}(\cos \vartheta) \begin{Bmatrix} \cos m\lambda \\ \sin m\lambda \end{Bmatrix} d\sigma,$$

$$k = \begin{Bmatrix} 1 & \text{for } m = 0 \\ 2 & \text{for } m \neq 0 \end{Bmatrix}, \tag{5.54b}$$

where σ denotes the unit sphere, and $d\sigma$ is the element of solid angle. The disturbing potential then follows from (5.53). Finally, *Bruns'* theorem (5.39) furnishes the *geoid undulation*

$$N(\vartheta, \lambda) = \frac{T(\vartheta, \gamma)}{\gamma} \tag{5.55a}$$

as a global function of position. Upon substituting equation (5.53) and recalling (5.43), we have

$$N(\vartheta, \lambda) = R \sum_{l=2}^{\infty} \sum_{m=0}^{l} (\delta C_{lm} \cos m\lambda + \delta S_{lm} \sin m\lambda) P_{lm}(\cos \vartheta). \tag{5.55b}$$

(5.53), (5.54a), and (5.55b) represent *global gravity field approximations*. These series expansions are required for large-scale problems, such as orbit determinations for earth satellites, and geophysical or geodynamical interpretations of deeper seated mass anomalies. An important application is the use of spherical harmonic models as a reference for local gravity field approximations, either by integral formulas (see below), or by least squares collocation, cf. [5.4.2], [5.4.3].

Gravimetric geoid computations with spherical harmonic expansions were carried out by UOTILA (1962) (up to $l = m = 4$) and by RAPP (1977) (up to $l = m = 52$), among others. Due to the irregular distribution of the terrestrial gravity data, the harmonic coefficients thus computed exhibit considerable uncertainties. More recent developments combine harmonic coefficients derived from satellite orbit analyses and results of satellite altimetry with terrestrial gravity data, cf. [5.4.4]. Generally, fully normalized harmonics [2.3.2] are used in recent models.

The series expansion (5.53) for the disturbing potential can also be represented by an integral. These *integral formulas* are used for *local gravity field approximations* (TSCHERNING 1981). If we write the gravity anomaly as an harmonic expansion

$$\Delta g(\vartheta, \lambda) = \sum_{l=0}^{\infty} \Delta g_l(\vartheta, \lambda) \tag{5.56}$$

then a comparison with (5.51) yields the relationship between the surface harmonics T_l and Δg_l. Potential theory states that Δg_l can be computed by integrating Δg over the surface of the earth. We obtain

$$T_l = \frac{R}{l-1} \Delta g_l = \frac{R}{l-1} \cdot \frac{2l+1}{4\pi} \iint_{\sigma} \Delta g \, P_l(\cos \psi) \, d\sigma.$$

According to the spherical law of cosines [2.3.1], the spherical distance ψ between the attracted point and the surface element $d\sigma$ is related to the coordinates of the attracted point (ϑ, λ) and attracting point (ϑ', λ'). Substitution of the equation above into (5.50) gives the formula derived by STOKES (1849):

$$T = \frac{R}{4\pi} \iint_{\sigma} S(\psi)\Delta g \, d\sigma. \tag{5.57}$$

The following sum, representable in closed form,

$$S(\psi) = \sum_{l=2}^{\infty} \frac{2l+1}{l-1} P_l(\cos \psi) = \frac{1}{\sin \dfrac{\psi}{2}} + 1 - 5 \cos \psi$$

$$- 6 \sin \frac{\psi}{2} - 3 \cos \psi \, \ln\left(\sin \frac{\psi}{2} + \sin^2 \frac{\psi}{2} \right) \qquad (5.58)$$

is known as *Stokes' function*. Using (5.55a), the geoid undulation becomes

$$N = \frac{R}{4\pi\gamma} \iint_{\sigma} S(\psi) \Delta g \, d\sigma. \qquad (5.59)$$

(5.57) can also be obtained by solving the integral equation (5.46).

Stokes' formula provides T or N pointwise by an integration of gravity anomalies which refer to the geoid. The *Stokes'* function may be viewed as a weighting function. Its zeros are near $\psi = 39°$ and $\psi = 118°$. At the attracted point ($\psi = 0$), it becomes infinite (∞), so that particular attention must be afforded to the neighborhood of the attracted point.

The deflections of the vertical are related to the disturbing potential by (5.40). The derivatives of (5.57) give the integrals formulated by VENING MEINESZ (1928) for the *deflections of the vertical* defined on the geoid [5.1.1]:

$$\begin{Bmatrix} \xi \\ \eta \end{Bmatrix}_0 = \frac{1}{4\pi\gamma} \iint_{\sigma} \frac{dS(\psi)}{d\psi} \Delta g \begin{Bmatrix} \cos \alpha \\ \sin \alpha \end{Bmatrix} d\sigma, \qquad (5.60)$$

where α is the azimuth of the line joining the attracted (computation) point P and the attracting point P' (Fig. 2.10).

The *Vening Meinesz function* $dS(\psi)/d\psi$ starts at the attracted point as unbounded, but then decreases rapidly. After $\psi \approx 100°$, the influence of the gravity anomalies on ξ, η is less than $1''$, so that the integration can frequently be limited to the area up to $\psi \approx 100$.

When *evaluating* the formulas of *Stokes* and *Vening Meinesz* in practice, the integration is replaced by a summation of finite surface elements. In this case, average values take the place of the functions $S(\psi)$ and $dS(\psi)/d\psi$ and the gravity anomalies. The grid lines of the geographic coordinates (degree subdivisions) are particularly suited for the delineation of the surface elements. In the vicinity of the computation point, annular partitions (concentric circles with radial subdivisions) are appropriate. The contribution of the *inner zone* enclosing the attracted point is given to a first approximation by

$$N_i = \frac{s_0}{\gamma} \Delta g, \qquad \begin{Bmatrix} \xi \\ \eta \end{Bmatrix}_i = - \frac{s_0}{2\gamma} \begin{Bmatrix} \partial(\Delta g)/\partial x \\ \partial(\Delta g)/\partial y \end{Bmatrix}. \qquad (5.61)$$

s_0 is the radius of the inner zone (e.g. $s_0 = 5$ km). N_i and ξ_i, η_i depend on the gravity anomaly and the horizontal gradient of the gravity anomaly at the computation point, respectively (x = north, y = east).

Mean gravity anomalies in degree subdivisions (or equal area blocks) are required to compute the harmonic coefficients (5.54) and to evaluate the integral formulas (5.59), (5.60). For smaller blocks (e.g. $5' \times 5'$, $15' \times 15'$, 10 km $\times$ 10 km), they are derived from point anomalies (e.g. GERKE and WATERMANN 1959, see [5.2.4]). With the high efficiency of Fast Fourier Transforms (FFT), a large number of data can be evaluated (SCHWARZ et al. 1990). This even permits to incorporate gridded *point gravity anomalies* (e.g. in a 5 km $\times$ 5 km grid) into the integral formulas. Mean values over larger blocks ($1° \times 1°$, $5° \times 5°$, $15° \times 15°$) are generally computed from the smaller blocks. Since uniform gravimetric surveys do not exist over the entire earth's surface (the polar regions and the oceans, particularly in the southern hemisphere are not as well surveyed as the continents), only a part of the mean values can be formed from observed gravity data. For unsurveyed areas, methods were developed to predict gravity anomalies [5.2.7]. Free-air anomalies [5.2.4] are applied nearly exclusively for geoid computations. Mean free air anomalies have been determined globally for $1° \times 1°$ block subdivisions (*Bureau Gravimetrique International*), of which (as of 1986) approximately 70% were obtained from observed data. Mean $30' \times 30'$ anomalies have been computed for some well surveyed regions (KIM and RAPP 1990). The accuracy of the mean values amounts to about ± 50 to $\pm 200 \, \mu ms^{-2}$. Although the contribution of the *inner zone* (5.61) remains small for the geoid undulation, it can attain several arc seconds in the case of the deflection of the vertical. Hence, in the determination of ξ_i, η_i, additional gravity measurements are generally required around the computation point.

A combination of the *spherical harmonic expansion* and *Stokes' formula* has usually been employed for the more recent geoid determinations, cf. [5.4.2]. The long-wavelength features of the gravity field and geoid are represented by harmonic expansions to low degree ($l = 15$ to 20) using (5.54a) or (5.55b). The values of the harmonic coefficients are borrowed from solutions in satellite geodesy [5.3.4] or from a combined solution [5.4.4]. *Stokes'* formula (5.59) furnishes the short-wavelength characteristics of the geoid, where Δg is replaced by the difference between the terrestrial gravity anomaly and the truncated harmonic function of (5.54a). The integration can then be limited to a spherical distance ψ_0 of $10°$ to $20°$. An optimal combination of a spherical harmonic model and the gravity anomalies is possible in the spectral domain. The integration radius is then determined by the error models for the data and by the admissible emission error (high frequency field component outside ψ_0), cf. [5.4.2]. In regions endowed with dense gravimetric surveys, this integral combination method delivers the geoid to a resolution of 10 to 20 km, and a relative accuracy of $\pm$ a few dm over some 100 km. The absolute accuracy depends on the global model, and amounts to approximately ± 1 m.

Of the regional gravimetric *determinations of the geoid*, the following are mentioned: the computation of the geoid for the northern hemisphere (Columbus geoid) carried out in 1950–1957 by W. A. HEISKANEN (1957) at the Ohio State University in Columbus; the geoid for Africa (OBENSON 1974) and the computations undertaken by the Goddard Space Flight Center (MARSH and VINCENT 1974).

For *Europe* and her bordering seas, gravimetric quasi-geoid heights and vertical deflections were computed in a $12' \times 20'$ grid, using the integral combination method (TORGE et al. 1984a). As data sets, the spherical harmonic coefficients of the GEM9 model [5.3.3], $1° \times 1°$ free-air anomalies ($\psi_o = 20°$ for N and $10°$ for ξ, η), and $6' \times 10'$ anomalies ($\psi_0 = 3°$) were used. The accuracy has been estimated to ± 0.5 m/200 km and ± 1.1 m /1000 km. For the vertical deflections, the accuracy is $\pm 1'' \dots 2''$, whereby the main error part is due to unmodelled local topography. This solution was extended to an astrogravimetric quasigeoid, by including about

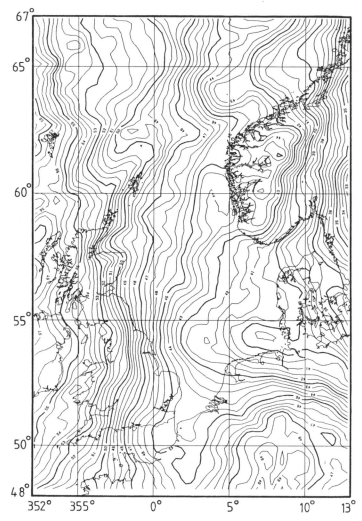

Fig. 5.12. European gravimetric quasigeoid EGG1, referred to GRS80, northwestern Europe part, contour line interval 0.5 m, after TORGE et al. (1984a)

5000 deflections of the vertical (BRENNECKE et al. 1983), Fig. 5.12. The deflections of the vertical supported the original gravimetric solution especially in areas where gravity data were lacking or of bad quality.

Gravimetric geoid computations for individual countries (e.g. U.S.A.: STRANGE et al. 1971, FRG: LELGEMANN 1974) can be employed, just as astrogeodetic determinations [5.1.6], in the reduction of observed spatial distances. A recent gravimetric quasigeoid computation for the Federal Republic of Germany is based on a tailored (360, 360)-model, cf. [5.4.4], gridded $(1' \times 1'5)$ point gravity anomalies, and a $30'' \times 50''$ digital terrain model (DENKER 1989). FFT-techniques were applied for the evaluation of the surface integral, cf. [5.4.2]. The accuracy of this solution is estimated to $\pm 0.01 \ldots 0.03$ m over distances of a few km to a few 100 km, and ± 0.1 m over 1000 km , see also DENKER et al. (1991). Thus the "cm-geoid" is approached which is needed for combining GPS-heights with the results of leveling (TORGE 1990b).

5.2.4 Gravity Reductions, Cogeoid

Gravity anomalies as boundary values on the geoid are required for the gravimetric determination of the geoid. The purpose of *gravity reductions* is to reduce the observed gravity values to the geoid and to displace the topographic masses exterior to the geoid in such a way that the geoid becomes a bounding surface. To this end, certain assumptions must be made as to the distribution of mass (density law); the gravimetrically determined geoid is subject to the errors of the density hypothesis.

With the displacement of the masses, the gravity potential changes: *indirect effect* of the gravity reduction. The level surface possessing the potential W_0 of the geoid after the masses have been displaced is called the *cogeoid* (compensated geoid). The vertical displacement δN of the cogeoid with respect to the geoid (positive outward) is computed from the change in potential δW at the geoid according to *Bruns' theorem* (5.39)

$$\delta N = \frac{\delta W}{\gamma}. \tag{5.62}$$

Stokes' formula gives the undulation of the cogeoid:

$$N^c = N + \delta N, \tag{5.63}$$

where the geoidal gravity has to be reduced beforehand to the cogeoid: *Bowie reduction*. Using a spherical approximation for the vertical component of the gravity gradient (5.43), this reduction is given by

$$\delta g_B = -2\frac{\gamma}{R}\delta N. \tag{5.64}$$

The evaluation of (5.62) evokes laborious computations, susceptible to errors, of the changes in potential due to the mass displacements. The indirect effect should therefore be as small as possible.

In addition, the gravity anomalies should exhibit as smooth a variation as possible. The simplifies the formation of representative mean values and the prediction of gravity anomalies. Finally, it is desired in the formulation of geophysical and geological problems that the gravity anomalies be suitable for the investigation of the mass distributions in the earth's interior.

We reduce the surface gravity value g to the geoid value g_0 at the point P_0 (Fig. 5.11) using the vertical component of the gravity gradient $\partial g/\partial H$, valid in free air, and the orthometric height H. A comparison with the normal gravity γ_0 at the ellipsoid point Q_0, corresponding to (5.52), gives the *free-air anomaly*

$$\Delta g_F = g + \delta g_F - \gamma_0. \tag{5.65}$$

In the *free-air reduction* δg_F, the unknown actual gradient is generally replaced by the normal vertical gradient $\partial \gamma/\partial h$ (3.63), where the value 3086 ns^{-2} at $\varphi = 45°$ is frequently sufficient:

$$\delta g_F = -\frac{\partial g}{\partial H} H \approx -\frac{\partial \gamma}{\partial h} H \approx 3.086 \, H_{(m)} \, \mu\text{ms}^{-2}. \tag{5.66}$$

The free-air reduction corresponds to a parallel displacement of the topographic masses by the height of the computation point, or in good approximation, to a condensation of the topographic masses onto the geoid, as suggested by *Helmert*. It provides approximate boundary values on the geoid; the indirect effect attains at most a few meters.

A few *refinements* are necessary in computing a geoid with ± 0.1 m accuracy (MORITZ 1974). First, the atmospheric mass, in accordance with [3.5.5], must be taken into account. Also, irregularities in topography should be removed by a terrain reduction (5.71). Finally, the spherical approximation [5.2.2] must be replaced by an ellipsoidal one.

The height dependent influence of the topographic masses has not been removed in (5.65). The free-air anomalies are therefore *correlated* with the *height of the point* and are not representative for a large area (GROTEN and REINHART 1968). This dependence can be ascertained and eliminated by an empirically obtained linear regression, or by a topographic reduction (i.e. through the Bouguer anomaly, see below). If one averages these smoothed values over one block (subdivision) and subsequently applies the height correlation term which is computed from the average height in this block, then this yields *mean free-air anomalies* freed from the local influence of height. *Mean heights* have been determined for smaller blocks. A global set of $5' \times 5'$ gridded land and seafloor elevations is stored at the World Data Center for Solid Earth Geophysics, Boulder, Colorado. High resolution models (e.g. $30'' \times 30''$) are being developed in many countries. Furthermore, spherical harmonic expansions of topography (e.g. RAPP 1982a; $l, m = 180.180$) are at one's disposal for global investigations.

If one eliminates the influence of the topographic masses by a *topographic reduction* δg_{Top} and subsequently reduces the gravity value by a free-air reduction δg_F, then one obtains the *Bouguer anomaly*:

$$\Delta g_B = g - \delta g_{Top} + \delta g_F - \gamma_0. \tag{5.67}$$

δg_{Top} can be computed from the law of gravitation. In this respect, the terrain may be divided into *vertical columns* using concentric rings and radii. From the notation of Fig. 5.13a, the vertical component of gravitation of each column is given by

$$b_z = G\rho\Delta\alpha(\sqrt{z_2^2 + r_1^2} - \sqrt{z_2^2 + r_2^2} - \sqrt{z_1^2 + r_1^2} + \sqrt{z_1^2 + r_2^2}). \tag{5.68a}$$

With the height H_P of the point and the height H of the column (Fig. 5.14), the following are obtained for the topographic reduction:

$$z_1^2 = (H_P - H)^2, \quad z_2 = H_P; \quad \delta g_{Top} = \sum b_z. \tag{5.68b}$$

If a digital terrain model is available, the use of *rectangular prisms* is more appropriate for computing the topographic reduction. The gravitational effect of a prism with limits $x_1 \, x_2, y_1, y_2, z_1, z_2$ and density ρ (Fig. 5.13b) is given by NAGY (1966):

$$b_z = G\rho\left|\left|\left| -x \ln(y+r) - y \ln(x+r) + 2 \arctan\frac{xy}{zr} \right|_{x_1}^{x_2} \right|_{y_1}^{y_2} \right|_{z_1}^{z_2}, \tag{5.69}$$

with $r = \sqrt{x^2 + y^2 + z^2}$.

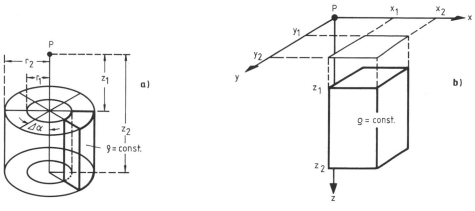

Fig. 5.13. Gravitation of elementary bodies a) vertical cylindrical column b) rectangular prism

The topographic reduction is frequently decomposed into the Bouguer plate reduction δg_P and the terrain reduction δg_T. The *plate reduction* accounts for the gravitation of an infinitely extended horizontal plate having a constant "Bouguer density" ρ, the thickness being the height H_P of the attracted point (Fig. 5.14). For $\Delta\alpha = 2\pi$, $r_1 = 0, r_2 = \infty, z_1 = 0. z_2 = H_P$, (5.68) transforms into the easily evaluable form

$$\delta g_P = 2\pi G\rho H_P = 0.419 \; \rho \; H_{P_{(m)}} \; \mu ms^{-2}. \tag{5.70}$$

(ρ in g cm^{-3}). The *terrain correction* creates a Bouguer plate by filling and removing topographic masses; for planar considerations, it is always positive. With $z_1 = 0$ and $z_2 = H_P - H = \Delta H$ (5.68a) becomes

$$b_z = G\rho\Delta\alpha(r_2 - r_1 + \sqrt{\Delta H^2 + r_1^2} - \sqrt{\Delta H^2 - r_2^2}); \quad \delta g_T = \sum b_z. \tag{5.71}$$

The Bouguer gravity anomaly now reads

$$\Delta g_B = g - \delta g_P + \delta g_T + \delta g_F - \gamma_0. \tag{5.72}$$

Again, the substantial effort which is required for the computation of δgt_T can be reduced by dividing the topography into rectangular prisms, and evaluating a digital terrain and (if available) also a density model. FFT-techniques provide economic solutions.

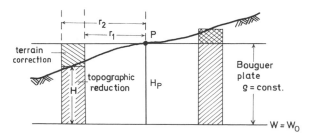

Fig. 5.14. Topographic gravity reduction, Bouguer plate reduction, terrain correction

The uncertainty in the topographic reduction is determined by the errors of the density hypothesis. For global and regional considerations, one frequently uses the mean density of the upper crust of the earth, $\rho = 2.67$ g cm^{-3}. The terrain correction attains values of 1 to 10 μms^{-2} in flat areas; in highlands and mountainous regions, it can take on values of 100 μms^{-2} and 1000 μms^{-2}, respectively.

Since the topographic masses are completely removed, the *indirect effect* for the Bouguer anomaly is very large (a few 100 m); it is not suited for geoid computations. However, the Bouguer anomaly has considerable significance in geophysics [5.5.3].

In accounting for the topography, the Bouguer anomalies display smooth variation; they are therefore employed in the formation of mean anomalies (see above) and in the prediction of anomaly values [5.2.7]. *Isoanomaly maps* (isoanomaly curve = line of equal gravity anomalies) serve in depicting the Bouguer anomalies. Small-scale (1 : 10 mill., 1 : 1 mill.) maps are produced by, among others, the Bureau Gravimetrique International; whereas, the national services (e.g. U.S. Geological Survey) mainly prepare maps of larger scale (1 : 250000, 1 : 500000). In the *U.S.A.*, a cooperative effort of the Society of Exploration Geophysicists (SEG), the Geological Survey, the Defense Mapping Agency, and the National Oceanic and Atmospheric Administration led to the collection of some million gravity point data on land, and in off-shore areas. Based on these data, a Bouguer anomaly map 1 : 2.5 mill. (contour line interval 50 μms^{-2}) has been compiled (HINZE 1985), Fig. 5.15. The anomalies are referred to the I.G.S.N.71 [4.2.4] and the GRS67 [3.5.5]. Terrain corrections were applied to a distance of 166.7 km in mountainous regions.

In the case of *isostatic anomalies*, the topographic masses are used in the regularization of the earth's crust under the assumption of an isostatic model [5.5.4]. The oceans are filled by the excess mass found beneath them. The new mass distribution corre-

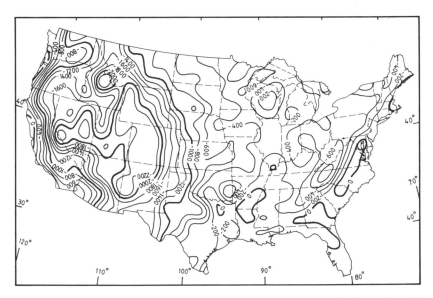

Fig. 5.15. Regional Bouguer gravity map of the United States composed of wavelengths longer than 250 km, referred to I.G.S.N.71 and GRS67, rock density 2670 kg/m^3, after KANE and GODSON (1985), contour line interval 200 μms

sponds to a crust of constant thickness and density. The isostatic reduction δg_I can be computed according to (5.68) or (5.69) in which the upper and lower limits of the vertical column to be regularized are substituted for z_1 and z_2, respectively. The difference between the densities of the regularized crust and mantle and the densities of the isostatic model is used for ρ in (5.68) or (5.69). The isostatic anomaly is given by

$$\Delta g_I = g - \delta g_{Top} + \delta g_I + \delta g_F - \gamma_0. \tag{5.73}$$

Disregarding those regions which are not in hydrostatic equilibrium, the isostatic anomalies are small and are characterized by smooth variation; they are well suited in the formation of mean values and for prediction purposes. The indirect effect can amount to 10 m. Because of this and due to the considerable computational effort, they are rarely used to determine the geoid. However, they provide valuable information in geophysics [5.5.5].

5.2.5 Solution of the Geodetic Boundary-Value Problem for the Surface of the Earth

As *M. S. Molodenski* (MOLODENSKII et al. A1962) has shown, the geodetic boundary-value problem for the earth's surface may be solved without hypothesis. In this case, the earth is approximated by the telluroid [3.5.6]. The telluroid point Q is attached to the physical surface point P by the conditions (see Fig. 5.4):

$$\varphi_Q = \Phi_P, \quad \lambda_Q = \Lambda_P, \quad U_Q = W_P. \tag{5.74a}$$

The "observed" quantities are the *free-air anomalies* (5.37) defined on the earth's surface:

$$\Delta g = g_P - \gamma_Q. \tag{5.74b}$$

g_P is the measured gravity, γ_Q is the normal gravity at the telluroid point Q, and is rigorously computed using the normal height H^N (3.71).

The disturbing potential (5.35) is caused by the perturbing masses which, according to *Molodenski*, can be thought of as an infinitely thin layer condensed on the telluroid Σ (Fig. 5.16). We introduce the product of the variable surface density $dm/d\Sigma$ and the gravitational constant G:

$$\mu = G \frac{dm}{d\Sigma}. \tag{5.75}$$

Corresponding to (2.8), the *disturbing potential* of a simple layer then becomes

$$T = \iint_\Sigma \frac{\mu}{l} \, d\Sigma. \tag{5.76}$$

We substitute T and its normal derivative into the differential equation (5.42). The ellipsoid is again approximated by a sphere ($r = R$). The integral equation thus found for μ may be solved iteratively by a series expansion; T is then also determined from (5.76). Upon introducing the unit sphere σ and limiting the series to its first two terms, we have (MORITZ 1971)

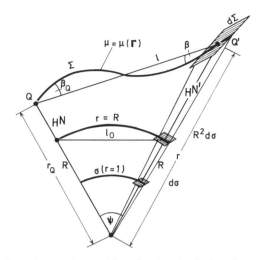

Fig. 5.16. Boundary value problem for the physical surface of the earth

$$T = \frac{R}{4\pi} \iint\limits_{\sigma} (\Delta g + G_1) S(\psi) \, d\sigma$$

with

$$G_1 = \frac{R^2}{2\pi} \iint\limits_{\sigma} \frac{H^{N'} - H^N}{l_0^3} \Delta g \, d\sigma, \qquad l_0 = 2R \sin \frac{\psi}{2}.$$

(5.77)

To a first approximation, G_1 corresponds to the gravimetric terrain correction δg_T [5.2.4]. The terrain-corrected free-air anomalies are also denoted as "*Faye*"-*anomalies*.

Here, $S(\psi)$ is *Stokes'* function (5.58), $H^{N'}$ and H^N are the ellipsoidal heights of the telluroid points Q' (attracting point) and Q (attracted point), that is, they are the normal heights of the corresponding surface points. For the *height anomaly*, *Bruns'* formula (5.39) furnishes

$$\zeta = \frac{R}{4\pi\gamma} \iint\limits_{\sigma} (\Delta g + G_1) S(\psi) \, d\sigma.$$

(5.78)

Molodenski's surface deflections of the vertical [5.1.1] are given with (5.40) by

$$\begin{Bmatrix} \xi^N \\ \eta^N \end{Bmatrix} = \frac{1}{4\pi\gamma} \iint\limits_{\sigma} (\Delta g + G_1) \frac{dS(\psi)}{d\psi} \begin{Bmatrix} \cos\alpha \\ \sin\alpha \end{Bmatrix} d\sigma - \frac{\Delta g}{\gamma} \begin{Bmatrix} \tan\beta_1 \\ \tan\beta_2 \end{Bmatrix},$$

(5.79)

where β_1 and β_2 are the terrain inclinations in north-south and east-west directions, respectively.

The principal terms in (5.77) through (5.79) correspond to the formulas of *Stokes* and *Vening Meinesz* (5.57)–(5.60). The correction G_1 and the additional term in (5.79) contain the influence of the features of the terrain (MORITZ 1968d). To ensure the convergence of the series expansion used in this derivation, extreme inclinations and singularities (mountain chains) need to be removed from the earth's surface; that is, the surface must be smoothed out. The solutions above are not subject to the density hypotheses of the geoid determination [5.2.4]. Since the earth's surface is not an equipotential surface, they are however considerably more complex than the solutions of the boundary-value problem for the geoid.

5.2.6 Physical Surface of the Earth and External Gravity Field

According to [5.1.1], the *spatial ellipsoidal coordinates* φ, λ, h of *points on the earth's surface* can be computed if we can determine either the geoid undulation N and the deflections of the vertical ξ_0, η_0 referred to the geoid, as in [5.2.4], or the height anomaly ζ and the deflections of the vertical ξ^N, η^N referred to the surface, as in [5.2.5].

The geoidal quantities, the astronomic latitude Φ and longitude Λ, and the orthometric height H together yield the following:

$$\varphi = \Phi + \delta\Phi - \xi_0, \qquad \lambda = \Lambda + \delta\Lambda - \eta_0 \sec \varphi, \qquad h = H + N. \qquad (5.80)$$

Φ and Λ observed on the earth's surface are reduced to the geoid with the aid of the curvature of the plumb line $\delta\Phi$, $\delta\Lambda$ (5.26).

The surface quantities combined with Φ, Λ and the normal height H^N give

$$\varphi = \Phi + \delta\varphi^N - \xi^N, \qquad \lambda = \Lambda - \eta^N \sec \varphi, \qquad h = H^N + \zeta. \qquad (5.81)$$

Here, the normal geographic latitude φ^N is transformed into the geodetic latitude φ using the normal curvature of the plumb line $\delta\varphi^N$ (5.3).

The errors ($\pm 0''5 \dots 1''$) of astronomical positioning and of gravimetric vertical deflections prohibit the use of (5.80), (5.81) for the determination of φ, λ, as $\pm 1''$ corresponds to a position error of ± 30 m. On the other hand, high-precision ($\pm 0.01 \dots 0.1$ m) geoid or quasigeoid heights (differences) allow the transformation of levelled heights H or H^N to ellipsoidal heights derived from *GPS* [4.4.7] or vice versa.

The *external gravity field* is determined, for example, by computing the disturbing potential T or the gravity anomaly Δg (free-air anomaly) in the space exterior to the earth. The subsequent transition to the gravity potential W and the gravity g requires the normal potential U and the normal gravity γ, respectively; these can be computed rigorously [3.5.2]. The *disturbing potential* at a point (r, ϑ, λ) in space is given by a generalization of *Stokes'* formula, derived by *Pizzetti*:

$$T_P = \frac{R}{4\pi} \iint_\sigma S(r, \psi) \Delta g \, d\sigma. \qquad (5.82)$$

Here,

$$S(r, \psi) = \frac{2R}{l} + \frac{R}{r_P} - \frac{3Rl}{r_P^2} - \frac{R^2}{r_P^2} \cos \psi \left(5 + 3 \ln \frac{r_P - R \cos \psi + l}{2r_P} \right) \qquad (5.83)$$

is the extended *Stokes'* function. In analogy to (5.59) and (5.60), we can obtain the separation N_P and the deflection of the vertical ξ_P, η_P from (5.82) at every point in the exterior space.

Since, according to (5.49), $r\Delta g$ is a harmonic function, the determination of the *gravity anomaly* Δg in space corresponds to the first boundary-value problem of potential theory (Dirichlet problem). The solution for a spherical approximation is given by *Poisson*'s integral:

$$\Delta g_P = \frac{R^2(r_P^2 - R^2)}{4\pi r_P} \int\!\!\!\int_\sigma \frac{\Delta g}{l^3}\, d\sigma. \qquad (5.84)$$

Hence, for a point P in space, T_P and Δg_P can be computed by integrating the gravity anomalies Δg given on the spherical bounding surface. Applying this to the physical surface of the earth, the influence of the topography again must be taken into account by additional terms.

To solve the integrals (5.82) and (5.84), mean values of the gravity anomalies Δg are formed over grid subdivisions or over sectors of concentric rings; the integration is replaced by a summation. In the computation of Δg, the influence of distant zones is small; it is generally sufficient to integrate up to a radius which is ten times the height of the computation point.

If it is supposed that the *physical surface of the earth* is *known* from geometric measurements (geometric methods of satellite geodesy [5.3.2], astrogeodetic measurements [5.1.2], and satellite altimetry [5.3.5]), then one can dispense with the telluroid [5.2.5] as an approximating surface. The geodetic boundary-value problem reduces to the task of determining the external gravity field from gravity anomalies on the earth's surface. This corresponds to the second (*Neumann*) boundary-value problem of potential theory (KOCH and POPE 1972), cf. [5.2.2].

5.2.7 Prediction of Gravity Anomalies

The solution of the geodetic boundary-value problem involves surface integrals which should extend over the entire surface of the earth. However, the gravity acceleration, and therefore, the gravity anomaly can only be determined for discrete points or in profiles (marine and airborne gravimetry), but not continuously over the surface.

This fact has been taken into account by a definition of the boundary-value problem given by BJERHAMMAR (1975). A solution is sought which corresponds to the discrete gravity anomalies given on the surface of the earth. Upon introducing a reference sphere entirely enclosed within the earth, an analytic downward continuation of the observed gravity anomalies Δg_P is carried out with the aid of *Poisson*'s integral (5.84), such that the *total* gravity information is contained in a limited number of "carrier points" on this sphere, the other points on the sphere having the gravity anomaly zero. Because there are only a finite number of observed points and "carrier points", (5.84) is converted to a matrix equation which after inversion yields the Δg at the "carrier points". The disturbing potential, the gravity anomaly, and the deflections of the vertical can then be determined at every point in the exterior space by using (5.82), (5.84), and the generalized formulas of (5.60). The observed anomalies are thus regained at the measured points; the gravity field between them is smoothed out.

Since parts of the earth's surface have not been surveyed gravimetrically, or only incompletely, unknown gravity anomalies must be estimated (predicted) in order to apply the integral formulas. For this purpose, suitable methods include, for example, interpolation with the aid of isoanomaly maps, representations of a certain area by the nearest measured value, and using the anomaly zero for an unsurveyed area (particularly suitable in the application of the isostatic anomalies whose values are irregularly scattered about zero). Optimum results and accuracy estimates are provided by least squares *prediction*. This process was thoroughly investigated by MORITZ (1970b); it can also be applied to data which are subject to errors.

The prediction is based on the uniform statistical behavior (homogeneity) of gravity anomalies, which is described by the *covariance function* $C(S)$ of Δg. $C(S)$ is the average product of the gravity anomalies Δg and $\Delta g'$ at a pair of points P and P'; it depends only on the distance S between these two points (isotropy):

$$C(S) = \text{cov}(\Delta g, \Delta g')_S = M\{\Delta g \Delta g'\}, \qquad S = \overline{PP'}. \qquad (5.85)$$

Here, M symbolizes the formation of the average over all pairs of points which are separated by a distance S. $C(S)$ characterizes the correlation of the gravity anomalies; $S = 0$ yields the variance

$$C(0) = \sigma^2(\Delta g) = M\{\Delta g^2\}. \qquad (5.86)$$

With increasing distance between the points, the correlation of Δg decreases; after a certain distance, $C(S)$ oscillates about zero.

In this analysis, the Δg-field is viewed as a stochastic process. Therefore, any systematic trend should be eliminated before considering the statistical treatment. For a global application, the mean value Δg_0 of Δg over the entire earth must equal zero, cf. [5.2.8].

The estimation of a global $C(S)$ for free-air anomalies was examined by KAULA (1959), as well as by TSCHERNING and RAPP (1974). When $S = 0$, then $\sigma^2(\Delta g) = (424\ \mu\text{ms}^{-2})^2$ for point anomalies, and

$$\sigma^2(\overline{\Delta g})_{1^\circ} = (303\ \mu\text{m}^{-2})^2$$

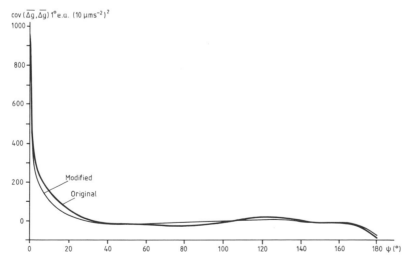

Fig. 5.17. Empirical covariance function of 1° equal area mean free-air anomalies, after TSCHERNING and RAPP (1974)

for mean $1°$-anomalies, the related empirical covariance function is shown in Fig. 5.17. It refers to $1°$-equal area anomalies (approximately quadratic compartments with constant area 110 km $\times$ 110 km). The prediction of point values is practical only for smaller, more densely surveyed areas. Mean anomalies (e.g. $5' \times 5'$, $30' \times 30'$, $1° \times 1°$) are usually predicted for regional and global investigations.

In the usual *linear prediction*, the gravity anomaly Δg at P is estimated by a linear function of the observed Δg at n points. If one designates the difference between the true value Δg and the predicted value $\widetilde{\Delta g}$ as the prediction error, then the requirement of a minimum error variance of the interpolated value leads to

$$\widetilde{\Delta g}_P = C_P^T \bar{C}^{-1} \Delta g. \qquad (5.87)$$

Here,

$$C_P = \begin{pmatrix} C_{P1} \\ \vdots \\ C_{Pn} \end{pmatrix}, \qquad \bar{C} = C + D, \qquad C = \begin{pmatrix} C_{11} & \cdots & C_{1n} \\ \vdots & & \vdots \\ C_{n1} & \cdots & C_{nn} \end{pmatrix}$$

$$D = \begin{pmatrix} D_{11} & \cdots & D_{1n} \\ \vdots & & \vdots \\ D_{n1} & \cdots & D_{nn} \end{pmatrix}, \qquad \Delta g = \begin{pmatrix} \Delta g_1 \\ \vdots \\ \Delta g_n \end{pmatrix},$$

where $C_{Pi} = M\{\Delta g_P \Delta g_i\}$ = crosscovariance of the gravity anomaly at P with the gravity anomaly at the observed point P_i,

$C_{ij} = M\{\Delta g_i \Delta g_j\}$ = autocovariance of the gravity anomalies at the observed points,

$D_{ij} = M\{n_i n_j\}$ = autocovariance of the observational errors n (noise).

For noiseless data, $D = O$.

The elements C_{Pi} and C_{ij} can be obtained for any station separation $\psi = S/R$ by the anomaly covariance function, yielding the covariances $\mathrm{cov}(\Delta g, \Delta g', \psi)$. The prediction results are relatively independent of the type of the covariance function, but realistic results can be expected only within the correlation length (station separation for which $\mathrm{cov}(\Delta g, \Delta g', \psi) = \frac{1}{2}\sigma^2(\Delta g)$).

5.2.8 Potential, Mass, and Position of the Gravimetric Reference Ellipsoid

In the solution of the geodetic boundary-value problem, the following assumptions were made:

1. The level ellipsoid and the geoid have the same *potential* $U_0 = W_0$. Then also $U_Q = W_P$ (5.39).

2. The level ellipsoid and the geoid have the same mass $M_{Ell} = M$, so that no zero-degree term T_0 appears in the spherical harmonic expansion of the disturbing potential (5.47).

3. The *center of the ellipsoid* and the *earth's center of mass* coincide, such that no first-degree Term T_1 enters in the expansion (5.47).

Since the spherical harmonic expansion for Δg (5.49) contains the factor $(l - 1)$, T_1 has no effect. The position of the ellipsoid can be selected arbitrarily without changing the gravity field. Hence, the center of the ellipsoid may be placed at the earth's center of mass ($=$ origin of the coordinate system). The gravimetric method thus yields results which refer to a *geocentrically positioned ellipsoid*.

If we admit the differences

$$\delta U = W_0 - U_0, \qquad \delta M = M - M_{Ell} \qquad (5.88)$$

in the spherical harmonic expansion for T and Δg, then the zero-degree term in Δg (5.54a) is given by

$$\Delta g_0 = -\frac{G}{R^2}\delta M + \frac{2}{R}\delta U. \qquad (5.89)$$

Stokes' formula (5.59), as well as the expansion (5.55b) are extended by the constant term

$$N_0 = \frac{G}{R\gamma}\delta M - \frac{1}{\gamma}\delta U. \qquad (5.90)$$

From potential theory, it is known that Δg_0 can be computed by integrating Δg over a unit sphere:

$$\Delta g_0 = \frac{1}{4\pi} \iint_\sigma \Delta g \, d\sigma. \qquad (5.91)$$

N_0 corresponds in a spherical approximation to a change in scale of the geoid, which can be determined by comparing a measured geoid distance s_0 with the corresponding computed (from ellipsoidal coordinates as obtained by the gravimetric method [5.2.6] or by satellite methods [5.3.1]) ellipsoid distance s_{Ell}:

$$N_0 = \frac{R}{s}(s_0 - s_{Ell}) - \frac{1}{s}\int_1^2 N' \, ds. \qquad (5.92)$$

The geoid undulations N' are obtained from *Stokes'* formula (5.59). δM and δU are computed from Δg_0 and N_0 according to (5.89) and (5.90).

With these results, the original reference ellipsoid $E(a, f, M_{Ell})$ can be transformed into the ellipsoid $E^*(a^*, f^*, M^*_{Ell})$, fulfilling the assumptions of equal mass and potential as the geoid (Fig. 5.18):

$$M^*_{Ell} = M_{Ell} + \delta M, \qquad U_0^* = U_0 + \delta U. \qquad (5.93)$$

The semimajor axis of this ellipsoid is given by

$$a^* = a + N_0. \qquad (5.94)$$

With $\gamma_0 \approx \gamma_a$, Δg_0 corresponds to a change in the equatorial gravity:

$$\gamma_a^* = \gamma_a + \Delta g_0. \qquad (5.95)$$

The geometric flattening f remains unchanged in this transition of ellipsoids. The ellipsoid E^* has the same volume as the geoid. Due to the incomplete coverage over the earth with gravity data, this method at present provides only uncertain results.

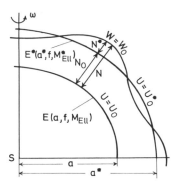

Fig. 5.18. Ellipsoid transformation in the gravimetric method

In case δM is determined from observations of space probes [5.4.6], then according to (5.89) and (5.90), one can dispense with the determination of either Δg_0 obtained from gravity measurements or N_0 from distance measurements.

5.3 Methods of Satellite Geodesy

The methods of satellite geodesy provide for the evaluation of observations to and from artifical earth satellites, as well as to the moon and to extragalactic radio sources [4.4]], (KAULA A1966, SCHNEIDER A1988, SEEBER A1989/1992).

5.3.1 Observation Equations

Satellite observations provide topocentric directions, ranges, and range differences to the satellite. The equation which relates the topocentric radius vector s of the satellite, is geocentric radius vector r, and the geocentric vector r_P of the station is (Fig. 5.19):

$$r_P + s - r = O. \tag{5.96}$$

Here, the topocenter and geocenter may not be equated as in the case of geodetic astronomy which dealt with observations of stars.

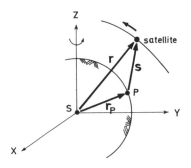

Fig. 5.19. Geocentric and topocentric position of the satellite

The observed vector s is formed by the spatial distance s [4.4.5] and the directions t_{Gr}, δ [4.4.4]:

$$s = se = s \begin{pmatrix} \cos \delta \cos t_{Gr} \\ \cos \delta \sin t_{Gr} \\ \sin \delta \end{pmatrix},$$ (5.97)

with the Greenwich hour angle

$$t_{Gr} = \alpha - \theta_0, \quad \theta_0 = \text{Greenwich sidereal time, cf. Fig. 4.34.}$$

The geocentric vector r is determined according to (4.73) by the orbital elements at epoch t_0, by the time t, and by the parameters of the terrestrial gravitational field:

$$r = r(a_0, e_0, \Omega_0, i_0, \omega_0, \overline{M}_0; t; GM, J_{lm}, K_{lm}).$$ (5.98)

The point of observation P and the satellite S have components

$$r_P = \begin{pmatrix} X_P \\ Y_P \\ Z_P \end{pmatrix}, \quad r = \begin{pmatrix} X_S \\ Y_S \\ Z_S \end{pmatrix}, \quad r - r_P = \begin{pmatrix} \Delta X \\ \Delta Y \\ \Delta Z \end{pmatrix}$$ (5.99)

in the earth-fixed system.

If we substitute (5.97) into (5.96), then for the directional vector (unit vector) we have

$$e = \frac{1}{s}(r - r_P).$$ (5.100)

Eliminating the distance s and using (5.99) yields the *directions*

$$t_{Gr} = \text{arc tan} \frac{\Delta Y}{\Delta X},$$ (5.101)

$$\delta = \text{arc tan} \frac{\Delta Z}{\sqrt{\Delta X^2 + \Delta Y^2}}.$$ (5.102)

For the *distance s*, we find that

$$s = \sqrt{\Delta X^2 + \Delta Y^2 + \Delta Z^2}.$$ (5.103)

Finally, the *difference in distances* to the satellite points S_1 and S_2 (4.77) is seen to be

$$s_2 - s_1 = \sqrt{(X_2 - X_P)^2 + (Y_2 - Y_P)^2 + (Z_2 - Z_P)^2} \\ - \sqrt{(X_1 - X_P)^2 + (Y_1 - Y_P)^2 + (Z_1 - Z_P)^2}.$$ (5.104)

The *observation equations* (5.101) through (5.104) provide the relationship between the observed quantities and the coordinates of the station and the satellite.

For the *adjustment*, the observation equations are linearized by a Taylor series expansion. The necessary approximate values are obtained from the geodetic coordinates of the stations, from the computed orbit of the satellite, and from previously determined values for the parameters of the gravitational field.

If the position of the satellite is represented by (5.98), then there are six unknown orbital parameters and an infinity (∞^2) of unknown harmonic coefficients. Additional parameters could possibly enter which describe other disturbing gravitational and nongravitational fields [4.4.2]. Even by necessarily limiting the spherical harmonic expansion of the gravitational field to a low degree, a complete determination of the many heterogeneous unknown quantities remains a problem. The solutions are more easily formulated, if a number of unknowns can be eliminated before the adjustment. The methods in [5.3.2] and [5.3.3] are based on this procedure.

The observation equation (5.103) also holds for *laser distance measurements to the moon* [4.4.5]. The coordinates of the moon are taken from the corresponding ephemeris (Astronomical Ephemeris); whereby, it is necessary to account for the distance between the reflector and the moon's center. Corrections must be introduced in the adjustment process for the parameters of the moon's orbit and for the physical librations (oscillations of the moon about its center of mass), STOLZ (1975).

5.3.2 Geometric Method

In the geometric method of satellite geodesy, the satellite is regarded as a high-flying and hence a far-reaching, visible target; the knowledge of its orbit is required only to locate the satellite. Observations to the satellite are carried out *simultaneously* at two or more stations. The unknown positions of the satellite may be eliminated in the observation equations (5.101)–(5.104); the only remaining parameters are the co-ordinates of the stations.

Since a large number of measurements generally exist for each pass of the satellite, it is appropriate to reduce them to a common epoch. In this way, a synchronization of the observations that were conducted at the various stations can be achieved. A *spatial smoothing* is made based on the fact that all measurements refer to the same orbital path. Here, the coordinates of the satellite for one passage are represented by series expansions as functions of time. For short arcs, the orbit can be considered as unchanging; the six orbital elements [4.4.1] of the satellite then enter as additional unknowns (short arc method), WOLF (1967a), SCHWARZ (1969).

Optimal solutions are obtained if simultaneous direction, range, and range difference measurements are involved in the construction of spatial *satellite networks* (CAMPBELL et al. 1973). The various observed quantities then complement each other.

Direction measurements provide the form of the network and combined with time measurements, they orient it in a geocentric global system (MORITZ 1970a). The spatial directions $e_{11}, e_{21}, e_{12}, e_{22}$ are determined from simultaneous measurements at P_1 and P_2 to the satellite positions S_1 and S_2 (Fig. 5.20). The point P in a network is then established by the directions to S_1 and S_2. The angles of intersection of the directions should not be too acute for a strong determination of the point.

The directions between the ground stations can then be derived from the directions to the satellite. The unit vectors $e_{11}, e_{21}, e_{12}, e_{22}$ span the planes $P_1 S_1 P_2$ and $P_1 S_2 P_2$, which are defined by their normal unit vectors

$$n_1 = \frac{e_{11} \times e_{21}}{|e_{11} \times e_{21}|}, \quad n_2 = \frac{e_{12} \times e_{22}}{|e_{12} \times e_{22}|}. \tag{5.105}$$

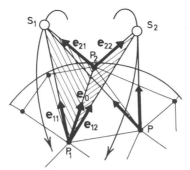

Fig. 5.20. Simultaneous direction measurements, satellite triangulation

The planes intersect in the line $P_1 P_2$ whose unit vector is

$$e_0 = \frac{n_1 \times n_2}{|n_1 \times n_2|}. \qquad (5.106)$$

By combining such spatial directions to obtain a *satellite triangulation* net, global or continental control networks have been constructed, in which the points are separated by 500 to 4000 km.

Range measurements to the satellite provide the scale of the spatial network. Simultaneous range measurements s_{11}, s_{21}, and s_{31} from three ground stations P_1, P_2, and P_3 determine the position of the satellite S_1 which is situated at the intersection of the three corresponding spheres (Fig. 5.21). The point P in such a range-network (*satellite trilateration*, BLAHA 1971) is determined by simultaneous measurements to the three satellite positions S_1, S_2, and S_3. To obtain favorable intersections, the satellite positions should not occupy the same orbital plane. The incorporation of ranges into

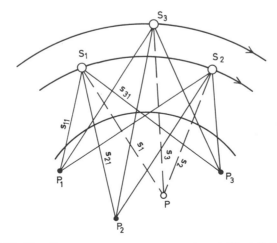

Fig. 5.21. Simultaneous range measurements, satellite trilateration

a satellite triangulation improves, in particular, the determination of heights of the ground stations.

The *spatial location* of the satellite network with respect to the earth's center of mass remains unknown in the geometric method. The *parallelism* of the network coordinate axes to the geocentric system is provided by the spatial direction measurements. If geocentric coordinates of one or more network stations are available from dynamic solutions (see below), or from absolute positioning employing the orbital method [5.3.4], the geometric system can be centered at the earth's center of mass.

Spatial triangulation originates with Y. VÄISÄLÄ (1946) who introduced *stellar triangulation* with the aid of high balloon targets. The *World Network of the National Geodetic Survey* in the U.S.A. came into existence through geometric stellar triangulation (Fig. 5.22). It contains 45 stations, any two from 4000 to 4500 km apart, and distributed over the earth's surface as evenly as possible. The observations were conducted from 1966 to 1970 with the Wild BC 4 cameras to the balloon satellite Pageos. The scale is obtained from seven 1200 to 3500 km long baselines which were measured in polygonal traverses with geodimeters and tellurometers. They are located in North America, Australia, Africa, and Europe. The mean scale uncertainty of the network amounts to $\pm 5 \times 10^{-7}$, the standard deviation of the coordinates is ± 4.5 m (SCHMID 1974). Continental densification nets (stations about 1000 km apart, denser in parts

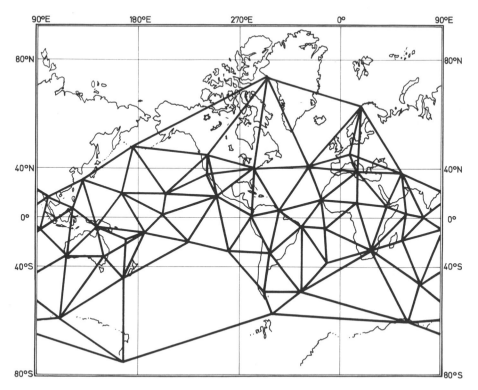

Fig. 5.22. Geometric global satellite network of the U.S. National Geodetic Survey, after SCHMID (1974)

of Europe) were constructed in North America and Europe. They are connected to each other by stations in Greenland and Iceland.

According to the *Secor-method* [4.4.4], the U.S. Army Map Service surveyed a network extending over the equatorial regions; due to insufficient directional control, the positional uncertainty of the approximately 40 stations is ± 25 to ± 30 m. The observation principle followed the scheme explained in Fig. 5.21.

A comprehensive *adjustment* (geometric method) of the direction and range (Secor) measurements of various organizations was instituted by the Department of Geodetic Science at the Ohio State University (OSU WN14). The standard deviation of the coordinates of the 158 stations was found to be ± 3.9 m (MUELLER 1974).

5.3.3 Dynamic Method, Harmonic Coefficients

In the dynamic method of satellite geodesy, the satellite is regarded as a sensor moving in the gravitational field of the earth. The observation equations then contain all the unknowns mentioned in [5.3.1]. We first concentrate on the *harmonic coefficients* describing the gravitational field of the earth, cf. [2.3.3]. Regarding their influence on a satellite orbit, it is appropriate to distinguish between secular, long-periodic, and short-periodic perturbations. The *zonal* parts of the gravitational potential cause primarily secular and long-periodic perturbations; whereas, the longitude dependent *tesseral* terms, in general, give rise only to short-periodic perturbations. If one integrates over one revolution U, then the perturbations varying with periods $U, 2U,$ ... are eliminated. Furthermore, for longer intervals of integration time, the influence of the *station coordinates* is so small that these may be introduced as known quantities.

In order to derive the relationship between the perturbations of the orbital elements and the *zonal* harmonic coefficients, we neglect the nonzonal terms in the spherical harmonic expansion of the perturbing potential R' (4.71). The integration of the equations of motion (4.72) over one revolution of the satellite yields the changes in the orbital elements as functions of the zonal harmonics. The principal terms of this expansion are given for the elements of interest Ω, ω, e, i by

$$\Delta\Omega = -3\pi\left(\frac{a_E}{\bar{p}}\right)^2 \cos i\, J_2 + \cdots$$

$$\Delta\omega = 6\pi\left(\frac{a_E}{\bar{p}}\right)^2 \left(1 - \frac{5}{4}\sin^2 i\right) J_2 + \cdots$$

$$\Delta e = -3\pi(1-e^2)\left(\frac{a_E}{\bar{p}}\right)^3 \left(1 - \frac{5}{4}\sin^2 i\right) \sin i \cos \omega\, J_3 + \cdots \tag{5.107}$$

$$\Delta i = 3\pi\left(\frac{a_E}{\bar{p}}\right)^2 \left(1 - \frac{5}{4}\sin^2 i\right) \cos i \cos \omega\, e\, J_3 + \cdots$$

with

$$\bar{p} = a(1-e^2).$$

Here, the semimajor axis of the ellipsoid is denoted by a_E in order to distinguish it from the semimajor axis of the satellite's orbit.

J_2 and the higher *even* zonal coefficients cause *secular perturbations* in Ω and ω. For $i < 90°$, Ω decreases in time (regression of the nodal line). The change in ω corresponds to a rotation of the orbital ellipse in the orbital plane (cf. Fig. 4.34). This rotation produces *long-periodic perturbations* in the quantities e, i, $\bar{p}$ because these contain ω. In this way, ω is related to the *odd* zonal coefficients. The even zonals can be determined from the perturbations in Ω and ω; while the odd zonals are obtained from the perturbations in i and e. The orbital perturbations for longer time intervals are computed by integrating (5.107), where the unit of time is one revolution of the satellite. If these perturbations are added to the orbital elements at the initial epoch, then one obtains the orbital elements at the desired time as functions of the zonal harmonics. Substitution into (5.96) then provides a system of equations for the determination of the zonal harmonics. The coefficients of the harmonics, according to (5.107), depend particularly on the orbital inclination i, and also on the eccentricity e and on the semimajor axis a. Therefore, in order to obtain independent equations, they must be used for satellites whose corresponding orbital elements i, e, and a are not the same.

Sources of error in the determination of the J_l arise from the choice of the maximum degree of the spherical harmonic expansion and because the orbital elements are not always sufficiently diverse. As a result of the mutual correlation among the J_l, the coefficients of higher degree are subject to change more significantly in the case of higher-order expansions.

The *tesseral* harmonics are responsible for small-amplitude (a few 100 m), short-periodic perturbations (period $\leqslant 1$ day, or $\leqslant 1$ revolution) in the orbital elements i, ω, Ω. Therefore, they can be determined only from sufficiently rapid, consecutive, and accurate observations of various satellites and at well distributed stations. Here, Doppler measurements are particularly suitable, being almost independent of the weather. In the analysis, the deviations of the *station coordinates* that are used from their actual geocentric coordinates must not be neglected; also, the other disturbing fields should be carefully eliminated. With equations (5.101) through (5.104), the results of the adjustment yield the geocentric coordinates of the tracking stations, the orbital elements at the initial epoch, and the harmonic coefficients.

In a first step, the geocentric gravitational constant GM [5.4.6] and the zonal harmonic coefficients may be taken as errorless quantities. In this way, GM and the mean angular velocity of the satellite, through (4.66), determine the semimajor axis of the orbital ellipse, and thereby, the scale of the system.

A few nonzonal terms of higher order can be determined with the aid of the phenomenon of *resonance*. Namely, if the ratio of the mean angular velocity of a satellite (4.66) to the rotational velocity of the earth is a whole number, then one can easily observe the resulting amplification due to resonance in the orbital perturbations.

With increasing efficiency of electronic computers, the computation of station coordinates, satellites' orbital parameters, and harmonic coefficients may be performed also in one adjustment.

Due to the "damping factor" $(a_e/r)^l$ in the potential expansion (2.51), the relative errors of the computed harmonic coefficients increase rapidly at higher degrees l. As a consequence, only the coefficients up to degree 20 (maximum 36) can be derived significantly from the analysis of satellite orbits, at heights >800 to 1000 km.

Global dynamic solutions (earth models) have been developed by the Smithsonian Astrophysical Observatory SAO (particularly optical direction and laser distance measurements), by the NASA — Goddard Space Flight Center GSFC (directions, as well as radar and laser distance measurements, SMITH et al. 1976), and by the French-German group GRGS/Toulouse-SFB78/Munich. Most of the more recent solutions incorporate also terrestrial gravity data and satellite altimetry, cf. [5.4.4].

Pure satellite solutions are the *Goddard Earth Models* Gem 9 ($\sim 20\%$ laser measurements, camera, radar, Doppler and laser data, $l, m = 20, 20$, geocentric coordinates of 150 stations, LERCH et al. 1979), and GEM-L2 (*Lerch* et al. 1985). The latter one includes the GEM9 data and about 440 000 laser distance measurements to the Lageos satellite, cf. [4.4.3]. The result includes a spherical harmonic model complete to degree and order 20 (see Table 5.2 for the numerical values of the low degree coefficients), the geocentric coordinates of about 120 tracking stations including about 20 Lageos observation sites (± 5 cm accuracy), and the value $GM = 398\,600.440 \times 10^9$ m^3 s^{-2}.

The estimated *errors* of the coefficients $\bar{C}_{lm}$, $\bar{S}_{lm}$ increase with increasing degree l, from the order of 10^{-10} to 10^{-9} for the zonal harmonics, and 10^{-9} to 10^{-8} for the tesseral harmonics. The long-wave geoid structures can be derived from GEM-L2 to an accuracy better than 0.1 m.

A 36, 36 (plus additional coefficients until degree 50) "satellite only" model is the GEM-T2 (MARSH et al. 1990a). It includes the parameters of 12 major tidal waves. The estimated error of the related (36, 36) geoid model is ± 1 m. One application of the model is to support the precise orbit determination (± 0.1 m) of the TOPEX-POSEIDON altimeter satellite, cf. [4.4.9].

Tab.5.2. GEM-L2 low order fully normalized [2.3.2] harmonic coefficients ($\times 10^6$), after LERCH et al. (1985).

Zonal Harmonics		Tesseral Harmonics			
l	$\bar{C}_l$	l	m	$\bar{C}_{lm}$	$\bar{S}_{lm}$
2	-484.165	2	1	-0.001	-0.003
			2	$+2.438$	-1.399
3	$+\ \ 0.958$	3	1	$+2.029$	$+0.250$
			2	$+0.904$	-0.616
			3	$+0.723$	$+1.415$
4	$+\ \ 0.541$	4	1	-0.535	-0.466
			2	$+0.355$	$+0.661$
			3	$+0.993$	-0.203
			4	-0.192	$+0.307$
5	$+\ \ 0.069$				
6	$-\ \ 0.151$				

For the Starlette satellite the "tailored" gravitational model PGS-1331 (36, 36) is available (MARSH et al. 1985).

Finally, we mention the *Deep Space Network* of the Jet Propulsion Laboratory. It consists of 8 globally distributed stations, which conduct Doppler measurements to space probes. From these observations, one can determine *GM* [5.4.4], the station's distance from the earth's rotational axis, and the difference in longitude between stations.

5.3.4 Orbital Method, Absolute and Relative Positioning

If the orbit of the satellite is known from continual orbit determinations, then the *geocentric coordinates* of an observer can be derived from observations at his station alone. The achievable positional accuracy is thereby limited by the accuracy of the computed orbit.

Already during the International Geophysical Year 1957/58, attempts were made to determine the geocentric coordinates of stations from optical-photographic *direction measurements* [4.4.4] to the moon, see Fig. 5.20. Due to the uncertainty in the coordinates of the moon and the reduction of the observed surface points to the moon's center, the accuracy that could be obtained in the coordinates was ± 50 m (MARKOWITZ 1958).

Presently the orbital method is extensively applied using satellite laser ranging, as well as microwave Doppler and distance measurements. We distinguish between absolute and relative positioning.

At *absolute positioning* the coordinates of the observation stations are directly derived from the satellite's ephemeris. Consequently they include the total amount of orbital errors and refraction uncertainties. *Relative positioning* is based on simultaneous measurements performed on two or more stations, to the same satellites. Orbital errors, including errors of the gravitational model, and refraction effects are correlated over distances of up to some 100 to 1000 km. Consequently they partly cancel in the coordinate differences of two stations which are observed simultaneously.

Long-arc orbit computations (up to 30 *d*) are needed for absolute positioning. Relative positioning requires *short-arc* computations (< 1 revolution), as simultaneous observations are difficult to assess for large station separations and for optical (laser) methods. An orbit improvement is then achieved by calculating corrections to the Keplerian elements, or by polynomial fitting.

Laser distance measurements [4.4.5] to the satellites Lageos and — to a lesser extent — Starlette [4.4.3] are used to observe global and regional networks established for geodynamic investigations, cf. [5.5.5]. "Tailored" gravitational models provide an orbital accuracy of "dm"-order of magnitude, cf. [5.3.3].

Most of these networks are related to the *NASA Crustal Dynamics Project*. About 20 permanent and some transportable laser systems participate in the observation of a global network, with stations distributed over the tectonic plates, Fig. 5.23. Mean geocentric station coordinates have been derived with an accuracy of ± 5 cm, from Lageos observation between 1976 and 1982 (TAPLEY et al. 1985). Short-arc techniques have been successfully applied at regional geodynamic networks, established in North America and Europe. At station separa-

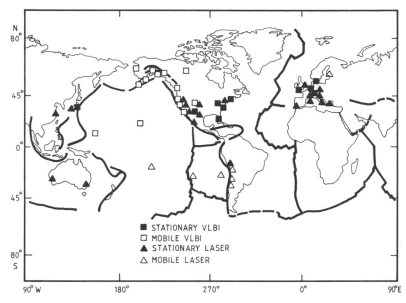

Fig. 5.23. Laser and VLBI stations in the NASA Crustal Dynamics Program, from SEEBER (A1989)

tions of some 100 to 1000 km, "cm"-accuracy has been achieved for Lageos orbits, and baselines have been derived with an accuracy of ± 2 cm.

The operational *navigation* and *positioning systems* Transit/NNSS [4.4.6] and *NAV-STAR/GPS* [4.4.7] are also based on the orbital method, for absolute and relative positioning. Tracking accuracy and gravitational models only allow orbital accuracies of $\pm$ few 10 m (broadcast ephemeris at Transit) and $\pm$ few m (GPS). Consequently, *absolute positioning* of single points cannot be improved beyond $\pm 3 \dots$ 5 m (reference system WGS72, SEPPELIN 1974), and $\pm 1 .. 2$ m (WGS84), resp., cf. [4.4.7]. This accuracy is reached in Doppler-positioning (broadcast ephemeris) by observing 30 to 50 satellite passes, corresponding to about one week of observations at middle latitudes. With GPS, real time positioning (*P*-code) gives ± 10m, and the few m accuracy is presently achieved after few days.

Geodetic applications generally make use of *relative positioning* in Transit-Doppler and in GPS surveys. The most simple case is the occupation of two stations with two receivers and simultaneous satellite observations (*translocation*). The derived coordinate differences describe the baseline vector between the stations. A network can thus be built up by combining single baseline vectors through an adjustment, taking their error variance-covariance matrices into account. If more than two receivers are available, simultaneous observations on several stations can be performed: *multi-station* concept. Optimization procedures may help to plan the network observation and evaluation in an effective manner (SNAY 1986). This includes the selection of geometrically favourable configurations, and the elimination of satellites with an elevation $< 10°$ over the horizon.

The multistation adjustment of a larger network, observed with several receivers over a sequence of subsequent observation periods, is characterized by a large amount of data and unknown parameters. This includes orbital corrections by applying short-arc methods (KOUBA 1983b). Sophisticated *software* packages are available for Doppler (e.g. BROWN 1976b) and for GPS networks (e.g. GURTNER et al. 1985, WÜBBENA et al. 1986, see also BEUTLER et al. 1988).

Transit-Doppler multistation solutions have given relative *accuracies* of $\pm 0.2 \ldots 0.5$ m, over distances of up to a few 100 km (60 to 80 accepted passes, broadcast ephemeris), SEEBER et al. (1982). *GPS-relative positioning* delivers *real-time accuracy* of ± 1 m (*P*-code), and $\pm$cm...dm-accuracy for distances of 10 km to 1000 km (carrier phase measurement), cf. [4.4.7], SEEBER (1987), SEEBER et al. (1987). As GPS derived ellipsoidal heights reach the accuracy of levelled heights at distances of some 10 km, the "cm-geoid" determination has become an actual problem, in order to combine these different heights, cf. [5.2.3], TORGE et al. (1989).

Doppler positioning has been, and is still applied for establishing, densifying, and controlling geodetic fundamental networks. GPS-techniques have rapidly entered into this application field in the last years, and have initiated a drastic change in geodetic strategies (TORGE 1988), cf. [6.1.1], [6.2.1].

5.3.5 Analysis of Satellite Altimetry

Satellite altimetry [4.4.9] provides the perpendicular distance h_a between the satellite and the instantaneous surface of the ocean (Fig. 4.45). This data can be analyzed for a geometric determination of *sea surface topography* and the *geoid* [3.3.3], as well as to obtain the details of the gravity field (ARNOLD 1974).

The following observation equation (ellipsoidal approximation) can be derived from Fig. 4.45 (GOPALAPILLAI 1974):

$$h_a = r - r_P + \frac{r_P}{8}\left(1 - \frac{r_P}{r}\right)e^4 \sin^2 2\varphi - (N + \delta h_i + \delta h_s). \tag{5.108}$$

In this equation, the geocentric distance r to the satellite is determined by tracking the satellite (computing its orbit). The distance r_P to the subsatellite point is given by (3.18) and (3.19), e is the first eccentricity (3.12), and δh_i denotes the difference between the instantaneous and the quasi-stationary sea surface [3.3.3]. This time-varying component of the sea surface topography is eliminated partly (oceanic waves) by the smoothing effect of the "footprint", representing the measurement "point", cf. [4.4.9]. Oceanic tides are reduced by applying tidal models, cf. [4.2.6]. Finally, long-term parts may be averaged out by introducing the mean values of repeated tracks. Equation (5.108) then furnishes the separation $(N + \delta h_s)$ between mean sea level and the ellipsoid. Isolating the geoid undulation N ($\leqslant 100$ m) from the quasi-stationary sea surface topography δh_s ($\leqslant 1 \ldots 2$ m) requires additional information, cf. also [5.4.4].

Global oceanographic *models* of the long-wave structure (wave-length >1000 km) of *sea surface topography* are available, with $\pm 0.1 \ldots 0.2$ m accuracy (LEVITUS 1982). Relative "cm" accuracy can be achieved in regional models.

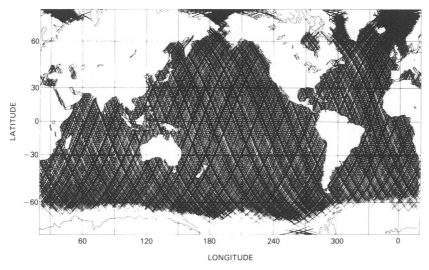

Fig. 5.24. SEASAT 18-day arc altimeter data distribution, from NASA Panel Report "Altimetric System", 1987

The satellite *altimeter missions* GEOS3 and SEASAT, cf. [4.4.9], have rendered high resolution determinations of the (quasistationary) sea surface topography for ocean regions between 72°N and 72°S latitude. Accuracies for one-second averages are ± 0.5m for GEOS3, and ± 0.1 m for SEASAT. The track separations vary between a few km (parts of GEOS3) and 100 km (SEASAT), and the along-track resolution is approx. 10 km, Fig. 5.24.

Main long-wave error source in SST- and related "altimeter-geoid" calculations is the satellite *orbit error*. It depends particularly on the *gravitational model* which is used to compute the orbit. An improved orbit determination is achieved by introducing "tailored" models, which are derived by especially including observations to the altimeter satellite. By this procedure, the orbital accuracy could be improved from ± 10 m to $\pm 1 \ldots 2$ m for GEOS3, and from ± 5 m to ± 1 m for SEASAT. Recent gravitational models allow to reduce the radial orbit error to the order of a decimeter, cf. [5.3.3].

Operational *tracking* of the altimeter satellites is performed by methods using radiowaves (e.g. Doppler measurements). The position accuracy of the tracking stations was in the few *m*-order for the GEOS-3- and SEASAT mission, and will be in the decimeter and subdecimeter order in the future, cf. [5.3.4]. Since residual orbital errors still by far exceed the altimeter measuring accuracy, non-dynamical methods are employed for further orbital improvement (SANDWELL et al. 1986). They use the *crossover discrepancies*, which are observed when the same ocean area is covered several times with altimeter profiles (MARSH et al. 1980). These discrepancies mainly reflect the vertical orbit errors and may be modelled by time or distance dependent polynomials, minimizing SST-differences at satellite ground track intersections in a crossover adjustment. In *regional* evaluations, profile shifts and tilts or low order areal polynomials already deliver a sufficient model approximation.

"*Altimeter geoids*" (containing the geoid and the quasistationary sea surface topography) have been derived from GEOS3 and SEASAT data on a global scope for $1° \times 1°$ and $0°\!.5 \times 0°\!.5$

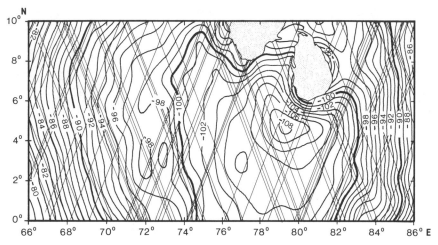

Fig. 5.25. SEASAT implied sea surface heights based on a $1° \times 1°$ data grid, contour line interval 1 m, after RAPP (1982b)

mean values, with accuracies of ± 1 m or better (MARSH et al. 1986), Fig. 5.25. On a regional scope, higher resolution (up to 20 km) and accuracies (± 0.1 m) can be achieved (BRENNECKE et al. 1982).

The long-wavelength (resolution 2000 km), circulation of the oceans has been modelled by spherical harmonics complete to degree and order 10 (precision ± 0.1 m), from SEASAT and GEOSAT altimetry in combination with satellite tracking data and surface gravimetry, cf. [5.4.4].

Employing the inverse of *Stokes'* formula (5.59), the geoid undulations N can be used to compute the *gravity anomalies* Δg (LELGEMANN 1976). In a spherical approximation (R = radius of the earth, γ_m = mean value of gravity), we have

$$\Delta g_P = -\frac{\gamma_m}{R} N_P - \frac{\gamma_m}{16\pi R} \iint_\sigma \frac{N - N_P}{\sin^3 \psi/2} d\sigma, \qquad (5.109)$$

where N is the geoid undulation at a particular surface element $d\sigma$ of the unit sphere σ, and ψ is the spherical distance between the computation point and $d\sigma$. The computational procedure in practice replaces the integration by a summation over finite compartments, cf. [5.2.3]. Due to the rapidly decreasing influence of the undulations with increasing ψ, the remote zones can be assigned approximate values for N, for example, those obtained from a global harmonic expansion [5.4.2].

In this way, mean $1° \times 1°$ free-air anomalies have been computed from GEOS3 and SEASAT data with accuracies of $\pm 50 \ldots 100$ μms^{-2} (RAPP 1986a). A set of $15' \times 15'$ point free-air anomalies was computed by BALMINO et al. (1987), taking the sea surface topography into account. By averaging numerous GEOSAT profiles, deflections of the vertical were derived with an accuracy of $\pm 0\overset{..}{.}2$, and an along track resolution of 12 km (SANDWELL and McADOO 1990).

These results, in turn, can be applied in the integral formulas of the gravimetric method [5.2.3].

5.4 Combined Methods of Evaluation

The classification of the geodetic methods of analysis into the astrogeodetic, gravimetric, and satellite methods is motivated by the observation techniques and the historical developments. The methods distinguish themselves according to their capabilities.

The *astrogeodetic methods* [5.1] provide spatial coordinates of surface points and the detailed structure of the continental vertical deflections and the geoid. The local accuracy is high; over larger distances, the accuracy is reduced by systematic influences affecting the orientation and scale. The systems refer to their respective geodetic datums; however, their axes are generally parallel to those of the geocentric system ($\pm 0.2'' \cdots \pm 1''$). The origin can deviate several 100 m from the earth's center of mass. The *gravimetric methods* [5.2] yield the external gravity field structures and the geoid, and coordinates referring to the center of mass, whereby the scale can be determined only approximately. Due to the insufficient knowledge of the details of the gravity field, the coordinates are subject to larger uncertainties. The *methods of satellite geodesy* [5.3] furnish the gravitational field and spatial coordinates in a geocentric system or in a system which is parallel to it. The gravitational field resolution is limited by the satellite's altitude to (at present) 500 to 1000 km.

In combining these methods, the information content of the data is more completely exploited, while systematic errors can be detected and eliminated. Combined solutions are obtained by collectively analyzing the heterogeneous data (a very large amount) or by combining the results gained through the various methods. The solutions can be limited to specific problems or they can attempt to optimally incorporate all data into a common model.

5.4.1 Astrogravimetric Leveling

Astrogravimetric leveling, developed by *Molodenski*, is a first attempt to combine the astrogeodetic and the gravimetric methods for a detailed determination of the geoid and the quasigeoid. It solves the problem of interpolating the deflections of the vertical [5.1.6] by incorporating gravimetric data (MOLODENSKII et al. A1962).

We start with the astronomically leveled *height anomalies* ζ (5.27), this time, using the surface deflections of the vertical ε^N, defined by Molodenski. If one combines (5.27) with the gravimetric deflections of the vertical (5.79) and restricts the area of integration B to approximately three times the distance between the points of the astrogeodetically determined deflections, then one obtains

$$\Delta \zeta_{12} = \zeta_2 - \zeta_1 = -\frac{\varepsilon_1^N + \varepsilon_2^N}{2} s + GK, \tag{5.110a}$$

where the gravimetric correction is

$$GK = \frac{R}{4\pi\gamma_m} \iint_B \Delta g' \bar{S}(\psi_1, \psi_2) dB \qquad (5.110\text{b})$$

and the Stokes' function is given by

$$\bar{S}(\psi_1, \psi_2) = \frac{2}{\psi_2} - \frac{2}{\psi_1} - \frac{s}{R}\left(\frac{\cos v_1}{\psi_1^2} + \frac{\cos v_2}{\psi_2^2}\right). \qquad (5.110\text{c})$$

Here, $\Delta g'$ is the free-air anomaly (5.74) modified by a terrain reduction (5.71); this quantity corresponds to the expression $\Delta g + G_1$ in (5.78). ψ_1 and ψ_2 are the angular distances from the surface element dB to the points P_1 and P_2 at which the deflections were obtained. The directions from P_1 and P_2 to dB reckoned from the line joining P_1 and P_2 are denoted by v_1 and v_2, respectively.

From (5.27) and (5.24), the difference in the *geoid undulations* is given by

$$\Delta N_{12} = N_2 - N_1 = \Delta\zeta_{12} + E_{12}^N - E_{12}, \qquad (5.111)$$

where E^N and E are the normal and orthometric corrections, respectively.

(5.110) and (5.111) permit the computation of $\Delta\zeta$ and ΔN from astrogeodetic deflections of the vertical at P_1 and P_2 and from gravity anomalies in the limited area B. The gravimetric correction GK accounts for the fact that the variation of the deflections of the vertical departs from linearity.

For irregularly varying deflections, the gravimetric correction can assume values that are larger than the "main term" in (5.110) and (5.111): 1 m for points 40 km apart. The accuracy of GK is determined by the free-air anomalies in the area B. In order to obtain centimeter to decimeter accuracy, gravimetric densification measurements are generally required. The difference $E^N - E$ in (5.111) attains only centimeter values.

5.4.2 Remove-Restore Methods in Gravity Field Determination

Integral formulas [5.1.6], [5.2.3], [5.2.5] and least squares collocation [5.4.3] are available for regional and local gravity field approximation, e.g. for geoid determination. Global spherical harmonic models are generally combined with regional terrestrial data, as gravity anomalies or vertical deflections. In high-resolution computations, the gravitational effect of the topography (provided by a digital terrain model and occasionally also density model) is also taken into account. A *remove-restore-technique* has been developed, based on model and topography reduced gravity field quantities (e.g. DENKER et al. 1986). For the disturbing potential T as the fundamental field quantity [5.2.1] this reads as

$$T_{red} = T - T_{Mod} - T_{Top}. \qquad (5.112)$$

Since all gravity field related data can be described as linear functionals L of T, the linearized observations l (e.g. gravity anomalies) are reduced correspondingly:

$$l(T_{red}) = l(T) - l(T_{Mod}) - l(T_{Top}). \qquad (5.113)$$

The linear relations between T and the most important field quantities vertical deflections, gravity anomalies, and geoid heights are given by (5.40), (5.44), and (5.55a).

By this procedure, the long-wave (e.g. up to 200 km wavelength for high-resolution global models) and the short-wave (e.g. with wavelengths 20 to 2 km or less) parts of the gravity field are removed from the data. The reduced gravity field has smaller values, and it is much smoother. After applying either integral formulas or least squares collocation on the reduced observations, the original field parameters have to be restored by restitution of the model and the topography part. The advantage of this technique is that only a limited data collection area is required for the evaluation, and that a statistical treatment of the residual field is facilitated. By relating all gravity field quantities to the basic quantity T, the combination of different data types is easily performed, see below and [5.4.3].

The method has been applied successfully with integral formulas and least squares collocation. *Integral formulas* in the original form require data of one type only, and presuppose a complete data coverage (interpolation problem). Main application are regional *geoid* (or quasi-geoid) computations, according to

$$N = N_{Mod} + N_{red}, \tag{5.114}$$

with, see (5.59),

$$N_{red} = \frac{R}{4\pi\gamma} \iint_{\Delta\sigma} (\Delta g - \Delta g_{Mod}) S(\psi) d\sigma. \tag{5.115}$$

The model parts Δg_{Mod} and N_{Mod} are obtained from a low order ($l_{max} = 20 \ldots 36$) spherical harmonic model, using (5.54a) and (5.55b). The integration area is determined by the admissible omission error, resulting from neglected gravity field parts $l > l_{max}$ (MARSH and VINCENT 1974).

A refined algorithm is provided by *least squares spectral combination* with optimum integral kernels (SJÖBERG 1979, WENZEL 1982). This method allows to combine also different types of data. It starts with a spectral decomposition of the disturbing potential parts coming from different data (global model, mean gravity anomalies of different block size etc.). The spectral components are then combined by a least squares adjustment, using spectral weights derived from error estimates of the data. Summing up the combined components finally yields the quantity searched for. The computation can be performed by closed integral formulas with optimum integral kernels. In contrast to the original Stokes or Vening-Meinesz functions, cf. [5.2.3], they are no longer infinite at the computation point, and they converge to zero more rapidly.

A very economic evaluation of the integral formulas is possible in the spectral domain, using *Fast Fourier Transform* (FFT) techniques (SIDERIS 1987). The convolution then becomes a simple multiplication, and the results are easily retransformed to the space domain by the inverse FFT. With high-resolution global models (up to $l_{max} = 360$), a planar approximation of the integral formulas is permitted. The terrestrial data must be gridded by interpolation, and the data collection area can be reduced remarkably. FFT-techniques also allow an efficient computation of the effects of the terrain on different gravity field quantities (SIDERIS 1990).

Some results of regional gravity field determinations with integral formulas using the procedures described above, are given in [5.2.3].

5.4.3 Least Squares Collocation

As KRARUP (1969) has shown, the prediction methods [5.2.7] may be used to compute any quantity of the earth's gravity field from arbitrary, measured quantities of this field. By combining the prediction with a determination of parameters through an adjustment, a very general method of least squares is devised which is designated *least squares collocation* (Lat.: collocare — to place together, combine), MORITZ (1975). The general form of the *observation equations* in the method of collocation is

$$l = AX + s + n. \tag{5.116}$$

Here, l is the vector of observations. It is composed of a systematic part AX ($X =$ vector of the parameters, $A =$ a given rectangular coefficient matrix, describing the linearized relations between observations and parameters) and two mutually independent random parts, s (signal vector, containing the residual gravity field quantities as gravity anomalies etc.) and n (vector of measuring errors, noise). Each of the random quantities s and n is supposed to have a mean value of zero; their statistical behavior is described by the covariance matrix C of the signal and the covariance matrix D of the noise. Due to the independence of s and n, we have

$$\bar{C} = C + D. \tag{5.117}$$

Collocation furnishes the parameters X (adjustment) by optimally removing the measuring errors (filtering), but in addition, allowing also for the computation of the signal s at the unsurveyed points (prediction). In applying the least squares condition of the adjustment procedure to both the signal quantities and the noise, the problem can be interpreted as an adjustment of condition equations with unknown parameters. The solution is given by

$$X = (A^T \bar{C}^{-1} A)^{-1} A^T \bar{C}^{-1} l, \quad \tilde{s}_P = C_P^T \bar{C}^{-1} (l - AX). \tag{5.118}$$

$\tilde{s}_P$ is the estimated component of the signal vector s at the point P.

In applications to global geodesy, the vector of observations l contains all measured quantities. Disregarding the noise, which can be added easily, these quantities may be decomposed into systematic and irregular parts. The systematic part AX comprises the parameters of the ellipsoidal reference system and the station coordinates. Other systematic effects, such as instrument constants and drift parameters can also be included in the model. The random part s contains the departures of the earth's gravity field from the ellipsoidal reference system; that is, the deflections of the vertical, the geoid undulations, the gravity anomalies, and the differences between the harmonic coefficients of the actual and normal gravity fields.

This model combines the determination of geometrical and physical parameters of the earth. All available observations are utilized, and the statistical properties of the gravity field are taken into account. This approach has been designated as "integrated geodesy" (EEG and KRARUP 1973). Observation equations for this model have been derived and linearized for adjustment computations (HEIN 1983, 1986).

The covariance matrix $\bar{C}$ (5.117) is required in order to derive the parameters of the figure of the earth X from (5.116), as well as the quantities s which characterize the anomalous gravity field. The error covariance matrix D is obtained from a priori estimates of the accuracies and correlations of the observations. Since all signal quantities refer to the same gravity field, the signal covariance matrix C must be derived from a fundamental function through propagation of covariances. For example, this function can be the covariance function $C(\psi)$ of the gravity anomalies (5.85), ψ = spherical distance on the unit sphere. A corresponding global approximation is available with the anomaly degree variance model of TSCHERNING and RAPP (1974):

$$
\sigma_l^2(\Delta g) = \begin{cases} 0 & \text{for } l = 0, 1 \\ 754 & \text{for } l = 2 \\ \dfrac{42528(l - 1)}{(l - 2)(l + 24)} 0.999\,617^{(l + 2)} & \text{for } l \geqslant 3 \end{cases} \quad (\mu\text{ms}^{-2})^2. \quad (5.119a)
$$

The relation (spherical approximation on the earth's surface) between the anomaly degree variance

$$
\sigma_l^2(\Delta g) = M\{\Delta g_l^2\} \tag{5.119b}
$$

and the covariance function $C(\psi)$ is given by the spherical harmonic expansion

$$
C(\psi) = \text{cov}(\Delta g, \Delta g') = \sum_{l=2}^{\infty} \sigma_l^2(\Delta g) P_l(\cos \psi). \tag{5.120}
$$

In regional applications, $C(\psi)$ has to be fitted to the gravity field structure in the area. This is mainly done by reducing the variance of the gravity signal (GOAD et al. 1984).

The propagation of covariances corresponds to the error propagation in integral transformations, e.g. as it is represented by the Stokes' formula. In order to derive the covariances between the basic quantity T and other gravity field quantities, the same linear functionals have to be applied to the covariances which exist between T and those quantities, e.g. (5.40), (5.44), and (5.55a).

For a set of given observations, the results of collocation possess the highest attainable accuracy. The main problem in practical applications is the inversion of the sizable matrix $\bar{C}$. Therefore, this process has been used only for selected data sets and/or in limited areas (TSCHERNING and FORSBERG 1986). In addition, the determination of the parameters X is generally excluded. Equation (5.116) then furnishes optimum estimates of the gravity field quantities (MORITZ 1970b). The global model and the topography part are generally reduced from the data, in order to facilitate numerical calculations, cf. [5.4.2]. The advantage lies in the combination of all (heterogeneous) observations, where these can be processed as discrete values and need not exist continuously as for the integral formulas of the gravimetric method. For homogeneous and continuously distributed observations, collocation is transformed into the integral formulas [5.2.3] (MORITZ 1976). The prediction of gravity anomalies (5.87), in turn, represents a special case here; the observation vector l contains the "measured" gravity anomalies $\Delta g'$, and the signal s_P is the gravity anomaly Δg_P at an unsurveyed point.

Recent investigations (DENKER 1988) have shown that presently available computer facilities allow collocation to be applied to sets of 3000 to 4000 observations. This permits the computation of the geoid or quasigeoid from point anomalies with a few km average distance, in blocks of 100 km × 100 km extension. If a high-resolution global model ($l_{max} = 360$) is used, point

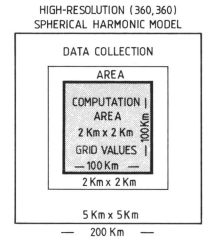

Fig. 5.26. Data collection scheme for geoid calculation by least squares collocation, after DENKER (1988)

data outside the computation area have to be collected only in a limited range (e.g. 100 km) in order to provide a satisfying overlap of adjacent blocks, Fig. 5.26.

5.4.4 Earth Models (Gravity Field and Geocentric Coordinates)

The results of terrestrial gravimetry and satellite geodesy are generally combined to determine the geocentric coordinates of the satellite observation sites, and the coefficients of the spherical harmonic expansion of the earth's gravitational field: *earth models*. The satellite observations yield station coordinates and the lower degree harmonics, while the terrestrial data and satellite altimetry provide the details of the gravity field. The solutions may be restricted to the harmonic expansion of the gravitational field: *geopotential models*. The following global *data sets* are available (1989):

— observations to artificial satellites: approx. 150000 optical directions [4.4.4], 1/2 mill. Doppler measurements [4.4.6], and more than 2 mill. laser distance measurements [4.4.5],
— mean $1° \times 1°$ free-air anomalies (about 35 000 values) and mean $30' \times 30'$ anomalies for some regions, cf. [5.3.2].
— mean $1° \times 1°$ and $30' \times 30'$ altimeter geoid heights from GEOS-3 and SEASAT data, cf. [5.3.5].

Recent *global earth models* are derived through the dynamical method of satellite geodesy [5.3.3], combining the satellite results with the other data sets in a least squares adjustment. A number of earth models has been computed since the 1960s. The more recent models consist of the geocentric coordinates of the tracking stations (100 to 200 stations, or more), a set of harmonic coefficients (currently complete up to about $l, m = 20, 20$ or $36, 36$, plus higher zonal and resonant harmonics), and the parameters of the level ellipsoid which best approximates the geoid [5.4.5]. The uncertainty in the station coordinates varies between ± 5 to ± 10 m (camera stations), ± 2 to ± 4 m (first generation laser stations), and ± 1 to ± 2 m (Doppler stations). The inclusion of third generation laser distance measurements reduces the standard deviations to $\pm$ a few cm. The harmonic coefficients up to $l = 8 \dots 12$ are determined by satellite data; beyond this, altimetric and gravimetric data affect and finally dominate the solutions. The resolution of the gravity field for the above mentioned expansions is 1000 km and 550 km, respectively. The corresponding long-wavelength features of the geoid are ascertained to about $\pm 1 \dots 2$ m, and $\pm$ a few 10 μms^{-2} for the gravity anomalies. The effect of the neglected higher order terms ($l > 36$) amounts to ± 2 m, and ± 350 μm^{-2}, respectively. Discrepancies among the various solutions may reach 2 or 3 times the uncertainties cited above. The low degree geoid structures (up to $l = 4$) agree within ± 0.2 m.

Earth models have been computed by the Smithsonian Astrophysical Observatory until the 1970's (SAO Standard Earths SE), by the NASA Goddard Space Flight Center (Goddard Earth Models GEM), and by the Groupe de Recherches de Géodésie Spatiale, France/SFB 78 TU München and DGFI I, F.R.G. (GRIM gravity models).

"Satellite only" models only use observations to satellites. We mention the SAO-SE III (90 stations, $l, m = 18, 18$, GAPOSCHKIN 1973), the GEM 9 (150 stations, $l, m = 20, 20$, LERCH et al. 1979) and the Lageos-dominated GEM-L2 (173 stations, $l, m = 20, 20$, 5d average earth rotation parameters) as well as the GEM-T2 ($l, m = 36,36$ and higher terms), cf. [5.3.3]. Among the models which combine satellite data with gravimetric and altimetric mean values are the GEM 10B ($l, m = 36, 36$, LERCH et al. 1981) and the GRIM3-L1 (includes Lageos data, 109 stations, $l, m = 36, 36$, REIGBER et al. 1985). The GRIM-4 model includes a 40, 40 gravitational field model plus additional terms up to degree 50, 13 oceanic tidal waves, coordinates for 217 tracking stations, and horizontal velocities for 14 laser stations, REIGBER et al. (1990).

Finally, the WGS72 and WGS84 reference systems have to be mentioned, which are used for the NNSS/Transit- and the NAVSTAR/GPS-Navigation, cf. [4.4.7].

The long-wave structures of the free-air anomaly field and the geoid, as derived from recent earth models, are shown in Fig. 5.27 and Fig. 5.28. The principal features of the geoid are the maxima near New Guinea ($+ 75$ m), in the North Atlantic, in the southwestern Indian Ocean, and in the Andes; as well as the minima to the south of India ($- 105$ m), in Antarctica, to the west of California, and near Puerto Rico.

Geopotential models of higher degrees (presently up to degree and order 360) have been derived by least squares adjustment of gravity field data or by their integration over the earth (RAPP 1986b).

In the *least squares adjustment*, the harmonic coefficients obtained from an earth model with low-order expansion of the gravity field (see above) are introduced as "observed" parameters with their variances, and combined with the $1° \times 1°$ or $30' \times 30'$ mean values of gravity anomalies $\Delta\bar{g}$ and altimetric geoid heights $\bar{N}$. Equations (5.54a) and (5.55b) then serve as observation equations for $\Delta\bar{g}$ and $\bar{N}$, with error estimates taken from separate investigations of the data sets. In the *integral method*, the harmonic coefficients are derived by integration of gravity anomalies over the earth's surface, following (5.54b). This method requires less computational effort

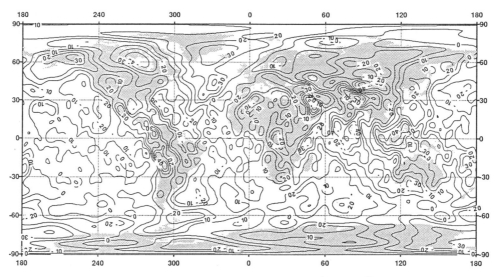

Fig. 5.27. Free-air anomalies, GRIM4-S1 gravity model, reference ellipsoid $a = 6378\,136$ m, $f = 1:298.257$, $GM = 398\,600.440 \times 10^9$ m^3 s^{-2}, contour line interval 10 mgal ($= 100\ \mu\mathrm{m}^{-2}$), from REIGBER et al. (1990)

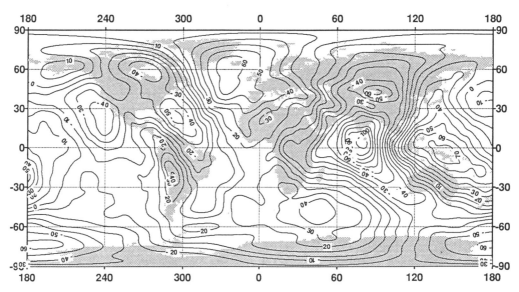

Fig. 5.28. Geoid heights, GRIM4-S1 gravity model, reference ellipsoid $a = 6378\,136$ m, $f = 1:298.257$, $GM = 398\,600.440 \times 10^9$ m s^{-2}, contour line interval 10 m, from REIGBER et al. (1990)

than the adjustment. However, homogeneous and globally complete data sets are required, so that a preprocessing becomes necessary. This includes gravity field transformations, e.g. from altimetric geoid heights to gravity anomalies according to (5.109), and interpolations for areas not covered by data, cf. [5.2.7].

An example for a least squares adjustment solution is the *geopotential model GPM-2* (WENZEL 1985) which is complete through $l_{max} = 200$. It includes the harmonic coefficients of the model GEM-L2 [5.3.3], which have been processed together with $1° \times 1°$ mean free-air anomalies, and $1° \times 1°$ mean altimetric geoid heights. The sea surface topography has been taken into account by employing the model of LEVITUS (1982). The accuracy of the results is estimated to ± 0.52 m (height anomalies), ± 298 μms^{-2} (gravity anomalies), and $\pm 4''4$ (vertical deflections). These values include the omission errors ± 0.42 m, ± 290 μms^{-2}, and $\pm 4''3$ resp., resulting from wave-lengths < 200 km ($\hat{=} l > 200$).

Among the models computed by the integral method are the OSU 89 A/B (Ohio State University) models (RAPP and PAVLIS 1990). They are complete to degree and order 360, and combine the model GEM-T2 with terrestrial $1° \times 1°$ and $30' \times 30'$ gravity anomalies, and with $30' \times 30'$ anomalies derived from satellite altimetry in oceanic areas.

Tailored geopotential models have been developed in order to better approximate the gravity field of *regional* extension (WEBER and ZOMORRODIAN 1988, KEARSLEY and FORSBERG 1990). A global high resolution expansion is used as starting model, and higher order coefficients (e.g. from $l = 60$) are modified so that regional data (mean gravity anomalies) are better reproduced. Regionally tailored models especially serve to support local gravity field approximations [5.4.2], [5.4.3]. As they remove significant parts of the regional field, data collection for integral formulas or least squares collocation may be limited to the computation area and a narrow zone (a few 100 km) around it. For Europe and her surroundings, tailored (360, 360) models have been developed, based on the global models GPM2 and OSU 86F, and adapted to the $12' \times 20'$ and $0°.5 \times 0°.5$ mean gravity anomalies in this area (BAŠIČ 1989). These models deliver "dm"-accuracy for the geoid over some 100 to 1000 km, cf. [6.2.4].

Successful attempts have been made to model the gravitational field and sea surface topography (SST), in combined solutions incorporating satellite altimetry (SEASAT, GEOSAT), surface gravimetry, and satellite tracking data, cf. [5.3.5]. A priori information about the gravity field (long-wave "satellite only" model) and SST (oceanographic information) were taken into account, and the satellite orbit parameters obtained corrections. Gravitational models thus derived are complete up to degree and order 50 (± 0.2 m on the oceans, MARSH et al. 1990), and SST models are complete to 10, 10 (± 0.1 m). The radial orbit error could be reduced to ± 0.2 m (see also DENKER and RAPP 1990).

If high resolution is to be obtained from the spherical harmonic expansion, then the terms of this expansion must be carried to a large degree. The great number of coefficients to be determined then leads to severe computational problems. They may be solved by special normal equation matrix arrangements and iterative procedures (WENZEL 1985).

Other representations of the gravitational potential have been also investigated. Among them are those using density value of a simple surface layer (simple density layer), KOCH (1968), cf. [5.2.5], or the ones which use discrete mass points to represent the field sources (BALMINO 1974). The advantage of these methods resides in the fact that the gravity potential at a point is determined mainly by the surface density or the mass near that point; the effect of more distant areas remains small. In applications, these representations are appropriately combined with low-degree harmonic expansions (MORRISON 1971).

As these representations are based on unrealistic mass distributions, and as computing facilities have developed rapidly, spherical harmonic expansions are nearly exclusively used today.

5.4.5 Centering and Strengthening Astrogeodetic Systems

Astrogeodetic systems (or others not oriented geocentrically) are transformed, in the most general case, to the global X,Y,Z-system by three translations, three rotations, and a change in scale (Fig. 5.29); WOLF (1963c), cf. [5.1.7]:

$$r = r_0 + (1 + m)Rr'. \tag{5.121a}$$

In this equation, $r^T = (X, Y, Z)$ is the geocentric position vector of P, $r_0^T = (X_0, Y_0, Z_0)$ contains the geocentric coordinates of the origin of the x,y,z-system, and corresponds to a translation of that system in space (datum shift). $r'^T = (x, y, z)$ is the position vector of P in the nongeocentric x,y,z-system, and m is the scale correction. The elements of the rotation matrix R are the independent Eulerian angles ε_x, ε_y, ε_z representing rotations about the x,y,z-axes. For small rotations, this matrix is given by

$$R = \begin{pmatrix} 1 & \varepsilon_z & -\varepsilon_y \\ -\varepsilon_z & 1 & \varepsilon_x \\ \varepsilon_y & -\varepsilon_x & 1 \end{pmatrix}. \tag{5.121b}$$

In order to apply (5.121) the geodetic coordinates φ, λ, h are converted into the Cartesian system using (3.34). The transformation parameters are then computed with the aid of at least three points whose coordinates are available in both systems.

Satellite geodesy provides geocentric coordinates with high accuracy.

The gravimetric method can also deliver geocentric coordinates, cf. (5.80) and (5.81). Due to the stringent requirements with respect to the gravity coverage of the earth

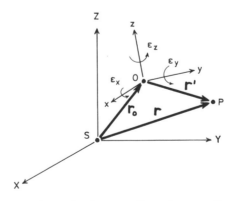

Fig. 5.29. Transformation between Cartesian coordinate systems

it was not possible to develop a corresponding gravimetric world geodetic system as proposed by HEISKANEN (1951).

In the case of the newer global earth models [5.4.4], the translations (and to some extent, also the rotations and scale changes) of the more important *astrogeodetic systems* were determined with the help of a number (up to 100) of satellite control points. Table 5.3 contains the parameters of some of these systems, cf. [5.1.4]:

Tab. 5.3. Datum Transformation Parameters (7 Parameter Solution) of Several Astrogeodetic Systems, Referring to the Geocentric System WGS84, cf. [4.4.7], after DMA (1987)

Geodetic Datum	Translations (m)			Rotations (″)			Scale Corr.
	X_0	Y_0	Z_0	ε_x	ε_y	ε_z	$m \times 10^6$
Australian 1966	−127	−50	153	0.0	0.0	−0.2	1.2
European 1950	−102	−102	−129	0.4	−0.2	0.4	2.5
North American 1927	−4	166	183	−0.3	0.3	−0.1	0.4
South American 1969	−56	−3	−38	0.1	−0.6	−0.2	−0.6

The uncertainty in these values is approx. ± 5 m for the translations. In most cases, the rotation angles and the scale corrections are statistically not significant. More accurate values and regional parameter variations due to network inhomogeneity may be obtained for limited regions, within the scope of special measurement projects, cf. [6.1.3], [6.1.8].

Differential relations are needed for adjustment computations. Of primary interest are the changes in the geodetic coordinates φ, λ, h resulting from translation, rotation, and scale change, as well as from changes in the ellipsoidal parameters (transformation of geodetic datums [5.1.2]). We introduce (3.34) into (5.121) and differentiate; then the required relationships are obtained by setting $dr = 0$, approximating with small variations δ, and solving for the coordinate changes (MERRY and VANIČEK 1974, TORGE 1980b). For a spherical approximation and with the neglect of rotations and scale changes, they are given by

$$\left.\begin{aligned}
a\,\delta\varphi &= \sin\varphi\cos\lambda\,\delta X_0 + \sin\varphi\sin\lambda\,\delta Y_0 - \cos\varphi\,\delta Z_0 + 2a\sin\varphi\cos\varphi\,\delta f \\
a\cos\varphi\,\delta\lambda &= \sin\lambda\,\delta X_0 - \cos\lambda\,\delta Y_0 \\
\delta h &= -\cos\varphi\cos\lambda\,\delta X_0 - \cos\varphi\sin\lambda\,\delta Y_0 - \sin\varphi\,\delta Z_0 - \delta a + a\sin^2\varphi\,\delta f.
\end{aligned}\right\}$$
(5.122a)

The changes in the deflection of the vertical $\delta\xi$, $\delta\eta$ and in the geoid undulation δN are computed from (5.122a) and the relations

$$\delta\xi = -\delta\varphi, \quad \delta\eta = -\cos\varphi\,\delta\lambda, \quad \delta N = \delta h,$$
(5.122b)

which follow from (5.1) and (5.5). Equations (5.122) are suitable for datum transformations when δr_0 is known. In particular, they can be used to determine the changes in the origin point P_1 of the geodetic system. Finally, by applying (5.122) also to the point P_1 and eliminating δr_0, one obtains the equations of *Vening Meinesz* (5.30).

Besides for the purposes of centering, the geocentric coordinates are also useful in *strengthening* the astrogeodetic systems. The terrestrial data on their behalf may stabilize the satellite networks. In a combined adjustment, the systematic effects, such as scale and orientation errors, as well as deformations (horizontal refraction) in the terrestrial network can be detected and taken into account together with eventual systematic errors of the satellite networks (WOLF 1980). The distance between the incorporated satellite network points should be proportioned such that the errors of the terrestrial and satellite methods are approximately of equal size. By uniting the terrestrial and satellite networks, one can either adjust each individually and determine a transformation by imposing a least squares condition on the common points; cf. [6.1.7]; or one can perform a general, rigorous adjustment. In the first case, the internal structures of the two systems are retained; while in the second case, undetected systematic errors can lead to network distortions (WOLF 1967b, KRAKIWSKY and THOMSON 1974).

5.4.6 Optimal Earth Parameters

Optimal earth parameters are based on the evaluation of all data available at a particular epoch. They serve for defining the *mean earth ellipsoid* being an optimal approximation to the geoid; the four parameters of the level ellipsoid [3.5.2] must be established accordingly. We distinguish between the physical and geometric determinations.

In the *physical definition*, the mass M_{Ell}, the gravity potential U_0, the dynamic form factor $J_{2(Ell)}$, and the rotational velocity ω_{Ell} are given the values which correspond to the earth (W_0 = value of the geoid potential):

$$M_{Ell} = M, \quad U_0 = W_0, \quad J_{2(Ell)} = J_2, \quad \omega_{Ell} = \omega. \tag{5.123}$$

All other ellipsoidal quantities are then known. From (3.49), (3.50), M and U_0 determine the semimajor axis a and the equatorial gravity γ_a.

The equally valid *geometric definition* is based on conditions giving the minimum of the squared geoid undulations N, the deflections of the vertical ξ, η, or the gravity anomalies Δg:

$$\iint_\sigma N^2 \, d\sigma = \text{min.}, \quad \iint_\sigma (\xi^2 + \eta^2) \, d\sigma = \text{min.}, \quad \iint_\sigma \Delta g^2 \, d\sigma = \text{min.} \tag{5.124}$$

N, ξ, η, Δg can be formulated as functions of the ellipsoidal parameters (HEISKANEN and MORITZ A1967, pp. 216–217).

Various methods are applied for the determination of the parameters. The geocentric gravitational constant GM is derived according to Kepler's third law and from observations of distant satellites (especially Lageos) and space probes, as well as from laser distance measurements to the moon [4.4.5]. The semimajor axis a can be determined, after the astrogeodetic systems are centered [5.4.5], from a condition of minimum geoid undulations. Most recently it has been obtained from an optimal fit between the ellipsoidal and orthometric heights at satellite tracking stations in a global solution [5.4.4], as well as by adjusting an ellipsoid to the satellite-altimetry results [5.3.5]. J_2 is derived mainly from satellite observations [5.3.3]. The computation of Earth models [5.4.4] in many cases includes the derivation of GM, a, and J_2. Methods in astronomy provide ω with high accuracy.

Recent *representative values* for the fundamental earth parameters are (CHOVITZ 1988):

$$GM = (398\ 600.440 \pm 0.003) \times 10^9 \text{ m}^3 \text{ s}^{-2}$$

(includes the atmospheric contribution),

$$a = 6378\ 136 \pm 1 \text{ m},$$

$$J_2 = (1082.626 \pm 0.002) \times 10^{-6}$$

$$\omega = 7.292\ 115 \times 10^{-5} \text{ rad s}^{-1}.$$

Time variations of these parameters are as follows: There is no real evidence for $\dot{G} \neq 0$, and $\dot{a} \neq 0$. Consequently GM and a can be assumed to be constant with time. A temporal change of J_2 was derived from satellite orbital analysis, with

$$\dot{J}_2 = (-2.8 \pm 0.3) \times 10^{-11}/a$$

as representative value, cf. [5.5.5].

Periodic variations of ω do not exceed the order of 10^{-12} rad s^{-1}, and are monitored by the International Earth Rotation Service. A secular variation of

$$\dot{\omega} = (-4.6 \pm 0.4) \times 10^{-22} \text{ rad s}^{-2}$$

has been found from astronomical data and the analysis of lunar laser ranging. It may be decomposed into a tidal deceleration (-6.0×10^{-22} rad s^{-2}), and an acceleration ($+1.4 \times 10^{-22}$ rad s^{-2}) reflecting a postglacial backsurge in the earth's mantle, cf. also [4.1.3].

5.5 Structure and Dynamics of the Earth's Body

The geosciences which include geology, geophysics, petrology, mineralogy, geochemistry, and geodesy deal with the investigations of the body of the earth. The results of geodesy (the figure of the earth and the external gravity field including their variations in time [1.2]) represent boundary conditions which must be considered when forming earth models. Also, the concepts acquired by the geosciences in regard to the structure and dynamics of the earth's body are significant in the formulation and implementation of geodetic studies.

From the geophysical literature we quote the works of BOTT (A1982), JEFFREYS (A1970), and STACEY (A1977). The interrelations between geodesy and other geosciences are treated in HEISKANEN and VENING MEINESZ (1958), LAMBECK (A1988), and MORITZ (A1990), see also MUELLER and ZERBINI (A1989).

5.5.1 The Radial Structure of the Earth

The results of various observations show that the earth does not possess a homogeneous structure.

By considering the mean density of the earth and the principal moment of inertia with respect to the rotational axis, it can be concluded that the *density increases towards the center of the earth*. The mass of the earth, obtained from GM [5.4.6] and the gravitational constant G [2.1.1], is $M = 5.974 \times 10^{24}$ kg. With the volume of the earth ellipsoid, $V = 1083 \times 10^{18}$ m^3, the *mean density* is given by

$$\rho_m = (5.515 \pm 0.001) \times 10^3 \text{ kg m}^{-3}.$$

The mean density of the crust of the earth amounts to only 2.8×10^3 kg m^{-3} [5.5.3], so that the density must increase toward the interior of the earth. Satellite observations yield the "dynamic form factor" $J_2 = (C - \bar{A})/a^2 M$ [2.3.4], where $\bar{A}$ is the mean equatorial principal moment of inertia. Astronomic observations have given a value of $1:305.44$ to the dynamical (mechanical) ellipticity

$$H = \frac{C - \bar{A}}{C}. \tag{5.125}$$

From this, the *principal moment of inertia* with respect to the *rotational axis* is computed:

$$C = 0.3307 \, a^2 \, M.$$

For a homogeneous spherical earth with radius R, we have $C = 0.4 \, R^2 \, M$; this again indicates an increase of density with depth.

As shown in *seismology*, the body of the earth has a *shell-like* construction. The shell boundaries are formed by the surfaces of discontinuity of elastic waves. *Global density models* are based on this layered structure and assume a spherically symmetric density distribution (BULLEN A1975, DZIEWONSKI and ANDERSON 1981). The density $\rho = \rho(r)$ is a function of the radial distance r from the earth's center of mass only. It can be computed under the assumption of a hydrostatic equilibrium [5.5.2] and with given boundary values. In these models, the earth's body is composed of the crust, the upper mantle (lower boundary at 650 km depth), the lower mantle (2900 km), the fluid outer core (5150 km), and the solid inner core. Departures from a centrally symmetric structure exist particularly in the crust and upper mantle, cf. [5.5.3].

Global earth models include a radial distribution of *elasticity* parameters. Hence, it is also possible to verify them by comparing the observed *tidal parameters* or *Love numbers* [2.4.2] with the corresponding model values. For the diurnal tide 01, earth tide observations [4.2.6] yielded the global mean values

$$\delta = 1.162, \quad \gamma = 0.679$$

for the gravimetric and clinometric *amplitude factors* (MELCHIOR A1983). With (2.74), (2.75) this leads to the *Love numbers*

$$h = 0.64, \quad k = 0.32.$$

Observed values for the *Shida number l* show a large scatter around 0.1. Spherical earth models yield values of

$$h = 0.61, \quad k = 0.30, \quad l = 0.08.$$

By introducing tidal models for an elliptical rotating earth with an elastic inner core, a liquid outer core, and an inelastic mantle (WAHR 1981, DEHANT 1987), and taking oceanic tidal models (SCHWIDERSKI 1980) into account, the discrepancies between observed and modelled values for the gravimetric tidal parameters reduce to a few 0.1% (BAKER et al. 1989)

Love numbers can be obtained independently from *space techniques* (satellite laser ranging, very long baseline interferometry). The tidal displacements of the station positions give the parameters h and l. The parameter k models the tidal potential, and enters into the perturbations of satellite orbits. From orbital analyses of the Lageos satellite [5.3.4], the values

$$h = 0.60, \quad k = 0.302, \quad l = 0.09$$

have been derived for the combined solid earth-ocean tidal response (GENDT and DIETRICH 1988). They agree to about 1% with the model values.

5.5.2 The Earth as a Body in Equilibrium

Originally, the earth existed in a liquid state. One may therefore assume the presence of approximately *hydrostatic pressure p* in its interior. It depends only on the weight of the above lying masses and increases toward the center of the earth. The fundamental hydrostatic equation is

$$dp = -\rho(r)g(r)\,dr. \tag{5.126}$$

For equipotential surfaces of the gravity field, we have (2.31)

$$dW = -g(r)\,dr. \tag{5.127}$$

Consequently, the relation

$$dp = \rho(r)\,dW \tag{5.128}$$

shows that the surfaces of equal pressure are also equipotential surfaces, as well as surfaces of equal density.

For a rotating spheroidal body in equilibrium, the equipotential surfaces assume the form of *ellipsoids*, if terms of $0(f^2)$ are neglected. The relationship between the flattening $f = f(r)$ and the density $\rho = \rho(r)$ is given by a differential equation which was formulated by *Clairaut*. Under the assumption that the density depends only on the radius, one obtains the solution for the external equipotential surface:

$$\frac{C}{a^2 M} = \frac{2}{3}\left(1 - \frac{2}{5}\sqrt{\frac{5\,m}{2\,f} - 1}\right). \tag{5.129}$$

Substituting the values, derived from satellite and astronomic observations, of the principal moment of inertia C [5.5.1] and of m (3.58), the *flattening of the equilibrium ellipsoid* is given by $f = 1/299.8$. The deviation with respect to the value $f = 1/298.25$ that is derived from J_2 for the earth ellipsoid is significant; cf. KHAN (1969). The assumption that the interior of the earth is in complete hydrostatic equilibrium is therefore not valid.

The larger flattening may be attributed to a high viscosity of the lower mantle of the earth. Due to tidal friction, the earth today has a smaller rotational velocity than in earlier times [4.1.3]; a state of hydrostatic equilibrium should result in a correspondingly smaller flattening. However, the viscosity of the lower mantle prevents the rapid formation of a state of equilibrium, thereby preserving a "fossil" flattening.

In addition, the observed values of the odd zonal and tesseral harmonic coefficients [5.3.3], [5.4.4] are not consistent with the requirements for equilibrium.

As discussed in [2.3.4], the coefficient C_3 represents the fact that the earth's mass is asymmetrically distributed with respect to the equator. This corresponds to a rise of the geoid at the north pole by about 20 m, and a similar subsidence at the south pole. The coefficients $C_{2,2}$ and $S_{2,2}$ indicate a deviation from a rotationally symmetric mass distribution, cf. [3.5.4].

The causes for these departures will be found in mass anomalies located in the crust and mantle of the earth, cf. [5.5.3].

A *geophysical earth model* should be consistent with the level ellipsoid as a geodetic normal figure. A corresponding density model can be found which, to a good approximation, is in hydrostatic equilibrium, cf. [3.5.1].

5.5.3 Interpretation of the Gravity Field, the Crust of the Earth, and the Upper Mantle

Vertical and lateral density variations are found in the earth's crust and in the upper mantle. The heterogeneous structure of the uppermost layers is recognized directly by the distribution of the *topographic masses* and from the results in *geology*. Variations in density exist at the boundaries between different types of rock, but also within the same type. The *geophysical* measurements supply information on the structure of the crust and the mantle. Primarily seismic velocity-depth distributions are available for the development of density models (S. MUELLER A1974, WOODHOUSE and DZIEWONSKI 1984).

The current concept of the *structure of the crust and the upper mantle* may be summarized as follows, Fig. 5.30. A *zone of sediments* with sharp variations in thickness is found in the uppermost layer. The velocity of seismic waves and the density both fluctuate strongly. Adjoining the sediments in continental areas is the

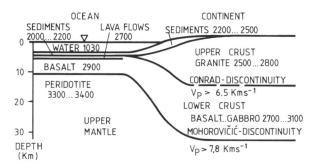

Fig. 5.30. Structure of the earth's crust with rock densities (kg/m^3) and velocities of seismic primary waves, from TORGE (A1989)

upper crust with a mean density of 2700 kg m^{-3}, which consists of acidic rocks (granite). At its lower boundary, the Conrad discontinuity, the velocity v_P of the longitudinal (primary) waves increases to about 6.5 km s^{-1}. This bounding layer which has not been detected everywhere is found at varying depths (northern Germany: 12 km, southern Germany: 20 km). The granitic zone does not exist beneath the oceans. The velocity v_P increases gradually in the adjoining lower crust which has a mean density of 2900 kg m^{-3}. Basic rocks such as a gabbro (basalt) are assumed to exist in this area. A layer of basalt lava flows or consolidated sediments is found below the oceans in the upper regions of the lower crust. The boundary of the upper mantle of the earth [5.5.1] forms the Mohorovičić discontinuity; below this zone, $v_P > 7.8$ km s^{-1}. The depth of the Moho is closely related to the topography; in continental areas, it amounts to 25 ... 70 km (30 to 40 km in the southeastern United States, 50 to 60 km in the western Alps, and 60 to 80 km in the Himalaya mountains) and beneath the oceans it is about 10 km, cf. [5.5.4].

Immediately below the Moho in the upper mantle, the mean density is 3300 to 3400 kg m^{-3}. The material here is assumed to consist of ultrabasic rocks (peridotite). A zone of lower wave velocity (low velocity) begins at a depth of 80 km (oceans) to 150 km (continents). The part of the mantle above this zone together with the earth's crust forms the rigid lithosphere. Its average thickness amounts to 100 km in oceanic and 150 km in continental areas. It is broken into plates which move with respect to one another. The low velocity zone (average thickness 100 to 200 km) lying below these plates and with small viscosity behaves over long periods like a liquid. It is designated the asthenosphere. Global tectonic processes are determined by the interactions of the asthenosphere and the lithospheric plates [5.5.5].

Substantial conclusions with respect to the horizontal structure of the crust and the mantle have been drawn from an analysis of the gravity field. The observed or derived quantities of this field contain various types of information. However, as Stokes' theorem [3.5.1] shows, it is not possible to make definitive assertions from their interpretations (inverse problem of potential theory). Deflections of the vertical provide indications not only concerning the structure near the surface, but also with respect to isostasy [5.5.4]. Gravity anomalies disclose higher, as well as more deeply lying mass anomalies. The Bouguer gravity anomalies [5.2.4] are particularly suitable for local and regional considerations. They reveal changes in density near the surface and in the earth's crust. Globally, they reflect a systematic behavior [5.5.4]. The long-wavelength features of the gravity field in the form of spherical harmonic coefficients, mean free-air and isostatic anomalies are suited for global analyses of deeper structures, KAULA (1970).

Wavelengths longer than several 1000 km are assumed to originate from density and/or temperature anomalies in the lower mantle and at the mantle-core boundary. Anomalies in the lower mantle particularly contribute to wavelengths of a few 1000 km. Lithospheric masses have a strong effect on wavelengths shorter than 1000 to 2000 km (PHILLIPS and LAMBECK 1980). Gravity field structures with wavelengths of a few 100 km generally originate from the earth's crust. The geoid contains information especially about the mass distribution at greater depth.

Correlation computations between gravity anomalies or geoid heights and other crust-mantle parameters (Moho depths, terrestrial thermal flux) partly have revealed significant relationships but also regional deviations. One example is the correlation of a rise in the *geoid* with a subsidence of the *Moho* (ČOLIĆ and PETROVIĆ 1984). Large *tectonic structures* such as young-folded mountains, continental grabens, deep sea trenches and oceanic ridges show pronounced correlations with the gravity field, cf. [5.5.5]. *Tidal anomalies* remaining after modelling the earth's body tides and the ocean loading effects can be analyzed with respect to the rheological characteristics of the crust and upper mantle (MELCHIOR and DE BECKER 1983). The corresponding investigations are impeded by the uneven distribution of observation stations and the numerous disturbing effects.

5.5.4 Isostasy

The topographic masses above sea level represent a disturbance with respect to hydrostatic equilibrium; the same can be said for the water masses of the oceans. If one assumes that below sea level the earth is in hydrostatic equilibrium, then by removing the topography and by filling the oceans, one should be able to create a spheroidal equilibrium figure with an accompanying normal gravity field [3.5.1]. However, from the systematic behavior of the deflections of the vertical, the gravity anomalies, and the geoid undulations, it follows that the visible mass excesses and deficiencies are at least partially compensated by corresponding mass distributions in the earth's interior. The theory of *isostasy* postulates that a distribution of hydrostatic pressure [5.5.2] exists below a surface of compensation.

During the Peruvian arc measurement [1.3.2], *P. Bouguer* discovered that the *deflections of the vertical* as computed from the masses of the mountains were larger than the observed values. The vertical deflections which had been observed by *G. Everest* in the South of the Himalaya were the base for the theories developed in 1855 by *Airy* and by *Pratt*. These deflections happened to be smaller than the corresponding values computed from topographic masses. As one example, the Indian geodetic survey obtained a $5\rlap{.}{''}2$ difference in the deflections of the vertical between two stations, while a value of $15\rlap{.}{''}9$ was computed.

Globally, the *Bouguer gravity anomalies* exhibit a systematic behavior. On the continents, they are generally negative (as low as $-2000\ \mu\mathrm{ms}^{-2}$), as opposed to the oceanic regions, where they are positive (up to $4000\ \mu\mathrm{ms}^{-2}$). A correlation with average height or depth may be demonstrated (HEISKANEN and VENING MEINESZ A1958). It can be approximately described by a regression of $-1000\ \mu\mathrm{ms}^{-2}/1000$ m average height, and $+1000\ \mu\mathrm{ms}^{-2}/1000$ m average depth. Finally, according to HELMERT (A1880/1884), the continental masses would have to produce *geoid undulations* of as much as 500 m; whereas, the observed values remain under 100 m.

The classical *isostasy models* of *Airy* and *Pratt* represent simplified special cases of the actual compensation mechanism.

The isostatic model developed by *G. B. Airy* in 1855 is based on a crust of constant density ρ_0 and varying thickness (Fig. 5.31). The compensation is accomplished locally within vertical columns. The normal column of height $H = 0$ has thickness T_0. Continental columns ($H > 0$) form mountain "roots" of thickness d_{cont}; "antiroots" with thickness d_{oc} are found beneath oceanic columns which are at a depth t. Thus, the crust penetrates with varying depth into the subcrustal masses (floating equilibrium). To establish the surface of compensation, we have the following conditions for

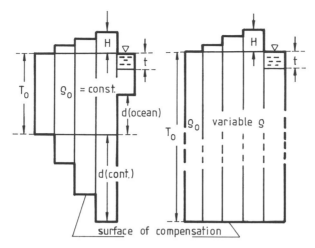

Fig. 5.31 (left). Isostatic model of Airy

Fig. 5.32 (right). Isostatic model of Pratt

equilibrium

$$(\rho_M - \rho_0)d_{\text{cont}} = \rho_0 H \qquad \text{for continents} \atop (\rho_M - \rho_0)d_{\text{oc}} = (\rho_0 - \rho_w)t \qquad \text{for oceans.} \right\} \qquad (5.130)$$

With the conventionally used values for crustal density $\rho_0 = 2670$ kg m^{-3}, the density of the mantle $\rho_M = 3270$ kg m^{-3} below the surface of compensation, and the density of seawater $\rho_w = 1030$ kg m^{-3}, the thickness of the root and antiroot are given by

$$d_{\text{cont}} = 4.45\, H, \quad d_{\text{oc}} = 2.73\, t. \qquad (5.131)$$

The thickness T_0 of the normal column can be estimated from isostatic gravity anomalies [5.2.4] which are obtained on the basis of a certain depth of compensation. For a depth of compensation of $T_0 = 30$ or 40 km, the isostatic anomalies are generally independent of height. This result is in good agreement with the results of seismology; the isostatic surface of compensation approximately corresponds to the Mohorovičić discontinuity [5.5.3].

The *isostatic model of J. H. Pratt* (1855) is based on a layer of constant thickness T_0 with lateral changes in density ρ (Fig. 5.32). The normal column ($H = 0$) has a density ρ_0; continental columns possess smaller densities, while those below the oceans are more dense. The conditions for equilibrium are given by

$$\rho_{\text{cont}}(T_0 + H) = \rho_0 T_0 \qquad \text{for continents} \atop \rho_w t + \rho_{\text{oc}}(T_0 - t) = \rho_0 T_0 \qquad \text{for oceans.} \right\} \qquad (5.132)$$

Using $\rho_0 = 2670$ kg m^{-3}, $\rho_w = 1030$ kg m^{-3}, the densities ρ of the columns for the continents and the oceans are evaluated to be

$$\rho_{\text{cont}} = 2670\,\frac{T_0}{T_0 + H}, \quad \rho_{\text{oc}} = \frac{2670 T_0 - 1030 t}{T_0 - t}. \qquad (5.133)$$

The depth of compensation T_0 can be determined by reasoning similarly as in the Airy model. From the variation of the topographic isostatic deflections of the vertical in the United States, *Hayford* obtained $T_0 = 113.7$ km for the depth for which the deflections are minimal. This depth is in agreement with the values assumed for the thickness of the continental lithosphere, cf. [5.5.3].

Corresponding isostatic anomalies differ only slightly when computed according to various models and depths of compensation; the validity of any model is therefore difficult to confirm by gravimetric methods. The mean anomalies, however, generally scatter unevenly about zero and attain maximum values of 500 μms^{-2}, disregarding the few uncompensated areas, cf. [5.5.5].

The free-air anomalies can be considered as isostatic anomalies with a depth of compensation equal to zero. They give a good perspective of the mass excesses and deficiencies when their correlation with height is removed [5.2.4].

5.5.5 Geodesy and Geodynamics

Geodesy contributes to the research in geodynamics by providing the external gravity field and by the determination of recent temporal changes of the earth's surface and the gravity field. Apart from geodesy, the principal disciplines participating in this research are astronomy, geochemistry, geology, geomorphology, geophysics, and oceanography.

The *gravity field* contains the integral information about the distribution of the terrestrial masses, cf. [2.1.1]. Short-wave field components mainly originate from the topography and the upper crust. When they are removed, the remaining field reveals lateral density inhomogeneities within deeper layers of the earth's body, cf. [5.5.3]. These indicate deviations from a hydrostatic equilibrium and hence regions of stress where actual movements may occur. The theory of *plate tectonics* together with that of *isostasy* are of fundamental importance for geodynamical model computations, with the observed gravity field as one essential constraint.

The theory of *plate tectonics* (MCKENZIE and PARKER 1967, MORGAN 1968) postulates 6 larger (Pacific, American, Eurasian, African, Indian-Australian, and Antarctic) and more than 20 smaller relatively rigid lithospheric plates, which move on top of the asthenosphere (LE PICHON et al. A1973), cf. [5.5.3] and Fig. 5.33. The plate boundaries are characterized by an accumulation of seismic and volcanic activity.

The plates are created in the regions of the *oceanic ridges* (central part) from hot, swelling material of the asthenosphere and then pressed apart, Fig. 5.34. When two plates collide, the heavier oceanic plate is forced to sink into the upper mantle and there is dissolved (subduction zones with high seismic activity). This process creates *deep-sea trenches*, and *island arcs* (e.g western Pacific) or *mountain ranges* (e.g. the Andes) are formed at the margins of those plates remaining at the earth's surface. Mountains are uplifted when two continental plates meet (Alpine-Himalaya-System). *Transform-faults* are found at the plate boundaries which are characterized by shear movements (e.g. San Andreas fault in California).

The former concepts of *continental drift* (WEGENER A1915) and *sea-floor-spreading* (progression of the ocean floor from the oceanic rifts), DIETZ (1961), HESS (1962), have

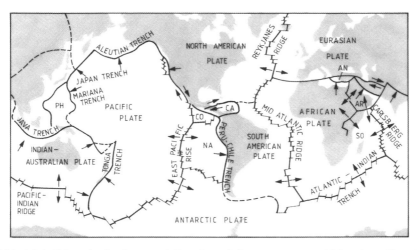

Fig. 5.33. Main lithospheric plates and direction of plate movements, AN = Anatolian, AR = Arabian, CA = Caribbean, CO = Cocos, NA = Nazca, PH = Philippines, SO = Somalia plate, from TORGE (A1989)

been integrated into the theory of plate tectonics. The driving mechanism of plate motion is postulated to consist of large scale thermal convection currents in the viscous mantle. Magnetic surveys in conjunction with age determinations of rocks have yielded rates of expansion of the ocean floor of 1 cm/year (Reykjanes ridge) and up to 15 cm/year (Pacific). From sea-floor spreading rates and geological and earth-quake shifts, a *model* of the *plate movements* during the last few million years has been developed (MINSTER and JORDAN 1978).

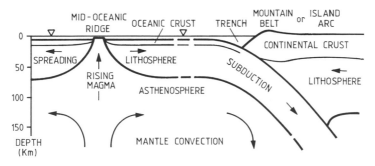

Fig. 5.34. Motion of lithospheric plates at diverging and converging plate boundaries, vertical scale exaggerated, from TORGE (A1989)

While *isostatic compensation* [5.5.4] is achieved for most parts of the earth, large *deviations* are found in areas of deep-sea trenches and the neighboring island arcs. These deviations are caused by orogenic processes in connection with plate tectonics. In zones of extended pleistocene glaciation like Canada and Fennoscandia, a hydro-static imbalance has ocurred after the melting of the ice masses, leading to a post-glacial uplift (see below).

We summarize some relationships between structures of plate tectonics and intraplate processes, and features of the gravity field, cf. also KAULA (1972), McKENZIE (1972):

— mantle-wide convection maintains many of the longer wave lengths (> 1000 km), larger amplitude (> 10 m) geoid heights,
— deep-sea trenches (e.g. Puerto Rico Trench) are characterized by negative free-air anomalies (up to $-3000\ \mu ms^{-2}$) and geoid heights (decline by 10 to 15 m),
— oceanic ridges show negative Bouguer anomalies (up to $-2000\ \mu ms^{-2}$), while free-air anomalies vary around zero,
— young folded-mountains exhibit negative Bouguer anomalies, ($-2000\ \mu ms^{-2}$ and more), and geoid rises (up to some 10 m),
— continental grabens are indicated by negative Bouguer anomalies (up to $-2000\ \mu ms^{-2}$),
— postglacial uplift regions show negative free-air anomalies (up to $-500\ \mu ms^{-2}$ and more) and a geoid depression.

With the increasing accuracy of geodetic measurements and evaluation techniques, the quantities that are determined in geodesy must be viewed as varying in time: "*four-dimensional geodesy*" [1.2], BRUNNER and RIZOS (A1990). To compare quantities observed at different epochs requires reductions in regard to the significant temporal changes. In the context of establishing global and regional systems, time-varying observations are generally reduced to a common reference epoch, cf. [2.4], [3.1]. On the other hand, *repeated geodetic measurements* contribute to the understanding of the dynamic character of the earth, i.e. of geodynamics.

Geodynamical processes affect the geodetic systems and observables in a variety of ways: The astronomic reference system is influenced by *precession and nutation* of the earth's axis [4.1.2] and changes in the *angular velocity* of the earth's rotation [4.1.3]. *Polar motion* [3.1] alters the orientation of the geodetic reference system. The *tidal forces* cause periodic variations in the gravity field of the earth [2.4.1] and movements of the earth's surface [2.4.2]. *Terrestrial mass displacements* give rise to time dependent changes in the gravity field [2.4.3] and in the physical surface of the earth (geodetic control points).

A (hypothetical) *expansion of the earth* would result in a change in the surface gravity and in the radius of the earth. Among the causes of such an *expansion* the following are mentioned: phase transition of the core material of the earth with a concurrent decrease in density; and, the decrease in the gravitational constant with time (relative decrease of about 10^{-10} to 10^{-11} per year) as required by the cosmological considerations of P. A. M. DIRAC (1938). Estimates lead to a suspected secular increase in the earth's radius of 0.1 ... 1 mm/year.

Here, we treat only the geodetically ascertained recent *horizontal* and *vertical motions* of the earth's surface, and *gravity variations*, which are due to terrestrial mass displacements (e.g. VYSKOČIL et al. A1983, HENNEBERG A1986). Large-scale changes are mainly related to global tectonics, postglacial isostatic compensation, and sedimentary compaction. They progress in secular or long-term fashion. Short-time changes concentrate on tectonic plate boundaries (see above), in connection with seismotectonic processes and volcanic events. In these regions, geodetic and gravimetric techniques contribute to the interdisciplinary attempt of earthquake forecasting (RIKITAKE A1982, BILHAM et al. 1989).

The time interval to be allowed between repeated geodetic measurements is governed by the expected changes and the attainable measuring accuracy. The observation stations must be perfectly recoverable (monumentation); local disturbances (geologic structure, groundwater fluctuations) should remain negligibly small.

We mention some *results* of repeated geodetic and gravimetric control surveys for the detection of global, regional and local changes.

Horizontal movements on *global level* are determined by satellite laser-ranging (SLR) and very long baseline interferometry (VLBI), as well as by laser distance measurements to the moon (BENDER and SILVERBERG 1975), cf. [4.4.5], [4.4.8]. Within the NASA Crustal Dynamics Project, cf. also [5.3.4], strain rates for the tectonic plates have been found which cover more than ten years (MA et al. 1989, SMITH et al. 1990). For sites located within the stable interior of the major plates, the derived interplate motions (uncertainties in the cm-order of magnitude) show good agreement with the geological models, Fig. 5.35.

Global gravity changes can be proved with the help of harmonic coefficients derived from analysis of satellite orbits, and with globally distributed absolute gravity measurements.

Temporal variations of *low degree zonal harmonics* ($l = 2, 3, 4$) have been derived from orbit analyses of Starlette and Lageos (CHENG et al. 1989). The suspected cause of the observed decrease of the dynamic form factor [5.4.6] is a post-glacial viscous rebound. A global *absolute gravity network* is being established since 1988, cf. [4.2.4]. Significant results about global gravity changes could be expected from repeated surveys after 10 years (MATHER et al. 1977). Observed gravity variations δg are related to the local height change δH by the free-air relation $\delta g/\delta H = -3\,\mu\mathrm{ms}^{-2}/\mathrm{m}$, cf. [5.2.4]. In addition, δg includes the gravitational effect of mass shifts

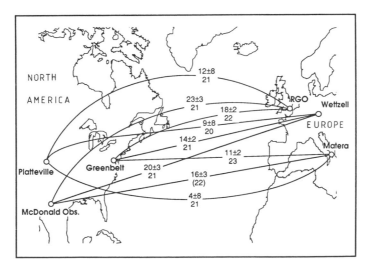

Fig. 5.35. Spreading rates across the north Atlantic in mm/a; top value from SLR analysis, bottom value predicted by the Minster and Jordan model, from SMITH et al. (1990)

inside the earth's body. By introducing a (simplified) model for the internal density changes, gravimetric techniques can be employed for monitoring vertical movements (TORGE 1986).

Relative movements within the area of *tectonic plate boundaries* are determined by terrestrial geodetic measurements [4.3] and by gravimetric methods [4.2]. A regional control is possibly by mobile SLR- and VLBI-systems, delivering "cm"-accuracy over some 100 to 1000 km distances. Global Positioning System (GPS) receivers can be employed more efficiently, cf. [4.4.7], [5.3.4]. They are used extensively in threedimensional networks with station separations varying between some 100 m and 1000 km (DAVIS et al. 1989). In regions of seismic and volcanic activity (California, Eastern Asia, Alpine-Himalaya Zone, Iceland), various geodetic methods are generally applied in order to determine the effects of changes in the stress field before, during, and after an active episode.

Earthquake and *aseismic deformation* studies in California started in 1908, and are now performed using space and terrestrial techniques (STEIN 1987). Recent gravity surveys, leveling, and laser-ranging revealed correlated changes in gravity elevations, and strain (JACHENS et al. 1983). The results of frequent laser distance measurements along the San Andreas Fault (1982–1986) were consistent with a uniform-in-time deformation, but also indicated coseismic offset and postseismic relaxation (SAVAGE et al. 1987). VLBI and GPS measurements especially provide regional deformation control within a few years of observation (DIXON et al. 1990).

Recent developments in monitoring crustal strain and finding earthquake precursors in the Circum-Pacific area are discussed by RIKITAKE (A1982). A GPS-network (20 stations) has been established in 1988 in the Yunnan/China earthquake region, in conjunction with terrestrial geodetic and gravimetric control (SEEBER and LAI 1990, TORGE et al. 1990), Fig. 5.36. Gravity

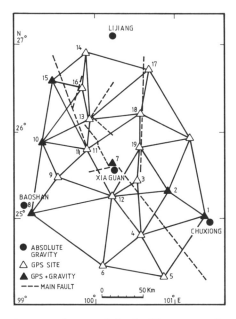

Fig. 5.36. GPS and gravity control network in the Yunnan earthquake region, after SEEBER and LAI (1990) and TORGE et al. (1990)

variations associated with the Tangshan earthquake (gravity change of 0.3 to 0.4 μms^{-2} before the earthquake) have been investigated by LI et al. (1989).

A region of a diverging plate boundary has been investigated in Northern Iceland since 1938. Here, an active rifting episode could be observed between 1975 and 1981. Horizontal movements amounted to a few m/km (WENDT et al. 1985), and observed gravity changes were well correlated with elevation changes (TORGE and KANNGIESER 1985), Fig. 5.37.

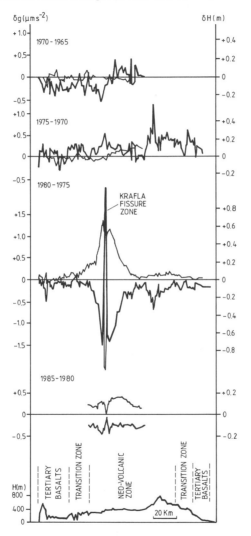

Fig. 5.37. Gravity and height changes along an EW-profile in northern Iceland ($\varphi = 65°40'$), observation epochs 1965, 1970, 1975, 1980, after TORGE (A1989)

Volcanic deformation in connection with magma injection has been studied mainly by laser distance measurements, leveling, and gravimetry. Examples are the Long Valley Caldera, California, uplift (up to 0.5 m) since 1980 (RUNDLE and WHITCOMB 1986), and the Mauna Loa, Hawaii, control network (LOCKWOOD et al. 1985).

Large-scale *vertical movements* occur particularly in zones of recent mountain building and postglacial compensating processes. Subsidence occurs in areas with sedimentary basins. Results in geology show that long-term variations in height on the order of 1 mm/year are not uncommon. Recent vertical movements have been generally investigated by precise leveling [4.3.5].

In order to draw conclusions on absolute movements, it is necessary to also obtain the recent *sea level fluctuations* from tide gauge observations [3.3.3]. *Gravity measurements* offer another chance to detect height changes. For large-area variations, the Bouguer relation $-2\ \mu ms^{-2}/m$ is frequently found between gravity and height changes (STRANG VAN HEES 1977, BIRO A1983).

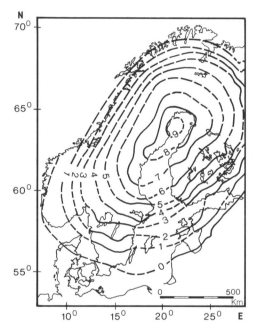

Fig. 5.38. Observed land uplift of Fennoscandia in mm/a, after KAKKURI (1986)

Isostatic rebound effects are investigated particularly in Fennoscandia and in Canada, by leveling, mean sea level observations and gravity measurements (KAKKURI 1986). The Fennoscandian land uplift shows a maximum of $+9$ mm/year, Fig. 5.38. The relation between gravity changes and land uplift was found to be $-2.2\ldots-2.3$ nms^{-2}/mm. In the area of the German coast of the North Sea and the Baltic, one suspects a subsidence of 0.5 to 1 mm/year. A maximum rise of 1 mm/year and more was discovered from relevelings in the Swiss Alps, covering a period of 80 years (GUBLER et al. 1981).

5.6 Lunar and Planetary Geodesy

As a result of the introduction of space probes and satellites in the exploration of space, geodetic methods can be summoned to investigate the moon (selenodesy) and the planets (planetary geodesy). According to [1.2], the formulation of the problem of geodesy encompasses the determination of control networks in a coordinate system firmly tied to the celestial body in question, the determination of the external gravity field, and the establishment of geometric and physical parameters of a simple reference body.

The fundamental distinction between the *measuring methods* to be applied here and the classical methods of global geodesy lies in the fact that the surface of the celestial body is generally not occupied. The observational data are obtained predominantly by *space probes* and *lunar* or *planetary satellites*. These act as sensors in the gravity field of the celestial body; in addition, they can be equipped with measuring systems to gain further knowledge of the surface. In exceptional cases, the data are directly obtained *to the surface* (landing of manned or unmanned space vehicles). The state of lunar and planetary geodesy is described by SJOGREN (1983), and BILLS and SYNNOTT (1987).

Prior to 1959, only earthbound *astronomic observations* were available for the determination of the parameters mentioned above (the first observation of the moon's surface was made through a telescope by *Galileo Galilei* 1609/1610). As of 1946 (radar contact with the moon), the optical measuring methods were supplemented by radar pulse measurements between the earth and the moon and planets. With these methods, the astronomers could obtain, among others, the distance to the moon (relative accuracy of $\pm 3 \times 10^{-4}$), as well as the equatorial semidiameter (± 0.5 to $\pm 5 \times 10^{-2}$), and to some extent also the flatting of the planets. Furthermore, the masses and rotational velocities of the moon and planets could be derived. A control network on the moon (lunar craters, front side) was constructed with respect to the geometric center of the moon (uncertainty of ± 0.5 to ± 2 km).

5.6.1 Lunar Geodesy (Selenodesy)

Various, mutually supplementing methods were and still are applied in selenodesy.

In analogy to the geocentric system [3.1], a moon-fixed *selenocentric system* is introduced as a coordinate system. Its origin is located at the moon's center of mass, and its Z-axis lies along the moon's rotational axis which intersects the equatorial plane perpendicularly. The X-axis points to the earth's center of mass. Upon introducing a selenocentrically situated reference sphere (see below), the corresponding coordinates are defined analogously as in [3.4.3]. The selenographic latitude is positive from the equator northward and negative southward; the northward direction corresponds to north on the earth. The selenographic longitude is reckoned positively eastward from the zero-meridian formed by the X- and Z-axes. The height is obtained with respect to the reference sphere. A mean pole and a mean zero-meridian must be used because of the (presumed) polar motion and due to the librations [5.3.1].

A fundamental *control network* (point spacing of approximately 1000 km) is formed on the moon's front side by *laser reflectors* which were deployed during the Apollo 11, 14, 15 and Luna 21 spaceflight missions. The laser distance measurements [4.4.5] carried out on the earth can then be used to derive, among other quantities, the selenocentric coordinates, DICKEY et al. (1984). The system is supplemented by

ALSEP (Apollo Surface Experiments Package) transmitters which were set up by the Apollo missions 12, 14, 15, 16, 17. It is possible to obtain the relative positions of these transmitters by differential interferometry. This method is based, in analogy to VLBI [4.4.8], on the analysis of the phase shift which results from simultaneous observations at two different terrestrial receiving stations (COUNSELMAN et al. 1973). The locations of the reflectors and the relative positions of the ALSEP transmitters can be determined to an accuracy of ± 1 m.

Photographs taken by probes, satellites, or space vehicles serve to establish further control points (easily identifiable craters, or other features). These photos are developed automatically and scanned; the information is then transmitted to the earth. The camera center in space is obtained from observations (Doppler measurements [4.4.6] and radar ranging) at terrestrial tracking stations. If the equations of motion of the satellite are developed in the selenocentric coordinate system, and if the method of evaluation is the dynamic method of satellite geodesy [5.3.3], then besides the selenocentric coordinates of the camera position, one also obtains the parameters of the gravity field (see below), KOCH (1970). Photographs of the stars which are taken by satellite-borne stellar cameras can be employed to spatially orient the camera axis. Finally, altimeter measurements from the satellite to the lunar surface provide the control in scale. With sufficient overlap of the photographs, the surface control points are then determined by an aerotriangulation (see e.g. KONECNY 1974).

Numerous photographs of the moon's surface were taken by the Luna moon probes and satellites (U.S.S.R., 1959–1970, Luna 3: 1959, the first photograph of the moon's backside), and by the Ranger (U.S.A., 1961–1965) and Surveyor probes (U.S.A., 1966–1968). A complete coverage was achieved with the aid of the Lunar-Orbiter satellites (U.S.A., 1966/67). The resulting control network presents coordinate uncertainties of $\pm$ a few 100 m to ± 15 km (moon's backside). A metric camera (focal length = 76 cm, photo size = 11.5 × 11.5 cm), a stellar camera, and a laser altimeter (± 2 m) were set up by the Apollo flights 15, 16, 17 (1971/72); a clock provided time determinations to ± 1 ms. Photogrammetric surveying (camera height at times < 50 km) furnished a control network with one point per 900 km^2 on the moon's front side and within 30° on either side of the equator ($\sim 20\%$ of the moon's surface); the relative uncertainty amounts to ± 30 m (DOYLE et al. 1977). A refined lunar topographic mapping (scale 1:5 mill., countour interval of 500 m) based on photogrammetric and laser altimetric data, lunar radar sounder and earth-based radar observation is under way (WU 1985). The topographic datum is defined in terms of spherical harmonics (low order spheroid).

For the determination of the *lunar gravity field*, the gravitational potential is expanded into a series of spherical harmonics, cf. SAGITOV et al. (A1986). The harmonic coefficients of this expansion and the selenocentric gravitational constant are obtained by evaluating tracking data using the dynamic method [5.3.3]. Since the probe cannot be tracked as it passes the side not seen by the earth, the gravity field can be determined there only with limited accuracy. The gravity field on the moon's front side is perturbed by large positive gravity anomalies (up to 3000 μms^{-2}) in the area of the annular maria (mascons = mass concentrations). They can be described by superimposing the gravitational effects of point or disk masses on the harmonic expansion. Gravity measurements were conducted on the moon's surface during the Apollo missions (± 50 μms^{-2}).

The existing analysis shows that the long-wavelength features of the gravity field vary quite smoothly (r.m.s. variation of $\pm 500\ \mu\mathrm{ms}^{-2}$). For the harmonic expansion (up to $l = 15$), only the coefficients up to $l = 10$ are well determined (FERRARI et al. 1980):

$$J_2 = 202.1 \times 10^{-6}, \quad J_{2,2} = -22.3 \times 10^{-6}, \quad J_3 = 12 \times 10^{-6}.$$

The selenocentric gravitational constant GM_M and the rotational velocity ω_M have the following values:

$$GM_M = 4902.8 \times 10^9\ \mathrm{m}^3\ \mathrm{s}^{-2}, \quad \omega_M = 2.661\ 699 \times 10^{-6}\ \mathrm{rad\ s}^{-1}.$$

The gravity on the moon's surface ($g = 1.63\ \mathrm{ms}^{-2}$) is approximately 1/6 of the gravity on earth.

In analogy to the geoid [3.3], one can select the level surface known as the *selenoid* to be the physically defined reference surface. Here, it is not possible to establish this surface through a mean sea level, but instead, one imposes the condition that it and the moon's surface enclose the same volume. In the case of insufficient knowledge of the geometry of the lunar surface, such a reference surface can also be fixed by some chosen vertical datum point. The *sphere* and the *triaxial ellipsoid* are suitable as geometrically defined reference surfaces which closely approximate the selenoid.

The radius of the mean lunar sphere is $R_M = 1738$ km. The mean density $\rho_M = 3340\ \mathrm{kg\ m}^{-3}$ follows from the total mass of $M_M = 735 \times 10^{20}$ kg. Using the dynamic form factor J_2 and the differences of the principal moments of inertia A, B, C, cf. [2.3.4],

$$\beta = \frac{C - A}{B} = 631 \times 10^{-6}, \quad \gamma = \frac{B - A}{C} = 227 \times 10^{-6},$$

as obtained from observations of the librations, we find $C/R_M^2 M_M = 0.390$; A and B depart only slightly from this value. From these results, one can infer that the density of the lunar body is approximately homogeneous ($C/R^2 M = 0.4$ for a homogeneous sphere). This agrees well with the direct determinations from rock samples on the Apollo and Luna missions. Lunar density models of shell-like construction which satisfy the observed boundary conditions (topography, gravity field, librations, seismicity) disclose a strongly varying crustal thickness with a mean value of 60 km (front side) and 100 km (backside), BILLS and FERRARI (1977).

Defining the physical reference surface to be the level surface passing through the Apollo 12 landing site ($W_{A12} = 2824.5 \times 10^3\ \mathrm{m}^2\ \mathrm{s}^{-2}$), the axes of a best-fitting triaxial ellipsoid differ only by a few 100 m. The height anomalies and deflections of the vertical attain values of ± 500 m and $\pm 10'$, respectively (BURŠA 1975).

5.6.2 Planetary Geodesy

For corresponding measurements concerning the planets, the techniques in use, besides the earthbound methods of *optical* and *radar astronomy*, employ *tracking data* (particularly Doppler measurements [4.4.6]) of space probes, as well as digital *photogrammetric* and *altimetric* data obtained by these probes. By observing the orbital perturbations of natural and artificial celestial bodies in the gravitational field of a planet, one is able to deduce its mass (as given in the product with the gravitational constant G) and the lower harmonic coefficients $J_{l,m}$, $K_{l,m}$ of the spherical harmonic expansion of the gravitational potential [2.3], cf. [5.3.3]. Astronomic measurements (especially radar observations) furnish the equatorial radii and the rotational velocities. Topographic information is gained from images and radar altimetry.

Among the *inner planets*, Venus and Mars, being closest to the earth, were thoroughly explored by the Mariner probes (U.S.A., Mariner 2, launch in 1962), as well as by the Venus and Mars probes of the U.S.S.R. Particular significance is attached to the Mars-Orbiter Mariner 9 (1971, image coverage, with resolution in part up to 100 m), and the Venus-Mercury probe Mariner 10 (1974, first accurate information on Mercury). The Pioneer Venus Orbiter (1978) provided detailed information on the topography (± 200 m) and gravity field of Venus. High-resolution results are expected from the NASA Magellan Venus Radar Mapper Spacecraft, which will be placed into orbit (275 to 2100 km altitude) in 1990 (SAUNDERS et al. 1990). Carrying a multimode radar system, it will be capable of imaging the surface (resolution of 300 m and better), and determining the topographic relief (± 50 m for 10 km blocks). Since 1976 a stereophotogrammetric coverage of Mars is available as provided by the Viking-Orbiters 1 and 2 (U.S.A.).

Until the 1970s, research of the *outer planets* was exclusively based on optical and radar observations from the earth. Jupiter and Saturn have been investigated by the Pioneer 10 and 11 (launch in 1973/74) and Voyager 1 and 2 (1977) space probes. New results for Uranus and the Uranian satellites were obtained during the Voyager 2 encounter in 1986.

Table 5.4 lists some *planetary parameters* of geodetic relevance (state of 1987).

Tab. 5.4. Geometrical and physical parameters of the planets, after SJÖGREN (1983), THE ASTRONOMICAL ALMANAC (1985), and BILLS and SYNNOTT (1987)

Planet	Equatorial Radius (km)	GM ($km^3 \, s^{-2}$)	$J_2 \times 10^6$	Mean Surface Gravitation (ms^{-2})	Mean Density ($kg \, m^{-3}$)	Harmonic Coeff. of Grav. Field
Mercur	2440	22032	60	3.70	5400	$J_2, J_{2,2}, K_{2,2}$
Venus	6052	324858	6	8.87	5200	up to 18, 18
Earth	6378	398600	1083	9.80	5500	up to 360, 360
Mars	3393	42828	1959	3.72	3900	up to 18, 18
Jupiter	71492	126687×10^3	14736	24.8	1300	J_2, J_4, J_6
Satum	60268	37931×10^3	16480	10.5	700	J_2, J_4
Uranus	25662	5794×10^3	3349	8.4	1300	J_2, J_4
Neptun	24830	6809×10^3	4300	11.6	1800	J_2

6 Geodetic Networks

Control networks for position, height, and gravity are established by geodetic and gravimetric surveying, within the frame of national geodetic surveys. This chapter describes only the design of the *fundamental networks* (first-order nets). They provide the basis for densification networks, and the final construction of national map series, but are also significant to global geodesy.

Although *threedimensional positioning* has already entered into the establishment of geodetic networks, national control systems still distinguish between *horizontal* [6.1], *vertical* [6.2], and *gravity* [6.3] networks. The separate treatment of horizontal positioning and heighting is, on one hand, due to the fact that the corresponding observations react differently to atmospheric refraction and to gravity. On the other side, most users ask for a horizontal control defined in a geometric system, while vertical control should refer to the gravity field (TORGE 1986). Remarks to the design of threedimensional networks will be found in [6.1.1] and [6.2.1]. The fundamental principles of geodetic surveying, including methods which are useful in the design of densification networks, are treated by BOMFORD (A1980) and KAHMEN and FAIG (A1988). Coordinate systems and coordinate transformations are treated by GROSS-MANN (A1976), SCHÖDLBAUER (A1981), HEITZ (A1985), and HECK (A1987).

We will not consider the *conformal mapping* of the earth ellipsoid on the plane which yields planar Cartesian coordinates that are required in applied geodesy (GROSSMANN A1976, KUNTZ A1983, RICHARDUS and ADLER A1974, LEE 1974).

6.1 Horizontal Control Networks

6.1.1 Design, Monumentation, Observations

The control points of horizontal control networks are designated trigonometric (triangulation) points (TP). First-order TP or primary triangulation points are separated by 30 to 60 km. Points of higher elevation served in establishing stations for which intervisibility exists or can be created through the construction of towers. The points are permanently monumented by underground and surface marks (stone plates, and stone or concrete pillars, bolts in bedrock). Safety marks aid in the verification and recovery of stations in the event of damage to the original marks.

Until recently, the *TP* have been determined by the methods of triangulation, trilateration, or by traverse surveys (ASHKENAZI 1973). Since the 1960's, satellite based positioning methods have been employed for large-scale control of terrestrial networks. With the Global Positioning System (GPS) an efficient threedimensional positioning method is now available (see below).

In *triangulation*, one observes all angles of the triangles formed by the TP [4.3.2]. The network scale is obtained from the lengths of individual triangle sides. In order to avoid an increase in systematic scale errors, such distance measurements [4.3.3] should be carried out at intervals of about 200 km. Laplace stations [5.1.4] control the orientation of the network. Primary triangulations can be laid out in the form of chains or areal networks. To cover larger regions, chains of triangles or quadrilaterals with diagonals have been frequently observed and tied together in the form of a framework. The meshes of this framework are then filled by first-order triangulation networks or by densificiation nets with shorter sides.

The method of *trilateration* has gained considerable significance through the development of electromagnetic measurements of distance [4.3.3]. Here, the lengths of all triangle sides and all possible diagonals are measured to obtain a sufficient number of redundant determinations in the net. Although the scale is continually controlled, the errors in orientation can accumulate rapidly, so that tight control through Laplace stations is required.

The design of control networks through *high-precision traverses* is very economical. In this method, the sides are measured by electronic distance meters and the traverse angles are measured by a theodolite utilizing forced-centering. By connecting these traverses at nodal points, polygonal networks may be constructed with high accuracy. Swerving of the net is prevented if the Laplace stations are sufficiently close to each other.

Fundamental triangulation networks can ultimately be formed by combining triangulation, trilateration, and high-precison traverses. The particular method will essentially depend on the terrain under consideration.

The relative *accuracy* of terrestrial horizontal control networks varies from $\pm 10^{-5}$ to $\pm 2 \times 10^{-6}$ s (s = station separation).

The existing control networks were determined generally between 1850 and 1950 by *triangulation*; the methods of *trilateration*, and particularly, *traverse surveys* have been used in the more recent geodetic surveys [6.1.6]. For a certain, generally specified configuration of stations and a desired accuracy of the control points, methods in *optimization* can furnish information regarding the design and frequency of observations (BOSSLER et al. 1973, GRAFAREND and SANSÓ A1985). Network optimization can be extended to include also the reliability of the results, and it has to take into account restrictions, such as maximum allowable cost of the survey.

Between 1950 and 1965, the *Shoran* and *Hiran* methods [4.3.3] were applied in the surveys of inaccessible and extended regions, as well as in bridging parts of oceans. The *Aerodist* methods [4.3.3] were employed to rapidly densify framework nets. A Shoran- and Hiran-trilateration of Canada was conducted from 1949 to 1958 (average length of a side: 400 km, $\pm 2 \times 10^{-5}$); Hiran chains connect North America over Greenland and Iceland to Europe (1953–1956). Also, such ties exist between Crete and Africa (1953), and between Florida and Trinidad.

Since the 1980s, *GPS-positioning* has entered into the design and construction of geodetic networks (GOAD A1985, GROTEN and STRAUSS A1988). As this method does not depend on station intervisibility and weather conditions, and as the observation time per station is very short, it offers a great flexibility, cf. [4.4.7]. With relative positioning accuracies of 10^{-6} to 10^{-7} s for distances of 10 to 1000 km, it is superior to classical horizontal positioning, cf. [5.3.4]. GPS-positioning may be used in different ways in geodetic networks, e.g. WOLF (1986), SEEBER (A1989/1992):

— Large-scale control and strengthening of existing classical networks, with respect to orientation, scale, and regional distortions, cf. [6.1.7],
— third and fourth order densification (station distances < 10 km) of existing networks, with relative "cm"-accuracy and better (AUGATH 1988),
— construction of new areal control, e.g. by establishing a base net (100 to 150 km station distance) and a densification net (distances of appr. 10 km). Further densification may be performed by GPS (possibly by single-frequency receivers) and/or by electronic tacheometers, cf. [4.3.3]. The relative accuracy of large-scale networks can be improved by orbit corrections, obtained from a regional tracking system, cf. [4.4.7].

6.1.2 Computations

The system of ellipsoidal or geodetic coordinates φ, λ [3.4.1] is used for reference; the *geodetic datum* [5.1.4] then orients such a system. In earlier geodetic surveys, the reference surface was a conventional ellipsoid computed from the adjustment of several arc measurements [1.3.3]. More recent geodetic surveys partly refer to a regionally best-fitting ellipsoid derived from the equations of the deflection of the vertical [5.1.7], or they are based on the ellipsoid of a Geodetic Reference System [3.5.5], cf. the table in [5.1.4]. The deflection of the vertical at the origin point was either set to zero or determined by an adjustment of the deflections of the vertical, with a minimum condition for the sum of the squared vertical deflections, cf. [5.1.7]. The geoid undulation at the origin point has frequently been established indirectly by reducing the observed baselines to the geoid and treating them as ellipsoidal quantities; the ellipsoid and the geoid then intersect at these lines. With one observed astronomic azimuth, Laplace's equation (5.8a) furnishes the orientation of the network.

The observed *azimuths* and horizontal *directions* or *angles* have usually been corrected only for the skew normal, and only orthometric heights were considered in the reduction of observed *distances* [5.1.4]. Coordinates have then been transferred from the origin to the network points by appropriate adjustment computations (see below). The neglect of the deflections of the vertical and the geoid undulations cause systematic orientation and scale errors; this approximate procedure is known as the "*development method*". At all first-order TP in the newer geodetic surveys, astronomic latitudes and longitudes are observed, or the deflections of the vertical are interpolated, so that reductions can be carried out which account for the deflections [5.1.4] and geoid undulations (astronomic leveling [5.1.6]).

To compute the geodetic coordinates, a *geodesic* is introduced on the ellipsoid [6.1.3] as the line joining the TP. The adjustment can be made either by the method of variation of coordinates or by the method of conditioned observations.

The *adjustment* according to *variation of coordinates* is generally applied today. The observation equations relate the observed azimuths, horizontal directions and distances to the coordinates φ, λ. These equations are formulated as the solution to the inverse problem [6.1.5]. In earlier times, the adjustment according to *conditioned observations* was preferred due to the smaller number of unknown parameters. The adjustment removes the misclosures which appear in the geometry of the network. Using the solution of the direct problem [6.1.5], the coordinates of the origin point may be transferred into this network which now has no misclosures (*network extension*). A combined adjustment of the networks of different order gains significance with the high accuracy of trigonometric and polygonometric densification networks, as well as with the possibilities of electronic data processing.

Results of *satellite positioning* may be introduced into the adjustment, after transforming them into the φ,λ-system. Parameters for datum shift and for changes of scale and orientation generally have to be introduced in the mathematical model. Differences of coordinates derived from GPS should be introduced as correlated data, and the different data sets have to be properly weighted, e.g. WOLF (1982), ASHKENAZI et. al (1988), cf. [3.2.3], [5.4.5]. More convenient is a threedimensional adjustment in the Cartesian X,Y,Z-system [5.1.2], holding heights and astronomical coordinates fixed (VINCENTY 1980).

6.1.3 Geodesics on the Rotational Ellipsoid

In order to carry out computations on the rotational ellipsoid, the points on the ellipsoid must be connected to one another by surface curves. We consider primarily the normal section (arc) and the geodesic.

The *normal section* is defined by the curve of intersection of the vertical plane [3.4.2] and the ellipsoid. Hence, the directions (5.13), which are observed by the theodolite and reduced to the ellipsoid, form angles between normal sections; spatial distances can also be reduced to lengths of normal sections (4.51). Since the surface normals of two points on the ellipsoid are in general skewed to each other, the reciprocal normal sections from P_1 and P_2 and from P_2 to P_1 do not coincide (Fig. 6.1). In order to obtain unique computations, the difference in azimuth $\alpha_1' - \alpha_1''$ must be taken into account; for $S = 50$ km, this difference amounts to at most only $0.''02$.

Usually, because of its favorable properties in differential geometry, a unique surface curve, the *geodesic*, is introduced. This line is the shortest connection on the ellipsoid between two points and extends generally between the two reciprocal normal sections (Fig. 6.1).

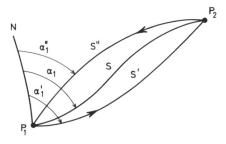

Fig. 6.1. Normal section and geodesic

To derive the equation of the geodesic, we start with the geodetic curvature κ_g. It corresponds to the curvature of the normal projection of a curve $r(S)$ onto the plane that is tangent to the surface. κ_g may be represented by the triple scalar product

$$\kappa_g = (r' \times r'') \cdot n. \tag{6.1}$$

r' is the tangent vector and r'' is the curvature vector (' denotes the first derivative and " denotes the second derivative with respect to arc length). n designates the normal vector to the surface. For the geodetic curvature of the geodesic, we have

$$(r' \times r'') \cdot n = 0, \tag{6.2}$$

that is, the local projection onto the tangential plane is a straight line. This *second-order differential equation* on the rotational ellipsoid and in the φ, λ-system becomes with $\lambda = \lambda(\varphi)$

$$\frac{d^2\lambda}{d\varphi^2} + \left(\frac{2}{p}\frac{dp}{d\varphi} - \frac{1}{M}\frac{dM}{d\varphi} \right)\frac{d\lambda}{d\varphi} + \frac{p}{M^2}\frac{dp}{d\varphi}\left(\frac{d\lambda}{d\varphi}\right)^3 = 0. \tag{6.3}$$

p is the radius of the parallel circle (3.18), N is the radius of curvature in the prime vertical (3.26), and M is the radius of curvature of the meridian (3.24). From the relations

$$\frac{d\varphi}{dS} = \frac{\cos \alpha}{M}, \quad \frac{d\lambda}{dS} = \frac{\sin \alpha}{N \cos \varphi} \tag{6.4}$$

which are taken directly from Fig. 6.2 and which hold in general, the first integration of (6.3) leads to *Clairaut's* equation

$$N \cos \varphi \sin \alpha = \text{const.} = N_m \cos \varphi_m. \tag{6.5}$$

The constant of integration corresponds to the radius of the parallel circle at the geographic latitude φ_m, at which the geodesic has an azimuth of 90°. Introducing the reduced latitude β (3.20), (6.5) becomes

$$\cos \beta \sin \alpha = \cos \beta_m. \tag{6.6}$$

Integrating (6.5) yields elliptic integrals. If one differentiates (6.5) with respect to S, then with (6.4), we have

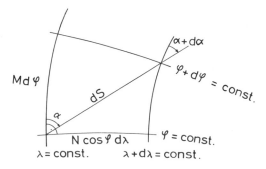

Fig. 6.2. Arc element in the system of the geodetic coordinates

$$\frac{d\alpha}{dS} = \frac{\sin \alpha \tan \varphi}{N}. \tag{6.7}$$

For series expansions, (6.4) and (6.5) resp. (6.7) form an important system of *first-order differential equations* for the geodesic.

The azimuth α_1' and arc length S' which refer to the normal section are reduced to the azimuth α_1 and the arc length S of the geodesic as follows:

$$\left.\begin{aligned} \alpha_1' - \alpha_1 &= \frac{e^2}{12a^2} \cos^2 \varphi_1 S^2 \sin 2\alpha_1 + \cdots \\[2ex] S' - S &= \frac{e^4}{360a^4} \cos^4 \varphi_1 S^5 \sin^2 2\alpha_1 + \cdots \end{aligned}\right\} \tag{6.8}$$

For $S = 50$ (or 200) km, the reduction in azimuth amounts to at most $0\rlap{.}''007$ (or $0\rlap{.}''112$), and the reduction in arc length is no more than 2×10^{-11} (or 2×10^{-8}) m. The latter can therefore always be neglected. The azimuth reduction attains the accuracy of first-order angle measurements only for very long lines.

6.1.4 Solution of Ellipsoidal Triangles

For the determination of geodetic coordinates from distance and azimuth [6.1.5], the unobserved sides and angles must be computed using ellipsoidal triangles. The solutions can be reduced to the computation of *ellipsoidal polar triangles*, by the formulas developed for the direct and inverse geodetic problems, cf. [6.1.5]. It has to be observed that, in addition to three geometric elements (angles and distances), two orientation parameters (latitude and azimuth) have to be known, in order to solve the problem.

For the lengths of sides in a first-order triangulation (< 100 km), the ellipsoidal computations can be replaced by calculations on a sphere. In this respect, the ellipsoid is approximated by the *Gaussian osculating sphere* tangent at $P_0(\varphi_0)$ and having a radius

$$R_0 = \sqrt{M_0 N_0}. \tag{6.9}$$

The latitude of tangency φ_0 can be chosen as the arithmetic mean of the geographic latitudes of the vertices of the particular triangle. Within a radius of 100 km about the point of tangency of the Gaussian osculating sphere, the errors in direction caused by the spherical approximation remain less than $0\rlap{.}''002$, and distance errors are less than 1 mm.

For the solution of a spherical triangle having sides a, b, c and angles α, β, γ, the *spherical law of sines* yields

$$\frac{\sin \alpha}{\sin \beta} = \frac{\sin \dfrac{a}{R}}{\sin \dfrac{b}{R}}. \tag{6.10}$$

Expanding $\sin(a/R)$ and $\sin(b/R)$ in series up to $0(1/R^3)$, one obtains relations corresponding to the law of sines for the plane. If the spherical angles are reduced by one third of the spherical excess, then this gives *Legendre's equation*:

$$\frac{\sin(\alpha - \varepsilon/3)}{\sin(\beta - \varepsilon/3)} = \frac{a}{b}. \tag{6.11}$$

If the spherical sides are given increments (additaments), then the result is the *Soldner method of additaments*:

$$\frac{\sin \alpha}{\sin \beta} = \frac{a - a^3/6R^2}{b - b^3/6R^2}. \tag{6.12}$$

The *spherical excess* ε appearing in (6.11) is the surplus over 180° of the angle sum of a spherical triangle. It is computed according to

$$\varepsilon = \frac{F}{R^2}, \tag{6.13}$$

where F is the area of the plane triangle computed from the lengths of the spherical sides. For an equilateral triangle with $S = 50$ km, $\varepsilon = 5.''48$.

6.1.5 Direct and Inverse Geodetic Problems

In ellipsoidal computations [6.1.2], the following problems arise:
1. To compute the geodetic coordinates φ_2, λ_2 of point P_2, as well as the azimuth α_2, given the coordinates φ_1, λ_1 of point P_1, the azimuth α_1, and the distance S.
2. To compute the azimuths α_1, α_2 and the distance S, given the coordinates φ_1, λ_1, φ_2, λ_2 of the points P_1, P_2.

These problems are known as the *direct* and *inverse geodetic problems*, respectively. In either case, one is concerned with the solution of the ellipsoidal polar triangle $P_1 N P_2$ (Fig. 6.3). If the geodesic is introduced as the surface curve between P_1 and P_2, then the problems above demand the integration of the differential equations of the geodesic and the solution for the desired quantities. As *elliptic integrals* emerge in the solutions, closed formulas are not available for the direct and the inverse geodetic problem. The numerous solutions can be divided into three groups (SCHNÄDELBACH 1974).

The solutions in the first group are based on the integration of the system of first order differential equations (6.4), (6.7) of the geodesic. Here, *Legendre* (1806) carried

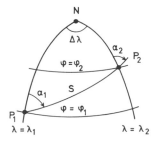

Fig. 6.3. Direct and inverse geodetic problems

out *Taylor series* expansions of the latitude, longitude, and azimuth differences as functions of arc length:

$$
\left.
\begin{aligned}
\varphi_2 - \varphi_1 &= \left(\frac{d\varphi}{dS}\right)_1 S + \frac{1}{2}\left(\frac{d^2\varphi}{dS^2}\right)_1 S^2 + \cdots \\[2mm]
\lambda_2 - \lambda_1 &= \left(\frac{d\lambda}{dS}\right)_1 S + \frac{1}{2}\left(\frac{d^2\lambda}{dS^2}\right)_1 S^2 + \cdots \\[2mm]
\alpha_2 - \alpha_1 &= \left(\frac{d\alpha}{dS}\right)_1 S + \frac{1}{2}\left(\frac{d^2\alpha}{dS^2}\right)_1 S^2 + \cdots
\end{aligned}
\right\}
\tag{6.14}
$$

Using the first derivatives (6.4), (6.7), one can also compute the higher derivatives. Since the series are expanded with respect to S, they converge slowly, so that in general, they are applied only up to a range of 100 km. At middle latitudes, an expansion to the fifth (φ, λ) resp. fourth (α) order then provides an accuracy of $\pm 0\rlap{.}{''}0001$, and $\pm 0\rlap{.}{''}001$ resp.

Numerical integrations are based on the subdivision of S into small increments, with subsequent application of (6.4), (6.5). By iterating with smaller increments and comparing the results, a given error limit can be reached. Solutions of this type stem from DORRER (1966), who used the Runge-Kutta method, and from KIVIOJA (1971), among others.

In the methods developed by *Bessel* (1826) and *Helmert* (1880), the ellipsoidal polar triangle (Fig. 6.3) is transferred to a concentric sphere (radius a). The computations are then rigorously performed on this sphere and a transformation is subsequently made back to the ellipsoid. The reduced latitude β is used for the spherical latitude; β is related to φ by (3.2.1). If one transfers the azimuth α_1 to the sphere, then by Clairaut's equation (6.6), the ellipsoidal azimuths are preserved in this transference. The relations between the ellipsoidal distance S and the spherical distance σ, as well as those between the ellipsoidal and spherical longitude differences $\Delta\lambda$ and $\Delta\lambda'$ are derived by combining the equations

$$
\frac{d\beta}{d\sigma} = \cos\alpha, \quad \frac{d\lambda'}{d\sigma} = \frac{\sin\alpha}{\cos\beta}
\tag{6.15}
$$

which are valid on the sphere, with the corresponding ellipsoidal formulas (6.4). After some manipulations, the following differential equations are obtained:

$$
dS = a\sqrt{1 - e^2\cos^2\beta}\;d\sigma, \quad d\lambda = \sqrt{1 - e^2\cos^2\beta}\;d\lambda'.
\tag{6.16}
$$

The resulting elliptic integrals can be solved either by expanding the square roots in series and subsequently integrating term by term (BODEMÜLLER 1954), or by numerical methods (MITTERMAYER 1968). This process exhibits favorable convergence since one solves for only small differences between the ellipsoidal and spherical quantities. It is therefore suitable also for computations involving very long geodesics (VINCENTY 1975).

Finally, the direct and inverse geodetic problems can be solved using a *conformal projection to the sphere* with subsequent spherical calculations and a transformation back to the ellipsoid (SCHNÄDELBACH 1971). Simple transformation equations are obtained by employing the Gaussian osculating sphere (6.9). Since the projection causes distortions, the azimuths and distances are subject to reductions. This method is also suitable for long lines.

6.1.6 National Networks: Examples

The *Primary Triangulation Net of* the *Federal Republic of Germany* (DHDN), as an example of a classic *areal* system, emerged between 1870 and 1950 from the combination of several individual networks (Fig. 6.4). The part of the network between the rivers Elbe and Main, and western border of Germany was held fixed. It consists of chains and densification nets and was triangulated by the Geodetic Survey of Prussia under the direction of *Schreiber* from 1870 to 1895 ("Schreiber's block").

The ellipsoid with

$$a = 6377\,397 \text{ m}, \quad f = 1:299.15,$$

computed in 1841 by *Bessel* from ten arc measurements served as a reference surface. The origin point was in Rauenberg near Berlin, where the deflection of the vertical was set to zero. The network was oriented by the astronomic azimuth of the triangle side connecting Rauenberg and Berlin-Marienkirche. The scale was obtained from five baselines from which the length of the nearest triangle side was derived by special base extension network. Since the baselines were reduced only to the geoid, the reference ellipsoid approximately coincides with the geoid in these lines [6.1.2] (WOLF

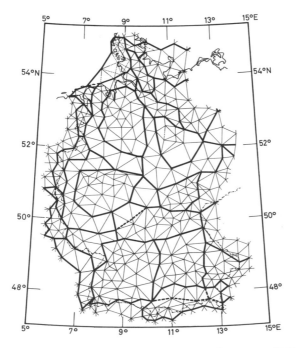

Fig. 6.4. Primary triangulation net of the Federal Republic of Germany (DHDN = Deutsches Hauptdreiecksnetz, state of 1957), from AUGATH (1988)

1987). The non-Prussian networks were tied to the northern block through common points along the network margins. The geodetic datum of "Schreiber's Block" was held fixed.

This procedure and the effects arising from the "development method" [6.1.2] caused geometric distortions in the net, which manifest themselves as scale variations up to 1×10^{-5}, overall deformations of 1 m and more, and regional strains of several 0.1 m. The average DHDN-transformation parameters with respect to a geocentric system have been derived through a Doppler-campaign (RINNER et al. 1982), with the translations $X_0 = 583$ m, $Y_0 = 68$ m, $Z_0 = 395$ m, a rotation $\varepsilon_z = 3\rlap{.}''4$, and a scale correction $m = 11.1 \times 10^{-6}$.

The horizontal networks in the U.S.A., the U.S.S.R., and other countries of larger areal extent are based on a *framework* constructed from triangulation chains along meridians and parallels. The areal extension of control through densification networks is then undertaken according as the development of the individual land areas progresses. Nodal networks arise at the junctures of the triangulation chains, where a baseline and a Laplace azimuth are generally included. These internally adjusted nodal networks are treated as constraints in the adjustment of the overall framework.

The framework of the *U.S.A.* has a mesh size of approximately 500 km; it was adjusted by the U.S. Coast and Geodetic Survey (*W. Bowie*) in the North American Datum 1927 [5.1.4] (BAKER 1974). Starting in the 1970s, the U.S. horizontal control network was revised by transcontinental *geodimeter traverses* ($\pm 10^{-6}$ s) and by *Doppler points* ($\pm 1 .. 2$ m) evenly distributed over the entire country (Fig. 6.5). Classical and new

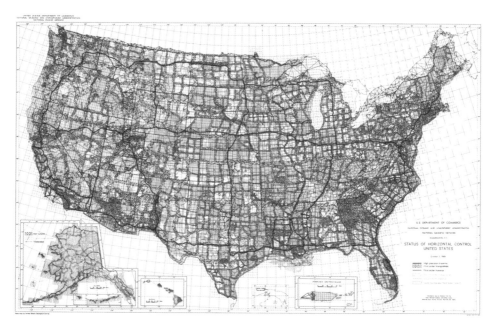

Fig. 6.5. United States horizontal control net, state of 1986, with high precision traverses (bold lines), first and second order triangulation and traverses. Courtesy of National Geodetic Survey, National Ocean Service, NOAA

data have been included into a recent readjustment of the North American networks, cf. [6.1.7]. The network of the *U.S.S.R.* (mesh size: 200 to 400 km) was adjusted in the Pulkovo 1942 datum (*T. N. Krassovski*). Numerous astrogeodetic deflections of the vertical were determined for the reductions to the ellipsoid; in addition, gravimetric data were amassed extensively for the interpolation of the deflections of the vertical [5.1.6], IZOTOV (1959). The reference ellipsoids of both systems were situated so as to achieve a good fit to the geoid [5.1.7]. The relative accuracy of these networks amounts to $\pm 10^{-5}$, which can lead to distortions of 10 to 15 m at the margins of the system.

Control in *Canada* originally was developed through triangulation chains and traverses. During the 1970s and 1980s, the entire country was covered by *Doppler control points* (± 1 m), with an average station separation of about 200 km. Since the 1980s, *GPS-positioning* is applied for network control and densification.

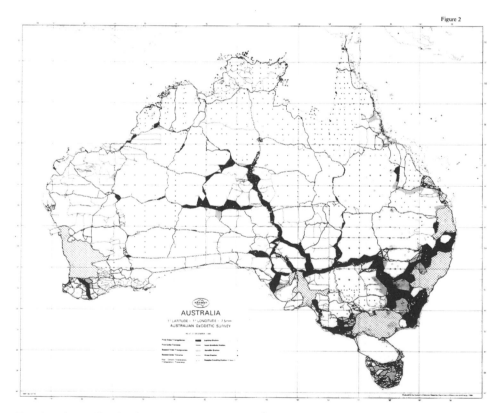

Fig. 6.6. Australian horizontal control net, state of 1986, with first and second-order triangulation (hatched areas), first and second-order traverses supported by Laplace-stations, high density trilateration, triangulation and traversing (dotted areas), Doppler satellite stations (open circles), and Aerodist and Hiran (connection to Papua New Guinea) stations (black circles), from National Report for 1983-87 "Geodesy in Australia," IUGG-IAG Gen. Ass. Vancouver 1987.

The *Australian* first-order control network was determined primarily through geodimeter *traverses* (Fig. 6.6); the nodal points are separated by several 100 km. Laplace azimuths have been observed, whenever possible. In the developed coastal regions, this polygonal network was densified by *triangulations* (chains and areal nets) and *traverses*; the less accessible areas have been filled by the *Aerodist method* [4.3.3]. *Doppler* satellite stations cover large parts of the country. A *Hiran* chain [4.3.3] connects north-eastern Australia with Papua New Guinea. A network adjustment led to the Australian Geodetic Datum 1966, cf. [5.1.4], [5.4.5]. The datum parameters for the origin point at Johnston were obtained by optimally fitting the ellipsoid to the geoid using 275 astrogeodetic deflections of the vertical that are distributed over Australia; the geoid undulation was set to zero (LAMBERT 1977). After including the more recent data, a readjustment of the primary geodetic network was performed, leading to the Australian Geodetic Datum 1984 (AGD84), ALLMAN and VEENSTRA (1984).

6.1.7 Network Unification and Large-scale Control

The unification of triangulation nets may be required in order to construct national triangulation systems out of various partial networks, or to create continental systems from the national networks. If the original observational data are still available and if the computational effort is warranted, then a *new adjustment* of the nets provides optimum results.

If the coordinates exist for a number of points in both systems, then the *unification of the networks* must be performed using these *common points*. Since the coordinates of the various systems originate from different measurements and computations (adjustments), they can not be strictly brought to coincidence ("heterogeneous coordinates"). The changes to one common *geodetic datum* are then determined by the condition

$$\Sigma(\delta\varphi^2 + \cos^2\varphi \; \delta\lambda^2) = \text{min.} \tag{6.17}$$

which is formed for the coordinate difference $\delta\varphi$, $\delta\lambda$ at the common points. Because of $\delta\varphi = -\delta\xi$ and $\cos\varphi\delta\lambda = -\delta\eta$, cf. (5.1), equation (6.17) corresponds to (5.32). The datum shift parameters are derived from the translational equations for the deflections of of the vertical (JORDAN-EGGERT-KNEISSEL IV, A1958/59, p. 1247 pp.). This method corresponds to a similarity transformation on the ellipsoid. The parameters of the transformation (displacements, rotation, scale change) are determined by an adjustment (Helmert transformation).

Satellite control points are used to an increasing extent for the unification and strengthening of classical terrestrial networks, cf. [5.3.4]. They do not only provide the parameters for transformation to the geocentric system, but also help detect network distortions with respect to scale and azimuth, cf. [5.4.5]. If the network unification is based on satellite stations, a three-dimensional adjustment model is preferable, cf. [3.4.3], [5.1.2].

We mention some *examples* for the control of classical networks by satellite methods, and for the unification and improvement of continental networks:

Doppler- and GPS-control points are now used in many regions, in order to control and connect existing networks. During the *African Doppler Survey* 1981–1986 (ADOS 1987), more than 300 Doppler stations have been established in 47 African countries, providing a common reference for the national networks.

Parts of the horizontal control network in *Finland* have been controlled by the method of *stellar triangulation* (average length of a side: 200 km), in which flashing lights served as targets, cf. [4.4.4]. The appropriate equipment was carried by weather balloons to altitudes of 30 to 40 km, and actuated from the ground by a quartz crystal clock. The azimuth and angle of altitude of the triangle sides were determined with uncertainties of $\pm 0.''3$ and $\pm 0.''5$, respectively. The scale of the triangulation was acquired from a first-order triangulation network and a specially designed long-sided traverse observed by laser geodimeters (KAKKURI 1973).

A unified *European triangulation* network was created around 1950 as a network frame, and included selected triangulation chains from geodetic surveys (WOLF 1949). The central part of this system was the Central European Network which was augmented by blocks in the southeast, southwest, and north (WHITTEN 1952). The reduction of the horizontal directions due to the deflection of the vertical was not implemented, part of the base lines were reduced only to the geoid, and the orientation was secured through Laplace stations. The geodetic datum (*European Datum 1950*, ED 50) was defined by the International Ellipsoid of 1924 (3.66a) and the values $\xi_1 = +3.''36$, $\eta_1 = +1.''78$ for the fundamental point at the Helmert-tower in Potsdam, cf. [5.1.4.]. ξ_1 and η_1 were determined in a vertical deflection adjustment, cf. [5.1.7]. N_1 was set to zero, and resulted from an optimal fit of the reduced base lines to the ellipsoid. Later on, areal densification nets were included into the network frame. Improvement of the European horizontal control network RETRIG (Réseau Européen de Triangulation) started in the 1950's.

The *European Datum 1987* (ED87) as adopted by IAG is the final solution of this two-dimensional continental network (EHRNSPERGER et al. 1987, PODER and HORNIK 1989), see Fig. 6.7.

Terrestrial data (horizontal directions, astronomical azimuths, electronic distance measurements and distances derived from invar base lines) as well as space data (three-dimensional coordinates of SLR/VLBI/Doppler-fundamental stations, NNSS-Doppler- and SLR (Lageos)-stations established during special campaigns) were included in the network adjustment. The terrestrial data were reduced to the ellipsoid (International Ellipsoid of 1924) using observed deflections of the vertical and the derived astrogeodetic geoid, cf. [5.1.6]. The rigorous adjustment employed the Helmert-blocking method (WOLF 1978). 16 national blocks were introduced, each with individual scale and orientation parameters, and tied together at common points along junction zones. As the ED50 coordinates of the station Munich ($\xi = -2.''18$, $\eta = 2.''20$) have been fixed, ED87 is not a geocentric system. The relation to the Conventional Terrestrial System [3.1] is mainly given by the reference frame of 12 fundamental stations. The translation parameters ($X_0 = -83$ m, $Y_0 = -97$ m, $Z_0 = -117$ m) are accurate to ± 1 m, parallelism of the axes is about $\pm 0.''1$, and scale is provided with $\pm 0.1 \times 10^{-6}$ The neighbourhood accuracy between network stations generally is better than $\pm 10^{-6}$ s.

A new *European Reference System* (EUREF) is now under construction. It consists of about 20 SLR/VLBI-sites fairly well distributed over the continent, and of about 100 connected GPS-stations. This three-dimensional system represents the global terrestrial system within Europe, and is intended to serve as frame for future GPS and other high-precision surveys.

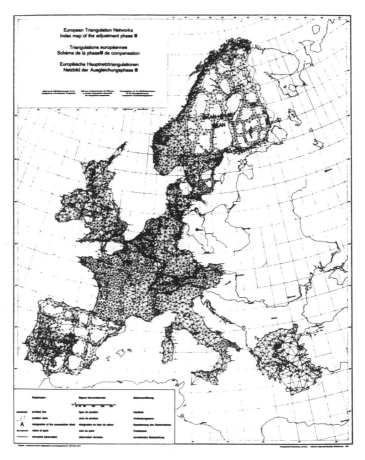

Fig. 6.7. European horizontal network RETRIG, after EHRNSPERGER et al. (1987)

A readjustment (1974–1986) of the *geodetic control networks* in *North America* (including U.S.A., Canada, Greenland, Mexico and Central America) has led to the *North American Datum of 1983* (NAD83), replacing NAD27 [6.1.6], SCHWARZ (1989), SCHWARZ and WADE (1990).

Terrestrial data include horizontal directions from fundamental triangulation (1. to 4. order in U.S.A.), astronomical azimuths, and electronic and taped distance measurements, cf. [6.1.6]. More than 1000 Doppler stations (200 km average station separation) provide an areal control and the translation to the geocenter while a number of VLBI base lines give the system's scale and orientation. The rigorous adjustment (about 1.8 Mill. observations, more than 900 000 unknowns, more than 260 000 stations) was realized by Helmert-blocking (1500 to 2000 stations per block), and used the height-constrained three-dimensional method (VINCENTY 1980). 3D-formulas [3.4.3], [5.1.2] were employed, holding heights and astronomical coordinates fixed, thus avoiding reductions to the ellipsoid. Deflections of the vertical and geoid heights were derived from astronomical and gravimetric data, cf. [5.2.3]. Computations were performed with respect to the ellipsoid of the Geodetic Reference System 1980 [3.5.5], in a geocentric position (BIH Terrestrial System of 1984). From comparisons with GPS results, r.m.s. discrepancies of $\pm$ few cm to ± 0.2 m have been found for distances between 10 and 300 km (SNAY 1990).

6.2 Vertical Control Networks

6.2.1 Design, Monumentation, Observations

Vertical control networks are determined by the method of geometric leveling; the control points are known as *bench marks* (BM). The BM-network is based on a first-order leveling net which is designed in loops having diameters of 100 km or less. The loops are composed of leveling lines which connect nodal points. These lines, in turn, are formed by leveling runs which connect neighboring bench marks (average spacing of 1 km).

The BM are generally marked above ground by bolts on buildings, in bedrock, or on concrete posts; and in areas of lesser stability (alluvium) by long pipes (pipe mark). Monuments established underground at larger intervals secure the network and serve as a basis for scientific investigations regarding changes of elevation. The leveling lines in general follow main traffic routes; the first-order lines should pass over the most stable regions.

The leveling is conducted according to the procedures of *precise leveling* [4.3.5].

Since regional and local changes in elevation can reach magnitudes of mm/year, the vertical control networks should be releveled at not too long time intervals (20 to 30 years). A higher repetition rate should be pursued in areas having experienced recent, large changes in elevation, cf. [5.5.5].

GPS positioning now delivers *ellipsoidal* height differences with cm- to dm-accuracy over distances of 10 to 1000 km, cf. [5.3.4]. Consequently, this very economic method has the potential of strengthening leveling networks provided that geoid or quasigeoid differences can be determined with corresponding accuracies, cf. [6.2.4].

6.2.2 Computations

The *reference surface for heights* (geoid, quasigeoid) [3.3.2] is established by tying it to the mean sea level. Due to the difficulties in the determination of mean sea level and because of the departure of this surface from a level surface [3.3.3], the reference surfaces for height in the various countries can differ by more than one meter.

Prior to the adjustment of the first-order leveling nets, the *observed raw height differences* must be corrected for the fact that the level surfaces are not parallel. By multiplication with surface gravity, the leveled height differences can easily be transformed into differences of *geopotential numbers*, cf. [4.3.5]. In most networks, the raw results have been converted to either differences of *orthometric heights* or differences of *normal heights* using the orthometric or normal correction, respectively [5.1.5]. Gravity measurements provide the necessary surface gravity values along the path of the leveling line.

In many countries, surface gravity values along the leveling lines were generally not available (until the 1950s), when vertical control networks were established. Therefore, actual gravity was replaced by normal gravity (3.64), which led to *normal* or *spheroidal orthometric heights*. The spheroidal orthometric correction for larger gravity anomalies can differ from the orthometric correction (5.17) by a few mm (flat terrain), and up to some dm (mountaineous area). The spheroidal orthometric heights therefore represent a poor approximation to the orthometric heights, their values depend on the path of leveling. They can be viewed as a first step towards normal heights (WOLF 1974). Nowadays these height systems are converted to systems of normal or orthometric heights.

Traditionally *adjustment* by conditions has been preferred in leveling networks, with the loop misclosures set to zero, but the method of variation of parameters is generally applied now.

Normal heights can be determined without an hypothesis. They have been introduced in eastern Europe (SCHNEIDER 1960), and in France. For the computation of *orthometric heights*, hypotheses must be formed regarding the mass distribution between the physical surface of the earth and the geoid. Here, the average value of gravity along the plumb line can be approximated by the value at the height $H/2$. It is obtained under the assumption of constant density and plate-like topography by removing the Bouguer plate (5.70), applying a free-air reduction (5.66) down to $H/2$, and subsequently restoring the plate, where the sign is again negative. Using the density 2670 kg m^{-3}, we obtain the solution (5.20). The heights computed on the basis of this hypothesis are called *Helmert heights*. In mountainous regions, the error resulting from this hypothesis can reach values on the order of cm. An improvement to the model is possible, according to NIETHAMMER (1932), by considering the density variations and the actual topography (terrain reduction (5.71)). Such a refined system of orthometric heights has recently been introduced in Austria, employing a high-resolution digital terrain and density model (HÖGGERL 1986, SÜNKEL 1988).

6.2.3 National Networks: Examples

The *Primary Leveling Network of the Federal Republic of Germany* (DHHN) is an example of an areal first-order leveling net. It is composed of network parts which were observed from 1912 to 1960 (HELLER and WERNTHALER 1955). New parts were tied to the existing net by constraining the latter. The loops of this net have diameters of 30 to 80 km (Fig. 6.8). The first-order lines pass over particularly stable areas; they are secured by underground marks in the form of granite pillars. At geologically well suited locations, three underground marks are combined in each case to form one group; at prominent places of unchanging elevation five marks are combined for one national first-order bench mark.

From the differences between the forward and backward leveling runs, the standard deviation is given by ± 0.3 to ± 0.4 mm $\sqrt{s_{km}}$. The loop misclosures deliver corresponding values of ± 0.4 to ± 0.7 mm $\sqrt{s_{km}}$. These discrepancies can be explained by the neglect of the correlations between the observations in the error analysis (LUCHT 1972).

Since 1879, the heights have referred to the level surface through the reference point of mean sea level; this surface is designated Normal-Null (NN), (*sea level datum*). The reference point of mean sea level is situated 37.000 m below the standard bench mark which was established

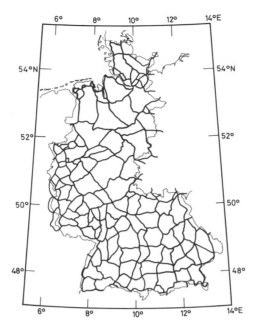

Fig. 6.8. Primary leveling net of the Federal Republic of Germany (DHHN = Deutsches Haupthöhennetz), from AUGATH (1988)

at the former Berlin Observatory in 1879. The standard benchmark of 1879 was replaced in 1912, due to the demolition of the observatory, by an underground mark about 40 km to the east of Berlin (standard benchmark of 1912). The height of the standard benchmark of 1879 was obtained via leveling lines (cm-accuracy in the transfer) from the tidal gauge at Amsterdam ("Normaal Amsterdamsch Peil" NAP). The heights represent the vertical distance from the reference surface: heights above mean sea level; the unit of measure is the international meter. Practically, the reference surface is defined by the aggregate of first-order points, particularly the underground marks.

As no gravity measurements were available when this network was established, only the spheroidal-*orthometric correction* was applied to the raw leveling results, cf. [6.2.2]. A readjustment in geopotential numbers is under way, after extensive leveling and gravimetric data acquisition along the leveling lines. Normal heights will probably be introduced for the official height system.

The *U.S.A.* and *Canada* are also covered by an areal distribution of precise leveling lines, which are tied to 26 tidal stations. The adjusted heights establish the *National Geodetic Vertical Datum of* 1929 (formerly the Sea Level Datum of 1929). The accuracy estimated from loop misclosures yields standard deviations which are generally less than or equal to ± 1 mm $\sqrt{s_{km}}$ (BAKER 1974). As the mean sea level of the tidal stations was held fixed (zero height) in the adjustment, distortions from neglected sea surface topography have been introduced into the height system, cf. [3.3.3]. These distortions may amount to 0.7 m from coast to coast, but should remain less than 0.1 m along the coast lines. A new adjustment of the North American Vertical Datum will be completed soon, cf. [6.2.4].

The first-order leveling lines in *Australia* run along the more developed areas of the coastal regions. A widespread coverage over the entire continent is being undertaken with third-order leveling lines. (3. order standard deviation ± 12 mm $\sqrt{s_{km}}$). Numerous ties to tidal stations permit comparisons with the sea surface topography [3.3.3].

6.2.4 Network Unification and Large-Scale Control

National vertical control networks have to be unified in order to solve problems of continental scope. They then serve for investigating mean sea level deviations from a common level surface (sea surface topography), cf. [3.3.3], for the detection of vertical crustal movements, cf. [5.5.5], and for height control in large-scale engineering projects. We mention two examples of continental vertical control networks.

The *United European Leveling Net* (Réseau Européen Unifié de Nivellement, REUN) was formed in 1954 from selected first-order leveling lines of the participating countries (western Europe), with loop circumferences of 500 to 1200 km. The net is connected to about 60 tide gauges located along the coast lines of the Mediterranean, the Atlantic, the North Sea, and the Baltic, (Fig. 6.9). It was adjusted in geopotential numbers. The loop misclosures attained maximum values of 0.2 gpu (the geopotential unit gpu approximately corresponds to the meter unit, cf. [3.3.2]). The REUN refers to the mean sea level of the North Sea as determined by the "Normaal Amsterdamsch Peil (NAP)" of 1950.0 (middle of the observation period 1940–1958). According to

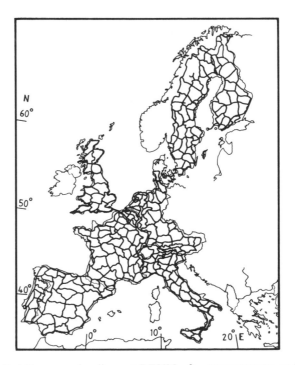

Fig. 6.9. United European leveling net REUN, after EHRNSPERGER and KOK (1987)

oceanographic information, this determination is 0.5 m below the geoid (LISITZIN A1974). A readjustment (UELN-73) has been performed, which includes new leveling data (about 100 000 km of leveling lines, 775 adjusted heights, maximum standard deviation with respect to NAP ±0.07 gpu), EHRNSPERGER and KOK (1987). Further development of REUN will be directed to a kinematic network (modeling of vertical crustal movements) and to an eventual use of tidal stations for strengthening the network.

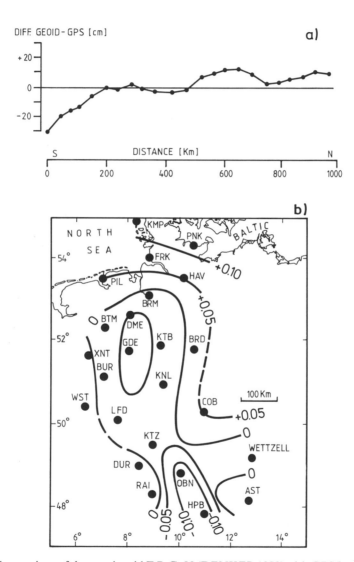

Fig. 6.10. Comparison of the quasigeoid F.R.G. 89 (DENKER 1989) with GPS/leveling results a) along the European GPS traverse between Munich and Flensburg (TORGE et al. 1989), b) areal control from the DÖNAV campaign (calculation IfE Hannover, Prof. Seeber), after TORGE (1990c)

The *North American Vertical Datum of 1988* (NAVD88) will be the result of a readjustment of the leveling data in U.S.A., Canada, Mexico, and Central America, after replacing destroyed bench marks, and extensive releveling. The adjustment will be performed using geopotential numbers, with observed or interpolated gravity values for the bench marks. In order to manage the computation work (620 000 bench marks), partitioning of the unknowns into blocks and least squares "Helmert-blocking" technique will be employed (WOLF 1978). The question of how to incorporate tidal heights (datum definition) is still under discussion (ZILKOSKI 1987).

As geometric leveling is time-consuming, and suffers from the accumulation of systematic errors over large distances, *GPS-derived ellipsoidal height differences* (cm-to dm-accuracy over distances from a few km to 1000 km, cf. [5.3.4]) can strengthen vertical control networks. In order to combine "GPS"-heights with "levelled" heights, differences in *geoid heights* or *height anomalies* have to be known with corresponding accuracy according to (5.5) and (5.6), TORGE (1987). Recent regional and local geoid or quasigeoid computations are capable of meeting this requirement, cf. [5.2.3], ENGELIS et al. (1985), DENKER et al. (1991), see Fig. 6.10. In local areas (10 to 20 km extension) with a smooth gravity field, GPS heights may even be transformed to the vertical control net by simple geometric transformation (ZILKOSKI and HOTHEM 1989).

6.3 Gravity Networks

6.3.1 Design, Monumentation, Observations, and Computations

Gravity networks form the framework for geodetic and geophysical gravity measurements. The first-order gravity net evenly covers a particular country with a number of points which are interconnected by relative gravimeter measurements of high precision cf. [4.2.2]. The relation of the net to a *gravity reference* level is determined by connecting it to a global gravity system or to absolute gravity measurements. Most of the existing nets already refer to the IGSN71 [4.2.4]. The scale of the net is obtained by calibrating the relative gravimeters on special calibration lines. With the development of transportable absolute gravimeters [6.2.1], gravity reference and network scale can be derived from a number of absolute gravity stations, well distributed over the survey region.

When choosing the stations, care should be taken to ensure that they are as stable as possible, cf. [4.2.4]. Easy lines of traffic should exist between stations, since a quick connection between two points is advantageous in the determination of drift. In large networks, gravity stations are frequently located at airports; these points, which are generally not permanent, must be tied to the actual first-order points by special centering measurements. In order to control the spatial position of a gravity point to a corresponding accuracy of ± 0.1 μms^{-2}, relative height and position should be locally controlled within accuracies of ± 1 mm and ± 1 cm respectively. In addition, one should make sure that no mass displacements have occurred in the vicinity of the point. This can be done by establishing gravimetric eccenters in the vicinity of the station.

The *survey procedure* for a first order gravity network includes instrumental investigations and calibration of relative gravimeters, the establishment of absolute gravity points with station separations of some 100 km (or the connection to IGSN71 stations), and the multiple observation of all network stations with several relative gravimeters. An optimization procedure may be employed in order to obtain maximum accuracy and reliability (TORGE A1989). The network adjustment is generally performed by variation of parameters which include the gravity values, and drift and calibration parameters, cf. [4.2.4]. Recently established gravity networks have an average accuracy of $\pm 0.1 \ \mu\mathrm{ms}^{-2}$

6.3.2 National Networks: Examples

In *Germany*, areal gravimetric surveys based on a net of relative pendulum stations (Potsdam Gravity System) have been performed between the 1930s and 1960s. A new *fundamental gravity network* (DSGN76) was observed in the Federal Republic of Germany from 1976 to 1977 (SIGL et al. 1981). This network consists of 21 stations, each being represented by a station center and 3 eccenters, Fig. 6.11. 4 stations were surveyed with the absolute gravimeter of the IMGC/Torino, cf. [4.2.1]. 44 network ties were measured twice in the sequence 1-2, 2-1 by two crews, each equipped with two LaCoste-Romberg gravimeters. The network adjustment yielded standard deviations of $\pm 0.06 \ldots 0.11 \ \mu\mathrm{ms}^{-2}$. The DSGN76 is densified in three orders (station density in 1st, 2nd and 3rd order is 1 station/1000 km², 1/100 km², and 1/5 km², respectively).

In the *U.S.A.*, a gravity base network with 59 stations was established in 1966/67 and renewed in 1975/76 with 4 LaCoste-Romberg gravimeters, observing closed loops.

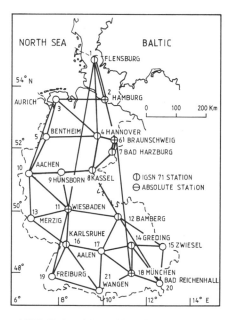

Fig. 6.11. Gravity base net 1976, Federal Republic of Germany (Deutsches Schweregrundnetz DSGN76), after SIGL et al. 1981

A fundamental absolute gravity net (about 50 stations, station separation 300 km) is currently under development, employing a JILA absolute gravimeter, cf. [4.2.1], PETER et al. (1989).

The *Canadian* Gravity Standardization Network (CGSN) consists of 241 first-order and some 5000 second-order stations (Fig. 6.12). It has been observed with LaCoste-Romberg gravimeters and is tied to ISGN71-stations. Recently the network has been strengthened by absolute gravity measurements at nine stations (JILA gravimeter), LAMBERT et al. (1989).

The *Australian* National Gravity Base-station Network (1980) includes 240 airport stations, tied by traverses with LaCoste-Romberg gravimeters, and controlled by 6 absolute measurements with the USSR absolute gravimeter.

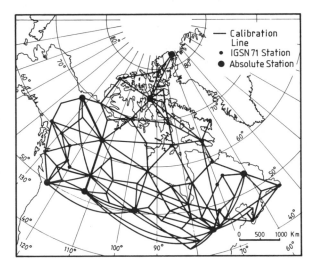

Fig. 6.12. First order Canadian gravity standardization network CGSN 1980, after LAMBERT et al. (1989)

References

Abbreviations frequently used:

AVN = Allgemeine Vermessungsnachrichten. H. Wichmann, Karlsruhe.

BGI = Bulletin d'Information, Bureau Gravimetrique International. Toulouse.

Boll. Geof. teor. appl. = Bolletino di Geofisica teorica ed applicata. Osservatorio Geofisico Sperimentale, Trieste.

Bull. Géod. = Bulletin Géodésique. Springer, Berlin-Heidelberg-New-York.

Can. Surv. = The Canadian Surveyor, Ottawa.

DGK = Veröffentlichungen der Deutschen Geodätischen Kommission bei der Bayerischen Akademie der Wissenschaften. München und Frankfurt a.M.

EOS = Transactions. American Geophysical Union, Washington, D.C.

Geoph. J. R. Astr. Soc. = Geophysical Journal of the Royal Astronomical Society. London.

Gerl. Beitr. Geoph. = Gerlands Beiträge zur Geophysik. Akademische Verlagsgesellschaft Geest & Portig K.-G., Leipzig.

J. Geophys. = Journal of Geophysics (Zeitschrift für Geophysik). Springer, Berlin-Heidelberg-New York.

JGR = Journal of Geophysical Research. American Geophysical Union, Washington, D.C.

Man. Geod. = Manuscripta Geodetica. Springer, Berlin-Heidelberg-New York.

Mitt. Inst. Theor. Geod. Bonn = Mitteilungen aus dem Institut für Theoretische Geodäsie der Universität Bonn.

OSU Rep. = Reports of the Department of Geodetic Science (formerly Rep. of the Institute of Geodesy, Photogrammetry and Cartography). The Ohio State University, Columbus, Ohio.

Rev. Geophys. = Reviews of Geophysics and Space Physics. Washington, D.C.

SAO Spec. Rep. = SAO Special Reports, Smithsonian Institution, Astrophysical Observatory, Cambridge, Mass.

Surv. Rev. = Survey Review. Tolworth, Survey, U.K.

Unisurv = Unisurv G — Univ. of New South Wales Reports. Kensington, N.S.W.

Wiss. Arb. Univ. Hannover = Wissenschaftliche Arbeiten der Fachrichtung Vermessungswesen der Universität Hannover.

ZfV = Zeitschrift für Vermessungswesen. K. Wittwer, Stuttgart.

A. Text Books, Manuals, and Symposia Proceedings

The Astronomical Almanach for the Year 1985. Washington-London 1985.

BARTELS, J. Gezeitenkräfte. In: S. Flügge (Herausg.): Handbuch der Physik, 48, Springer-Verlag Berlin-Göttingen-Heidelberg, 734–774, 1957.

BIALAS, V. Erdgestalt, Kosmologie und Weltanschauung. K. Wittwer, Stuttgart 1982.

BIRÓ, P. Time variation of height and gravity. H. Wichmann Verlag, 1983.

BOMFORD, G. Geodesy. 4. ed., Clarendon Press, Oxford 1980.

BONATZ, M., P. MELCHIOR (eds). Proceed. 8th Internat. Symp. on Earth Tides, Bonn 1977. Inst. f. Theor. Geod., Univ. Bonn 1977.

BOTT, M. H. P. The interior of the earth. 2. ed., Elsevier Science Publ., Amsterdam 1982.

BROUWER, D., G. M. CLEMENCE. Methods of celestial mechanics. Academic Press, New York 1961.

BRUNNER, F. K. (ed.). Geodetic refraction. Springer-Verlag, Berlin-Heidelberg-New York 1984.

BRUNNER, F. K., CHR. RIZOS (eds.). Developments in four-dimensional geodesy. Lecture Notes in Earth Sciences 29, Springer-Verlag, Berlin-Heidelberg-New York 1990.

BULLEN, K. E. The earth's density. Chapman and Hall, London 1975.

DEHLINGER, P. Marine gravity. Elsevier Scient. Publ. Co., Amsterdam etc. 1978.

DEUMLICH, F. Surveying instruments. W. de Gruyter, Berlin-New York 1982.

EICHHORN, H. Astronomy of star positions. F. Ungar Publ. Co., New York 1974.

GAPOSCHKIN, E. M., B. KOLACZEK (eds.). Reference coordinate systems for earth dynamics. D. Reidel, Dordrecht 1981.

GOAD, C. C. (ed.). Proc. First Int. Symp. on Precise Positioning with the Global Positioning System. Rockville, Md., 1985.

GRAFAREND, E., F. SANSÓ (eds.). Optimization and design of geodetic networks. Springer-Verlag, Berlin-Heidelberg-New York 1985.

GROSSMANN, W. Geodätische Rechnungen und Abbildungen in der Landesvermessung. 3. ed., K. Wittwer, Stuttgart 1976.

GROTEN, E. Geodesy and the earth's gravity field. F. Dümmler, Bonn 1979.

GROTEN, E., R. STRAUSS (eds.). GPS-techniques applied to geodesy and surveying. Lecture Notes in Earth Sciences 19, Springer-Verlag, Berlin-Heidelberg-New York 1988.

HECK, B. Rechenverfahren und Auswertemodelle der Landesvermessung. H. Wichmann, Karlsruhe 1987.

HEISKANEN, W. A., H. MORITZ. Physical geodesy. W.H. Freeman and Co., San Francisco and London 1967.

HEISKANEN, W. A., F. A. VENING MEINESZ. The earth and its gravity field. McGraw-Hill, New York 1958.

HEITZ, S. Coordinates in geodesy. Springer-Verlag, Berlin-Heidelberg-New York 1985.

HELMERT, F. R. Die mathematischen und physikalischen Theorien der höheren Geodäsie. Teubner, Leipzig 1880/1884. Reprint Minerva GmbH, Frankfurt a.M. 1961.

HENNEBERG, H. G. (ed.) Recent crustal movements, 1985. Tectonophysics 130, No. 1–4, 1986.

HOBSON, E. W. The theory of spherical and ellipsoidal harmonics. Cambridge Univ. Press 1931 (reprint 1955).

HOTINE, M. Mathematical geodesy. ESSA Monogr. 2, Washington 1969.

HRADILEK, L. Threedimensional terrestrial triangulation-applications in surveying engineering. K. Wittwer, Stuttgart 1984.

INGHAM, A. E. Sea surveying. J. Wiley and Sons, London 1975.

JEFFREYS, SIR HAROLD. The earth — its origin, history and physical constitution. 5. ed., Cambridge Univ. Press 1970.

JORDAN-EGGERT-KNEISSL. Handbuch der Vermessungskunde. 10. Aufl., J.B. Metzler, Stuttgart. Band IV. M. Kneissl: Mathematische Geodäsie (Landesvermessung), 1958/1959.

KAHMEN, H. Elektronische Meßverfahren in der Geodäsie. 2. Aufl., H. Wichmann, Karlsruhe 1978.

KAHMEN, H., W. FAIG. Surveying. W. de Gruyter, Berlin-New York 1988.

KAULA, W. M. Theory of satellite geodesy. Blaisdell Publ. Co., London 1966.

KELLOGG, O. D. Foundations of potential theory. J. Springer, Berlin 1929 (Dover Publ., New York 1953).

KING, R. W., E. G. MASTERS, C. RIZOS, A. STOLZ, J. COLLINS. Surveying with Global Positioning System. F. Dümmler, Bonn 1987.

KUNTZ, E. Kartennetzentwurfslehre. H. Wichmann, Karlsruhe 1983.

LAMBECK, K. The earth's variable rotation. Cambridge Univ. Press 1980.

LAMBECK, K. Geophysical geodesy. Clarendon Press, Oxford 1988.

LAURILA, H. S. Electronic surveying and navigation. J. Wiley and Sons, New York 1976.

LE PICHON, X., J. FRANCHETEAU, J. BONNIN. Plate tectonics. Developm. in Geotectonics, vol. 6, Elsevier, Amsterdam-London-New York 1973.

LEVALLOIS, J. J. Mesurer la terre — 300 ans de géodésie Francaise. Association Francaise de Topographie, Paris 1988.

LISITZIN, E. Sea level changes. Elsevier, Amsterdam etc. 1974.

MARUSSI, A. Intrinsic geodesy. Springer-Verlag, Berlin-Heidelberg-New York 1985.

MELCHIOR, P. The tides of the planet earth. Pergamon Press, Oxford etc. 1983.

MOLODENSKII, M. S., V. F. EREMEEV, M. I. YURKINA. Methods for study of the external gravitational field and figure of the earth (1960). Israel Progr. for Scient. Transl., Jerusalem 1962.

MORITZ, H. Advanced physical geodesy. H. Wichmann-Abacus Press, Karlsruhe-Tunbridge Wells 1980.

MORITZ, H. The figure of the earth. H. Wichmann, Karlsruhe 1990.

MORITZ, H., I. I. MUELLER. Earth rotation. F. Ungar Publ. Co., New York 1987.

MUELLER, I. I. Spherical and practical astronomy. F. Ungar Publ. Co., New York 1969.

MUELLER, I. I., S. ZERBINI (eds.). The interdisciplinary role of space geodesy. Lecture Notes in Earth Sciences 22, Springer-Verlag, Berlin-Heidelberg-New York 1989.

MUELLER, S. (ed.). The structure of the earth's crust based on seismic data. Elsevier, Amsterdam etc. 1974.

NETTLETON, L. L. Gravity and magnetics in oil prospecting. Mc Graw-Hill, New York etc. 1976.

PELZER, H., W. NIEMEIER (eds.). Determination of heights and height changes. F. Dümmler, Bonn 1987.

RICHARDUS, P., R. K. ADLER. Map projections. Am. Elsevier Publ. Co., New York 1974.

RIKITAKE, T. Earthquake forecasting and warning. Center for Academic Publ. Japan/Tokyo — D. Reidel Publ. Co., Dordrecht-Boston-London 1982.

RUNCORN, S. K. (ed.). International dictionary of geophysics. Pergamon Press. Oxford etc. 1967.

SAGITOV, M. U., B. BODRI, V. S. NAZARENKO, KH. G. TADZHIDINOV. Lunar gravimetry. Academic Press, London-Orlando 1986.

SCHNEIDER, M. Himmelsmechanik. 2. Aufl., BI-Wissenschaftsverlag, Mannheim 1984.

SCHNEIDER, M. Satellitengeodäsie. BI-Wissenschaftsverlag, Mannheim-Wien-Zürich 1988.

SCHNEIDER, M. (ed.). Satellitengeodäsie. VCH Verlagsges., Weinheim 1990.

SCHÖDLBAUER, A. Rechenformeln und Rechenbeispiele zur Landesvermessung. H. Wichmann, Karlsruhe 1981.

SCHWARZ, K. P. (ed.). Inertial technology for surveying and geodesy. Proc. Third Int. Symp., Banff, Canada 1985. The Division of Surveying Eng., The Univ. of Calgary, Canada 1986.

SEEBER, G. Satellitengeodäsie Satellite geodesy. W. de Gruyter, Berlin-New York 1989/1992.

SIGL, R. Geodätische Astronomie. H. Wichmann, Karlsruhe 1975.

SIGL, R. Introduction to potential theory. Abacus Press, Cambridge 1985.

SMART, W. M. Textbook on spherical astronomy. Cambridge Univ. Press, London 1960.

STACEY, F. D. Physics of the earth. 2. ed., J. Wiley and Sons, New York-London-Sidney-Toronto 1977.

STOKER, J. J. Differential geometry. Wiley-Interscience, New York 1969.

SÜNKEL, H. (ed.). Mathematical and numerical techniques in physical geodesy. Lecture Notes in Earth Sciences 7, Springer-Verlag, Berlin-Heidelberg-New York 1986.

TOMASCHEK, R. Tides of the solid earth. In: S. Flügge (Herausg.): Handbuch der Physik, 48, 775–845, Springer-Verlag, Berlin-Göttingen-Heidelberg 1957.

TORGE, W. Gravimetry. W. de Gruyter, Berlin-New York 1989.

VANÍČEK, P., E. J. KRAKIWSKY. Geodesy: The Concepts. 2. rev. ed., Elsevier Science Publ., Amsterdam-New York 1986.

VIEIRA, R. (ed.). Proc. 10th Internat. Symp. on Earth Tides, Madrid 1985.

VYSKOČIL, P., A. M. WASSEF, G. GREEN (eds.). Recent Crustal movements, 1982. Developments in Geotectonics 20 (Tectonophysics Vol. 97), Elsevier, Amsterdam etc. 1983.

WEGENER, A. Die Entstehung der Kontinente und Ozeane (1915). 4. Aufl., Vieweg u. Sohn, Braunschweig 1962.

WELLS, D. (ed.). Guide to GPS-positioning. Canadian GPS Associates, Fredericton, New Brunswick 1987.

B. Individual Publications

ADOS 1987. African Doppler Survey 1981–1986: Results. Regional Centre for Services in Surveying, Mapping and Remote Sensing, Nairobi 1987.

ALLMAN, J. S., C. VEENSTRA. Geodetic model of Australia 1982. National Mapping Techn. Report No. 33, 1984.

ANDERLE, R. J. Determination of polar motion from satellite observations. Geophys. Surveys 1, 147–161, 1973.

ANDERLE, R. J. Polar motion determined by Doppler satellite observations. Bull. Géod. 50, 377–390, 1976.

ANDERSEN, N., J. GRABOWSKI, O. REMMER. The hydrostatic levelling across the Fehmarn Belt. In: H. Pelzer, A. Witte (eds.), Precise vertical positioning, F. Dümmler, Bonn 1991 (in press).

ANGUS-LEPPAN, P. V. A system of observations for four-dimensional geodesy. Proc. I.A.G.-Symp. "The Earth's Gravitational Field and Secular Variations in Position". Univ. of New South Wales. Sydney, 702–709, 1973.

ANGUS-LEPPAN, P. V. Refraction in geodetic levelling. In: F. K. Brunner (ed.), 163–180, 1984.

ARNOLD, K. Considerations on satellite altimetry. Gerl. Beitr. Geoph. 83, 90–94, 1974.

ASHKENAZI, V. Triangulation, trilateration or traverse. Vladimiro K. Hristov-Septuagenario. Academia Scientarum Bulgarica, 121–126, Sofia 1973.

ASHKENAZI, V., T. MOORE, M. E. NAPIER, C. DE LA FUENTE. Using GPS to control a triangulation network. Surv. Rev. 29, 287–294, 1988.

ASSOCIATION INTERNATIONALE DE GÉODÉSIE. Geodetic Reference System 1967. Publ. Spéc. du Bull. Géod., Paris 1971.

AUGATH, W. Experiences with Trimble receivers in the control network of the F.R.G. In: E. Groten, R. Strauß (eds.), 131–143, 1988.

BAKER, L. S. Geodetic networks in the United States. Can. Surv. 28, 445–451, 1974.

BAKER, T. F., R. J. EDGE, G. JEFFRIES. European tidal gravity: an improved agreement between observations and models. Geophys. Res. Letters 16, 1109–1112, 1989.

BALMINO, G. La representation du potentiél terrestre par masses ponctuelles. Bull. Géod. no. 111, 85–108, 1974.

BALMINO, G., A. BERNARD. Satellite gravity gradiometry for the determination of the geopotential. In: Proceed. of an ESA Special Workshop on "Solid Earth Science and Application Mission for Europe" (SESAME), 95–101. Chiemsee, F.R. Germany 1986. (ESA SP-1080).

BALMINO, G., B. MOYNOT, M. SARRAILH, N. VALES. Free air gravity anomalies over the oceans from SEASAT and GEOS3 altimeter data. EOS 68, 17–19, 1987.

BAŠIĆ, T. Untersuchungen zur regionalen Geoidbestimmung mit "dm" Genauigkeit. Wiss. Arb. Univ. Hannover, Nr. 157, 1989.

BECKER, J.-M. The experiences with new levelling techniques ML and MTL. In: H. Pelzer and W. Niemeier (eds.), 159–174, 1987.

BENDER, P. L., E. C. SILVERBERG. Present tectonic plate motions from lunar ranging. Tectono-physics 29, 1–7, 1975.

BENDER, P. L., D. G. CURRIE, R. H. DICKE et al. The lunar laser ranging experiment. Science 182, 229–238, 1973.

BERGER, J., J. LEVINE. The spectrum of Earth strain from 10^{-8} to 10^2 Hz. JGR 79, 1210–1214, 1974.

BEUTLER, G., I. BAUERSIMA, W. GURTNER, M. ROTHACKER, T. SCHILDKNECHT. Static Position-ing with the Global Positioning System (GPS): State of the art. In: E. Groten, R. Strauß (eds.), 363–380, 1988.

BEYER, L. A., R. E. VON HUENE, T. H. MCCULLOH, J. R. LOVETT. Measuring gravity on the sea floor in deep water. JGR 71, 2091–2100, 1966.

BILHAM, R., R. YEATS, S. CERBINI. Space geodesy and the global forecast of earthquakes. EOS 70, 65, 73, 1989.

BILLS, B. G., A. J. FERRARI. A lunar density model consistent with topographic, gravitational, librational and seismic data. JGR 82, 1306–1314, 1977.

BILLS, B. G., S. P. SYNNOTT. Planetary geodesy. Rev. Geophys. 25, 833–839, 1987.

BIRARDI, G. The establishment of a net of vertical deflection points in Italy by means of a photo-astronomical procedure. Boll. di Geod. e Scienze Affini 35, 113–152, 1976.

BJERHAMMAR, A. Discrete solutions of the boundary value problem in physical geodesy. Tellus 27, 97–106, 1975.

BLAHA, G. Investigations of critical configurations for fundamental range networks. OSU Rep. no. 150, Columbus, Ohio 1971.

BODEMÜLLER, H. Die geodätischen Linien des Rotationsellipsoides und die Lösung der geodä-tischen Hauptaufgaben für große Strecken unter besonderer Berücksichtigung der Bessel-Helmertschen Lösungsmethode. DGK, B Nr. 13, München 1954.

BOEDECKER, G., TH. FRITZER. International Absolute Gravity Basestation Network. IAG-SSG 3.87 Status Report March 1986. Veröff. Bayer. Komm. für die Internat. Erdmessung der Bayer. Akad. d. Wissensch., Astron.-Geod. Arb., Heft Nr. 47, München 1986.

BOMFORD, G. The astrogeodetic geoid in Europe and connected areas 1971. Travaux de l'Assoc. Intern. de Géodésie 24, 357–370, Paris 1972.

BOSSLER, J. D., C. C. GOAD, P. L. BENDER. Using the Global Positioning System (GPS) for geodetic positioning. Bull. Géod. 54, 553–563, 1980.

BOSSLER, J. D., E. GRAFAREND, R. KELM. Optimal design of geodetic nets 2. JGR 78, 5887–5897, 1973.

BOUCHER, C. GPS receiver technology. In: S. Turner (ed.), Applied Geodesy, 11–15. Springer, Berlin-Heidelberg-New York 1987.

BOWIN, C., TH. C. ALDRICH, R. A. FOLINSBEE. VSA Gravity Meter System: Tests and recent developments. JGR 77, 2018–2033, 1972.

BOWRING, B. R. The accuracy of geodetic latitude and height equations. Surv. Rev. 28, 202–206, 1985.

BRENNECKE, J., D. LELGEMANN, W. TORGE, H. -G. WENZEL. Validation of SEASAT-l altim-etry using ground truth in the North Sea region. DGK, B Nr. 263, Frankfurt a.M. 1982.

BRENNECKE, J., D. LELGEMANN, E. REINHART, W. TORGE, G. WEBER, H.-G. WENZEL. A European astro-gravimetric geoid. DGK, B Nr. 269, Frankfurt a.M. 1983.

BROWN, D. C. Doppler Surveying with the JMR-1 receiver. Bull. Géod. 50, 9–25, 1976a.

BROWN, D. C. Doppler positioning by the short arc method. Proc. Int. Symp. on Sat. Doppler Positioning, 97–140, Las Cruzes, USA, 1976b.

BROZENA, J. M., M. F. PETERS. An airborne gravity study of eastern North Carolina. Geophy-sics 53, 245–253, 1988.

BROZENA, J. M., G. L. MADER, M. F. PETERS. Interferometric Global Positioning System: Three-dimensional positioning source for airborne gravimetry. JGR 94, 12153–12162, 1989.

BRUNS, H. Die Figur der Erde. Publ. Königl. Preuß. Geod. Inst., Berlin 1878.

BUREAU GRAVIMETRIQUE INTERNATIONAL. Carte des anomalies de Bouguer Europe-Afrique 1:10 000 000, 3. ed., Paris 1971.

BURŠA, M. Sur certaines relations entre les parametres de l'ellipsoide terrestre et le champ de gravitè, en particulier par rapport au systeme de reference A.I.G. 1967. Bull. Géod. no. 97, 261–289, 1970.

BURŠA, M. Parameters of the selenopotential and the lunar deflections of the vertical. Bull. Astron. Inst. CSSR 26, 140–148, 1975.

CAMPBELL, J. Basislängenänderungen — abgeleitet aus VLBI-Beobachtungen im Projekt IRIS. In: M. Schneider (ed.), 269–289, 1990.

CAMPBELL, J., B. WITTE. Grundlagen und geodätische Anwendung der Very Long Baseline Interferometry (VLBI). ZfV 103, 10–20, 1978.

CAMPBELL, J., G. SEEBER, B. WITTE. Kombination von Doppler-, Laser- und photographischen Beobachtungen in Satellitennetzen. DGK, B Nr. 200, München 1973.

CARROLL, D. G., C. W. WESSELS. A 1975 astrogeodetic geoid for the United States. XVI. Gen. Ass. IAG-I.U.G.G., Grenoble 1975.

CARTER, W. E., D. S. ROBERTSON, J. R. MACKAY. Geodetic radio interferometric surveying: application and results. JGR 90, 4577–4587, 1985.

CARTWRIGHT, D. E., J. CREASE. A comparison of the geodetic reference levels of England and France by means of the sea surface. Proc. Roy. Soc. London A 273, 558–580, 1963.

CARTWRIGHT, D. E., A. C. EDDEN. Corrected tables of tidal harmonics. Geoph. J.R. Astr. Soc. 33, 253–264, 1973.

CARTWRIGHT, D. E., R. J. TAYLER. New computations of the tide-generating potential. Geoph. J.R. Astr. Soc. 23, 45–74, 1971.

CHENG, M. K., R. J. EANES, C. K. SHUM, B. E. SCHUTZ, B. D. TAPLEY. Temporal variations in low degree zonal harmonics from Starlette orbit analysis. Geophys. Res. Letters 16, 393–396, 1989.

CHOVITZ, B. H. Threedimensional model based on Hotine's mathematical geodesy. Can. Surv. 28, 568–573, 1974.

CHOVITZ, B. H. Parameters of common relevance of astronomy, geodesy, and geodynamics. The Geodesist's Handbook — Bull. Géod. 62, 359–367, 1988.

ČOLIĆ, K., S. PETROVIĆ. Correlation between gravity anomalies, geoid heights and Mohorovičić discontinuity depths in the Dinaric-Pannonian region of Yugoslavia. Proceed. IAG-Symp., XVIII. IUGG-Gen. Ass., Hamburg 1983, Vol. 1, 137–146, OSU, Columbus, Ohio 1984.

COOK, A. H. The external gravity field of a rotating spheroid to the order of e^3. Geoph. J.R. Astr. Soc. 2, 199–214, 1959.

COUNSELMAN III, C. C., H. F. HINTEREGGER, R. W. KING, I. I. SHAPIRO. Precision selenodesy via differential interferometry. Science 181, 772–774, 1973.

CULLEY, F. L. Measuring around the earth by electronic tracking of satellites. Surveying and Mapping 25, 515–521, 1965.

DAVIS, J. L., W. H. PRESCOTT, J. L. SVARC, K. J. WENDT. Assessment of Global Positioning System measurements for studies of crustal deformation. JGR 94, 13635–13650, 1989.

DEHANT, V. Tidal parameters for an inelastic earth. Phys. Earth Planet. Inter. 49, 97–116, 1987.

DEICHL, K. Zur Messung mit Pendelastrolabien und ihrer Auswertung. ZfV 100, 499–509, 1975.

DENKER, H. Hochauflösende regionale Schwerefeldbestimmung mit gravimetrischen und topographischen Daten . Wiss . Arb. Univ. Hannover, Nr . 156, 1988.

DENKER, H. A new gravimetric quasigeoid for the Federal Republic of Germany. DGK, B Nr. 291, München 1989.

DENKER, H., R. H. RAPP. Geodetic and oceanographic results from the analysis of 1 year of GEOSAT data. JGR 95, 13151–13168, 1990.

DENKER, H., D. LELGEMANN, W. TORGE, G. WEBER, H.-G. WENZEL. Strategies and requirements for a new European geoid determination. Proc. Int. Symp. on the Definition of the Geoid, Vol. 1, 207–222, Ist. Geogr. Mil. Ital., Firenze 1986.

DENKER, H., TH. GROTE, W. TORGE. High resolution quasigeoid determination by different methods — some results in northwestern Germany. In: H. Pelzer, A. Witte (eds.), Precise vertical positioning, F. Dümmler, Bonn 1991 (in press).

DICKEY, J. O., J. G. WILLIAMS, X. X. NEWHALL, C. F. YODER. Geophysical applications of lunar laser ranging. Proc. IAG-Symp., XVIII. IUGG-Gen. Ass. Hamburg 1983, Vol. 2, 509–521, OSU, Columbus, Ohio 1984.

DIETZ, R. S. Continent and ocean evolution by spreading of the sea floor. Nature 190, 854–857, 1961.

DIRAC, P. A. M. A new basis for cosmology. Proc. Roy. Soc., London, A 165, 199–208, 1938.

DIXON, T., G. BLEWITT, K. LARSON, D. AYNEW, B. HAGER, P. KROGER, L. KRUMEGH, W. STRANGE. GPS measurements of regional deformation in southern California. EOS 71, 1051–1056, 1990.

DMA. Department of Defense World Geodetic System 1984. DMA Techn. Rep. 8350.2, 1987.

DODSON, A. H., P. FLEMING. The Geomensor CR 204: Baseline test results. Surv. Rev. 29, 351–357, 1988.

DOODSON, A. I. The harmonic development of the tide-generating potential. Proc. Roy. Soc. London A 100, 305–329, 1921.

DORRER, E. Direkte numerische Lösung der geodätischen Hauptaufgaben auf Rotationsflächen. DGK, C Nr. 90, München 1966.

DOYLE, F. J., A. A. ELASSAL, J. R. LUCAS. Selenocentric geodetic reference system. NOAA Techn. Rep. NOS 70 NGS 5, Rockville, Md. 1977.

DRAHEIM, H. Die Geodäsie ist die Wissenschaft von der Ausmessung und Abbildung der Erdoberfläche — Eine Umfrage zur heutigen Situation in der Geodäsie. AVN 78, 237–251, 1971.

DUCARME, B. A fundamental station for trans-world tidal gravity profiles. Phys. Earth and Planet. Inter. 11, 119–127, 1975.

Dziewonski, A. M., D. L. ANDERSON. Preliminary reference earth model. Phys. Earth and Planet. Inter. 25, 297–356, 1981.

ECKER, E., E. MITTERMAYER. Gravity corrections for the influence of the atmosphere. Boll. Geof. teor. appl. 11, 70–80, 1969.

EDGE, R. J., T. F. BAKER, G. JEFFRIES. Improving the accuracy of tidal gravity measurements. In: R. Vieira (ed.), 213–222, 1986.

EEG, J., T. KRARUP. Integrated geodesy. Dan. Geod. Inst., int. rep. no.7, Copenhagen 1973.

EGGE, D. Zur sequentiellen Auswertung von Doppler-Satellitenbeobachtungen. Wiss. Arb. Univ. Hannover, Nr. 141, 1985.

EHRNSPERGER, W., J. J. KOK. Status and results of the 1986 adjustment of the United European Levelling Network — UELN-73. In: H. Pelzer and W. Niemeier (eds.), 7–45, 1987.

EHRNSPERGER, W., H. HORNIK, R. KELM, H. TREMEL. Das Europäische Datum 1987 (ED87) als Gebrauchsnetz für die Landesvermessung. ZfV 112, 93–104, 1987.

ENGELIS, T., R. H. RAPP, Y. BOCK. Measuring orthometric height differences with GPS and gravity data. Man. Geod. 10, 187–194, 1985.

ERKER, E. The Austrian geoid — local geoid determination using modified conservative algorithms. In: Austr. Geod. Comm. (ed.), The gravity field in Austria. Geod. Arb. Öst. f. d. Int. Erdmessung, N.F., Bd. IV, 19–46, Graz 1987.

FALLER, J. E., I. MARSON. Ballistic methods of measuring g — the direct free-fall and symmetrical rise-and-fall methods compared. Metrologia 25, 49–55, 1988.

FALLER, J. E., Y. G. GUO, J. GSCHWIND, T. M. NIEBAUER, R. L. RINKER, J. XUE. The JILA portable absolute gravity apparatus. BGI 53, 87–97, 1983.

FARRELL, W. E. Deformation of the earth by surface loads. Rev. Geophys. 10, 761–797, 1972.

FERRARI, A. J., W. S. SINCLAIR, W. L. SJOGREN, J. G. WILLIAMS, C. F. YODER. Geophysical parameters of the earth-moon system. JGR 85, 3939–3951, 1980.

FISCHER, I. The figure of the earth-changes in concepts. Geophys. Surveys 2, 3–54, 1975.

FISCHER, I. Mean sea level and the marine geoid — an analysis of concept. Marine Geodesy 1, 37–59, 1977.

FISCHER, I., M. SLUTSKY et al. New pieces in the picture puzzle of an astrogeodetic geoid map of the world. Bull. Géod. no. 88, 199–221, 1968.

FLACH, D. The Askania borehole tiltmeter in field operation. Proceed. 7th Int. Symp. on Earth Tides, Sopron 1973, 243–247, Budapest 1976.

FRICKE, W. Fundamental catalogues, past, present and future. Celestial Mechanics (1985). Veröff. Astron. Recheninstitut NO. 31, Heidelberg 1985.

FRICKE, W., H. SCHWAN, T. LEDERLE (eds.). Fifth Fundamental Catalogue (FK5). Veröff. Astron. Recheninstitut Heidelberg, NO. 32, G. Braun, Karlsruhe 1988.

FROOME, K. D. Mekometer III: EDM with sub-millimetre resolution. Surv. Rev. 21, 98–118, 1971.

GAPOSCHKIN, E. M. (ed.). 1973 Smithsonian Standard Earth (III). SAO Spec. Rep. 353, Cambridge, Mass. 1973.

GENDT, G., R. DIETRICH. Determination of geophysical parameters based on LAGEOS laser ranging data. Gerl. Beitr. Geoph. 97, 438–449, 1988.

GERARDY, TH. Die Anfänge von Gauss' geodätischer Tätigkeit. ZfV 102, 1–20, 1977.

GERKE, K., H. WATERMANN. Die Karte der mittleren Freiluftanomalien für Gradabteilungen $6' \times 10'$ von Westdeutschland. DGK, B Nr. 46 II, Frankfurt a.M. 1959.

GILLIES, G. T. The Newtonian Gravitational Constant. Metrologia 24 (Suppl.), 1–56, 1987.

GOAD, C. C., C. C. TSCHERNING, M. M. CHIN. Gravity empirical covariance values for the Continental United States. JGR 89, 7962–7968, 1984.

GOODKIND, J. M. Continuous measurement of nontidal variations of gravity. JGR 91, 9125–9134, 1986.

GOPALAPILLAI, S. Non-global recovery of gravity anomalies from a combination of terrestrial and satellite altimetry data . OSU Rep. no. 210, Columbus, Ohio 1974.

GRAFAREND, E. Three-dimensional geodesy and gravity gradients. OSU Rep. no. 174, Columbus, Ohio 1972.

GRAFAREND, E. Three dimensional geodesy I — The holonomity problem —. ZfV 100, 269–281, 1975.

GRAFAREND, E., W. NIEMEIER. The free nonlinear boundary vale problem of physical geodesy. Bull. Géod. no. 101, 243–262, 1971.

GROTEN, E. (ed.). Report on high precision gravimetry, Vol. II. Nachr. aus dem Karten und Verm. wesen Reihe II, Nr. 41, Frankfurt a.M. 1983.

GROTEN, E., J. BRENNECKE. Global interaction between earth and sea tides. JGR 78, 8519–8526, 1973.

GROTEN, E., E. REINHART. Gravity prediction in mountainous areas. Boll. Geof. teor. appl. 10, 28–43, 1968.

GUBLER, E., H.-G. KAHLE, E. KLINGELÉ, St. MUELLER, R. OLIVIER. Recent crustal movements in Switzerland and their geophysical interpretation. Tectonophysics 71, 125–152, 1981 .

GURTNER, W., G. BEUTLER, I. BAUERSIMA, T. SSCHILDKNECHT. Evaluation of GPS carrier difference observations: The Bernese second generation software package. Proc. Positioning with GPS, Vol. I, 363–372, Rockville, USA, 1985.

HAASBROEK, N. D. Gemma Frisius, Tycho Brahe and Snellius and their triangulations. Publ. Netherl. Geod. Comm., Delft 1968.

HAMMER, S. Relative precision of vertical and horizontal gravity gradients measured by gravimeter. Geophysics 44, 99–101, 1979.

HAMMER, S. Airborne gravity is here. Geophysics 48, 213–223, 1983.

HAMMOND, J. A., J. E. FALLER. Results of absolute gravity determinations at a number of sites. JGR 76, 7850–7855, 1971.

HARRISON, J. C. Cavity and topographic effects in tilt and strain measurement. JGR 81, 319–328, 1976.

HAYFORD, J. F. The figure of the earth and isostasy from measurements in the United States. U.S. Coast and Geodetic Survey, Washington, D.C. 1909.

HEIN, G. W. Erdmessung als Teil einer integrierten Geodäsie — Begründung, Stand und Entwicklungstendenzen. ZfV 108, 93–104, 1983.

HEIN, G. W. Integrated geodesy — state of the art 1986. In: H. Sünkel (ed.), 505–548, 1986.

HEISKANEN, W. A. Ist die Erde ein dreiachsiges Ellipsoid? Gerl. Beitr. Geophys. XIX, 356–377, 1928.

HEISKANEN, W. A. On the world geodetic system. Publ. Isostat. Inst. Int. Ass. Geod. no. 26, Helsinki 1951.

HEISKANEN, W. A. The Columbus Geoid. EOS 38, 841–848, 1957.

HEITZ, S. An astro-geodetic determination of the geoid for West Germany. Nachr. a.d. Karten- u. Verm. wesen, II Nr. 24, Frankfurt a.M. 1969.

HEITZ, S. Ein dreidimensionales Berechnungsmodell für Punktbestimmungen mit Berücksichtigung orthometrischer Höhen. ZfV 98, 479–485, 1973.

HEITZ, S. Bezugs- und Koordinatensysteme für globale geodätische Methoden im Subdezimeter-Genauigkeitsbereich. ZfV 103, 156–162, 1978.

HELLER, E., R. WERNTHALER. Entwicklung und Genauigkeit des neuen deutschen Haupthöhennetzes. DGK, B Nr. 17, München 1955.

HESS, H. H. History of ocean basins. In: A. E. Engel, H. L. James, B. F. Leonard (eds.), Petrologic studies — Buddington Memorial Volume, 599–620, Geol. Soc. Am., New York, N.Y. 1962.

HINZE, W. J. (ed.). The utility of regional gravity and magnetic anomaly maps. Society of Exploration Geophysicists, Tulsa, Oklahoma, 1985.

HIRVONEN, R. A. New theory of the gravimetric geodesy. Publ. Isostat. Inst., Int. Ass. Geod., no. 32, Helsinki 1960.

HÖGGERL, N. Die Ausgleichung des österreichischen Präzisionsnivellementsnetzes. Österr. Z. f. Verm. wesen und Photogrammetrie 74, 216–249, 1986.

HÖPCKE, W. Eine Studie über die Korrelation elektromagnetisch gemessener Strecken. AVN 72, 140–147, 1965.

HÖPCKE, W. On the curvature of electromagnetic waves and its effects on measurement of distance. Surv. Rev. 18, 298–312, 1966.

HUGGETT, G. R. Two-color Terrameter. Tectonophysics 71, 29–39, 1981.

HUGGETT, G. R., L. W. SLATER. Precision electromagnetic distance-measuring instrument for determining secular strain and fault movement. Tectonophysics 29, 19–27, 1975.

ILIFFE, J. C., A. H. DODSON. Refraction effects on precise EDM observations. Surv. Rev. 29, 181–190, 1987.

IZOTOV, A. A. Reference-ellipsoid and the standard geodetic datum adopted in the USSR. Bull. Géod. no. 53, 1–6, 1959.

JACHENS, R. C., W. THATCHER, C. W. ROBERT, R. S. STEIN. Correlation of changes in gravity, elevation, and strain in southern California. Science 219, 1215–1217, 1983.

JEKELI, C. The Gravity Gradiometer Survey System (GGSS). EOS 69, 105, 116–117, 1988.

JELSTRUP, J. Crossing of fjords with precise levelling. Bull. Géod. no. 38, 55–63, 1955.

Kääriäinen, J. Observing the earth tides with a long water-tube tiltmeter. Publ. Finn. Geod. Inst. no. 88, Helsinki 1979.

Kakkuri, J. Versuche mit dem automatischen Doppelinstrument Zeiss Ni2 beim Strom-übergangsnivellement. ZfV 91, 160–164, 1966.

Kakkuri, J. Stellar triangulation with balloon-borne beacons. Publ. Finn. Geod. Inst. no. 76, Helsinki 1973.

Kakkuri, J. Newest results obtained in studying the Fennoscandian lanp uplift phenomenon. Tectonophysics 130, 327–331, 1986.

Kane, M. F., R. H. Godson. Features of a pair of long-wavelength (>250 km) and short-wavelength (<250 km) Bouguer gravity maps of the United States. In: W. J. Hinze (ed.), 46–61, 1985.

Kanngieser, E., K. Kummer, W. Torge, H.-G. Wenzel. Das Gravimeter-Eichsystem Hannover. Wiss. Arb. Univ. Hannover, Nr. 120, 1983.

Kaula, W. M. Statistical and harmonical analysis of gravity. JGR 64, 2401–2421, 1959.

Kaula, W. M. Earth's gravity field: Relation to global tectonics. Science 169, 982–985, 1970.

Kaula, W. M. Global gravity and tectonics. In: E.C. Robertson (ed.), The nature of the solid Earth, 385–405, McGraw-Hill, New York 1972.

Kearsley, A. H. W., R. Forsberg. Tailored geopotential models — applications and short-comings. Man. Geod. 15, 151–158, 1990.

Khan, M. A. General solution of the problem of hydrostatic equilibrium of the earth. Geoph. J. R. Astr. Soc. 18, 177–188, 1969.

Kim, J.-H., R. H. Rapp. The development of the July 1989 $1° \times 1°$ and $30' \times 30'$ terrestrial mean free-air anomaly data bases. OSU Rep. no. 403, Columbus, Ohio 1990.

King, G. C. P., R. G. Bilham. Strain measurement instrumentation and technique. Phil. Trans. Roy. Soc. London A 274, 209–217, 1973.

Kivioja, L. A. Computation of geodetic direct and indirect problems by computers accumulating increments from geodetic line elements. Bull. Géod. no. 99, 55–63, 1971.

Kobold, F. Höhenwinkelmessung, Lotabweichungen und Meereshöhen. ZfV 80, 255–262, 1955.

Koch, K.-R. Alternate representation of the earth's gravitational field for satellite geodesy. Boll. Geof. teor. appl. 10, 318–325, 1968.

Koch, K.-R. Lunar shape and gravity field. Photogr. Engineering 36, 375–380, 1970.

Koch, K.-R., A. J. Pope. Uniqueness and existence of the geodetic boundary value problem using the known surface of the earth. Bull. Géod. no. 106, 467–476, 1972.

Konecny, G. Photogrammetrische Verfahren zur Auswertung von Satellitenbildern des Mondes. AVN 81, 122–141, 1974.

Kouba, J. A review of geodetic and geodynamic satellite Doppler positioning. Rev. Geophys. 21, 41–50, 1983a.

Kouba, J. An efficient short-arc orbit computation. Bull. Géod. 57, 138–145, 1983b.

Krakiwsky, E. J., D. B. Thomson. Mathematical models for the combination of terrestrial and satellite networks. Can. Surv. 28, 606–615, 1974.

Krarup, T. A contribution to the mathematical foundation of physical geodesy. Publ. Danish Geod. Inst. no. 44, Copenhagen 1969.

Kukkamäki, T. J. Über die nivellitische Refraktion. Publ. Finn. Geod. Inst. no. 25, Helsinki 1938.

Kukkamäki, T. J. Tidal correction of the levelling. Publ. Finn. Geod. Inst. no. 36, 143–152, Helsinki 1949.

Kukkamäki, T. J. Errors affecting levelling. Proc. NAD-Symp. Ottawa 1–10, 1980.

Kumar, M. World Geodetic System 1984: A modern and accurate global reference frame. Marine Geod. 12, 117–126, 1988.

KUNTZ, E., D. MÖLLER. Gleichzeitige elektronische Entfernungsmessungen mit Licht- und Mikrowellen. AVN 78, 254–266, 1971.

LAMBERT, A., J. O. LIARD, N. COURTIER, A. K. GOODACRE, R. K. MCCONNELL, J. E. FALLER. Canadian absolute gravity program. EOS 70, 1447, 1459–60, 1989.

LAMBERT, B. P. Australian geodetic surveys, present and future. The Austral. Surveyor 28, 331–339, 1977.

LANGBEIN, J. O., M. F. LINKER, A. F. MCGARR. Precision of two-color geodimeter measurements: Results from 15 months of observations. JGR 92, 11644–11656, 1987.

LEDERSTEGER, K. Die geodätischen Bezugsflächen und ihre Ausmaße. ZfV 81, 95–107, 1956.

LEE, L. P. The computation of conformal projections. Surv. Rev. 22, 245–256, 1974.

LELGEMANN, D. Zur gravimetrischen Berechnung des Geoids der Bundesrepublik Deutschland. DGK, A Nr. 77, Frankfurt a.M. 1974.

LELGEMANN, D. On the recovery of gravity anomalies from high precision altimeter data. OSU Rep. no. 239, Columbus, Ohio 1976.

LERCH, F. J., S. M. KLOSKO, R. E. LAUBSCHER, C. A. WAGNER. Gravity model improvement using GEOS-3 (GEM9 and 10). JGR 84, 3897–3916, 1979.

LERCH, F. J., B. H. PUTNEY, C. A. WAGNER, S. M. KLOSKO. Goddard earth models for oceanographic applications (GEM 10B and 10C). Marine Geodesy 5, 145–187, 1981.

LERCH, F. J., S. M. KLOSKO, G. B. PATEL, C. A. WAGNER. A gravity model for crustal dynamics (GEM-L2). JGR 90, 9301–9311, 1985.

LEVALLOIS, J. J. The history of the International Association of Geodesy. In: The Geodesist's Handbook, Bull. Géod. 54, 249–313, 1980.

LEVALLOIS, J. J., H. MONGE. Le géoid Européen, version 1978. Proc. Int. Symp. on the Geoid in Europe and Mediterranean Area, Ancona 1978, 153–164, Soc. Ital. di Fotogr. e Topogr., 1978.

LEVITUS, S. Climatological atlas of the world ocean. NOAA, Geophys. Fluid Lab., Profess. Paper 13, Dep. of Commerce, Washington, D.C. 1982.

LI RUIHAO, SUN HEPING, HU YENCHANG. Investigation of gravity variation associated with crustal deformation of the Tianjin area before and after the Tangshan earthquake. Tectonophysics 167, 341–347, 1989.

LISTING, J. B. Über unsere jetzige Kenntnis der Gestalt und Größe der Erde. Nachr. d. Kgl. Gesellsch. d. Wiss. und der Georg-August-Univ., 33–98, Göttingen 1873.

LOCKWOOD, J. P., N. G. BANKS, T. T. ENGLISH et al. The 1984 eruption of Mauna Loa Volcano, Hawaii. EOS 66, 169–171, 1985.

LUCHT, H. Korrelation im Präzisionsnivellement. Wiss. Arb. Univ. Hannover, Nr. 48, Hannover 1972.

LUNDQUIST, C. A., G. VEIS. Geodetic parameters for a 1966 Smithsonian Institution Standard Earth. SAO Spec. Rep. 200, Cambridge, Mass. 1966.

MA, C., J. W. RYAN, D. CAPRETTE. Crustal dynamics project data analysis-1988, VLBI geodetic results 1979–87. NASA Tech. Memor. 100723, 1989.

MARKOWITZ, W. Geocentric coordinates from lunar and satellite observations. Bull. Géod. no. 49, 41–49, 1958.

MARKOWITZ, W. SI, the international system of units. Geophys. Surveys 1, 217–241, 1973.

MARSH, J. G., S. VINCENT. Global detailed geoid computation and model analysis. Geophys. Surveys 1, 481–511, 1974.

MARSH, J. G., T. V. MARTIN, J. J. MCCARTHEY, P. S. CHOVITZ. Mean sea surface computation using GEOS-3 altimeter data. Marine Geodesy 3, 354–378, 1980.

MARSH, J. G., F. J. LERCH, R. G. WILLIAMSON. Precision geodesy and geodynamics using Starlette laser ranging. JGR 90, 9335–9345, 1985.

MARSH, J. G., A. C. BRENNER, B. D. BECKLEY, TH. V. MARTIN. Global mean sea surface based upon the Seasat altimeter data. JGR 91, 3501–3506, 1986.

MARSH, J. G., F. J. LERCH et al. The GEM-T2 gravitational model. JGR 95, 22043–22071, 1990a.

MARSH, J. G., C. J. KOBLINSKY, F. LERCH, S. M. KLOSKO, J. W. ROBBINS, R. G. WILLIAMSON, G. B. PATEL. Dynamic sea surface topography, gravity, and improved orbit accuracies from the direct evaluation of Seasat altimeter data. JGR 95, 13129–13150, 1990b.

MARUSSI, A. Fondements de géométrie différentielle absolue du champ potential terrestre. Bull. Géod. no. 14, 411–439, 1949.

MARUSSI, A., H. MORITZ, R. H. RAPP, R. O. VICENTE. Ellipsoidal density models and hydrostatic equilibrium. Phys. Earth and Planet Inter. 9, 4–6, 1974.

MATHER, R. S. Four dimensional studies in earth space. Bull. Géod. no. 108, 187–209, 1973.

MATHER, R. S. Geodetic coordinates in four-dimensions. Can. Surv. 28, 574–581, 1974a.

MATHER, R. S. Quasi-stationary sea surface topography and variations of mean sea level with time — an interim report (1973). Unisurv 21, 18–73, 1974b.

MATHER, R. S. On the evaluation of stationary sea surface topography using geodetic techniques. Bull. Géod. no. 115, 65–82, 1975.

MATHER, R. S. The role of the geoid in four-dimensional geodesy. Marine Geodesy 1, 217–252, 1978.

MATHER, R. S., E. G. MASTERS, R. COLEMAN. The role of non-tidal gravity variations in the maintenance of reference systems for secular geodynamics. Unisurv G 26, 1–25, 1977.

McADOO, D. C., D. T. SANDWELL. GEOSAT's exact repeat mission. EOS 69, 1569, 1988.

McCONNELL, R. K., D. B. HEARTY, P. J. WINTER. An evaluation of the LaCoste-Romberg model D Microgravimeter. BGI 36, I-35-45, 1975.

McKENZIE, D. P. Plate tectonics. In: E. C. Robertson, F. F. Hays, L. Knopoff (eds.), The nature of the solid earth, 323–360, McGraw-Hill, New York, N.Y., 1972.

McKENZIE, D. P., R. L. PARKER. The North Pacific: an example of tectonics on a sphere. Nature 216, 1276–1280, 1967.

MELCHIOR, P. Earth tides. Geophys. Surveys 1, 275–303, 1974.

MELCHIOR, P., M. DE BECKER. A discussion of world-wide measurements of tidal gravity with respect to oceanic interactions, lithosphere heterogeneities, Earth's flattening and inertial forces. Physics Earth and Planetary Inter. 31, 27–53, 1983.

MERRY, C. L., P. VANÍČEK. The geoid and datum translation components. Can. Surv. 28, 56–62, 1974.

MINSTER, J. B., T. H. JORDAN. Present-day plate motions. JGR 83, 5331–5354, 1978.

MITTERMAYER, E. Eine nichtiterative Lösung der 1. geodätischen Hauptaufgabe auf den Rotationsellipsoiden von Bessel, Hayford und Krassowsky für geodätische Linien beliebiger Länge. DGK, C Nr. 116, München 1968.

MOLODENSKI, M. S. Grundbegriffe der geodätischen Gravimetrle. VEB Verlag Technik, Berlin 1958.

MORELLI, C., C. GANTAR et al. The International Gravity Standardization Net 1971 (I.G.S.N. 71). I.U.G.G.-I.A.G. Publ. Spec. no. 4, Paris 1974.

MORGAN, W. J. Rises, trenches, great faults, and crustal blocks. JGR 73, 1959–1982, 1968.

MORITZ, H. Mass distributions for the equipotential ellipsoid. Boll. Geof. teor. appl. 10, 59–65, 1968a.

MORITZ, H. Über das Geodätische Bezugssystem 1967. ZfV 93, 81–88, 1968b.

MORITZ, H. Kinematical geodesy, DGK, A Nr. 59, München 1968c.

MORITZ, H. On the use of the terrain correction in solving Molodensky's problem. OSU Rep. no. 108, Columbus, Ohio 1968d.

MORITZ, H. Methoden zur Berechnung von Satellitentriangulationen. AVN 77, 353–359, 1970a.

MORITZ, H. Least-squares estimation in physical geodesy. DGK, A Nr. 69, München 1970b (OSU Rep. no. 130, Columbus, Ohio).

MORITZ, H. Series solution of Molodensky's problem. DGK, A Nr. 70, München 1971.

MORITZ, H. Precise gravimetric geodesy. OSU Rep. no. 219, Columbus, Ohio 1974.

MORITZ, H. Least-squares collocation. DGK, A Nr. 75, München 1975 (OSU Rep. no. 175, Columbus, Ohio 1972).

MORITZ, H. Integral formulas and collocation. Man. Geod. 1, 1–40, 1976.

MORITZ, H. Der Begriff der mathematischen Erdgestalt seit Gauß. AVN 84, 133–138, 1977.

MORITZ, H. Geodetic Reference System 1980. In: C. C. Tscherning (ed.), The geodesist's handbook 1984 — Bull. Géod. 58, 388–398, 1984.

MORITZ, H. Equilibrium figures in geodesy and geophysics. Proc. 6th Int. Symp. "Geodesy and Physics of the Earth", Potsdam 1988, Part II, Veröff. Zentralinst. f. Physik der Erde Nr. 102, 58–98, Potsdam 1989.

MORRISON, F. Density layer models for the geopotential. Bull. Géod. no. 101, 319–328, 1971.

MOSKVIN, G. J., V. A. SOROCHINSKY. Navigational aspects of GLONASS. GPS World, 50–54, Jan./Febr. 1990.

MOURAD, A. G. Geodetic measurements in the ocean. Marine Geodesy 1, 3–35, 1977.

MOURAD, A. G., D. M. FUBARA, A. T. HOPPER, G. T. RUCK. Geodetic location of acoustic ocean-bottom transponders from surface positions. EOS 53, 644–649, 1972.

MUELLER, I. I. Global satellite triangulation and trilateration results. JGR 79, 5333–5347, 1974.

MUELLER, I. I., O. HOLWAY III, R. R. KING JR. Geodetic experiment by means of a torsion balance. OSU Rep. no. 30, Columbus, Ohio 1963.

NAGY, D. The gravitational attraction of a right angular prism. Geophysics 31, 362–371, 1966.

NAT. ACAD. SCIENCES. National Academy of Sciences, Comm. on Geodesy — Geodesy: Trend and prospects. Nat. Acad. of Sciences, Washington, D.C., 1978.

NIEDERS. MIN. D. INNERN. Aufbau und Erhaltung des trigonometrischen Festpunktfeldes (TP-Erlaß). Hannover 1969.

NIEDERS. MIN. D. INNERN. Aufbau und Erhaltung des Nivellementfestpunktfeldes (NivP-Erlaß). Hannover 1971.

NIETHAMMER, TH. Nivellement und Schwere als Mittel zur Berechnung wahrer Meereshöhen. Veröff. Schweiz. Geod. Komm., Basel 1932.

OBENSON, G. A 1973 gravimetric geoid of Africa. Geoph. J. R. Astr. Soc. 37, 271–283, 1974.

PAIK, H. J., J.-S. LEUNG, S. H. MORGAN, J. PARKER. Global gravity survey by an orbiting gravity gradiometer. EOS 69, 1601, 1610–1611, 1988.

PESCHEL, H. Das motorisierte Präzisionsnivellement — leistungsfähigstes Verfahren genauer Höhenmessungen. Vermessungstechnik 22, 57–64, 1974.

PETER, G., R. E. MOOSE, C. W. WESSELS, J. E. FALLER, T. M. NIEBAUER. High-precision absolute gravity observations in the United States. JGR 94, 5659–5674, 1989.

PHILLIPS, R. J., K. LAMBECK. Gravity fields of the terrestrial planets: Long-wavelength anomalies and tectonics. Rev. Geophys. 18, 27–76, 1980.

PODER, K., H. HORNIK (eds.). The European Datum 1987 (ED87). Internat. Assoc. of Geodesy, RETRIG Subcomm., Publ. No. 18, München 1989.

RAMSAYER, K. Genauigkeitsuntersuchungen der Schwerereduktion von Nivellements. DGK, A Nr. 31, München 1959.

RAMSAYER, K. Untersuchung der Genauigkeit eines Raumpolygonzugs. ZfV 96, 429–439, 1971.

RAPP, R. H. Determination of potential coefficients to degree 52 from 5° mean gravity anomalies. Bull. Géod. 51, 301–323, 1977.

RAPP, R. H. Degree variances of the earth's potential, topography, and its isostatic compensations. Bull. Géod. 56, 84–94, 1982a.

RAPP, R. H. A summary of the results from the OSU analysis of Seasat altimeter data. OSU Rep. no. 335, Columbus, Ohio 1982b.

RAPP, R. H. The need and prospects for a world vertical datum. In: Proc. of the Internat. Assoc. of Geodesy, Symp. XVIII., IUGG Gen. Ass., Hamburg 1983, Vol. 2, 432–445, Dep. of Geod. Science and Surveying, The Ohio State Univ., Columbus, Ohio 1983.

RAPP, R. H. Gravity anomalies and sea surface heights derived from a combined GEOS-3/Seasat altimeter data set. JGR 91, 4867–4876, 1986a.

RAPP, R. H. Global geopotential solutions. In: H. Sünkel (ed.) 365–415, 1986b.

RAPP, R. H., J. Y. CRUZ. Spherical harmonic expansions of the earth's gravitational potential to degree 360 using 30′ mean anomalies. OSU Rep. no. 376, Columbus, Ohio 1986.

RAPP, R. H., N. K. PAVLIS. The development and analysis of geopotential coefficient models to spherical harmonic degree 360. JGR 95, 21885–21911, 1990.

REIGBER, C., G. BALMINO, H. MÜLLER, W. BOSCH, B. MOYNOT. GRIM gravity model improvement using LAGEOS (GRIM3-L1). JGR 90, 9285–9299, 1985.

REIGBER, Ch., P. SCHWINTZER et al. The GRIM4-S1 gravity model. Crustal Dynamics Princip. Invest. Meeting, Greenbelt, Md., 1990.

RICHTER, B. Das supraleitende Gravimeter. DGK, C Nr. 329, Frankfurt a.M. 1987.

RINNER, K. Distance measurement with the aid of electromagnetic waves. Geophys. Surveys 1, 459–479, 1974.

RINNER, K. Über geometrische Aufgaben der Meeresgeodäsie. ZfV 102, 354–366, 1977.

RINNER, K., G. SEEBER, H. SEEGER. Die Deutsch-Österreichische Dopplerkampagne. DGK, B Nr. 260, München 1982.

RÖDER, R. H., H.-G. WENZEL. Relative gravity observations at BIPM, Sèvres in 1985 and 1986. BGI No. 59, 177–183, 1986.

RÖDER, R. H., M. SCHNÜLL, H.-G. WENZEL. Gravimetry with an electrostatic feedback system. BGI No. 57, 72–81, 1985.

RÖDER, R. H., M. SCHNÜLL, H.-G. WENZEL. SRW feedback for LaCoste-Romberg gravimeters with extended range. BGI No. 62, 46–50, 1988.

ROSSITER, J. R. Mean sea level. In: Runcorn (A 1967), 929–934.

RUEGER, J.-M., F. K. BRUNNER. EDM-height traversing versus geodetic leveling. Can. Surv. 36, 69–88, 1982.

RUMMEL, R. Satellite gradiometry. In: H. Sünkel (ed.), 317–363, 1986.

RUMMEL, R., O. L. COLOMBO. Gravity field determination from satellite gradiometry. Bull. Géod. 59, 233–246, 1985.

RUMMEL, R., P. TEUNISSEN. Height datum definition, height datum connection and the role of the geodetic boundary value problem. Bull. Géod. 62, 477–498, 1988.

RUMMEL, R., Ch. REIGBER, K. H. ILK. The use of satellite-to-satellite tracking for gravity parameter recovery. Proc. ESA Workshop on Space Oceanography, Navigation and Geodynamics (SONG), ESA-SP-137, 151–161, 1978.

RUNDLE, J. B., J. H. WHITCOMB. Modeling gravity and trilateration data in Long Valley, California, 1983–1984. JGR 91, 12675–12682, 1986.

VAN RUYMBEKE, M. Sur un pendule horizontal équipé d'un capteur de déplacement a capacité variable. Bull. Géod. 50, 281–290, 1976.

SAKUMA, A. Gravitational acceleration, mass, and electrical quantities. In: B. N. Taylor and W. D. Phillips (eds.), Precision measurement and fundamental constants II, Nat. Bur. Stand. (U.S.) Spec. Publ. 617, 397–404, 1984.

SANDWELL, D. T., D. C. McADOO. High accuracy/resolution gravity profiles from 2 years of GEOSAT/ERM. JGR 95, 3049–3060, 1990.

SANDWELL, D. T., D. MILBERT, B. C. DOUGLAS. Global nondynamic orbit improvement for altimetric satellites. JGR 91, 9447–9451, 1986.

SAUNDERS, R. S., G. H. PETTENGILL, R. E. ARVIDSON, W. C. SJOGREN, W. T. K. JOHNSON, L. PIERI. The Magellan Venus Radar Mapping Mission. JGR 95, 8339–8355, 1990.

SAVAGE, J. C., W. H. PRESCOTT, M. LISOWSKI. Deformation along the San Andreas Fault 1982–1986 as indicated by frequent geodolite measurements. JGR 92, 4785–4797, 1987.

SCHMID, H. H. Worldwide geometric satellite triangulation. JGR 79, 5349–5376, 1974.

SCHNÄDELBACH, K. Computation of geodesics with electronic desk calculators. DGK, B Nr. 188, 79–93, München 1971.

SCHNÄDELBACH, K. Entwicklungstendenzen in Rechenverfahren der mathematischen Geodäsie. ZfV 99, 421–430, 1974.

SCHNEIDER, E. Die Normalhöhen in der Praxis. Vermessungstechnik 8, 90–94, 1960.

SCHÜLER, R., G. HARNISCH et al. Absolute Schweremessungen mit Reversionspendeln in Potsdam 1968–1969. Veröff. Zentralinst. Physik der Erde Nr. 10, Potsdam 1971.

SCHUTZ, B. E., B. D. TAPLEY, J. B. LUNDBERG, P. HALAMEK. Simulation of a Geopotential Research Mission for gravity studies. Man. Geod. 12, 51–63, 1987.

SCHWARZ, CH. R. The use of short arc orbital constraints in the adjustment of geodetic satellite data. OSU Rep. no. 118, Columbus, Ohio 1969.

SCHWARZ, Ch. R. (ed.). North American Datum of 1983. NOAA Prof. Paper NOS 2, Nat. Geod. Survey, Rockville, Md., 1989.

SCHWARZ, CH. R., E. B. WADE. The North American Datum of 1983: Project methodology and execution. Bull. Géod. 64, 28–62, 1990.

SCHWARZ, K. P. Zur Erdmessung des Eratosthenes. AVN 82, 1–12, 1975.

SCHWARZ, K. P., M. G. SIDERIS, R. FORSBERG. The use of FFT techniques in physical geodesy. Geophys. J. Int. 100, 485–514, 1990.

SCHWIDERSKI, E. W. On charting global ocean tides. Rev. Geophys. 18, 243–268, 1980.

SCHWIDERSKI, E. W. Atlas of ocean tidal charts and maps, part I: The semidiurnal principal lunar tide M2. Marine Geodesy 6, 219–266, 1983.

SEEBER, G. Aufgaben und Methoden der Meeresgeodäsie. ZfV 100, 169–179, 1975.

SEEBER, G. Inertiale Vermessungssysteme und ihre Anwendungsmöglichkeiten in der Geodäsie. ZfV 104, 460–471, 1979.

SEEBER, G. Die Rolle des NAVSTAR Global Positioning Systems für die Lösung geodätischer Aufgaben. ZfV 109, 1–11, 1984.

SEEBER, G. Point Positioning in marine geodesy (1979–1983). Marine Geodesy 9, 365–380, 1985.

SEEBER, G. Use of the GPS for the determination of precise height differences — models and results. Boll. Geod. Scienc. Aff. 16, 325–332, 1987.

SEEBER, G., LAI XIAN. A GPS survey in the Yunnan earthquake experimental field — objectives and first results. IUGG-IAG Proc., IAG Symp. no. 101, 149–154, Springer, New York-Berlin-Heidelberg 1990.

SEEBER, G., W. TORGE. Zum Einsatz transportabler Zenitkameras für die Lotabweichungsbestimmung. ZfV 110, 439–450, 1985.

SEEBER, G., D. EGGE, M. HOYER, H. W. SCHENKE, K. H. SCHMIDT. Einsatzmöglichkeiten von Doppler-Satellitenmessungen. AVN 89, 373–388, 1982.

SEEBER, G., D. EGGE, A. SCHUCHARDT, J. SIEBOLD, G. WÜBBENA. Experiences with the TI 4100 NAVSTAR Navigator of the University of Hannover. Proc. 1st Int. Symp. Precise Positioning with GPS, Vol. 1, 215–226, Rockville U.S.A., 1985.

SEEBER, G., A. SCHUCHARDT, G. WÜBBENA. Beobachtungen eines großräumigen GPS-Netzes mit Zweifrequenz-empfängern. ZfV 112, 397–401, 1987.

SEPPELIN, TH. O. The Department of Defense World Geodetic System 1972. Can. Surv. 28, 496–506, 1974.

SIDERIS, M. G. On the application of spectral techniques to the gravimetric problem. Proc. IAG Symp., Vol. II, 428–442, XIX. IUGG Gen. Ass., Vancouver 1987.

SIDERIS, M. G. Rigorous gravimetric terrain modelling using Molodensky's operator. Man. Geod. 15, 97–106, 1990.

SIGL, R., A. BAUCH. Das Universal Theo 002; sein Einsatz bei zwei genauen Verfahren der geodätischen Astronomie. AVN 83, 113–128, 1976.

SIGL, R., W. TORGE, H. BEETZ, K. STUBER. Das Schweregrundnetz 1976 der Bundesrepublik Deutschland (DSGN76), Teil I. DGK, B Nr. 254, München 1981.

SILVERBERG, E. C. Mobile satellite ranging. In: I. I. Mueller (ed.), Applications of geodesy to geodynamics, OSU Rep. no. 280, 41–46, Columbus, Ohio 1978.

SJÖBERG, L. Integral formulas for heterogeneous data in physical geodesy. Bull. Géod. 53, 297–315, 1979.

SJOGREN, W. L. Planetary geodesy. Rev. Geophys. 21, 528–537, 1983.

SMITH, D. E., F. J. LERCH, J. G. MARSH, C. A. WAGNER, R. KOLENKIEWICZ, M. A. KHAN. Contributions to the national geodetic satellite program by Goddard Space Flight Center. JGR 81, 1006–1026, 1976.

SMITH, D. E., R. KOLENKIEWICZ et al. Tectonic motion and deformation from satellite laser ranging to LAGEOS. JGR 95, 22013–22041, 1990.

SNAY, R. A. Network design strategies applicable to GPS surveys using three or four receivers. Bull. Géod. 60, 37–50, 1986.

SNAY, R. A. Accuracy analysis for the NAD 83 Geodetic Reference System. Bull. Géod. 64, 1–27, 1990.

SPELLAUGE, R. Elektromagnetische Streckenmessungen im Radiosicht- und Überhorizont-bereich über See. Wiss. Arb. Univ. Hannover, Nr. 47, Hannover 1972.

STANLEY, H. R. The GEOS-3 Project. JGR 84, 3779–3783, 1979.

STANSELL, T. A. The MX 1502 Satellite Surveyor. Proc. 2nd Int. Geod. Symp. on Satellite Doppler Positioning, Vol. 1, 497–534, Austin 1979.

STEIN, R. S. Contemporary plate motion and crustal deformation. Rev. Geophys. 25, 855–863, 1987.

STOKES, G. G. On the variation of gravity on the surface of the earth. Transact. Cambridge Phil. Soc. 8, 672–695, 1849.

STOLZ, A. Geodetic uses of lunar laser ranging. Bull. Géod. no. 115, 5–6, 1975.

STRANGE, W. E., S. F. VINCENT, R. H. BERRY, J. G. MARSH. A detailed gravimetric geoid for the United States. NASA GSFC Rep. TM-X 65691, Greenbelt, Md. 1971.

STRANG VAN HEES, G. L. Zur zeitlichen Änderung von Schwere und Höhe. ZfV 102, 444–450, 1977.

STURGES, W. Sea level slopes along continental boundaries. JGR 79, 825–830, 1974.

SÜNKEL, H. Digital height and density model and its use for orthometric height and gravity field determination for Austria. Boll. di Geodesia e Scienze Affini 47, 139–144, 1988.

SÜNKEL, H., N. BARTELME, H. FUCHS, M. HANAFY, W.-D. SCHUH, M. WIESER. The gravity field in Austria. In: Austr. Geod. Comm. (ed.), The gravity field in Austria. Geod. Arb. Öst. f. d. Int. Erdmessung, N.F., Band IV, 47–75, Graz 1987.

TAMURA, Y. A harmonics development of the tide generating potential. Bull. d'Inf. Marées Terrestres 99, 6813–6855, 1987.

TAPLEY, B. D., G. H. BORN, M. E. PARKE. The Seasat altimeter data and its accuracy assessment. JGR 87, 3179–3188, 1982.

TAPLEY, B. D., B. E. SCHUTZ, R. J. EANES. Station coordinates, baselines and earth rotation from LAGEOS laser ranging 1976–1984. JGR 90, 9235–9248, 1985.

TEGELER, W. Untersuchungen zur Genauigkeit der trigonometrischen Höhenmessung im Flachland und Mittelgebirge. Wiss. Arb. Univ. Hannover, Nr. 45, Hannover 1971.

TORGE, W. Untersuchungen zur Höhen- und Geoidbestimmung im dreidimensionalen Testnetz Westharz. ZfV 102, 173–186, 1977.

TORGE, W. Drei- und Zweidimensionale Modellbildung. In: H. Pelzer (ed.), Geodätische Netze in Landes- und Ingenieurvermessung, 113–130, K. Wittwer, Stuttgart 1980a.

TORGE, W. Geodätisches Datum und Datumstransformation. In: H. Pelzer (ed.), Geodätische Netze in Landes- und Ingenieurvermessung, 131–140, K. Wittwer, Stuttgart 1980b.

TORGE, W. Observation strategy and -technique in gravimetry. In: B. G. Harsson (ed.), Optimization of geodetic operations, 126-210, Norges Geografiske Oppmäling, Publ. 3/1984.

TORGE, W. Dreidimensionale Netze. In: H. Pelzer (ed.), Geodätische Netze in Landes- und Ingenieurvermessung II, 313–333, K. Wittwer, Stuttgart 1985.

TORGE, W. Gravimetry for monitoring vertical crustal movements: potential and problems. Tectonophysics 130, 385–393, 1986.

TORGE, W. Accuracy and stability of height reference surface. In: H. Pelzer, W. Niemeier (eds.), 69–82, F. Dümmler, Bonn 1987.

TORGE, W. More than five years of GPS experiments — rethinking of geodesy. In: E. Groten, R. Strauß (eds.), 363–380, 1988.

TORGE, W. Absolute gravimetry as an operational tool for geodynamics research. In: F. K. Brunner, Ch. Rizos (eds.), 15–28, 1990a.

TORGE, W. Approaching the "cm-geoid" — strategies and results. Mitt. d. geod. Inst. d. TU Graz, Folge 67, Graz 1990b.

TORGE, W. The geoid in Europa: Status, requirements, prospects. Cahiers du Centre Européen de Géodynamique et el Séismologie, vol. 2, 119–126, Luxembourg 1990c.

TORGE, W., E. KANNGIESER. Regional and local vertical crustal movements in northern Iceland, 1965–1980. JGR 90, 10173–10177, 1985.

TORGE, W., H.-G. WENZEL. Comparison of earth tide observations with nine different gravimeters at Hannover. In: M. Bonatz and P. Melchior (eds.), 632–640, 1977.

TORGE, W., H.-G. WENZEL. Dreidimensionale Ausgleichung des Testnetzes Westharz. DGK, B Nr. 234, München 1978.

TORGE, W., G. WEBER, H.-G. WENZEL. High resolution gravimetric geoid heights and gravimetric vertical deflections of Europe including marine areas. Marine Geophys. Res. 7, 149–175, 1984a.

TORGE, W., G. WEBER, H.-G. WENZEL. 6′ × 10′ free air gravity anomalies of Europe including marine areas. Marine Geophys. Res. 7, 93–111, 1984b.

TORGE, W., R. H. RÖDER, M. SCHNÜLL, H.-G. WENZEL, J. E. FALLER. First results with the transportable absolute gravity meter JILAG-3. Bull. Géod. 61, 161–176, 1987.

TORGE, W., T. BAŠIČ, H. DENKER, J. DOLIFF, H.-G. WENZEL. Long range geoid control through the European GPS traverse. DGK, B Nr. 290, München 1989.

TORGE, W., R. H. RÖDER, M. SCHNÜLL, L. TIMMEN, LAI XIAN, JIA MINYU, SUN HEPING, XING CANFEI. High precision gravity control network in Yunnan/China. BGI no. 67, 118–127, 1990.

TSCHERNING, C. C. Comparison of some methods for the detailed representation of the earth's gravity field. Rev. Geophys. 19, 213–221, 1981.

TSCHERNING, C. C., R. FORSBERG. Geoid determination in the Nordic countries from gravity and height data. Proc. Int. Symp. on the Definition of the Geoid, Vol. 1, 325–352, Ist. Geogr. Mil. Ital., Firenze 1986.

TSCHERNING, C. C., R. H. RAPP. Closed covariance expressions for gravity anomalies, geoid undulations, and deflections of the vertical implied by anomaly degree variance models. OSU Rep. no. 208, Columbus, Ohio 1974.

UOTILA, U. A. Harmonic analysis of world-wide gravity material. Publ. Isostat. Inst. Int. Ass. Geod. no. 39, Helsinki 1962.

VÄISÄLÄ, Y. An astronomical method of triangulation. Sitz. Ber. Finn. Akad. d. Wiss. schaften, Nr. 8, 99–107, 1946.

VANÍČEK, P., C. L. MERRY. Determination of the geoid from deflections of the vertical using a least squares surface fitting technique. Bull. Géod. no. 109, 261–280, 1973.

VANÍČEK, P., D. E. WELLS. Positioning of horizontal geodetic datums. Can. Surv. 28, 531–538, 1974.

VENEDIKOV, A. P. Analysis of earth tidal data. In: M. Bonatz, P. Melchior (eds.), 129–152, 1977.

VENING-MEINESZ, F. A. A formula expressing the deflection of the plumb-lines in the gravity anomalies and some formulae for the gravity field and the gravity potential outside the geoid. Proc. Koninkl. Ned. Akad. Wetenschaft 31, 315–331, Amsterdam 1928.

VENING-MEINESZ, F. A. New formulas for systems of deflections of the plumb-line and Laplace's theorem. — Changes of deflections of the plumb-line brought about by a change of the reference ellipsoid. Bull. Géod. no. 15, 33–51, 1950.

VINCENTY, T. Direct and inverse solutions of geodesics on the ellipsoid with application of nested equations. Surv. Rev. XXIII, 88–93, 1975.

VINCENTY, T. Height-controlled three-dimensional adjustment of horizontal networks. Bull. Géod. 54, 37–43, 1980.

WAALEWIJN, A. Hydrostatic levelling in the Netherlands. Surv. Rev. 17, 212–221, 267–276, 1964.

WAHR, J. Body tides on an elliptical, rotating, elastic and oceanless earth. Geophys. J. R. Astr. Soc. 64, 677–704, 1981.

WEBER, G., H. ZOMORRODIAN. Regional geopotential improvement for the Iranian geoid determination. Bull. Géod. 62, 125–141, 1988.

WELLS, W. C. (ed.). Spaceborne gravity gradiometers. NASA Conference Publ. 2305, Proc. of a workshop held at NASA Goddard Space Flight Center, Greenbelt, Md, Febr. 28–March 2, 1983, NASA 1984.

WENDT, K., D. MÖLLER, B. RITTER. Geodetic measurements of surface deformations during the present rifting episode in NE Iceland. JGR 90, 10163–10172, 1985.

WENZEL, H.-G. Zur Genauigkeit von gravimetrischen Erdgezeitenbeobachtungen. Wiss. Arb. Univ. Hannover, Nr. 67, Hannover 1976.

WENZEL, H.-G. Geoid computation by least-squares spectral combination using integral kernels. Proc. Gen. Meeting IAG, Spec. Issue J. Geod. Soc. of Japan, 438–453, Tokyo 1982.

WENZEL, H.-G. Hochauflösende Kugelfunktionsmodelle für das Gravitationspotential der Erde. Wiss. Arb. Univ. Hannover, Nr. 137, 1985.

WENZEL, H.-G., W. ZÜRN. Errors of the Cartwright-Tayler-Edden 1973 tidal potential displayed by gravimetric earth tide observations at BFO Schiltach. Bull. d'Inf. Marées Terrestres 107, 7559–7574, 1990.

WHITTEN, C. A. Adjustment of European Triangulation. Bull. Géod. no. 24, 187–203, 1952.

WILLIAMS, D. C., H. KAHMEN. Two wavelength angular refraction measurements. In: F. K. Brunner (ed.), 7–31, 1984.

WILSON, P. (ed.). Laser ranging instrumentation. Proc. 4th Int. Workshop on Laser Ranging Instrumentation (Austin 1982), Bonn 1982.

WILSON, P., M. CONRAD. Ein modulares, transportables Laser-Entfernungsmßsystem (MTLRS). ZfV 107, 410–419, 1982.

WOLF, H. Über die Ausgleichung von Dreiecksnetzen — Allgemeine Grundlagen und ein Neuvorschlag. Veröff. Inst. f. Erdmessung 1, 97–122, Bamberg 1949.

WOLF, H. Dreidimensionale Geodäsie. Herkunft, Methodik und Zielsetzung. ZfV 88, 109–116, 1963a.

WOLF, H. Die Grundgleichungen der dreidimensionalen Geodäsie in elementarer Darstellung. ZfV 88, 225–233, 1963b.

WOLF, H. Geometric connection and re-orientation of threedimensional triangulation nets. Bull. Géod. no. 68, 165–169, 1963c.

WOLF, H. Computation of satellite triangulation by spatial fitting of the orbit. DGK, B Nr. 153, 75–92, München 1967a.

WOLF, H. Possibilities for the joint adjustment of satellite and terrestrial triangulation and trilateration network. DGK, B Nr. 153, 93–99, München 1967b.

WOLF, H. Die wissenschaftliche Ausstrahlung Helmert's in die Gegenwart. In: DGK, E Nr. 12, 15–28, Aachen 1970.

WOLF, H. Über die Einführung von Normalhöhen. ZfV 99, 1–5, 1974.

WOLF, H. The Helmert-block method, its origin and development. In: Proc. 2nd Int. Symp. on Problems Related to the Redefinition of North American Geodetic Networks, Arlington, Va., 319–326. Nat. Geod. Inform. Branch, NOAA, Rockville, Md. 1978.

WOLF, H. Scale and orientation in combined Doppler and triangulation nets. Bull. Géod. 54, 45–53, 1980.

WOLF, H. Stochastic aspects in combined Doppler and triangulation nets. Bull. Géod. 56, 63–69, 1982.

WOLF, H. Möglichkeiten zur Gestaltung geodätischer Netze mit GPS-Messungen. ZfV 111, 397–405, 1986.

WOLF, H. Datums-Bestimmungen im Bereich der deutschen Landesvermessung. ZfV 112, 406–413, 1987.

WOODHOUSE, J. H., A. M. DZIEWONSKI. Mapping the upper mantle: three-dimensional modeling of earth structure by inversion of seismic waveforms. JGR 89, 5953–5986, 1984.

WU, S. S. C. Topographic mapping of the moon. Earth, Moon, and Planets 32, 165–172, 1985.

WÜBBELMANN, H. Hydrodynamic levelling across the Fehmarn Belt — Theoretical aspects and results —. In: H. Pelzer, A. Witte (eds.), Precise vertical positioning, F. Dümmler, Bonn 1991 (in press).

WÜBBENA, G., A. SCHUCHARDT, G. SEEBER. Multistation positioning results with TI 4100 GPS receivers in geodetic control networks. Proc. 4th Int. Geod. Symp. Satellite Positioning, Vol. II, 963–978, Austin, USA, 1986.

ZILKOSKI, D. B. The North American Vertical Datum of 1988 (NAVD88) — Tasks, impacts, and benefits. In: H. Pelzer, W. Niemeier (eds.), 47–67, 1987.

ZILKOSKI, D. B., L. D. HOTHEM. GPS satellite surveys and vertical control. J. of Surveying Engineering 15, 262–281, 1989.

ZÜRN, W., H. WILHELM. Tides of the earth. In: Landolt-Börnstein, New Series V, vol. 2, Geophysics of the solid earth, the moon and the planets, 259–299, Springer-Verlag, Heidelberg — New York — Tokyo 1984.

Index

Names of the authors cited in the text are not included in the index.

Walter de Gruyter
Berlin · New York

Wolfgang Torge
Gravimetry

1989. XII, 465 pages. 253 figures and 36 tables.
USA, Canada, Mexico: Cloth US $ 99.95   ISBN 0-89925-561-2
All other countries: Cloth DM 178,–   ISBN 3-11-010702-3

This book is intended to give a systematic account of gravity measurements and their evaluation. It provides an overall synopsis of the state of the art, with particular emphasis on recent developments, including the operational use of transportable absolute instruments and superconducting gravimeters, gravimetry and gradiometry on moving platforms, and the significance of gravity data for solving geodynamical problems. The book will be an indispensable reference for scientists and engineers concerned with gravity data field determination, in geodesy, geophysics, and physics, as well as in space and terrestrial navigation. Ranging from gravity field theory to examples of gravity surveys and applications, this volume covers the whole spectrum of current gravimetry and should be of interest to anyone who wishes to explore the subject.

Contents:
Introduction · Task of Gravimetry · Historical Development · National and International Organizations · **Theory of the Gravity Field** · Coordinate Systems · Fundamental Relationships in the Gravity Field · Geometry of the Gravity Field · Gravity Field Models · Height Systems · Disturbing Quantities in the Gravity Field · Statistical Description of the Gravity Field · **Space-Time Structure of the Exterior Gravity Field** · Normal Gravity Field of the Earth · Free-Air Anomalies · Global and Regional Structures of the Terrestrial Gravity Field · Temporal Gravity Variations · Gravity Fields of Moon and Planets · **Importance of Gravity in Natural and Engineering Sciences** · Gravity in Physics · Gravity Field and Geodesy · Gravity Field and Geophysics · Gravity Field and Geodynamics · Gravity Field and Orbit Computations · **Absolute Gravity Measurements** · Free-Fall Methods: Fundamentals · Free-Fall Experiments and Results · Pendulum Method · **Relative Gravity Measurements** · Dynamic Method · Static Method · Design Features of Spring Gravimeters · Calibration of Relative Gravimeters · Static Spring Gravimeter · Error Sources and Accuracy · **Gravity Measurements in Inaccessible Areas and on Moving Platforms** · Gravity Measurements in Inaccessible Areas · Gravity Measurements on Moving Platforms · Sea and Airborne Gravimeters Systems · Error Sources and Accuracy · Inertial Gravimetry · **Gravity Gradiometry** · Fundamentals · Stationary Gravity Gradiometry · Gravity Gradiometry on Moving Platforms · **Gravimetric Surveys** · Gravity Reference Systems · Gravity Networks · Regional and Local Gravimetric Surveys · Archival of Results · **Determination of Temporal Gravity Changes** · Measurement Instruments and Observation Methods · Gravitational Effects of Non-Tectonic Origin · Measurement of Gravimetric Earth Tides · Gravity Changes by Terrestrial Mass Displacements of Geodynamic Origin · **References** · **Index**

"This is a book which presents a systematic introduction to gravity measurements and provides a well-balanced survey of the state-of-the-art. The comprehensive description of the theory of the gravity field and its space-time structure on approx. 50 pages furnishes the book to a (stand-alone) reference for geodesists, geophysicists, geologists, engineers, and navigation people – to everybody who is concerned with gravity. Many illustrations, tables, photos, and practical examples assist the reader in understanding the subject of gravimetry. This monograph will become the 'bible' for every gravimetrist. It is hard to believe that there might be a better way for bringing gravimetry to students than just to recommend this monograph as lecture notes. Thus, the book can be recommended without any reservation. It is a 'must' for every geoscientist's library."
manuscripta geodaetica

Price subject to change

Walter de Gruyter
Berlin · New York

Heribert Kahmen · Wolfgang Faig

Surveying

1988. XVII, 578 pages. 474 figures and 23 tables.
USA, Canada, Mexico: Cloth US $ 129.95   ISBN 0-89925-022-X
All other countries: Cloth DM 198,–   ISBN 3-11-008303-5

The field of surveying has been subjected to drastic changes in recent years. Conventional equipment is being upgraded and replaced by electronic instrumentation, and digital computers play a major role in every aspect of surveying. By integrating modern concepts, equipment, technologies, field and evaluation procedures with conventional instrumentation, methods and tasks, this book provides a comprehensive treatment of present day surveying.
Thanks to its balanced presentation of both practical and theoretical information on all aspects of surveying the book will prove to be valuable for academic training and further education of professionals in a wide spectrum of the geosciences and related fields, such as surveying, civil engineering, cartography, architecture, geography, planning, etc. as well as for practicing professionals.

Contents: Fundamentals · Elements of Surveying Instruments · Theodolites and Angular Measurements · Distance Measurements · Fundamentals of Plane Coordinate Computations · Determination of Plane Horizontal Coordinates · Fundamentals of Horizontal Geodetic Networks · Field Surveys with Simple Instrumentation and Their Evaluation · Differential Levelling · Trigonometric Heighting · Barometric Heighting · Three-Dimensional Positioning · Route Surveying · Engineering Surveys · References · Author Index · Subject Index.

"This book is a translation of the very popular pocket books **Vermessungskunde I, II and III**, Sammlung Göschen, first published in 1910 by de Gruyter. Since their first issue these booklets have been revised, updated and extended several times. They are presently in their 17th, 14th and 12th German edition, respectively, and have always belonged to the basic textbooks of all German speaking students of surveying and of adjacent disciplines. The contents cover all elementary topics in surveying and contain everything a student should know up to the level of this first examination. The books do not assume any previous knowledge and are written so clear and selfcontained that they likewise serve well as reference for practitioners and for private studies. They stress the more side of the surveying profession: instrumentation, field surveying, staking, computations . . .

In summary, *Surveying* is a first-rate book on an elementary level which can be highly recommended to all students of surveying, to practitioners and to all those students and professionals who only occasionally are involved in surveying."

manuscripta geodaetica

Price subject to change